CONTENTS

TABLES AND FIGURES

Is this America? The Land of the Free and Home
of the Brave?

—*Fannie Lou Hamer*

T he title of this volume is *The Case for Affirmative Action on Campus:
Concepts of Equity, Considerations for Practice.* However, as our nation's institutions of higher education are truly microcosms of the
larger society in which they are embedded, this volume might well be reti-
tled, *The National Crisis: A Case Study of its Effects in Higher Education.*

What is this national crisis I speak of? It is the yawning distance between
the nation's aspiration to be an exemplar of democratic practice and equality
and the realities on the ground. It is the failure of America to fully come to
terms with the present effects of past discrimination, and to make combating
present discrimination a priority. It is the institutional arrangements, policies, and practices based upon race, gender, and other characteristics that still
operate as built-in headwinds, blocking the success and upward mobility of
people stuck at the bottom. It is the nation's massive failure to provide low-
income people and members of minority groups with equal and fair access
to quality education. Formal equal opportunity can do little good if people
lack equal access to educational opportunities that would allow them to take
advantage of this policy.

The nation will soon have a majority minority population. Immigrants,
many poor and undereducated, are changing national demographics. Income
and wealth inequality between and among discrete groups and individuals
are increasing. Indeed, the gap between rich and poor in America is greater
now than it has been in half a century, and exceeds that of any other developed nation today.

At all levels of educational achievement and attainment, America is lag-
ging behind other nations in fields critical to economic growth and national
competitiveness in the global marketplace. Students who need the most help
receive the least from public systems. A cycle of intergenerational transfer of
poverty because of a lack of quality education is in full swing and becoming
more intractable right before our eyes.

In the Information Age, driven by the revolution in technology, America
is challenged to embrace and adapt to a new, urgent imperative to broaden

and enhance human capital development. The emergent new world order requires nothing less. A commitment to fairness and democracy and, yes, the American dream, requires nothing less.

Put another way, it is contrary to the national interest to have swelling numbers of poorly educated, economically deprived, unhealthy, unhappy people with limited hope for prosperous jobs and a decent standard of living because of a lack of education. If our nation is to redeem its place of leadership among the world's community of nations, it must find a way to improve the quality of the education provided to the mass of its people. It is a matter of enlightened self-interest, economics, and national security. Our system of education needs to be populated by, and serve well, *all* Americans.

While much emphasis in public debate is put on closing the achievement gap in elementary and secondary education, in reality what we have is an education quality and access gap that consigns many students to failure and underachievement. Those students are disproportionately poor and members of minority groups. Gaps in higher education demand urgent attention as well. Today's high school dropouts earn far less than high school graduates, and high school graduates earn far less than those with 4-year college degrees. Few doubt that high-end jobs of the future will require some degree of higher education.

One would have hoped that given their mission—the generation and propagation of knowledge and the uplifting of humankind—institutions of higher education and their leaders would have been at the forefront of efforts to help the nation come to terms with the legacy of racism, discrimination, and exclusion. One would have hoped that institutions of higher education would have been pacesetters in devising policies and practices to broaden and improve higher education access. One would have hoped they would have helped the nation understand and embrace equality and justice as core constitutional values. One would have hoped . . .

However, in many instances, as the chapters in this volume document, institutions of higher education and their leaders have been part of the problem rather than the solution. Too many focus on being "selective" rather than responsive to the realities of education for so many low-income Americans, promote open pocketbooks rather than open hearts and minds, and model "elitism" rather than a concern for the common good.

Many of the legal cases decided before *Brown v. Board of Education* (1954) involved segregation in higher education. Even today, a number of states are still being monitored to ensure compliance with requirements designed to dismantle historically dual, racially exclusionary, and unequal systems of higher education. The debate in the academy about what constitutes merit and who "deserves" to be granted access to higher education rages on, while inequality and poverty grow.

While some higher education leaders and policy makers have nobly, and at high personal cost, risen to the challenge to lead the way to higher ground, too many have been, and are, on the wrong side of history. Our nation is the loser when higher education institutions fail to inspire us, lift us up, help us to become bigger than ourselves, and develop the better components of our nature.

Purpose

Access to education and opportunity, as a means to gain resources, power, and influence, has always been a hotbed of competition and contestation. The chapters in this volume document the many ways African Americans, in particular, were denied education and other human and civil rights during the days of legalized human trafficking of Africans, called slavery. They challenge us not to forget the legacy of the inferior and segregated educational opportunity offered to Blacks. They remind us of the concentration of low-income and/or Black students in inadequately resourced public elementary and secondary schools, where these students are taught by the least-experienced teachers and have the least access to technology and needed supportive services. They describe the ferment, frustration, and wasted effort and talent in higher education because of polarization over what is needed and what is right.

They describe the various civil and human rights struggles waged by African Americans and their allies in the streets, in the courts, in the academy, and in the court of public opinion to first abolish de facto segregation in education, and then eliminate the consequences of de jure segregation. This work also tells the compelling story of the waves of public protest against a segregated status quo, and enactment of half-step policies, identity formation patterns, and political trade-offs that have pitted groups against one another. It describes the peaks and valleys in the long march toward fairness, and reports on the halting progress made in the face of adversity. Each chapter is rich with detail, accessible legal history, theory, and possible explanations for the deep impulse felt by some to segregate themselves from others who are perceived to be different. The authors capture the stimulating intellectual and policy debates and explore the pros and cons of policies that are facially neutral but have the purpose or effect of placing some people or groups at a disadvantage while privileging others. Even in this first decade of the 21st century, *a luta continua*.

Focus on Affirmative Action

No set of policies or practices has been a greater source of angst, social division, and contention than so-called affirmative action policies. Whenever settled patterns of privilege undergo disruption, pushing back from multiple quarters is to be expected.

Affirmative action is best understood as an umbrella concept that subsumes different types of policies and practices tailored to meet specific, context-derived problems of discrimination and unfairness. Affirmative action strategies range from outreach and recruitment to targeted training and investment to goals, timetables, and set-asides. Affirmative action strategies may be voluntary or compulsory, embedded in public policy or private practice.

In the early years of affirmative action strategies, they were understood primarily as a means to ameliorate the effects of past or present discrimination against African Americans. Whether through judicial proceedings or public policy, if discrimination against African Americans could be established or was voluntarily admitted by the perpetrator, for example, an employer, a school, a public benefits program, then the remedy might include affirmative action approaches. This remedy was meant to restore the victim to the place he or she would have occupied, *but for discrimination*. Affirmative action was and is primarily about restorative justice.

The clearest case for affirmative action strategies exists within the community of African Americans who were first enslaved then segregated by law for over half a century and then denied equal access to education. Clearly, as a group, African Americans were hobbled by these practices. This assertion is difficult to refute, but some still argue that because African Americans are now treated equally, they are no longer entitled to any policy redress such as affirmative action. Statistics and a large body of contemporary decisional law suggest the contrary.

Much debate in the United States about affirmative action is really quite parochial. It is beyond the scope of this volume to explore how related policies and practices, variously named, are a staple in many countries all over the world. Many readers may not even be aware of international human rights instruments that sometimes require affirmative action and their expansive definition of covered people. Suffice it to say that in South Africa, what we in the United States call affirmative action is known as *corrective action*, a term that conveys the idea of redress of cognizable grievances. In India, "reservation" policies are in place to help Dalits and other disadvantaged and historically "backward" and excluded castes gain access to opportunities.

Brazil has begun to implement affirmative action efforts to help pry open opportunities for work and education for its huge population of African descent.

Whenever a society's hierarchical system has exploited some for the benefit of others, the hierarchy becomes subject to change, and methods to promote inclusion are needed. One might even say that an analogue to affirmative action exists in Iraq's fledgling efforts to ensure inclusion of Sunni and Shiite Muslims in its new government. The idea of affirmative action, much maligned in some quarters, is an approach to undo negative consequences of past unfair practices.

In America, as the development and implementation of affirmative action matured, other identifiable groups, in addition to African Americans, began to take advantage of the opportunity to press for recognition of discrimination. Women of all stripes, Latinos, religious minorities, sexual preference groups, people with disabilities, national origin minorities, and immigrants all stepped up their activism in search of redress. A backlash against group-sensitive remedies began to flourish, and the courts and policy makers grew more timid.

In this context, the concept of diversity as a positive benefit flowing from inclusionary policies came into popular use in discourse, policy circles, and the courts. Everyone benefits from inclusion, the logic of the new framework went, and therefore, for example, measures in higher education to promote inclusion and diversity of many different types are good. No longer was a demonstrated showing of past bad deeds or exclusion of discrete groups emphasized. Instead, institutions of higher education were called upon to illustrate their willingness to provide a better education for all by ensuring a diverse student body. As the U.S. Supreme Court held in *Grutter v. Bollinger* (2003), a diverse student population has documented educational benefits, helps break down racial and ethnic stereotypes, and fosters development of a racially integrated and diverse leadership class. The business community, which filed many briefs in the *Grutter* case, and its companion case, *Gratz v. Bollinger* (2003), heralded the benefits of a diverse workforce in the global village.

Presently, it is far from clear that diversity as a rationale for even voluntary integration or inclusion will be deemed lawful for much longer. When the Supreme Court under its new chief justice decided the *Meredith v. Jefferson County* case, involving the Louisville, Kentucky, public schools, and a companion case involving the public schools of Seattle, Washington, it outlawed the use of race or diversity for any purpose—benign as well as punitive, inclusionary, or exclusionary. The court found there is no compelling state interest that would justify acknowledgment of group characteristics in public education or the value of diversity. The authors of this volume acknowledge the importance of the *Meredith* decision and the subsequent impact it will have on the pursuit of diversity in higher education.

If the decision outlaws diversity as the basis for public school assignments, what will happen to the campus civil rights crisis? Already bans on affirmative action remedies exist in several states, as well as precipitous declines in admissions of low-income or minority-group students. Some institutions of higher education have abandoned efforts to become more inclusionary out of sheer fear of being sued.

Ironically, although race is not deemed a permissible consideration for the admission of students in higher education, many institutions have no problem considering wealth. Since alumni at many institutions receive preferences for their children, especially wealthy alumni, it appears that "them that's got shall get" is the ascendant framework for opportunity allocation. The interests of students who have attended competitive private schools are also served by the emphasis on grades as a proxy for merit. What will happen to the nation if this mind-set of exclusion persists?

Looking Ahead

This book will help anyone who wishes to understand the etiology of the nation's struggles with diversity in higher education, and it will further the current discussions surrounding affirmative action in important and substantive ways. Written with the interests of excluded minorities at its center, this work proposes strategies worth pursuing, if inclusion in higher education is the aim to be achieved.

Archbishop Desmond Tutu once said, "It is difficult to awaken a man pretending to be asleep." And so it is. Much of the nation is still snoring while the world around us has changed rapidly. It is no longer a question of whether the nation must change to become more inclusive, especially in higher education. It is a question of how, at what pace, and at what price change will occur.

Can America tolerate having millions of people without high school degrees or who are functionally illiterate? How many poor people must the nation amass before education as a means of poverty alleviation is understood and supported? How long will it be before people with resources and intellectual/public policy and thought-leaders recognize their interdependence with "the least of these?" Is importation of talent from abroad or outsourcing of work in critical fields related to science, technology, engineering, and mathematics in the national interest? Can America afford to continue to avert its eyes from the millions who could, with access to quality education, become civic leaders, business innovators, and more active participants in public life?

In the 1960s Fannie Lou Hamer, a Black Mississippi sharecropper, led a movement at high personal cost to help Black people gain representation at the National Democratic Convention. In a now famous address, she asked the plaintive question that resonates throughout this volume: "Is this America? Is this the land of the free and the home of the brave?"

I close with this admonition by poet Langston Hughes, "Let America be America again. Let it be the dream it used to be."

Lynn W. Huntley, President and Chief Executive Officer
The Southern Education Foundation

INTRODUCTION

T *he Case for Affirmative Action on Campus* is a synthesis of scholarly literature pertaining to affirmative action as social policy. The book provides a concise analysis of the historical, legal, psychosocial, and sociological perspectives forwarded by recent affirmative action research. Key judicial decisions and issues are covered, and their impact on program implementation within the landscape of higher education is explored. The sources and material will be relevant to readers interested in the implications of legislative background and policy development for postsecondary decision making. The volume will contribute to an increased understanding of current theoretical and philosophical positions, as well as construct a practicable application for the concept of affirmative action.

Irrespective of previous discrimination or its prior effects, legal challenges to affirmative action illustrate a lack of consensus regarding the idea of providing equal access to some while fostering preferential treatment of others. As efforts have been made to equalize opportunities, the degree to which opportunity enhancement programs made possible by affirmative action will continue remains questionable in light of the climate surrounding affirmative action in higher education. Moreover, while the rhetoric at many institutions of higher learning places a premium on diversity, actual campus climates may be less supportive of practices that promote a culturally pluralistic faculty and staff that recruit, retain, and matriculate underrepresented students. Hence, this book is an examination of the history and present state of equal-opportunity-enhancing efforts and of the implications of maintaining or eradicating affirmative action at institutions of higher learning. This collegiate discussion has major importance for national policy and praxis.

The Case for Affirmative Action on Campus explores the ways affirmative action has shaped and reshaped higher educational opportunities, highlighting student access (e.g., among African Americans, Hispanics, and women) prior to affirmative action, and examining how these opportunities have changed since the advent of the legal mandates that define the nation's current affirmative action policy and practices. Accordingly this volume also:

1. outlines the ideological and legal construction of color-blind legislation, resulting in the de facto exclusion of people of color from institutions of higher education;
2. addresses the role of the courts in affecting affirmative action practices in higher education institutions as workplaces and places of study;
3. highlights underrepresentation among collegians of color and examines research regarding student opinion on race-based policies at 2- and 4-year institutions;
4. details the pervasiveness of the affirmative action debate across educational sectors and the use of race as one of a myriad of factors considered in college admissions; and
5. explores affirmative action as a pipeline issue for future inclusionary policies focused specifically on new approaches to attaining diversity at colleges and universities.

Judicial and legislative actions, including the Civil Rights Act of 1964, Title IX, Section 504 of the Rehabilitation Act of 1973, and the Americans with Disabilities Act (ADA; 1991), prohibiting discrimination on the basis of race/ethnicity, national origin, gender, and disability, were enacted when American postsecondary institutions were traditionally homogenous and lacking in diversity. While access to American colleges and universities was historically reserved for White middle-class males, things changed in 1965 when Executive Order No. 11246 ratified affirmative action, which has since developed into one of the perennial debates of contemporary times. At the core of the debate remains the age-old question of who should have access to college.

Historically, the lack of consensus regarding affirmative action has addressed topics ranging from higher learning opportunities for the sons of nonlandowners during colonial times to the merits of educating women and freed slaves to the higher education needs of immigrants, international students, and those from poverty-stricken families. At present, the discourse is squarely centered on how to best affirm diversity and encourage greater participation among underrepresented collegiate populations.

Affirmative action is a government policy that seeks to remedy long-standing discrimination directed at specific racial/ethnic minorities and women. To this end, affirmative action provides procedures and guidelines to ensure that eligible and interested citizens, regardless of race, ethnicity, gender, religion, or age, receive equal opportunities for participation in higher education, employment, government contracts, housing, and other social welfare issues. Affirmative action does not fully restrict all forms of discrimination or make them illegal. Rather, it attempts to redress historical inequities by providing traditionally underrepresented groups with more equal access to most public and private arenas. However, as the discontents of diversity continue, marginal progress has been made in renegotiating and affirming cultural pluralism in American schools.

Much public conversation surrounding affirmative action focuses on the idea of preferential treatment. This book examines the ideological conflicts that permeate this dialogue that frame affirmative action as the undue favoring of racial/ethnic minorities without addressing other forms of nepotism and access. The authors address the importance of affirmative action as an antidiscrimination measure for enhancing educational mobility and postsecondary opportunities for graduating high school students.

As with society writ large, the U.S. educational system must respond to a swelling population of students from a myriad of backgrounds and experiences. Consequently, the interrelated systems of education and its structures must engage the complex nuances of multiple cultures, languages, and contexts within the classroom and within the college campus. At the postsecondary level these nuances require particular attention as they relate to who gets into college and how well students perform academically. One of the daunting age-old, yet contemporary, challenges facing postsecondary education in the United States is the attempt to marry educational opportunity with educational outcome while being inclusive of all students.

As the continued ambiguity surrounding affirmative action calls for further study of unexplored, unanswered, and under-investigated questions about better facilitating diversity in American postsecondary institutions, the main objectives of this volume are:

1. to highlight historical and legal perspectives of diversity;
2. to review legislative actions affecting affirmative action at postsecondary institutions;
3. to address whether diversity is a compelling interest relative to the educational, social, and economic mobility of a multiethnic student populace; and
4. to consider how students from marginalized groups navigate movement from secondary schools to colleges during an era of affirmative action retrenchment.

Antecedents to the modern-day discussions regarding affirmative action date from legal challenges waged prior to the implementation of affirmative action programming in the early 1970s. Although the use of race in granting educational access has continually been questioned, in the 1950s the groundwork for what would become equal educational opportunity began to be laid. In the case of *Brown v. Board of Education* (1954) the U.S. Supreme Court maintained that the precedent of "separate but equal" set in *Plessy v. Ferguson* (1896) was no longer constitutional. *Plessy v. Ferguson* held that segregation was legal if comparable educational facilities and opportunities were provided for Blacks and Whites. As a result of the *Brown v. Board of Education* (1954) verdict, it was assumed that educational institutions would no longer resist the enrollment of African Americans. In *Florida ex.rel. Hawkins v. Board of Control* (1956), the unconstitutionality of "separate but equal" was extended beyond elementary and secondary schools, enforcing higher education desegregation.

In tandem, the 1950s and 1960s gave rise to the notion of racial diversification and policy implementation as a national priority. However, systems of segregation, prejudice, and discrimination continued as the promotion of equality for all was not widely accepted. As a case in point, numerous African American students continued to enroll in historically Black colleges and universities and/or in northern colleges even in the face of national efforts to equalize educational opportunities (Aragon & Zamani, 2002; Brown, 1999). Be that as it may, when affirmative action was first initiated, President Lyndon B. Johnson viewed it as a means to an end—that end being the end of discrimination—and equal participation opportunities for racial/ethnic minorities and women (Edley, 1996).

From the onset various forms of affirmative action in postsecondary education have been challenged. A common misconception that many White Americans hold is that diversity strategies of this kind are a form of tokenism and preferential treatment (Feinberg, 1996; Kluegel & Smith, 1986; Sears, Henry, & Kosterman, 2000). On the contrary, student affirmative action policies advocate for equal educational opportunities for African Americans, Hispanic Americans, Native Americans, and women, in order to increase the number of underrepresented students in the applicant pool. Student affirmative action programs serve to eliminate barriers to educational attainment for women and students of color by attempting to set right historical discrimination, as well as the present-day effects of past inequities (Crosby, 2006; Trent, 1991a).

At its inception, the U.S. Constitution established the need for affirmative action. The civil rights innovations outlined in this document were not available to all the inhabitants of the new nation. Most African Americans were slaves, and therefore valued as property and counted as three-fifths of a person. For the most part, Native Americans received no consideration at all. Although counted, women had very few rights. In spite of a variety of legal and social changes, these groups continued to suffer blatant discrimination well into the second half of the 20th century.

The 14th Amendment provided the legal basis for affirmative action policies. Added to the Constitution in 1868, this amendment extends legal protection to all U.S. citizens. Specifically, Section One of the Equal Protection Clause of the 14th Amendment asserts that, "No state shall . . . deny to any person within its jurisdiction, the equal protection of laws." For many years, this clause was either selectively enforced or completely ignored. It was not until *Brown v. Board of Education* in 1954 that the notion of equal protection received serious national consideration. Specifically citing the 14th Amendment, the Supreme Court held that racial segregation in elementary and secondary education is unconstitutional because it promotes an unequal educational system. Following this ruling, President John F. Kennedy issued Executive Order No. 10925 in 1961, which asked federal contractors to adopt diversity programs in an effort to help end segregation. This order provided the legal foundation for affirmative action programs.

In the spirit of the Equal Protection Clause, the Civil Rights Act of 1964 bans discrimination on the basis of race, color, religion, sex, or national origin. To ensure compliance, federal funds are denied to those institutions that violate this mandate. More specifically, Title VI of the Civil Rights Act of 1964 (amended as 42 U.S.C. Section 2000e-2 [a]) states that:

> It shall be an unlawful employment practice for an employer to fail or re-fuse to hire or to discharge any individual or otherwise to discriminate against any individual with respect to his compensation, terms, conditions, or privileges of employment because of such individual's race, color, religion, sex, or national origin; or . . . to limit, segregate, or classify his employees or applicants for employment in any way which deprive or tend to deprive any individual of employment opportunities or otherwise adversely affect his status as an employee, because of such individual's race, color, religion, sex, or national origin.

To ensure compliance, the federal government established the Office of Federal Contract Compliance Programs (OFCCP) and the Equal Employment Opportunity Commission (EEOC). Established in 1965 under Executive Order No. 11246, the OFCCP reviews, monitors and enforces an institution's affirmative action plan. The OFCCP posits that each employment agency is responsible for designing an "acceptable" affirmative action program, which it defines as follows:

> An acceptable affirmative action program must include an analysis of areas within which the contractor is deficient in the utilization of minority groups, . . . and further, goals and timetables to which the contractor's good faith efforts must be directed to correct the deficiencies and to achieve prompt and full utilization of minorities, . . . at all levels and in all segments of its work force where deficiencies exist (41 C.F.R. Section 60–2.10)

Similar to the OFCCP, the EEOC also helps to enforce antidiscrimination laws and regulations. Created in Title VI of the Civil Rights Act of 1964, the EEOC enforces other related legislation including the Equal Pay Act of 1963, the Age Discrimination in Employment Act of 1967, and Title I of the Americans with Disabilities Act of 1990. The EEOC investigates discrimination charges filed by individuals. If an employer is in violation, the EEOC first attempts to bring about voluntary resolution. If this fails, the EEOC may choose to file suit against the employer in federal court. At the conclusion of such a case, the EEOC issues a "notice of the right to sue," which allows an individual to file an additional suit in federal court.

To comply with affirmative action regulations, most colleges and universities reformed their admissions and hiring practices. Throughout the 1970s higher education institutions established affirmative action programs and antidiscrimination policies designed to increase the number of women and minority students and faculty members in all fields and disciplines. This included actively encouraging women and minorities to apply for faculty and administrative positions, aggressively recruiting students from traditionally underrepresented groups, and offering support programs to help at-risk students succeed. Even so, affirmative action policy did not resolve all the discrimination problems affecting higher education. Instead, it became one of them. Many people questioned the constitutionality of affirmative action, including some White women, even though, as a group, White women received the greatest benefit from these programs.

Since the late 1970s, several cases have challenged the constitutionality and legality of affirmative action mandates. The earliest and most influential of these cases relative to higher education is *Regents of the University of California v. Bakke* (1978). Although the opinion rendered by the court supported the goal of striving to create a diverse student body, at the same time the court also stated that the use of racial distinctions is highly suspect and requires meticulous judicial review. Regarding the specific program in question, at the University of California, Davis, School of Medicine, the court rejected it as unlawful because it used a fixed quota, or set-asides, to attain diverse enrollment. Rather than settle the constitutional debate surrounding affirmative action, the *Bakke* decision made it more muddled and confused.

Wygant v. Jackson Board of Education (1986) further limited an institution's ability to act on affirmative action legislation by developing the "strict scrutiny" test. Seeming to clarify the *Bakke* decision, *Wygant* required that the use of racial classification support a compelling interest of state and be narrowly tailored to satisfy that particular interest. The court's ruling in this case also stated that historic social discrimination was not by itself a compelling reason for an affirmative action policy, and that a public employer should only enact such a policy if it is indeed needed.

In the cases of *Podberesky v. Kirwan* (1994) and *Hopwood v. State of Texas* (1996), U.S. Circuit Courts applied the Supreme Court decisions in *Bakke* and *Wygant*. In *Podberesky* the U.S. District Court for the District of Maryland ruled that a scholarship program for African American students at the University of Maryland was not a compelling state interest and therefore failed the "strict scrutiny" test. In 1994 the U.S. District Court of Appeals for the Fifth Circuit held that the University of Texas School of Law's admission policy of accepting less qualified minority applicants was unlawful because it employed a quota system. In 1996 this same court held that the Equal Protection Clause of the 14th Amendment does not permit the University of Texas to establish admissions policies that give preferential treatment to one race over another.

As a result of the *Hopwood* decision, many people have concluded that affirmative action programs are unconstitutional, and many states have begun to rethink their use of affirmative action programs (Lederman, 1997a). Most notably, in 1996 California voters approved a law banning the use of such programs in state and local agencies including the state's public colleges and universities. Yet, because many states are not bound to follow the Fifth Circuit's 1996 decision, the national debate over affirmative action continues. Washington State, California, Florida, and Michigan are officially anti-affirmative-action states, and anti-affirmative-action groups are aggressively targeting additional states to influence voters to oppose public affirmative action efforts (Martin, 2006).

The confusion that resulted from the Supreme Court's *Bakke* decision continues to make it difficult for lower courts to rule on issues related to affirmative action programs. Michigan is the latest battle site for this debate. Highlighting the two-faced approach used by the Supreme Court in its

Bakke ruling, the cases of *Gratz v. Bollinger* (2000) and *Grutter v. Bollinger* (2001) first uphold, and then reject, the use of affirmative action programs in college admissions. In the *Gratz* case, the U.S. District Court for the Eastern District of Michigan, South Division, ruled that the University of Michigan's consideration of race as a factor in its admission of undergraduate students to the College of Literature, Science and Arts, is both a lawful and "narrowly tailored" way of achieving diversity in its student population. However, in the *Grutter* case, the same court ruled that the University of Michigan Law School's use of race in its admission decisions violates both the 14th Amendment and Title VI of the Civil Rights Act of 1964, and is therefore, unconstitutional. This was overturned by the Supreme Court.[1]

Knowledge of the legal history of affirmative action is essential to understanding the current debate surrounding the place of affirmative action in postsecondary education. Colleges and universities are faced with the awesome task of implementing policies, creating programs, and carrying out practices that ensure social justice for students from all walks of life and reflect inclusionary procedures that provide equal educational opportunities, against the contentious backdrop of racialized politics and public polarity.

As institutions engage in the arduous task of making the case for affirmative action, contemporary educational leaders and policy makers must systematically understand the historical context and the contemporary forces behind the current contention surrounding affirmative action on many campuses. *The Case for Affirmative Action on Campus* comprehensively provides that material, and offers strategies to augment existing policies and to effectively facilitate institutional support for fostering inclusive college environments and multiethnic campus communities.

---

[1] See Appendix A.1 for complete timeline of legislative and judicial developments pertaining to affirmative action.

I

NAVIGATING THE ROCKY TERRAIN OF THE POST–CIVIL RIGHTS ERA

Placing the struggle for civil liberties in a historical context helps us to understand the varying interpretations of equal treatments and constitutional rights as they have developed in the United States. For centuries race has played a role in access to equal opportunities and shaping the policy landscape to recognize the public benefits of full participation across society for all American people. This chapter provides an overview of the convergence of racial differences with issues of access and equity with the basic goal of providing each U.S. citizen with freedom as a natural right and protection against discrimination in public and private domains.

In the last century, U.S. society became increasingly culturally pluralistic because of immigration and minority birth rates, among other factors. However, before the civil rights initiatives of the 1950s and 1960s, there was very little racial/ethnic diversity in American corporations or institutions of higher learning (Allen, 2004; Bowen & Bok, 1998; Fleming, 1984). During this era, opportunities in employment and higher education grew for members of historically disadvantaged, disenfranchised, and underrepresented groups, particularly African Americans, increasing their level of participation.

According to Spring (2006), people of color have been discriminated against since the arrival of the first Europeans in the Americas. Consequently initial civil rights policies and programs were established to redress discriminatory treatment African Americans suffered because of the heinous systems of slavery, Jim Crow, and continued de facto discrimination spanning more than three centuries. The well-known case of *Dred Scott v. Sandford* (1857) is one of many examples of the United States' rejecting the citizenship rights of African Americans. In the *Dred Scott* decision, Chief Justice Roger Taney declared that "they [African Americans] had no rights which the white man was bound to respect" (Rubio, 2001, p. 11). The Emancipation Proclamation signed by President Abraham Lincoln on January 1, 1863, was not an effort to uphold and give Blacks the rights they deserved but an attempt to prevent Civil War between the Confederate states and the northern territory over the question of slavery.

In 1865 the 13th Amendment to the U.S. Constitution abolished slavery, however, equal protection for African Americans (and other deprived groups such as Native Americans and women) was not guaranteed. Following the Civil Rights Act of 1866 and the passage of the 14th Amendment in 1868, surface-level social justice emerged, even as the conflict between de jure and de facto forms of inequity continued. In 1870 the 15th Amendment to the U.S. Constitution addressed the disparate treatment in voting rights, although injustices along racial lines persisted for many decades to follow.

During the period following the Civil War and Reconstruction (1861–1877), the first affirmative action programs debuted (Rubio, 2001). Representative John Coburn, a Republican from Indiana, coined the legal term *affirmative action* during Reconstruction to challenge the privilege, power, and dominion assumed by White citizens. Coburn stated:

> In other Reconstruction-era debates the word "affirmative" was actually used in the context of protecting black civil rights. But here it is linked to safeguarding black civil rights from the white affirmative action of state-sanctioned discrimination and refusal to stop white supremacist terrorism. (Rubio, 2001, p. 35)

More than 70 years after Coburn's call for the first *affirmative* acts to secure equality for Blacks, the National Labor Relations Act of 1935 referenced the need for affirmative action policy on behalf of union members and organizers who had been subjected to employment discrimination (Skrentny, 1996). Colker (2005) refers to affirmative action policy as supportive of the antidifferentiation language of the Civil Rights Act of 1964, intended by Congress to provide protection against racial and gender discrimination across the board. This differs from the antisubordination model of civil rights, in which people without disabilities cannot seek protection under statutes designed to protect individuals with disabilities (Colker, 1986, 2005). For example:

> In the early days of the enforcement of the act, the courts did not have to consider whether it reflected an antisubordination or antidifferentiation

perspective because the plaintiffs were racial minorities or women who had claims of discrimination under either legal theory. The courts soon concluded, however, that the act did not embody a pure antidifferentiation perspective and allowed whites and men to bring race and gender discrimination claims. At first, however, the courts also tolerated affirmative action for racial minorities and women, even though those programs conflicted with a pure antidifferentiation perspective. Over time, however, the courts have more and more narrowly construed the ability of employers to institute affirmative action programs and hence have moved the Civil Rights Act to a more pure antidifferentiation model (Colker, 2005, p. 99).

In sum, while the government has promoted and encouraged affirmative action, it has not monitored its implementation, much of which has been largely voluntary on the part of employers and educational institutions (Bergmann, 1999). Thus, affirmative action, as a means of diversifying the American labor market and schools, has yielded mixed results; some progress has been made, but parity is still elusive for people of color and women.

Historical Accounts and Contemporary Clashes in U.S. Civil Rights

The courts began to lay the groundwork for equal educational opportunity in the 1950s. In the case of *Brown v. Board of Education* (1954), the Supreme Court maintained that the precedent of "separate but equal" set in *Plessey v. Ferguson* (1896) was no longer constitutional. After the court's decision in the *Brown* case, the assumption was that educational institutions would no longer resist the enrollment of African Americans. While *Brown* began to dismantle segregation in elementary and secondary schools, *Florida ex.rel. Hawkins v. Board of Control* (1956) extended the unconstitutionality of separate but equal by enforcing desegregation in institutions of higher education (Brown, 1999; Ogletree, 2004; Sokol, 2006; Trent, 1991a).

The late 1950s witnessed continued integration confrontations including the Little Rock Nine incident, which required federal troops and the National Guard to escort the first Black students into Little Rock Central High School in Arkansas. By February 1960 young adults were engaged in student sit-ins to protest discrimination, and in coalition-building efforts, such as the Student Nonviolent Coordinating Committee (SNCC), and freedom ride organizing by the Congress of Racial Equality (CORE). In spite of the 1956 *Florida ex.rel. Hawkins v. the Board of Control* ruling that ordered desegregation in postsecondary contexts, on October 1, 1961, James Meredith enrolled at the University of Mississippi, which was surrounded by 5,000 federal troops called in to respond to outbreaks of violence, rioting, and protest directed toward the integration of the state's flagship campus (Brunner & Haney, 2006; Sokol, 2006).

During the civil unrest of the 1960s, and the racially charged crises that manifested at several colleges and universities during that time, legal efforts took shape to end racial divides and ensure equality across racial/ethnic groups (Wilson, 2001). As growing numbers of minorities began to openly criticize institutional policies and programs and demand change, racial inequities intensified even further. Concomitantly, the idea of racial diversification and affirmative action policy implementation became a national priority, even though the concept of equality for all was still vehemently challenged by segregation, prejudice, and discrimination. In an effort to prohibit discrimination, President John F. Kennedy introduced Executive Order No. 10925 in 1961, mandating that institutions receiving federal funds use affirmative action principles to ensure nondiscriminatory hiring practices. In 1964 President Lyndon B. Johnson signed the Civil Rights Act of 1964. Soon after, Congress passed the Voting Rights Act of 1965, and President Johnson issued Executive Order No. 11246, which later evolved into a series of policies and programming commonly referring to as *affirmative action* (Fleming, Gill, & Swinton, 1978; Rubio, 2001; Spann, 2000).

Enacted on September 24, 1965, to remove the barriers that restricted access to gainful educational and employment opportunities for people of color, affirmative action was created to obliterate discrimination toward racial/ethnic minorities, hold institutions accountable for fostering diversity, and promote the inclusion of disadvantaged groups (Busenberg & Smith, 1997; Crosby, 2006; Fleming et al., 1978; Skrentny, 1996). More specifically, any organization conducting business with the federal government had to become more inclusive in its hiring practices, and educational entities had to provide equal access in admissions.

Prior to the national effort to equalize educational opportunities, African American students frequently attended historically Black colleges and universities (HBCUs) and northern colleges (Brown, 1999; Trent, 1991a). By 1971 affirmative action programs were required at all institutions of higher learning, targeting predominately White institutions (Fleming et al., 1978).

Affirmative action mandates required measures that were deemed to be temporary in the areas of recruitment/outreach, hiring, promotions, and increases in salary. In higher education, affirmative action policies were meant to combat discrimination of diverse collegians. Affirmative action at the collegiate level has addressed the exclusivity of the "ivory towers" via admissions, scholarships, and financial aid (Brunner, 2006a). Special efforts were made to promote educational equity for African Americans, Hispanic Americans, Native Americans, and women (Trent, 1991a). As such, student affirmative action programs serve to redress historical discrimination, as well as the present-day effects of past discrimination (Crosby, 2006; Trent, 1991a).

Affirmative action evolved from Title VI of the Civil Rights Act of 1964 in an effort to bolster the 14th Amendment in solidifying equal protection for all citizens. However, even though Title VI of the Civil Rights Act of 1964 made it unlawful for American institutions receiving federal funds to discriminate against any individual on the basis of race, color, religion, sex, or national origin (42 USC 2000(d)-2000(d)(1)), segregation continued to exist in many educational institutions. Those that did adopt affirmative action policies were made to defend their efforts to include the underrepresented and disadvantaged (Fleming et al., 1978; Howard, 1997; Trent, 1991a).

Affirmative action has been questioned and legally challenged since its inception. The challenges illustrate a lack of consensus about the extent to which affirmative action ensures equal access and equality of opportunity. The ongoing backlash in higher education results from the mistaken impression that affirmative action is a form of preferential treatment or tokenism (Chideya, 1999; Feinberg, 1996; Zamani & Brown, 2003). Katznelson (2005) argues that given the historical roots of racial discrimination, the modern-day impact of previous injustices, and the effects of current racial biases, there is still a pressing need for affirmative action policies and programming.

Demographic Realities and Participation Trends

The term *racial/ethnic minority* is a misnomer from a global perspective because, worldwide, there are more people of color than Whites. Additionally, U.S. society is becoming increasingly multiethnic as racially diverse groups, including biracial and multiracial populations, grow. In 2005, one in three people in the United States was a person of color, as shown in Table 1 (U.S. Census Bureau, 2006).

Before long, the term racial/ethnic minority will also become outmoded in the United States. Demographers forecast that people of color will collectively represent the majority of the U.S. population by the year 2050 (U.S. Census Bureau, 2000, 2004). Against the backdrop of these changing demographics, institutions of higher learning have become less homogenous.

TABLE 1
Racial/Ethnic Composition of the Total U.S. Population

	United States
Total Population	299,398,485
	Percentage
One Race	98.0%
White alone	73.9%
Black or African American alone	12.4%
American Indian and Alaska Native alone	0.8%
Asian alone	4.4%
Native Hawaiian and Other Pacific Islander alone	0.1%
Some other race alone	6.3%
Two or more races	2.0%
Hispanic or Latino origin (of any race)	14.8%
White alone, not Hispanic or Latino	66.2%

From U.S. Census Bureau, *American Community Survey* (2006). Retrieved on May 9, 2008, from http://factfinder.census.gov/servlet/STTable?_bm = y&-geo_id = 01000US&-qr_name = ACS_2006_EST_G00_S0501&-ds_name = ACS_2006_EST_G00 e&-_lang = en&-_cal ler = geoselect&-state = st&-format =

However, the racial and ethnic makeup of these colleges and universities does not reflect the demographics of the larger populace.

K–12 Education

According to the *Digest of Education Statistics* (National Center for Education Statistics [NCES], 2006a), enrollment in public elementary and secondary schools rose 24% between 1985 and 2006, and students of color (i.e., African American, American Indian/Alaska Native, Asian American, and Hispanic) made up over two-fifths of students enrolled in pre-K–12 schools. An NCES report titled *Status and Trends in the Education of Racial and Ethnic Minorities* (KewalRamani, Gilbertson, Fox, & Provasnik, 2007) states that while Whites have experienced decreases in enrollment, the proportion of racial/ethnic minority students enrolled in public schools increased during 1993 to 2003, particularly in urban enclaves, with Hispanic students accounting for the majority of the growth.

As the racial and ethnic makeup of elementary and secondary school enrollment has shifted, the scarcity of resources and the practice of performance-based funding have made high-stakes testing and assessment primary components of any discussion, debate, or description of current educational practices. Achievement gaps by race/ethnicity continue to persist long term, which is evident in White students outperforming African American and Hispanic students in reading and mathematics on the National Assessment of Educational Progress (NAEP). While the score gaps between Blacks and Whites across age groups were smaller in 2004 than in the early 1970s for each assessment, the score gaps for Hispanic and White students were not different for 13-year-olds on the reading assessment or for 9-year-olds on the mathematics assessment (KewalRamani et al., 2007). As for achievement levels for Asian/Pacific Islander students in contrast to Whites, higher percentages of each group scored at or above proficient on the main NAEP reading assessment than did American Indian/Alaska Native, African American, and Hispanic students in 4th, 8th, and 12th grades. Additionally, a larger proportion of Asians/Pacific Islanders scored at or above proficient on the mathematics assessment than did all other races/ethnicities (KewalRamani et al., 2007). KewalRamani and colleagues also reported that relative to mathematics proficiency, 15-year-old Asian students outscored African American and Hispanic students on the 2003 Program for International Student Assessment (PISA) mathematics literacy assessment; also noteworthy is Hispanic students scoring higher than African American students, and U.S. 15-year-old students scoring lower than average in contrast to their peers abroad.

Postsecondary Education

Of the 1992 college-qualified high school graduates, 78% of Hispanic, 83% of White, and 83% of African American students expected to earn bachelor's degrees. College enrollment at degree-granting institutions increased by 17% between 1982 and 1992 (NCES, 2005). The percentage of undergraduate college students who are members of racial/ethnic minority groups increased from 17% to 32% between 1976 and 2004 (KewalRamani et al., 2007). It is important to note, however, that the degree of change in this data is primarily because of the growing numbers of Hispanic students (increasing from 3% to 10%) and Asian/Pacific Islander students (increasing from 2% to 6%) who attended college during that time period. While the proportion of African American students fluctuated during the early years of this period, enrollments only increased from 9% to 12% between 1976 and 2002. While the proportion of students of color has increased, the share of White students has decreased. Racial/ethnic minority students compose close to one-third of all undergraduates combined. Despite educational policy and efforts to promote equity in postsecondary attendance, participation of non-Asian students of color in higher education reflects stratification and differential postsecondary attainment outcomes (KewalRamani et al., 2007; Velez, 1985).

The American Council of Education (ACE) Status Report on Minorities (Harvey & Anderson, 2005) contends that there has been a 37% increase in postsecondary enrollment for African American students between 1991 and 2002, though enrollment figures illustrate stratification by institutional tier (2- or 4-year) and prestige. There was a 3% increase in persistence rates for African American students (from 51% to 54%) between 1994 and 2000. However, despite increases in African American matriculation and enrollment, persistent postsecondary participation gaps still exist between Blacks and Whites. The percentage of first-time African American college entrants completing programs within a 5-year time span remained the lowest among the racial/ethnic groups reporting that began their postsecondary education during 1995 and 1996 (*Educational Statistics Quarterly*, 2005). Degree conferral is highest for Asian American students (62%), followed by Whites (58%) and Hispanics (42%), with African American students last (36%).

Reflecting a major shift in the homogenous environments of college campuses of earlier years, by the year 2000 more than half of all undergraduates were women, and a bit more than two-fifths were 24 years old or older, marking the growth of a nontraditionally aged student demographic (National Postsecondary Student Aid Study, 2000). Women account for the majority of the growth that has occurred since the 1980s. However, a gender gap has emerged that varies by race/ethnicity. For example, Asian American women account for 54% of undergraduate Asian American students; White women make up 56% of Whites pursuing undergraduate study, while Hispanic women are 59% of undergraduate collegians for their ethnic group, and American Indian/Alaska Native females are 61% of undergraduates in their group. The most pronounced gender gap in postsecondary enrollment is among African American collegians. As a case in point, 54% of African American undergraduates were female in 1976; by 2004 African American females made up almost two-thirds (i.e., 64%) of Black undergraduate college students (KewalRamani et al., 2007).

Historically, community colleges have opened their doors to students defined as nontraditional because of their age, gender, race/ethnicity, low income level, first-generation immigration status, or physical disabilities. Two-year institutions have enrolled students of color, namely American Indian,

African American, and Hispanic students in higher proportions than 4-year colleges and universities for the last 20 years (Aragon & Zamani, 2002; Rendon & Garza, 1996; Rendon & Matthews, 1994). According to the American Association of Community Colleges (AACC, n.d.), 34% of community college students are racial/ethnic minorities consisting of 6% Asian American, 13% Black, 14% Hispanic, and 1% Native American (NCES, 2006b; Phillippe & Gonzalez, 2005).

Nearly half of all African American college students enrolled in postsecondary education 20 years ago attended community colleges, and the same holds true today (AACC, n.d.; National Advisory Committee on Black Higher Education and Black Colleges and Universities, 1979; National Postsecondary Aid Study, 2000; Phillippe & Gonzalez, 2005). Like African Americans, the number of Hispanics attending 2-year versus 4-year institutions has remained virtually unchanged over the last quarter century. In 1976 55% of Hispanic students attending college enrolled at 2-year institutions, and in 1995 the percentage rose to 56% (Sable & Stennett, 1998). Hence, it is worthy to note that the participation and growth of women, African American, Hispanic, first-generation, and low-income students have largely been at 2-year institutions of higher learning (Aragon & Zamani, 2002; Cohen & Brawer, 2003; Jacobs, 1999; London, 1992; Zamani, 2006).

Non-Asian students of color enter higher education at lower rates than their White and Asian American counterparts. Subsequently, African American, American Indian, and Hispanic students have not reached parity, particularly with their White peers. Given this fact, diversity initiatives and opportunity enhancement (the use of race as one of several factors in admissions decisions) are necessary to help bridge the gap in postsecondary educational attainment between 2-year colleges and 4-year institutions and graduate/professional degree programs (see Table 2). Research confirms the importance of "affirmative acts," especially in light of the shifting demographics of this country's populace (Bergmann, 1999; Katznelson, 2005; Smith, 1998, 2006; Trent, 1991b; Zamani & Brown, 2003).

Retrenchment and the Politics of Access Policy Opinions

Organized attempts to dismantle affirmative action have been made in several states. The University of California, University of Texas, University of Washington, and University of Michigan have been faced with the burdensome task of defending the promotion of campus diversity through the use of affirmative action. Even as women and people of color participate in higher education in greater numbers than ever, a national conversation continues

TABLE 2

Number of Degrees Conferred by Racial/Ethnic Group, 2005–2006

Degree Granted	Total Conferred [All Fields]	White, Non-Hispanic	Black, Non-Hispanic	Hispanic	Asian/PI	American Indian/AN	Non-resident Alien
Associate	713,066	485,297	89,784	80,854	35,201	8,552	13,378
Bachelor's	1,485,242	1,075,561	142,420	107,588	102,376	10,940	46,357
Master's	594,065	393,357	58,976	58,976	34,029	3,504	71,761
Doctor's	56,067	31,601	3,122	3,122	3,257	230	15,975
First Professional	87,655	63,590	6,223	6,223	10,645	710	2,041

Note. The Chronicle of Higher Education (2008, August 29). The Almanac Issue, 2008–9. Degrees conferred by racial and ethnic group, 2005–6, p. 20

surrounding the legitimacy of affirmative action (Crosby, 2006; NCES, 2005; Wilson, 2001). In light of the persistent backlash surrounding affirmative action in higher education, just how long opportunity enhancement programs will continue is questionable (Bergmann, 1999; Chideya, 1999; Fleming, 2000; Fleming et al., 1978).[1] There is no monolithic view of Americans' beliefs regarding access policies. Given that institutions of higher learning mirror the cultural pluralism of U.S. society as a whole, identity politics surface at colleges and universities representing the differing political ideologies of diverse student bodies.

Research examining student attitudes about affirmative action as they relate to race, gender, and income is limited. A great deal of literature discusses in detail how Whites across the political spectrum view affirmative action (Sears, Henry, & Kosterman, 2000; Sidanius, Singh, Hetts, & Federico, 2000; Sniderman, 1991, 1993a). There has been, however, limited inquiry and a lack of consensus regarding the attitudes of people of color toward affirmative action and how this relates to their political leanings. This may, in part, be because of the general misconception that members of racial/ethnic minority groups share similar politics and beliefs (Falcon, 1988; Shingles, 1992; Sigelman & Welch, 1991). People of color are often portrayed as homogenous in regard to social policy concerns, as if they represent a singular point of view (Sigelman & Welch, 1991; Sniderman, 1993b). Racial/ethnic minorities have multiple identities, as they are also members of social groups and microcultures that are based on characteristics including gender, socioeconomic status, age, ability, religion, and sexuality. As a result, a continuum of political ideologies contribute to what is often termed a minority consciousness. The division in political ideologies between African Americans, Asian Americans, and Hispanics is likely because of the historical differences in the experiences of each group, their perceptions regarding minority status, and their present societal positioning as it relates to social and educational attainment (Falcon, 1988).

According to Shingles (1992), minority consciousness extends from conservatism to liberalism to radicalism. Conservatives generally echo a preference for the status quo and do not challenge the distribution of societal

---

[1] Following the U.S. Supreme Court's ruling in *Gratz v. Bollinger* (2003) and *Grutter v. Bollinger* (2003), the pendulum is still swinging toward retrenchment of affirmative action. On November 7, 2006, Michigan residents voted to abolish affirmative action by supporting an amendment to the state constitution. The referendum, referred to as the Michigan Civil Rights Initiative (MCRI), called to a vote whether to repeal affirmative action or what was framed as "state-sponsored discrimination" by conservatives. Interestingly, voting in favor of the MCRI eliminated consideration of race, color, gender, ethnicity, or national origin—in hiring and promotions, in awarding contracts, and in admissions to taxpayer-financed educational institutions despite the high court's decision to uphold affirmative action, finding that diversity is a compelling state interest.

resources or the stratification of their group's positioning in the present social order (Shingles, 1992; Van Dyke, 1995). Liberals are considered to be individuals who question unequal participation of all citizens, advocate for governmental intervention in ensuring equity, and maintain a basic belief in economic, political, and social reform (Feldman & Zaller, 1992). Radicals reject the existing social order and link racism and sexism to the underlying principles of American politics (Shingles, 1992).

Conservatism and liberalism are the ideologies that generally influence the political behavior of diverse racial/ethnic groups in the United States. Political ideologies are directly related to how individuals justify their views about social matters, as there is a convincing degree of association between racial attitudes and political views (Hinich & Munger, 1994; Kerlinger, 1984; Sniderman, 1991, 1993a). Thus, the political views of various groups might serve to explain their attitudes about affirmative action. Additionally, the way in which people of color view their status, individually and collectively, have important ramifications for how they regard social policy issues, particularly race-conscious forms of affirmative action.

Determinants of Stigma, Stereotypes, and Social Race Relations

Some of the controversy surrounding affirmative action programs stems from the contention that diversity initiatives may be harmful to the intended beneficiaries. Certain groups, including individuals with disabilities, those with disfigurements, racial/ethnic groups, and the poor/underclass, can be met with intense reactions from dominant group members. The social meaning attached to particular behaviors and attributes of these groups is often referred to as stigma (Jones et al., 1984).

Stigma can be described as a pervasive belief that a person or group bears a mark of disgrace. To members of the dominant culture, this mark of disgrace is often a perceived difference that is used to negatively categorize the group (Ainlay, Becker & Coleman, 1986; Goffman, 1963). The stigmatized are commonly looked upon with great disdain, considered deviant and less than human. As a consequence, members of stigmatized groups are frequently subject to unfair treatment and hurtful sentiment.

Discrimination and prejudice are the means through which stigma most repeatedly surfaces. In theory, stigma extends to various forms of discriminatory treatment that the blemished person and/or group experiences. Fostering antidiscriminatory policies and diversity initiatives is a laudable contribution as most disadvantaged society members are generally members of stigmatized groups (Crocker & Major, 1989). Crocker and Major noted that some stigmatized groups, including African Americans and women, have fewer economic opportunities and lower economic outcomes than White males. The vast majority of our nation's poor population includes disproportionately high numbers of non-Whites and women. For instance, 28% of the U.S. poor are African American, although African Americans constitute 12.4% of the population. Hence, twice as many African Americans live at or beneath the poverty line, while slightly more than one-quarter of Hispanics live in poverty (Bergmann, 1999; U.S. Census Bureau, 2006). These statistics illustrate how discrimination occurs as a result of stereotypic beliefs, putting up economic and interpersonal obstacles before people perceived to be different by the dominant group.

Crocker and Lutsky (1986) and Ashmore and Del Boca (1981) define a stereotype as a set of generalized beliefs about a particular group. Ashmore and Del Boca (1981) forwarded three perspectives to explain why stereotypes permeate society:

1. The *Cognitive Perspective* contends that the stereotyping process results from one's basic cognitive functioning (Hamilton, 1981). In this case, research has noted that there are a number of human information-processing features that bias judgment and forward stereotypes whereby stereotyping is not uniquely different from other cognitive structures or processes (p. 28).

2. The *Motivational or Psychodynamic Perspective* suggests that stereotypes are roused by social and psychological needs. It is argued that stereotypes (e.g., being lazy, filthy, hypersexual, and so forth) are projected onto others because the markers may fear the existence of unfavorable traits within themselves. The motivational approach is a method of feeding one's ego to increase self-esteem, direct hostility away from oneself and toward the marked group.

3. The *Sociocultural Perspective* asserts that erroneous beliefs about people of color and other markable groups emerge from social agents such as family and the media. This perspective holds that people's biased perceptions toward marked groups is transmitted from direct experience and information received from others producing cultural ingroups and outgroups. (p. 28)

The persistence of stereotypes has influenced the preconceptions and expectancies of members of the majority, making it very difficult to discard these false beliefs. Prevailing false beliefs that mark stigmatized groups often make it impossible for members of these groups to secure access to equal opportunities. The stratification of society reflects structural inequities that characterize the imbalance of power between various groups. The overall social order promotes a system in which persons of power are more likely to achieve an affluent status. Given high levels of prestige, people with power maintain the ability to exercise social control over stigmatized groups (Becker & Arnold, 1986). Consequently, stigma is directly related to social inequities.

Ainlay, Becker, and Coleman (1986) state, "Many stigmatized people also begin to understand that the stigmatizer, having established a position of false superiority and consequently the need to maintain it, is enslaved to the concept that stigmatized people are fundamentally inferior" (p. 222). Hence, the institutionalization of stigma is systemic. For instance, those lacking formal education may feel further stigmatized because of the institutionalization of educational inequities. More explicitly, less education has been found to contribute to social class inequities for people from particular racial/ethnic groups, lower-income populations, and people with disabilities. Thus, people are stigmatized based on ascribed characteristics and attributes that subsequently position them at the lower echelon of the social hierarchy.

The Scarlet Letter *A* and Affirming Diversity

Affirmative action programming has sought to challenge the status quo and uneven stratification of societal resources. The number of racial/ethnic minorities that are economically and socially disadvantaged is disproportionate to that of White Americans (Bergmann, 1999; Kluegel, 1990; Kluegel & Smith, 1986; Spring, 2006; Tuch & Sigelman, 1997). Often the dominant culture tends to victimize the victim by framing the problems of the less fortunate as pathological. Members of the dominant culture rationalize that the social disadvantages facing many disenfranchised people of color are their own fault and result from poor values and dysfunctional family structures. What is not recognized is the systemic nature of discrimination or the necessity of public policies to enforce social justice. Therefore, it is not surprising that Whites (largely males) are most apt to oppose affirmative action (Feagin & O'Brien, 2004).

In facilitating diversity initiatives, however, one must examine what potential beneficiaries, and the general public, deem to be fair. As stated earlier, affirmative action is perceived by some as a disadvantage to women and minorities. Critics suggest that stigmatization hampers the beneficiaries of affirmative action, causing some members of these groups to share the negative sentiment about programming earmarked on their behalf. Do the costs outweigh the benefits? Northcraft and Martin (1982) interviewed 32 individuals requesting that the participants hypothetically match five recent hires to five résumés. Each participant was told that affirmative action obligations had to be satisfied by the company and that a Black person would have to be hired to satisfy the affirmative action requirements. In this quasi-experimental study, one of the applicants reviewed was designated as Black. The overall results revealed that participants paired the Black employee with the weakest résumé at a rate that exceeded probable chance. However, when there was not any mention of affirmative action requirements to hire someone Black, the matching of credentials did not occur in the same fashion. In short, research has illustrated how African Americans and other applicants of color frequently receive less than favorable evaluations when a commitment to affirmative action is expressed.

In a qualitative study, Ayers (1992) examined whether beneficiaries of affirmative action saw their experiences with affirmative action as fair or unfair. Thirteen women of color associated with a zealous College of Liberal Arts affirmative action program were asked to respond to questions about fairness in principle and practice. The researcher hypothesized that the subjects would find affirmative action more unfair in practice than in principle. The research noted that participants expressed dissatisfaction with affirmative action regarding the standard of excellence being questioned and the lack of commitment by the college. Opponents of affirmative action would suggest that the findings are not necessarily representative of the views held by the majority of women and minorities who should oppose benefiting from "racial preferences" in principle and practice (Clegg, 2004).

It is a common misperception that affirmative action goals compromise standards. The notion of affirmative action as tokenism implies the stigma of incompetence. Although affirmative action has contributed to the existence and growth of the African American middle class, the White counterparts of these successful achievers may assume that these African Americans received their positions solely because of race and not because of their intelligence, skill, talent and/or creativity (Cose, 1993). Many of the assumptions associated with affirmative action policies leave beneficiaries with a sense of attributional ambiguity.

Researchers have forwarded an alternative explanation for the stigmatized experience of affirmative action beneficiaries, which they have labeled *attributional ambiguity* (Blaine, Crocker, & Major, 1995; Major, Feinstein, & Crocker, 1994). The term attributional ambiguity is used to describe the views of beneficiaries about being treated negatively because of group membership or because of the perception that they lack individual merit. Goffman (1963) stated, "Given that the stigmatized individual in our society acquires identity standards which he applies to himself in spite of failing to conform to them, it is inevitable that he will feel some ambivalence about his own self" (p. 106). Blaine et al. (1995) conducted three experiments where in the first study they found increases in negative affect and a lower perceived work ethic when a position was offered out of sympathy to a stigmatized person rather than on the basis of qualifications. Findings from their second study illustrated that sympathy had a negative effect when prejudice and discrimination or mobility problems faced by the stigmatized individual were attributed to employee selection. In the third investigation, sympathy was shown to have negative effects when it was based on individual or group-based problems imposed by the stigmatizing condition. Hence, affirmative action programs could reinforce perceived incompetence relative to peer evaluations and subsequently create resistance toward affirmative action even among marginalized people affirmative action seeks to benefit (Major et al., 1994).

The small amount of research suggesting that affirmative action is stigmatizing in nature lacks the empirical stringency necessary for generalization beyond the respective studies. Additionally, this research has not effectively illustrated the extent to which potential beneficiaries feel stigmatized as a result of affirmative action. Although women's views of affirmative action have been investigated to a degree, the opinions of people of color have not been widely addressed (Turner & Pratkanis, 1994). Hence, there is no evidence to suggest that women and minorities share a monolithic view of affirmative action.

The Impact of Stigmatization and Stereotyping on Affirmative Action

According to Turner and Pratkanis (1994), affirmative action may be viewed as stigmatizing by being self-threatening when in conflict with societal norms and values. Nonetheless, stigmatization can only affect those members of marked groups that buy into American standards of idealism and meritocracy. Conservatives like Amy Chua, Stephen Carter, Linda Chavez, Ward Connerly, D'nesh D'Souza, Condoleezza Rice, Richard Rodriguez, Thomas Sowell, and Clarence Thomas are all people of color who are avid opponents of affirmative action. They contend that affirmative action is akin to racial preferencing and reverse discrimination. At times, these individuals even make their neoconservative White peers appear relatively progressive given their active, aggressive lobbying for racial/ethnic minorities to endorse the abolishment of affirmative action, which they view as degrading and promoting unfairness in educational settings and workplaces (*Black Issues in Higher*

Education, 2004a; Carter, 1991; D'Souza, 1992; Sowell, 2004). Paradoxically, these very visible people of color, who are aggressively calling for the abolition of affirmative action, are beneficiaries of the very policy initiatives they seek to dismantle.

Identifying With the Mainstream

> The new black conservatives assume that without affirmative action programs, white Americans will make choices on merit rather than on race. Yet they have adduced no evidence for this. Most Americans realize that job-hiring choices are made both on reasons of merit and on personal grounds. And it is this personal dimension that is often influenced by racist perceptions. (West, 1986, p. 644)

Black Conservatives and Affirmative Action

The Black and Brown conservative elite were able to break through the good ol' boys' network, not just by pulling themselves up by the bootstraps, but because of the legal enforcement of race as a consideration in recruiting and hiring practices. The congruence of the racial and political ideologies of neo-conservative minorities is suggestive of Cross's (1978) Nigrescence model typical of identity development moving from Black self-hatred to a positive Black self-image. Helms (1993) refers to this anti-self behavior as the *preencounter stage*, in which there is a devaluing of one's Blackness reflective of the lowest stage of Black identity development. Ultimately individuals move through three additional stages (i.e., *Encounter, Immersion,* and *Emersion*) before reaching the fifth and final stage referred to as *Internalization* reflective of attaining a sense of satisfaction with one's Blackness. In other words, there are African Americans and other racial/ethnic minorities that exhibit identity alienation, undermine positive racial ideology and harbor internalized hatred, all stemming from living in the context of patriarchal White supremacy. Subsequently, when members of racial/ethnic minority groups offer positive self-evaluations of ability and performance, this can reasonably be viewed as a manifestation of social destigmatization.

Destigmatization and Pervasive Stereotypes

> I'm not a threatening black person to them. . . . That's probably why I got hired. . . . But I also got hired because I'm good. I have all the tools.
> —Branford Marsalis (as cited in Copage, 1996)

Destigmatization comes about when people or groups are more positive about themselves and begin to feel less susceptible to the effects of stigma

(Ainlay et al., 1986; Jones et al., 1984). Jones and colleagues (1984) use the Black Power movement as an example of destigmatization. They state, "Instead of attempting to reduce the attributional salience of race, the Black power movement attempted to increase the salience while changing the valence from negative to positive. One Black organization after another followed the 'Black is beautiful' theme with varying degrees of enthusiasm, and the White majority was at least forced to reevaluate their silent assumptions about Blacks being content with their (inferior) place" (p. 305).

In the past 30 years, stigmatized groups have increasingly influenced society's image of them, in large part because of the appearance and growth of organizations, including the National Association for the Advancement of Colored People (NAACP) and the Urban League, that have led powerful antidiscrimination campaigns (Jones et al., 1984). The process of destigmatization is gradual, however, and negative attitudes about people of color continue to pervade the consciousness of society. Additionally, destigmatization efforts are sometimes halted when contemporary forms of racial antipathy that reinforce traditional modes of prejudice are reawakened and fuel a sense of worthlessness among the stigmatized (Ainlay et al., 1986).

Research by Pinel, Warner, and Chua (2005) examines whether stigma consciousness increases among African American and Hispanic students following attendance at a predominately White institution (PWI). The authors also sought to determine if attending majority-populated colleges influenced the academic performance and self-concept of African American and Hispanic students. In comparing 44 academically stigmatized African Americans and Hispanics to 79 nonstigmatized White and Asian American peers, the researchers found that males who experienced greater consciousness across degrees of stigma also experienced higher disengagement and lower grade point averages (GPAs). Increases in stigma consciousness for female respondents corresponded to poorer self-concept and lower engagement levels. Interestingly, stigmatized female students had low GPAs irrespective of their level of stigma consciousness.

In his text, *The Politics of Stereotype: Affirmative Action and Psychology*, Salinas (2003) suggests that behind efforts to eliminate affirmative action lie factors such as teachers' low expectations of students of color, the public's perception of the welfare queen, and many other negative stereotypes that adversely affect and further marginalize students of color. It is his contention that the culmination of years of stereotyping has a powerful impact on targeted people who, in turn, buy into the fallacy that they do not belong and cannot perform as well as their White counterparts. This phenomenon is harmful to students of color and greatly affects their psychosocial adjustment, their ability to perform within testing situations, and their overall persistence and matriculation.

High-Stakes Testing, Stereotype Threat, and Affirmative Action

According to Fleming (2000), the history of testing in the United States reflects prejudicial ideologies and racist assumptions of inferiority with regard to African Americans' intelligence. Given the testing movement's beginnings, one should consider which came first, psychometric bias or social bias? Is it the long history of social bias that includes racial stereotyping, discrimination, and intolerance that fuels psychometric bias? Or, is it psychometric bias in the form of unreliability in the instrumentation, the variance in testing conditions, or structural inequities in the educational preparation of students by race/ethnicity, gender, and class that perpetuate oppressive circumstances for marginalized groups?

Salinas (2003) argues that the impetus for the passage of California's Proposition 209 (1996), which ended the state's affirmative action programs, was the widely held stereotype that unqualified, unproductive, and undeserving racial/ethnic minorities are advancing in education and employment because of affirmative action. However, research investigating affirmative action, academic abilities, and standardized testing does not promote a consensus of thought on this topic (Cohen & Steele, 2002; Fleming, 2000; Gordon, 2001; Gordon & Bridglall, 2007; Steele, 2001). Derrick Bell (2006) states, "As presently administered, the scores on standardized tests more accurately measure the economic status of the test takers than they measure their potential for success in school or on the job. They reward as worthy of merit the already well-off while serving as one more barrier to disadvantaged test takers, white as well as black" (p. 42–43). For that reason, talented students from low-income families (a disproportionately high number of the financially underserved are students of color) are not identified as gifted, even though they have the ability to excel given the right teaching methods and circumstances (Delpit, 1995; Nieto & Bode, 2008; Sternberg, 2005).

African Americans who score well on high-stakes tests may have become acculturated to mainstream values and culture, which may contribute to the reason they scored high and may be less interested in Black ideological issues (Fleming, 2000). However, it is important to note that while some African Americans have ascended into the middle class, the Black-White achievement gap that results in differing outcomes for White and Black students remain, even with all things being equal. Scholars such as Jacqueline Fleming (1984, 2000) and Claude Steele (2000, 2001) assert that the elimination of affirmative action would make the presumable objectivity of ACT and SAT college entrance exams more pronounced. Additionally, the interaction of class with race/ethnicity and gender further exacerbates disenfranchisement for individuals of stigmatized groups in testing situations. In his expert testimony in defense of affirmative action, Claude Steele (2000) candidly discussed how students' life experiences are divergent and shaped by race/ethnicity, gender, and class. He noted:

> For example, consider what being African American, even from the middle-class, can predispose a person to experience: Assignment to lower academic tracks throughout schooling; being taught and counseled with lower expectations by less skilled teachers in more poorly funded schools; attending school in more distressed neighborhoods or in suburban areas where they are often a small, socially isolated minority; living in families with fewer resources; and having peers who—alienated by these conditions—may be more often disinterested in school. Clearly these race-linked experiences are enough to lead students from this group to have lower scores on the SAT at the point of applying to college without any reference to innate ability. A similar scenario could be described for many Hispanic groups in this society and for American Indians (especially those living on reservations). (p. 132)

Steele's (2001) research has been crucial in the battle over affirmative action as his work has proven that standardized tests only tap a small portion (roughly 18%) of the skill set required of good students. Therefore, test performance and grade performance do not translate well. To explain the performance gap, Steele and colleagues posit that stereotype threat can negatively affect the test performance of racial/ethnic minority students and women. When an individual is faced with a negative stereotype about his or her group—for example, the verbal perspicacity of Blacks or the inferior mathematical abilities of women—they are prone to become distracted and/or upset, which can interfere with their performance, particularly on high-stakes tests (Cohen & Steele, 2002; Steele, 2000, 2001; Steele & Aronson, 1995).

Sternberg (2006) examined how a wide array of teaching situations/methods such as prep courses, online tutorials, and test-taking approaches (e.g., making educated guesses, answering easier items first, practice subject tests, etc.) might provide a more effective predictor of college success on SAT measures for divergent learners participating in *The Rainbow Project*. The Rainbow Project's chief aim was to reduce ethnic group differences and augment the predictive validity of the SAT for college performance. Overall, the measures The Rainbow Project had taken to assess analytical, practical, and creative skills resulted in a reduction in racial/ethnic group differences on the SAT, with Latinos benefiting most. Additionally, the findings support the idea that the traditional psychometric view of cognitive aptitude in predicting college readiness is outmoded, as new standardized measures that focus on a broader range of abilities are taking hold (Sternberg). On a related note, the Educational Testing Service (ETS) has been considering how to produce and disseminate versions of the SAT that would take race/ethnicity and socioeconomic status into account. According to Glazer (1999), ETS introduced a race-blind model of the test, offering institutions a "Strivers" score, which is an adjusted score that takes race and social class into consideration. However, opponents of affirmative action such as Abigail Thernstrom (1999) have found fault with the Strivers score, calling it a cloaked strategy to promote racial preferences for non-Asian minorities and to allow higher numbers of Black and Hispanic students at elite institutions (Bowen & Bok, 1998).

The lack of available assessments and limited instructional deliveries highlight the devalued status of cultural identity and explain how characteristics such as race/ethnicity and gender skew institutional perceptions of identity that can induce academic success or contribute to academic failure among disenfranchised students. With continuing national efforts to discontinue affirmative action, some scholars (Gordon, 2001; Gordon & Bridglall, 2007; Sternberg, 2005) insist that an affirmative development of academic abilities, or the promotion of a theory of successful intelligence, would allow divergent learners to improve their abilities, capitalize on their strengths, and have the opportunity to succeed. For this reason diversity policy initiatives should be established as a deliberate attempt to increase cultural, social, and intellectual capital. Viewing affirmative action as a means to further the development of students' academic strengths is a needed response to unequal schooling contexts. Thus, the affirmative development of academic abilities would demand the eradication of educational inequities and differential access to resources, including socialization of intellect to multiple cultural contexts, exposure to high-performance learning communities, and special attention to attitudes, dispositions, and efficacy of students. It would also reduce the incidence of stereotype threat, even among the most academically high-achieving women and students of color.

Notes

As terms associated with social groups often change overtime and across contexts, it is important to note that African American and Black, as Hispanic and Latino/Latina, and American Indian and Native American, are used interchangeably in this text.

The terms *community colleges* and *2-year institutions* are used synonymously throughout the text.

THE LANGUAGE OF ENTITLEMENT AND FRAMING OF AFFIRMATIVE ACTION

T his chapter seeks to problematize the notion of White entitlement and the compelling interest of the state. This places affirmative action in an ideological perspective and bolsters support for policies and programs that account for historical inequalities in higher education. It is time to rejuvenate the legal rationales of the 1960s that have been abandoned for empty rhetoric that falsely suggests there is a level playing field.

Policy that attempts to end historical inequities and racial discrimination is often called into question in the popular rhetoric as an example of racial preference. This rhetoric implies that individual rights are compromised as unqualified applicants receive jobs and opportunities they do not deserve. These assumptions are usually part of a historical barrage of taunts fueled by conservative pundits. Bell (2000), Bonilla-Silva (2001), Crenshaw (2003), Harris (1993), Hudson (1999), and others have all written about the historical legacy of exclusion regarding people of color in education, housing, and employment. Currently their research is often minimized and replaced with language advocating for color-blind, race-neutral policies by affirmative action opponents.

White Entitlement and the Myth of Racial Preference

The current attacks against affirmative action can be viewed as a reclaiming of White entitlement within institutions of higher learning. While many may argue this to be an interpretive statement unsupported by hard evidence, one only has to engage the rhetoric of the Center for Individual

Rights (CIR). CIR's process of examining educational policies in higher education focus on the perceived displacement of White students in favor of students of color from underrepresented groups in the admissions process. In short, CIR policy recommendations advocate for the removal of any race-specific language in public policy.

When policy makers ignore the existence of race/ethnicity in their language and ideas, their de facto enforcement continues to disadvantage people of color. Inequities by race/ethnicity have long been a problem in U.S. society. However, the stream of problems that flow from these inequities never converged with appropriate solutions because of the pervasive politics of difference that surround us. Applying Kingdon's (2003) multiple-streams policy approach to the realm of affirmative action allows us to see how solutions to racial discrimination are prolonged in American history. For example, the slave trade began when the first Africans were brought to Jamestown, Virginia, in 1619, yet it was not until 1865 that the 13th Amendment to the U.S. Constitution abolished slavery. Why did it take nearly 250 years for a policy window to open that would condemn the institution of slavery? And how is it that it took another 100 plus years to develop policies that would affirm access and eradicate racial discrimination?

The current policy landscape reveals a backlash to affirmative action policies in higher education. Proposition 209 in California and the *Hopwood v. State of Texas* (1996) decision in Texas provide glaring examples, resulting in drastic reductions in Black and Latino/Latina undergraduate and graduate admissions in these states. Legal remedies, while necessary to address societal ills, are often too limited in scope to fully tackle systemic inequities stemming from institutionalized/individual racism and sexism. Unfortunately, the diminishing percentage of African American and Latino collegians is inconsequential to contemporary opponents of affirmative action.

In the book *There Goes My Everything: White Southerners in the Age of Civil Rights, 1945–1975*, Sokol (2006) candidly captures the tensions that occurred in the Deep South over a 30-year period. The author clearly depicts the sanctions that ensured that only Whites were given the opportunity and privilege to actualize their inalienable rights. For many other citizens, these rights remained wishful pursuits. An ethnocentric, occidental worldview is deeply rooted in the American contradictions that surround diversity and pluralistic democracy. Ringer contends that challenges to multiculturalism began during colonial times, and that a "racist duality" is woven into the very fabric of American life, as evidenced by the historical origins and foundation of the country (Ringer as cited by Grant, 2006, p. 162). CIR places

its rhetoric of American ideals of individualism at the center of its oppositional stance to affirmative action. This is suggestive of the White patriarchal
hegemony that is central to the fabric of life in the United States. However,
the CIR often fails to recognize that individual rights were created in the
interest of Whites, particularly White male landowners, as illustrated by
Bobo and Kluegel (1993), Haney Lopez (1996), and Harris (1993). The current attack against affirmative action is an attempt to reclaim property rights
(i.e., entitlement and self-interest) that are guaranteed by White birthright.

Framing Affirmative Action: Based on Race, Gender, or Need

Individual and group self-interests bear great influence on attitudes toward
affirmative action. Public opinion on social policies is often based on how
the issues are framed and presented to the public (Bobo, 2000; Bobo,
Kluegel, & Smith, 1993, 1997; Kinder & Sanders, 1996; Springer & Baez,
2002). More often than not, affirmative action is not seen by the public as
establishing fair competition and a level playing field for members of groups
that still suffer the effects of past discrimination. Additional research is still
needed on the perceptions of whether affirmative action is exclusively race-
targeted, gender-specific, or class-based.

One goal of affirmative action is to increase the representation of people
of color in upwardly mobile positions. Race-conscious affirmative action asserts that the majority of African Americans and other underrepresented
groups have not reached parity with Whites in relation to educational and
employment opportunities. Thus, race-conscious affirmative action is consistent with American ideas of fairness, as it has brought more people of color
to the attention of employers and higher education admissions officers
(Feinberg, 1996; Rendón, 2005).

Why Race Does Matter

Affirmative action is often framed in Black and White. Race-conscious social
policy implementation is commonly referred to as *affirmative action programming*. However, it is erroneous to consider race-conscious diversity initiatives
as euphemisms for the broad scope of affirmative acts that also include gender, economic need, and a host of other factors. When affirmative action is
framed exclusively as a race-conscious initiative, its opponents are quick to
conjure up labels, including tokenism, preferential treatment, reverse discrimination, and minority set-asides.

I believe there are some sincere White people. But I think they should prove it. (Malcolm X, as cited in Copage, 1993).

A person's racial/ethnic background often affects his or her view on affirmative action (Bobo & Kluegel, 1993; Fleming, 2000; Kluegel & Smith, 1983). However, there is a discrepancy among Whites in terms of how they react to policies targeting diverse racial/ethnic groups (Kluegel, 1990; Smith & Kluegel, 1984). The majority of Whites contend, however, that their views are egalitarian and they support opportunity-enhancing programming (Parker, Baltes, & Christiansen, 1997; Sears et al., 2000). Research suggests that White Americans often agree with affirmative action in theory but not in practice, particularly when policies are specifically race conscious (Dovidio, Mann, & Gaertner, 1989; Fleming, 2000; Kluegel & Smith, 1986). Levels of support do waiver, though, when the affirmative action policies in question are specifically race conscious (Dietz-Uhler & Murrell, 1993; Zamani, 2002).

Perceptions of Policy—Who Benefits?

Legitimizing Ideologies and Opposition to Affirmative Action.

Black civil rights organizations struggled for generations against employment discrimination, and it was their organizing that secured the most significant reforms to combat it. African Americans have also borne the brunt of recent attacks on affirmative action and the larger project of white racial revanchism that drives them. Indeed, so single-mindedly do contemporary critics of affirmative action focus on Blacks that one would never know from their arguments that the policy has served other groups. This sleight of hand has left both affirmative action and African Americans more vulnerable than they would be if the policy's other beneficiaries were acknowledged." (MacLean, 1999, p. 43)

Negative attitudes toward people of color may manifest themselves in opposition to affirmative action (Dovidio et al., 1989; Kluegel & Smith, 1983). Negative racial attitudes (i.e., racial affect) are a form of racism expressed by an individual's attitudes and beliefs about people from different racial/ethnic groups. Racial affect can be subtle or overt and often reflects an individual's opinion regarding changes in social stratification and the status quo.

Literature pertaining to the attitudes of potential beneficiaries toward affirmative action has found that African Americans are generally supportive of race-conscious programming efforts at 4-year institutions (Dovidio,

Gaertner & Murrell, 1994; Dovidio et al., 1989; Kinder & Sears, 1981; Mc-Conahay, 1986; Smith, 1998, 2006; Zamani, 2003). In contrast to African Americans, Latino/Latina students' support was dependent upon their socio-economic status (SES) and whether English was their second or native language. Latino/Latina collegians with a higher SES and/or English as their native language were found to be more resistant toward affirmative action in college admissions than their counterparts with lower a SES and for whom English was a second language (Sax & Arredondo, 1999).

"Engendering" Differences in Policy Stance

Differences of opinion regarding affirmative action are not exclusive to race/ethnicity. In addressing gender differences relative to affirmative action, studies have addressed White women's perceptions of affirmative action and what encourages support or disfavor for said policy initiatives (Chacko, 1982; Dovidio et al., 1989; Heilman, Simon, & Repper, 1987; Kluegel & Smith, 1983; Nacoste, 1987; Smith & Kluegel, 1984; Turner & Pratkanis, 1994). Smith (1993) conducted a study with 485 students at the University of Michigan regarding racial attitudes and views on affirmative action. The findings revealed that students entered college ambivalent about affirmative action, but after the first year White males became less supportive of affirmative action, while female support for these policies increased. Race/ethnicity and gender have been found to moderate perceptions of affirmative action, with Blacks and Latinos/Latinas exhibiting greater positive reactions than other groups, citing their support for affirmative action's attempt to further distributive, procedural, and organizational justice (Parker et al., 1997).

Zuniga, Williams, and Berger (2005) investigated whether student involvement in diversity-related activities produced action-oriented democratic outcomes, including challenging personal prejudices and committing to social justice causes. When controlling for extraneous factors, there was a greater likelihood for women to possess the motivation to reduce their own prejudices and actively promote inclusion than men. Thus, institutions of higher learning have the potential to sway opinions regarding diversity initiatives such as affirmative action via curricular offerings, residence life, and other student activities that demonstrate the importance of practicing democratic, egalitarian values. MacLean (1999) asserts that it is important to grasp affirmative action in relation to women, particularly White women. She states, "White women—are so often cast as *"free riders"* in the discourse, as passive beneficiaries living off the labor of others" (p. 43). Therefore when considering race and gender, the stakes are raised. The available data about women in higher education is as follows:

- Among 2004 high school graduates, young women were more apt to attend college than their male counterparts (72% versus 61%; roughly one-third of women between 25 to 64 years of age held a college degree in 2004, an increase of more than 20% since 1970 (Bureau of Labor Statistics, 2005).
- Women make up 58% of the nation's 13 million college undergraduates; the majority of students in graduate school are female, and women outnumbered men in 2002 for doctorates earned but are the minority of tenured professors (Cable Network News [CNN], 2004; Trower, 2002).
- Only 10% of tenured faculty are female, the vast majority being White women (Trower, 2002).
- Across disciplines, Whites compose 80.3% of full-time faculty and 85.2% of part-time instructional faculty and staff (White men account for 50% of full-time faculty and 44% of part-time instructors); meanwhile, African Americans make up 5% of full-time and of part-time faculty, and Hispanics are 3.5% of full-time and part-time instructors (NCES, 2005).
- One-third of assistant and associate professorships combined and one-sixth of full professorships are held by women, while women of color account for only 6% of all tenure and tenure-track positions (University of Michigan, 1998).

Taylor-Carter, Doverspike, and Cook (1996) attempted to integrate the results of the existing research on the effects of affirmative action on female beneficiaries. In their article, the authors framed affirmative action as a form of preferential treatment and identified macro- and microremedies for sustaining it. Macroremedies included changing attitudes of organizational members and creating displays of support from top management for affirmative action efforts. The microremedies entailed increasing organizational socialization and bolstering self-efficacy among female beneficiaries. Overall, Taylor-Carter and colleagues felt that these measures would assist in better integrating women into the workplace and had the potential to decrease feelings of isolation and low self-concept. Simultaneously, these policies could debunk negative female stereotypes, which, in turn, could increase perceptions of fairness. In critique, their viewpoint frames affirmative action as a tokenistic measure, and the evidence offered in support of psychological damage to the intended beneficiaries from diversity policy/programming efforts is inconclusive.

Although research has illustrated higher levels of support for diversity initiatives among women, when the efforts are race conscious, White women, like their White male counterparts, are less likely to support them. Whites generally do not support race-conscious policies (Bell, 2001; Bergmann, 1999; Crosby, 2006; Springer & Baez, 2002; Steele, 2001). In relation to issues of access, White women are no more racially tolerant than their male counterparts, despite the fact that they have benefited from affirmative action programs (Smith, 1998, 2006; Zamani, 2002). In other words, gender inequality did not prompt women to be more supportive of race-conscious affirmative action. The marginalization that White women experience in the form of sexism is different from the double jeopardy facing women of color, who are frequently targets of sexism and racism. Gender identity, while important for women of color, is not necessarily the most salient ingredient in their identity formation. Race/ethnicity, while incidental to many White women, is a major component in women of color's identity construction and in the way they are viewed/treated by society. The interaction of race/ethnicity and gender produces added layers of inequity for women of color.

Is It All About the Benjamins or the Lack Thereof?

A fashionable colloquialism in contemporary pop culture references the need to horde monetary and material wealth. Within this concept lies the euphemism coined for currency (the Benjamins). In recent years an alternative form of affirmative action has been proposed that moves away from the goal of remediation for groups that suffered historical discrimination and institutional racism (Boris, 1998; Crosby, 2006; Feinberg, 1996). This suggested form of "need-based" affirmative action is thought to be a compromise by some, as policies would no longer target just racial minorities and women but would be extended to include all people who demonstrate economic need. In response Feinberg (1996) argued that race-conscious and gender-specific affirmative action address three moral issues that need-based affirmative action policies do not adequately meet: (a) historical debt, (b) equality of opportunity, and (c) economics and the distribution of societal resources.

Some scholars contend that public opinion finds fault with the notion of a moral-based affirmative action that attempts to pay a historical debt to people who have been previously discriminated against, irrespective of their present-day situation (Boris, 1998; Feinberg, 1996; Trent, 1991a). In response, because the United States was built on dishonesty and free labor, there is a need to redress the vestiges of past immoral behavior sanctioned by the law of the land. From the 1600s to the 1960s, African Americans endured legalized prejudicial treatment. The legacy of slavery, as well as other forms of ethnic discrimination and sexism in American history, has long been responsible for straining race relations. Affirmative action was born as a series of legal amendments designed to uproot the long history of immoral, legally sanctioned discrimination in the United States, particularly toward indigenous groups (Native Americans), African Americans, Latinos/Latinas, and Asian Americans.

While injustices to African Americans launched the modern civil rights movement, other marginalized groups also asserted themselves to challenge historic discrimination. In *Deculturalization and the Struggle for Equality*, Joel Spring (2006) succinctly discusses the history of racism and disenfranchisement of dominated groups across the United States. A plethora of examples captures how endemic discrimination was for people of color. From the omission of citizenship rights for Native Americans in the 14th Amendment to the cultural genocide of enslaved African Americans to the invasion of the West, which stripped Mexicans of their land, to the economic exploitation of Asians, the social creation of differences served to perpetuate educational, economic, and political subordination of people of color.

The histories of people of color share the imposition of the dominant group to colonize, oppress, control, and have power over minority cultures in the United States (Feagin & O'Brien, 2004; Fraga, Meier, & England, 1988; Garcia, 1986; Spring, 2006; Wu, 2002). An African proverb states, "If you want to know the end, look at the beginning." The beginning of race relations in this country serves as the antecedent to the contemporary culture wars over affirmative action in higher education. It is clear that human and educational rights have come at great cost—this cost is what Spring calls *deculturalization*. Deculturalization involves the destroying of a people's culture with the intent to replace it with a new cultural norm through educational processes (Spring, 2006). Along these lines, multicultural education sought to include the experiences of dominated groups in the curriculum to eliminate prejudice, sexism, and affirm all students within an academic context.

Considering that race has historically been used to confiscate the rights of certain groups and protest policy mandates meant to improve persistent disparities, it comes as no surprise that affirmative action is often viewed as a burden imposed on present-day society to address historical discrimination. Much of the conflict arises when contemporary White Americans do not feel a sense of obligation for previous discrimination and do not ac-knowledge the wrongful deeds of their ancestors or the existence and effects of White privilege. Even though the institution of slavery was not introduced by today's society, it has contributed to supporting and stabilizing the coun-try's economy in a way that benefits the majority of its populace (Bonacich 1975, 1989; Lopez-Vasquez, 2005).

Although women and racial minority groups were excluded from full participation in American society, opponents of affirmative action believe that justifying gender and race-conscious policies leads to the elevation of group rights and the exclusion of individual rights. Given the firmly en-trenched notion of individualism in American ideology, affirmative action has been questioned by its opponents for promoting group rights and prefer-ential treatment at the expense of Whites, males in particular. On the other hand, need-based affirmative action supporters argue that ideas of fairness are addressed more appropriately by using lower economic status as the crite-ria for program targeting.

Many students and their families fret over the expenses associated with college attendance. Whether they are a racial/ethnic minority or White, stu-dents are vexed by the cost of attending the school of their choice, particu-larly if they are first-generation immigrants or have poor, low-income and working-class backgrounds. While there has been a shift from grant-based aid to loan-based aid, often the financial aid packages fall short of meeting the monetary obligations. Subsequently, some policy analysts argue that color-blind, economic-based affirmative action measures are welcome.

Supporters of affirmative action that opt to endorse need-based initia-tives do so in light of the unequal distribution of income, position, and status in the United States. The theory is that societal stratification is such that need-based affirmative action initiatives will also serve the goals of race- and gender-specific policies by meeting the needs of women, people of color, and low-income people in general (Barras, 1998). Prior to the attack on race-conscious programs, the majority of Whites were comfortable with the socio-economic gap between themselves and African Americans (Hartigan, 1999; Kluegel, 1990). Need-based affirmative action presumes that inequities for all people should be addressed and can be remedied. This perspective only entertains the economic factors of affirmative action and does not acknowl-edge previous injustices to people of color and women.

Issues of social class inequities are not necessarily a more recalcitrant so-cietal affliction than the malady of racism. In *Equity and Excellence in Ameri-can Higher Education*, William Bowen and colleagues (2005) look at the issue of differential access by arguing for need-based affirmative action. By their estimations, socioeconomic status as a measure of disenfranchisement is more pronounced for poor White children because they do not receive additional consideration by race and/or gender-targeted measures. Nevertheless, the authors fail to acknowledge that poor Whites still enjoy White privilege and are not systematically placed at a disadvantage because of flagrant racial discrimination.

A cumulative consequence exists, a double jeopardy of sorts, relative to the degree of disenfranchisement that more severely confines the economic, educational, political, and social upward mobility of people of color. It is negligent to suggest that there is comparative suffering or disadvantage between Whites and people of color when Whites make up about 66.2% of the U.S. populace, but only roughly 8% live at or beneath the poverty level (Webster & Bishaw, 2007). The percentage of people of color living under the poverty line, by contrast, is disproportionately higher, with 25% of African Americans, approximately 20% of Latinos/Latinas, and 11.6% of Asian/Pacific Islanders living in poverty. Additionally, American Indians and Alaska Natives have the highest rates of people in greater abject

FIGURE 1

**Percentage of People in Poverty in the Past 12 Months
by Race and Hispanic Origin: 2006**

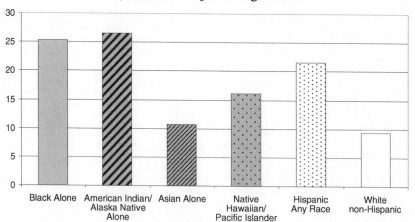

From Webster, B. H. & Bishaw, A. (2007, August). *American Community Survey Reports, ACS-08, Income, Earnings, and Poverty Data from the 2006 American Community Survey*, p. 20. Washington, DC: U.S. Government Printing Office.

poverty, even though they make up the smallest percentage of the overall population (0.8%).

Views Regarding Race Relations, Diversity Policies, and Self-Interest

Conflicts concerning race-conscious policy initiatives often reflect how people of different racial/ethnic groups get along with one another. In a study addressing the climate for cross-racial relations, a telephone survey of 1,170 African American, Hispanic, and White respondents, ages 15–24, concluded that these youth are cynical about improved race relations (Collison, 1992). Fifty percent of those surveyed viewed race relations as "generally bad." Research on social policies has indicated that race sharply polarizes positions taken by different racial/ethnic groups (Bobo, 2000; Bobo & Smith, 1994). National opinion surveys have found that the overwhelming majority of Whites oppose government programs that provide special assistance to African Americans (Bobo & Kluegel, 1993; Tuch & Sigelman, 1997; Zamani, 2002). The extant literature suggests that the driving force in American race relations is the degree to which Whites and people of color differ on social policy issues because of their values, absorption of pervasive stereotypes, and general beliefs about inequality (Bobo & Kluegel, 1993; Bobo & Smith, 1994; Kinder & Sanders, 1996; Krysan, 2000; Sidanius et al., 2000).

The policy attributes of affirmative action represent a wide range of ideas and practices from antidiscrimination provisions to special considerations to increased opportunities for African Americans (Kluegel & Smith, 1983; Tuch & Hughes, 1996a). As discussed previously, researchers have found that the vast majority of Whites oppose government assistance in the form of race-conscious programming (Bobo & Kluegel, 1993; Tuch & Hughes, 1996a, 1996b). Self-interest research focuses on the tendency of Whites to reject initiatives that seek to rectify the effects of prior and present racial discrimination (Bobo & Kluegel, 1993; Kluegel & Smith, 1983). Thus, the rejection of affirmative action based on self-interest may be attributed to notions of unfairness regarding social policies and programs that seek to assist marginalized groups.

Kluegel and Smith (1983) describe self-interest as one's concern with the maintenance of the status quo. Self-interest can be defined at the individual and group level. Individual self-interest refers to private interests in rates of return or loss for a person and direct family members. In contrast, group self-interest would involve making group-based appraisals when taking race-conscious policies into account according to one's categorical identification or affiliation (Bobo & Smith, 1994; Sears & Kinder, 1985).

Economic self-interest addresses notions of financial threat and personal livelihood (Kluegel & Smith, 1983). Closely related to individual and group self-interest, economic self-interest puts forward competitive and cooperative forms of self-interest. With respect to White opposition to affirmative action, Kluegel and Smith (1983) define competitive self-interest as perceived or direct competition with African Americans and other racial minority groups for societal resources, including access to jobs, promotions, and schooling. Competitive self-interest relates to both individual self-interest and group self-interest. On the other hand, cooperative self-interest anticipates reaping benefits from initiatives made in the best interest of others. In extending self-interest to members of disadvantaged groups, cooperative self-interest extends to group self-interest.

It has been argued that race-conscious initiatives are less favored than class-based or income-earmarked programming efforts because of the competitive individual and group self-interest of Whites (Bobo & Kluegel, 1993; Wilson, 1987). Therefore, to some extent the attitudes of Whites may be affected by self-interest. Jackman (1996) suggests, "Self-interested individuals tend to evolve attitudinal strategies that promote the interests of their group, since their long-term fate is linked to those other members of society who share similar life chances and who are subject to the same general constraints as themselves" (p. 764). Thus, race-neutral policies may not be as threatening to Whites because they assert self-interested positions and pursue ways of protecting their advantageous racial status (Jackman, 1996; Rendón, 2005; Stoker, 1996).

Although self-interest has largely been discussed in reference to Whites, the literature has considered self-interest in reference to women and African Americans. Given gender disparities, it is expected that women would be less likely to oppose affirmative action. Kluegel and Smith (1983) proposed that women might favor all opportunity-enhancing programs if they expect to benefit from affirmative action programs for women. Similarly, the self-interest of people of color should be cooperative in nature. On the basis of group self-interest, differences in racial policy issues are presumed to occur. Research has maintained that African Americans typically show more support for affirmative action than do Whites of the same economic standing (Bobo & Kluegel, 1993; Dovidio et al., 1989; Dovidio et al., 1994; Sax & Arredondo, 1999; Smith, 1998; Zamani, 2003). Thus, low-socioeconomic Whites are more apt to favor class-based policies that meet their individual and group self-interests. Similarly, Kravitz and Meyer (1995) found that, among Latino/Latina undergraduates, attitudes toward race-conscious affirmative action are significantly associated with self-interest. Interestingly, however, the researchers found that the impact of affirmative action programs targeting Latinos/Latinas bear considerable impact on individual but not collective self-interest.

The particular group a person ascribes to could bear some relationship to one's racial identity and policy attitudes. Social scientists have conducted research that examines the relationships between identity, stigma, social stratification, and self-interest (Ainlay et al., 1986; Crocker & Major, 1989; Jones et al., 1984). Sears and Jessor (1996) contend that the perceived group interest of Whites is contingent upon indicators of White group identity or self-categorization including frequent thoughts of themselves as White as opposed to other classifications. Sears and Jessor describe White identity as the perceived closeness to Whites as a group. However, according to Hartigan (1999, p. 51), "whiteness is not a simple attribute that they share with whites in other parts of the city and country." Most Whites do not refer to or think of themselves in terms of racial/ethnic identity (Nieto & Bode, 2008; Tatum, 2003, 2007). One of the ways Whiteness is articulated is in the emergence of solidified group self-interest among Whites in opposition to affirmative action. What follows is the assertion by Whites that people of color receive more opportunities while Whites are given less. An issue of equal importance is the role that identity, stigma, and stratification play in African American and Hispanic self-categorization in accounting for levels of support or resistance toward race-conscious policies.

In tandem with the sociological conception of self-interest is *interest convergence*. Interest convergence theory examines racial bias and intolerance from a self-interest frame of reference. Coined by Bell (1992), interest convergence theory postulates that the covert signs of racism paint an illusory picture that racial discrimination no longer exists, hence, the dominant group tolerates advances for people of color in terms of a quid pro quo; that is only when it suits their interests (Bell, 1987, 1995a, 1995b). For instance, members of the dominant group may purport to be egalitarian regarding the constitutional protection of people of color. However, concrete disagreement occurs in the event that remediation for previous injustice alters the status of Whites.

Consistent with interest convergence is the rise in discrimination toward minority group members that is a direct response to expansion and population growth among racial/ethnic minorities (Blalock, 1967). This theory is based on perceived social threat. Whites are often fearful of having to compete with people of color for scarce resources. This reaction of the dominant group to population growth among racial/ethnic minorities was a precursor to the racial divide currently surrounding affirmative action. The increasingly strong divergence of opinion between Whites and people of color is one manifestation of cultural contempt as it relates to matters of public policy.

White Privilege and Racist Policy Formation

It should be stated that the aforementioned arguments are interpretive, in that they employ theories of self-interest, interest convergence, and the politics of racial/gender identity to examine paradoxical popular rhetoric. This section seeks to challenge the conventional wisdom on affirmative action's opposition from an ideological perspective. The hope is to reveal an agenda that first and foremost wants to win the hearts and minds of the mainstream public. Legal victories aren't paramount in these efforts. Instead, the goal is to secure visibility and popular support in opposing affirmative action. If language is shifted to make affirmative action policies appear discriminatory, the conservative right will secure the necessary moral victory, solidifying its efforts to cast doubt on the necessity of affirmative action.

While chapter 1 outlined the basic tenets and original purposes of affirmative action, this section will consider, from an ideological perspective, how the laws, policies, and programs make a simple historically based assumption that some individuals and groups in the United States have always been excluded from access to various opportunities that promote quality of life and daily sustenance (Hudson, 1999). Because political bodies remain connected to the original racist premise of many public policies in the United States, accessing rights is still difficult for many individuals and groups.

The previous sentence deserves specific attention. Beyond the inflammatory assumptions that may result from our argument, an operational definition of racism is needed with regard to public policy. Policies are "racist" because of their continued subjugation of people of color as interpreted by the existing legal, social, economic, and political systems. An example would be the Immigration and Naturalization Act of 1790. Groups from western Europe were granted citizenship solely on the basis of being born on United States soil, while indigenous and African populations were still considered property and three-fifths of a human being. It is noted that these relationships served the interest of the state, but one can make the argument that current anti-affirmative-action policies continue to serve the interests of the majority, based on the assumption that nominal racial progress has "leveled" the playing field.

Cheryl Harris (1993), in examining the rights of Whites, makes a crucial segue when addressing the historical legacy of property rights and entitlement. "The origins of property rights in the United States are rooted in racial domination. Even in the early years of the country, it was not the concept of race alone that operated to oppress Blacks and Indians; rather, it was the interaction between conceptions of race and property which played a critical role in establishing and maintaining racial and economic subordination" (Harris, 1993, p. 5–6). Arguably, admission to institutions of higher education should be considered in the same mode as these assumed property rights. In this case, admission to institutions of higher education operates as a form of entitlement, while affirmative action policies have served as an interruption to the White property claim of merit. Entitlement is ideological in that it is assumed, but its assumption is based on de facto enforcement of the law.

Whiteness has been identified "as property if by property one means all of a person's legal rights" (Harris, 1993, p. 10). Rights were culturally and genetically inherited for Whites while they were regularly denied to people of color; affirmative action policies threaten this association. In the Supreme Court decision for the University of Michigan (*Gratz v. Bollinger*, 2003; *Grutter v. Bollinger*, 2003), the plaintiffs, Jennifer Gratz and Susan Grutter, were not suing for entrance into second- and third-tier institutions. Instead, they filed suit to challenge the admissions practice of the most prestigious institution in the state of Michigan based on their belief that they were as, if not more, qualified than the people of color granted admission to the University of Michigan-Ann Arbor that year. People of color were identified as wrongly benefiting from policies geared to disenfranchise deserving Whites.

Ideologically, affirmative action disturbs the privilege of Whiteness. In so doing, it challenges an institution that influences what groups have traditionally been given rights and power, and what groups have legally and socially suffered oppression, restricting and limiting their opportunities. Conservative public interest law firms like CIR would argue that they simply offer free legal representation to "deserving clients who cannot otherwise afford or obtain legal counsel and whose individual rights are threatened" (Center for Individual Rights, 2005b). The question becomes, who are these "deserving" clients and why are they deserving? More important, is the notion of being deserving reflected in the laws and social practices that render other groups undeserving or less meritorious? And what exactly is it that these individuals have a license to possess?

In developing a salient argument, ideological constructs of property, privilege, and entitlement require some unpacking. To the undiscerning eye, CIR's previous statement would appear neutral. However, a key element in CIR's project of winning the hearts and minds of the mainstream public is its ability to conceal racist intent. In essence, the exercise becomes preserving White (and mostly male) privilege without returning to de jure segregation. In doing so, Hudson (1999) identifies four strategies used by the conservative polity. Developed largely in response to the Civil Rights Act of 1964, the four components are:

- majority (i.e., White) and individual rights as the foundation(s) of American democracy;
- the acceptance of a narrow and restrictive definition of racism— limited primarily to varieties of individual prejudice—while systemic and cultural racism were exempt from critical analysis;
- the acceptance of deterministic and/or normative explanations of racial, gender, and class inequality that "blamed the victims" and;
- an historical understanding of racism, racial inequality and other forms of oppression, i.e., a type of "ditto-head" know nothingism (Hudson, 1999, p. 266).

The second and fourth points are crucial as they serve as rationale for conservative factions to wrongly appropriate the language of the civil rights movement. Right-wing groups are quick to use Martin Luther King's quote that one day people "will not be judged by the color of their skin but by the content of their character" (King, 1963).

Simultaneously, they conveniently ignore King's (1964) opinion in *Why We Can't Wait*, stating, "Whenever this issue of compensatory or preferential treatment for the Negro is raised, some of our friends recoil in horror" (p. 146). Because systemic, institutionalized racism is more difficult to present as state's evidence, conservative bodies rest on the logic of racism as isolated incidents of bigotry (Hudson, 1999; Ogletree, 2004). In order for this rationale to flourish, conservative ideologues seek to control popular discourse by minimizing the impact of racial discrimination.

The language of Executive Order No. 11246 (1965) and No. 11375 (1967) prohibiting discrimination on the basis of sex, gender, race, color, religion, and national origin are ideologically juxtaposed. Where the original premise was to prohibit discrimination in the workforce and in education, conservatives use the latter as a rationale to argue that affirmative action policies are the new brigade of discriminating measures, infringing on the individual rights of Whites (antidifferentiation). On the surface, this argument against affirmative action appears neutral. It has been argued that at this juncture racism does its greatest work because it has been "submerged in the popular consciousness" (Bell, 2000, p. 139).

Returning to the concept of interest convergence, its conceptual underpinnings are compelling in that Bell (1987, 1992) contends that the existence of exclusionary racial neutrality is due to displays of racism being less visible and majority group members acting in the interest of people of color not in the name of justice, but out of self-interest in order to gain or create greater dominance for themselves. In most affirmative action cases it does not serve the interests of the plaintiffs to support enforcement policies aimed at addressing issues of past discrimination. Instead, affirmative action is interpreted as a group of policies that infringe upon the individual rights of Whites, and, in turn, provide a legal rationale for civil proceedings. Within this context, vestiges of past discrimination against people of color are presumed irrelevant as Whites perceive themselves as the "out" group, wrongfully punished for crimes they did not commit.

The Battle of Propaganda: CIR and the Discourse of Infringement

Founded in 1989 by Michael McDonald and Michael Greve, CIR was created on the premise that public interest law firms could "change the law over time." Ironically, CIR's structure was modeled after liberal firms like the American Civil Liberties Union and Public Citizen. Nevertheless, CIR's language is explicit in supporting a conservative lean, maintaining the protection of individual and economic rights. What is not explicit, however, is how these supposed "rights" are weighted in court cases, specifically those that are prosecuting state and private bodies on behalf of Whites. Unsurprisingly, few, if any, clients of color have been plaintiffs in CIR cases. In fact, substantial portions of CIR support come from institutions with White supremacy agendas. Theodore Cross (1999) identifies CIR as receiving support from the overtly racist Pioneer Fund, which openly promotes "racial difference" while supporting scholarly work that advocates for the genetic superiority of Whites (Cross, 1999, p. 97). Because of the severity of such findings, it becomes important not to separate CIR from its funding sources. It is also important to look deeper and explore the scare tactics and propaganda circulated as CIR literature since 1996.

CIR (1998) publishes a handbook titled *Racial Preferences in Higher Education: The Rights of College Students*. In this publication, neutral language is used to illustrate entitlement. A section from the forward reads as follows:

> CIR has compiled this handbook—and a companion handbook for college and university trustees—in order to provide practical knowledge about what is legally permissible in college and university admissions programs. In making this information available to the public, we hope to place the

law governing racial preferences directly into the hands of those most affected by college and university policies. (p. iii)

Upon first sight the language appears transparent. However, after critical
examination, one would pose the following question: Who are those "most
affected by college and university policies" concerning race? One could argue
that this statement could be referring to people of color on predominantly
White campuses with tense racial climates often hostile to African Americans, Latinos/Latinas, Asian Americans, and Native American populations.

CIR has interpreted affirmative action laws as advocating racial quotas
instead of supporting diversity as a compelling state interest. The policies it
criticizes as promoting racial preferences are precisely those thought to negatively affect individuals and groups that feel they have entitlement rights to
these institutions of higher education. Cross poses the correct question in
asking whether there is historical precedent set in the exclusion of people of
color in colleges and universities in the United States (Cross, 1999). CIR,
again working in a historical vacuum, conveniently assumes minimal racial
progress supersedes systemic racism.

Subsequent sections in the handbook (CIR, 1998) are titled "What
Schools Cannot Do" and "Confronting Race Preferences." Both contain resource guides on how to interpret data distributed by university departments
and how to secure documents containing racial data. The introduction begins with "Nearly every elite college in America violates the law" (p. v). From
this sentence we might assume that the colleges in compliance with the law
would look like Bob Jones University, banning interracial dating, discouraging cross-racial socialization, and committed to remaining over 90% White.

Intentional in its attempt to attract attention to its efforts to ban affirmative action policies, CIR defines as its primary role the litigation of prec-
edent-setting cases. The hope is to alert White college students at elite universities of their ability to sue an institution if they sense wrongdoing. Explained further in later sections of this volume, visible programs for people
of color at traditionally White campuses are not in compliance with what
CIR has deemed "true" measures of diversity. Instead, as more racial categories are removed from consideration for admissions, the fairer CIR views the
policies as it forges ahead in its quest to maintain the status quo.

In Defense of the Status Quo: CIR and the
Absence of History

Cultural amnesia is at work with regard to CIR's continuance of placing
history on the back burner when it comes to the struggles of people of color

at predominately White institutions. Joy Williamson (2003), in her history of African American student organizing at the University of Illinois at Urbana-Champaign, documents the absence of programs aimed at including students of color. Because traditionally White institutions (TWIs) were hostile to the inclusion of students of color, federal and local programs were created to guarantee this inclusion. Despite some strides, it would be short-sighted to think that inclusion has been achieved. African American, Latino/Latina, Asian American, and Native American cultural centers were developed to ensure that students would have access to the same social, cultural, and educational programming offered to White students. These cultural centers were often met with opposition, and now, current policies provide an opening for institutions to rationalize downsizing or eliminating these centers, which they always viewed contentiously.

Popular critiques often question why White students don't have a cultural center. The most practical answer would be that there has always been a White cultural center, the university itself. Before the inclusion of students of color en masse in colleges with a traditionally White student population, history, culture, and social context were (and still are) reflected in the design and function of the university. By and large "diversity" days, weeks, and months at PWIs are housed in departments with the title of "Campus Life" or "Multicultural Services." Unfortunately, many of these departments operate as havens for university officials who prefer a "safe" cultural exchange between members of the student body. Here issues of race, class, and gender are substituted for food, festivals, and fun. Any in-depth, critical analysis of race is entertained only when the school finds itself in crisis concerning an overtly racist incident. In light of these realities the creation of cultural centers was an attempt to provide meaningful exchange for all students, centered on the concerns of students and communities of color. When student input does occur in campus life and multicultural programs, it functions in a nominal capacity, primarily operating in spaces that offer a sanitized interpretation of the life, history, and culture of students of color. In this sense, diversity is confined to practices that do not challenge or question the dominant hegemony. These practices, in turn, become surface measures masquerading as contributions to the cultural diversity of the campus community.

CIR rhetoric pushes for the removal of cultural centers and similar programs, arguing that they promote student segregation and divisions on college campuses. What CIR conveniently overlooks is that PWI campuses are contested spaces that often serve as reflections of the society at large. Any inclusive measure challenging the status quo is never safe. Despite conservative promotion of racial progress by means of racial/ethnic minority assimilation—or in other words, acculturation and deculturalization—a litany of questions remain to be answered with regard to issues of race.

Naming Nepotism: The Slippery Slope of Special Admits

The diversity segment of CIR's (1998) handbook contains a small section providing a rationale for the legality of legacy admissions (when students are admitted to an institution because one of their parents or immediate relatives is an alumnus or alumna). Though controversial, as they are not directly related to academic aptitude, such preferences are not considered illegal because they do not rely on race or ethnic origin. This rationale is ideologically contradictory, particularly given CIR's lack of attention or interest in pursuing legal disputes focused on private programs, including those for descendants of Civil War veterans or White ethnic groups (*Black Issues in Higher Education*, 2004a).

Also referred to as *admission by exception*, Moore (2005) asserts that this kind of nepotism provides preferences and privileges that far exceed those resulting from race- and gender-specific affirmative action. The University of California System admits up to 4% of students who are not fully eligible. Nonetheless, the suitability of the aforementioned special admits remains virtually unexamined in the discourse regarding affirmative action.

Language is of critical importance in the interpretation of access policies and programs. Although students may meet the minimum requirements to apply for admission, being eligible to apply is a different matter than actually gaining admission, which is based on a set of criteria or "preferences" that institutions use when deciding who will be accepted (Moore, 2005). Hence, the nepotism that allows access to rich kids, politicians' children, alumni legacies, and athletes does not prevent students who are not eligible and do not meet the admissions requirements from being offered admission at highly selective campuses (Moore). Universities can legally discriminate because of a technicality—the "special abilities" students can offer to the institution. Despite the fact that academic aptitude has no bearing on these students' admittance, CIR contends that these groups are integral to the livelihood of the institution, while diversity is not. Conversely, because race can be used as *one* of the factors weighted in admissions, CIR considers it a violation of the Civil Rights Act of 1964 and therefore illegal. The example of college revenue sports are of particular interest and importance to this discussion.

In the National Collegiate Athletic Association (NCAA) Division I athletics, the revenue-generating sports are men's basketball and football. Depending on the athletic success of the institution, they can be critical components of a school's financial portfolio. Coupled with television contracts for bowl games and basketball tournaments, collegiate athletics are a multibillion dollar industry. Interestingly, integral to this is the African American male athlete. Derrick Bell's (1992) interest convergence theory once more has conceptual utility as it asserts that African American progress is only considered when consistent in achieving the needs of Whites. As such, Black athletes serve the interests of PWIs through financial contributions including increased alumni donations and revenue-generating collegiate sports.

African American athletes constitute the overwhelming majority of athletes in Division I revenue sports, though college completion eludes many of these talented students (Gaston-Gayles, 2004; Shulman & Bowen, 2001). Although a small percentage of the student body, they are often (in addition to alumni contributions and research grants) largely responsible for generating school revenue. If we factor in legacy admits, the two groups could account for over half of an institution's revenue. Although crude in concept, it would be in the best interest of CIR to argue legacy admits and athletes as measures for diversity.

Regardless of the fact that Division I revenue athletes are predominantly African American while the vast majority of legacy admits at top-tier institutions remain White, a conservative organization like CIR could argue diversity despite the disparate numbers, because legacy admits outnumber Black athletes and other racial/ethnic minorities participating in collegiate sports by a considerable margin. Hence, the status quo is upheld while universities ensure fiscal security.

Because said processes are critical to the form and function of elite institutions of higher education, the ideology of affirmative action in the admissions process deserves attention in that it poses a direct interruption to policies that serve to exclude students of color from elite institutions. Dispelling popular notions around what group is "deserving" stands in opposition to organizations like CIR while calling for a deeper historical analysis of racial exclusion in the United States. By providing the rationale for such interruptions, the next chapter offers an examination of the thinking behind diversity, which includes a discussion of how race would challenge the aforementioned dynamic and confront the dominant culture and social capital of majority students at TWIs.

3

ACCESSING THE HISTORICAL REPOSITORIES OF SOCIAL AND CULTURAL CAPITAL IN HIGHER EDUCATION

T he contentious debate over affirmative action is, in part, because of the insidious nature of White supremacy and patriarchal hegemony, and the unwillingness to correct historical discrimination on the part of those subscribing to these ideologies. American institutions have been coconspirators in the clever cover-up and continuous denial and justification of White property rights, which resulted in centuries of civil rights violations. The discussion in chapters 1 and 2 illuminate how the 14th Amendment was not truly enforced, consequently making Executive Order No. 11246 (1965), also know as affirmative action, necessary. This chapter endeavors to frame the necessity of affirmative action in addressing issues of access and equity in higher education with regard to social and cultural capital.

As capital is accumulated differentially, racially/ethnically diverse members of society have not traditionally been considered important or worthy of being sought after, as various forms of capital in the United States have served to promote the interests of mainstream America. Historically, Whites have enjoyed a social system of exchange that benefits them through perpetuation of higher expectations, higher status, and the power to be oppressive to persons of color in this society. The discussion that follows outlines historical challenges to postsecondary educational equity and the construction of legal precedents key to understanding the practice of affirmative action in a contemporary context. In addition, this chapter examines various forms of capital in concert with Critical Race Theory (CRT) in analyzing Whiteness as the ascribed characteristic in accessing the reservoir of racialized rights that underpin the arguments for color-blind college admissions.

While its future remains uncertain, affirmative action has provided access to college for various disenfranchised students, particularly African Americans (Bowen & Bok, 1998; Cross & Slater, 1999). Attending college enables individuals to expand their personal and professional growth. Higher education opportunities are important because college attendance and completion are strongly associated with social and economic mobility (Bonacich, 1989; Gordon, 2001; Gordon & Bridglall, 2007; Hartmann & Whittaker, 1998; Marcotte, Bailey, Borkoski, & Kienzl, 2005; Pascarella & Terenzini, 1991; Paulsen & St. John, 2002). Correspondingly, postsecondary enrollment has been linked to earnings differentials between low-, middle-, and upper-income groups, between Whites and non-Asian minorities, and between genders (Bobo & Smith, 1994; Dutt, 1997; Lerman, 1997; McDonough, 1994, 1997; Paulsen & St. John, 1997).

Social mobility and economic disparities are also affected by whether a student is the first in his or her family to attend college. Commonly, these students come from families where high school completion may have been considered the pinnacle of success. Consequently, first-generation college students are generally concentrated within low-income and racially and ethnically diverse communities (Horn & Nuñez, 2000; London, 1992; Padron, 1992; Pascarella, 2004; Thayer, 2000).

African American and Hispanic students have not participated in higher education to the same extent as White students from middle- and upper-income families with greater financial resources (Chideya, 1995; Jackson, 1990). As a result of financial constraints, academic deficiencies and poor standardized test performance, certain groups of individuals have not found traditional baccalaureate degree education readily available, and subsequently have not enjoyed the same level of social and cultural capital in academe as their middle-class White counterparts (Gordon, 2001; Gordon & Bridglall, 2007; Padron, 1992; Richardson & Skinner, 1992). As a case in point, legal contests to affirmative action as one means of increasing participation among students of color continue despite the fact that wealthy White teens outnumber students benefiting from affirmative action, with 15% of affluent White freshmen attending highly selective colleges and failing to meet the institutions' minimum admissions standards (Schmidt, 2007a).

Legislative Antecedents Affecting Affirmative Action in Higher Education

From its onset, affirmative action has been met with resistance by its critics and praised by its advocates. One of the earliest challenges to affirmative action surrounded the appropriateness of race in college admissions. In the case of *DeFunis v. Odegaard* (1974) the trial court found the use of race in admissions at the University of Washington Law School to be unconstitutional. The law school was accused of having separate admissions procedures for students of color by giving less weight to their predicted first-year averages. As such, *DeFunis* argued that underqualified students of color had been accepted via affirmative action programs to the disadvantage of White students. The Washington State Supreme Court overturned this ruling on appeal by holding that it was in the state's interest to promote a racially balanced student body, in addition to addressing the shortage of African American and Hispanic attorneys.

Another early test to affirmative action was the *Regents of the University of California v. Bakke* (1978), which involved Alan Bakke who sued the university on the grounds of reverse discrimination when he was twice denied admission to the University of California at Davis Medical School. The Supreme Court ruled that Bakke's civil rights had been violated in the use of strict set-asides. The court further ruled that strict numerical quotas were not admissible in higher education admissions. However, the court also ruled that the use of race as one factor among many for the purpose of increasing diversity was constitutional, given the legacy of historical discrimination and its continuing present-day effects. Nonetheless, while *Bakke* made the use of quotas illegal, in the 1980 case of *Fullilove v. Klutznick* the Supreme Court ruled that 15% of public works funds could be set aside for qualified minority contractors, thus making the use of quotas/set-asides permissible if modestly tailored (Brunner, 2006a, 2006b).

Affirmative action concerns with regard to hiring/contracting have frequently influenced employment at K–12 and postsecondary educational institutions. Similar to *Fullilove* (1980), cases such as *Wygant v. Jackson Board of Education* (1986), *United States v. Paradise* (1987), *City of Richmond v. Cronson* (1989), and *Adarand Contractors v. Pena* (1995) were the predecessors of *Hopwood v. State of Texas* (1996), which departed from the precedent set in *Bakke* (1978). A complete discussion of the *Hopwood* case can be found on pp. 56–57.

Although women had been historically discriminated against in education and industry, vestiges of prior gender discrimination have not received the same treatment as issues of race discrimination. In 1982 Mississippi's system of single-sex colleges was struck down. The court denounced the justification of women's colleges based on remediation for past discrimination. In the case of *Mississippi University for Women v. Hogan* (1982), it was ruled that public educational institutions for women only were no longer justifiable.[1]

Furthermore, the court forwarded that remediation for the previous discrimination of women did not equate to the injustices suffered by people of color (Caso & Corry, 1996). Turning to the workplace, women (White females in particular) have benefited in hiring and are considered to have reached parity with their male counterparts in many venues since the inception of affirmative action, though pay equity and differential promotions still persist (Hartmann & Whittaker, 1998; Hecker, 1998).

Legal developments in higher education have not been limited to issues of access and admissions. In *Podberesky v. Kirwan* (1994), the use of race-conscious scholarships at the University of Maryland at College Park was questioned. The Benjamin Banneker Scholarship was a merit-based award earmarked for African American students. Given the history of Maryland's campus climate and racial tensions, this scholarship sought to address under-representation and attract academically talented African American students to the university. Podberesky sued the university, challenging the Banneker scholarship for providing scholarships only to African American students. *Podberesky v. Kirwan* illustrates how increasingly difficult it has been for institutions of higher learning to designate a fellowship or scholarship specifically for racial/ethnic minorities (Graca, 2005; Jackson, 1990). The federal court ruled that it was not permissible to maintain separate financial merit awards according to race (Shapiro, 1995).

In 1995 the University of California (UC) Board of Regents ruled that the use of affirmative action for student admissions and merit-based, race-conscious scholarships would no longer be allowed at any of the colleges and universities within the California system (Terry, 1998). In 1996 Proposition 209 sought to ban the use of affirmative action in the state of California. The proposition passed by voter referendum, thereby prohibiting student affirmative action and the use of affirmative action in employment decisions for business and education. As a result of Proposition 209, challenges to dismantle affirmative action policies and programs are under consideration in several other states including Texas and Washington (Johnston, 1997). Advocates of affirmative action sought to appeal passage of Proposition 209, and in November of 1997, the U.S. Court of Appeals denied lifting the ban on affirmative action in admission and employment decisions in California because of the overall support for the state referendum.

Admittance of African American and Hispanic students fell precipitously following the passage of Proposition 209, while the numbers for Whites slightly decreased and/or remained stable, and the numbers for Asians increased (nearly 43% of UC Berkeley students are Asian). In 2003 when UC Berkeley offered 355 Black students and 1,222 Latino/Latina students admission, a comprehensive review was requested by the board of regents to determine if campuses were continuing to use affirmative action in violation of state law, because these numbers were higher than the statistical model predictions of how many Black and Latino/Latina students should have been admitted (234 and 1,076 respectively; *Black Issues in Higher Education*, 2004b).

Anti-affirmative-action legislation in California led to a more aggressive attack on affirmative action programs in higher education around the country. Concurrent with efforts to dismantle affirmative action in California was *Adarand v. Pena* (1995). *Adarand* concerned the use of race in awarding construction contracts. This case was without any mention of education. Nonetheless, it had far-reaching effects on diversity initiatives implemented in higher education. The rejection of judicial scrutiny for federal set-aside programs heightened the controversy surrounding the use of affirmative action in higher education. The *Adarand* verdict spurred greater resistance to affirmative action, prompted an anti-affirmative-action climate, and led to a series of cases that have sought to dismantle affirmative action in higher education and in general (Amar & Katyal, 1996; Rosen, 1996). One such case was *Hopwood v. State of Texas* (1996).

Hopwood v. State of Texas (1996) concerned four White students who filed a suit against the University of Texas School of Law in Austin after being denied admission. CIR was involved in the *Hopwood* case in which students charged that the university had separate admissions criteria for African American and Hispanic applicants. The Fifth Circuit Court ruled in their favor prohibiting the law school from using preferential treatment to diversify the student composition. University officials sought an immediate appeal of the *Hopwood* case in 1996, but the Supreme Court held that the Fifth Circuit Court ruling would stand, banning the use of race and student affirmative action at Texas's public campuses (Healy, 1998a, 1998b). Following the ban on the use of race in admissions, Texas introduced a race-neutral admissions law in 1997 referred to as the Texas 10 Percent Plan. This law guarantees admission for the top 10% of high school graduates. Some argue that under this plan the University of Texas system is more diverse than it has ever been, while others feel that the law should be revisited to cap the number reserved for the top 10%, allowing for consideration of other factors besides academic standing (*Black Issues in Higher Education*, 2004c, 2004d, 2005).

In the years following *Hopwood* (1996), various foundations and institutions of higher learning have been struck with lawsuits disputing the use of affirmative action in awarding fellowships, scholarships, and internships for students of color (Barnes, 1996; Wright, 1997). Correspondingly, CIR has gone after summer enrichment programs, scholarships, and orientation and pipeline programs targeting racial/ethnic minorities in academia and the corporate sector (*Black Issues in Higher Education*, 2004a). It is not surprising that following its success in dismantling affirmative action at the University of Texas's law school, CIR continued to pursue graduate/professional admissions suits while also turning its attention to undergraduate admissions.

Two very important postsecondary cases concerning affirmative action are *Smith v. University of Washington Law School* (1997) and *Johnson v. Board of Regents of the University of Georgia* (1999). The *Smith* case involved three White applicants who disputed the University of Washington law school's decision to deny their admittance. The plaintiffs filed suit in 1997 following their rejection. One of the applicants had been denied admission 3 years in a row (Schmidt, 2002). The law school based its decisions on GPA, Law School Admission Test (LSAT) scores, and potential to contribute to campus diversity, without the use of formulas. The Ninth Circuit Court found that the university had a compelling interest in promoting racial diversity, citing 1978's *Bakke* decision. While the Supreme Court refused to hear the *Smith* case, a year later voters were presented with a state referendum to vote on the use of race in admissions (Schmidt).

As for the latter case of *Johnson v. Board of Regents of the University of Georgia* (1999), three White applicants who were rejected admission at the undergraduate level filed suit, claiming that the university employed set-asides and a formula that gave students of color an advantage in the admissions process. In 2001 the 11th Circuit found that the university had a discriminatory admissions policy and struck down the consideration of race as one of several admissions factors, asserting that campus diversity was not a compelling state interest. The court also suggested that the U.S. Supreme Court review the case. The University of Georgia opted not to appeal to the U.S. Supreme Court.

Following the new precedent set in *Hopwood v. State of Texas* (1996) and *Johnson v. Board of Regents of the University of Georgia* (1999), many institutions of higher learning voluntarily began to review their admissions procedures and diversity initiatives, fearful of impending litigation. For example, the University of Massachusetts at Amherst decided to forego the use of race in admissions. In an effort to increase enrollment of students of color, the University of Massachusetts had provided an edge to African American, Hispanic, and American Indian applicants in admissions and financial aid decisions (Healy, 1999a). In revising its policy of using race as an admissions factor, the university stated that low-income applicants and students of color would receive the same "plus" factor in the admissions process. The university anticipated a decrease in the enrollment of students of color given the alterations in policy. However, the university beefed up its recruitment efforts in response to the declining enrollment of students of color. The university's decision to rethink the use of race in its admissions policy was a response to the review and retreat of affirmative action efforts at peer institutions. Nonetheless, cases such as *Almonte v. Pierce* (1987) and *Monterey Mechanical Co. v. Wilson* (1997), which allowed organizations to use targeted outreach initiatives for members of historically underrepresented groups to broaden the applicant pool as long as others were not discouraged from applying or excluded from consideration, will likely be cited in future challenges to race-conscious and/or gender-specific recruiting efforts.

The University of California at Los Angeles (UCLA) responded to the anti-affirmative-action climate with an educational venture referred to as the Early Start Program (Chiang, 1998). Los Angeles Valley College and UCLA forged a program to address the retrenchment on affirmative action that has led to declining enrollments of students of color at UCLA. Early Start comprises 10th and 11th grade students at John H. Francis Polytechnic Mathematics, Science, and Technology Magnet School who enroll in college credit courses. The students enroll in the Valley College honors transfer program as juniors and are expected to complete 43 credit hours of college course work. Eligible students are selected from a pool of candidates who have a 3.0 minimum GPA and pass entrance exams in algebra and English. Students maintain dual enrollment while virtually guaranteeing a seat for themselves at UCLA. As participants in the program, students receive an opportunity to take tuition-free courses and skip their freshman year. Early Start welcomes students of all backgrounds; however, the majority of students from Francis Polytechnic are students of color (Chiang, 1998).

Most recently, the use of affirmative action in admissions at the University of Michigan was targeted for civil rights violations with regard to law school and undergraduate admissions by CIR (Lederman, 1997b). *Grutter v. Bollinger* (2003), the University of Michigan law school case, and *Gratz v. Bollinger* (2003), involving undergraduate admissions, were launched in 1997 on behalf of White students who were denied admission (Schmidt, 2002). In the case of *Gratz*, a class-action suit was filed on the basis of discriminatory treatment at the undergraduate level. The lawsuit was spearheaded by Jennifer Gratz, a White female with a GPA of 3.8 and an ACT score of 25, who was denied admission to the university's College of Literature, Science, and the Arts. Patrick Hamacher, a White male with a 3.0 adjusted GPA and a score of 25 on the ACT, was rejected 2 years after Gratz's unsuccessful application. The students represented in this case asserted that different standards were used for admitting students of different racial/ethnic backgrounds (Eckes, 2004). However, unlike the *Hopwood* (1996) case that revolved around *Adarand v. Pena* (1995), the *Gratz* case was based on the 14th Amendment and Title VI of the Civil Rights Act of 1964 (Lederman, 1997b).

With the *Grutter* (2003) case, a White female applicant sued following denial of admittance to University of Michigan's school of law. It was Barbara Grutter's opinion that her undergraduate GPA of 3.8 and 161 on the LSAT should have secured the Michigan native's slot in the law school. Although the admissions committee placed great weight on undergraduate GPA and LSAT scores, other attributes of applicants such as geographic background, race, and gender were considered among a litany of possible admissions contributions as argued by university officials and counsel in defense of the institutions' use of affirmative action in admissions. The Sixth Circuit Court of Appeals overturned a lower court's ruling that the University of Michigan, Ann Arbor, discriminated against Whites in its admissions procedures, citing that race was employed appropriately in obtaining a "critical mass" of students of color that would greatly add to the campus climate (Graca, 2005; Schmidt, 2002, 2003). The U.S. Supreme Court ruled in *Grutter v. Bollinger* (2003) in a 5–4 decision that the law school's admission policies were narrowly tailored given the individualized review of applicants. However, unlike the so-called slam dunk victory for the university in the *Grutter* case, permitting race as one plus factor among many, the ruling of the high court on *Gratz* regarding undergraduate admissions was less favorable. The bonus-point system was struck down in a 6–3 decision ruling it unconstitutional under the Equal Protection Clause of the 14th Amendment.

Irrespective of the level of entry, whether undergraduate, graduate, or professional school, the use of race as one factor among many in admissions considerations has been questioned. In addition to pressing lawsuits against the University of Michigan and other institutions prior to *Gratz* (2003) and *Grutter* (2003), CIR continues to place universities on notice for possible litigation. Among those institutions that have been threatened with potential lawsuits are the University of Chicago and the University of Illinois at Urbana-Champaign (*Black Issues in Higher Education*, 2004e; Grahnke, 1999). The University of Illinois has various support services at its Chicago and Urbana-Champaign campuses that are aimed at early outreach, recruitment, and retention of students of color, including

- American Indian Fellowship Program
- Educational Opportunity Program

- Illinois Minority Science Internship Program
- Illinois Consortium of Educational Opportunity Program (ICEOP)
- Minority Student Retention Program
- Support for Underrepresented Groups in Engineering Fellowship (SURGE)
- Research Apprentice Program in Applied Science (RAP)
- Summer Bridge/Transition Program
- Summer Research Opportunities Program (SROP)
- Principal's Scholars Program
- Mathematics Merit Workshop
- Minority Academic Partnership Plan (MAPP)
- Law Minority Access Program (Law MAP)
- Ronald E. McNair Post-Baccalaureate Achievement Program (University of Illinois, 1997)

CIR contends that the University of Illinois and other state institutions of higher education that have diversity development programs, such as scholarships and affirmative action programs earmarked for students of color, do not employ a balanced, equalizing process that considers grades and standardized tests without taking race or ethnicity into account (Grahnke, 1999).

A Call to the States

Illinois is one of several states that has debated the use of affirmative action, though a state referendum has not materialized (Grahnke, 1999). Following attempts to dismount affirmative action in Texas, an attempt to dismantle affirmative action in Washington State was promoted (Tharp, 1998). Voters passed Washington's Initiative 200 by state referendum in a 54% to 46% decision. Very similar to its predecessor, Proposition 209 in California, Initiative 200 ended affirmative action practices by the state and local government.

Unlike California, Washington State is not very culturally diverse. Its population is 83% White, and of its 5.6 million people, no one racially/ethnically diverse group exceeds 6% of the population (Tharp, 1998). Although race and ethnicity are no longer considered in the admissions process at the University of Washington, increasing attention has been drawn to factors such as socioeconomic status and personal disadvantage as a means of addressing diversity. The Office of Financial Management in the state of Washington compiled information from 4-year institutions and found that the key beneficiaries of special and/or alternative admissions, as well as hiring, at

Washington 4-year institutions were White (Kelly, 1996). Kelly reported the following:

> Special/alternative admission standards have long been derided by critics of affirmative action as a "lowering of standards" which diminishes academic excellence and limits opportunities for those who are better qualified. To the degree that alternative admission standards can be viewed as lowering the bar, whites are jumping that bar far more often than African Americans in Washington's 4-year schools.
>
> Because access to Washington's 4-year public institutions is capped by the state legislature, demand for enrollment slots has almost always outstripped availability. This is particularly true when demand for postgraduate slots is considered in isolation. (p. 78)

All told, Whites were receiving opportunities of access under affirmative action in public higher education at greater rates than underrepresented students of color, prior to and following the installation of Initiative 200 on December 3, 1998.

Like Washington, Georgia has a unique landscape and demography. In fact, in the early 1990s the University of Georgia proposed removing gender from consideration in admissions decisions to offset the low numbers of males enrolling at the institution. However, Georgia's admissions policies pertaining to race were challenged in a 1997 lawsuit. In the fall of 1999, the president of the University of Georgia announced that the school would not abandon the consideration of race as a factor in admissions, reaffirming the university's commitment despite the legal trend of litigation threats and voter initiatives (Collison, 1999). While the university's stance didn't find universal appeal, the governor of Georgia, Roy Barnes, supported the university's position.

On February 22, 2000, the state of Florida's legislature approved Governor Jeb Bush's One Florida Plan, with the goal of ending affirmative action across state entities (Brunner, 2006b). In April of 2000, Governor Bush announced his One Florida Plan also known as the Florida 20 Percent Plan. According to Bush, One Florida is an attempt to mend and not end affirmative action programs by eradicating racial preferences and establishing college admissions that are color blind. According to Kweisi Mfume, head of the NAACP, the One Florida Plan is "Jim Crow Jr." (as cited in Leo, 2000, p. 15). To be eligible for the plan students must complete 19 college prep courses, and the top 20% of every public high school would be admitted irrespective of race (similar to the Texas 10 Percent Plan and California's post–Proposition 209 Four Percent Plan which guarantees the top 4% of students at each California high school automatic admission to the UC system).

The move by Jeb Bush was scrutinized as an attempt to position him and his brother, President George W. Bush, as antipreferences but pro–affirmative action. However, critics suggest that the 20 Percent Plan is not a panacea. The hard fact remains that there is a stratification of African American and Hispanic students in low-performing schools, which, in turn, perpetuates de facto segregation (Leo, 2000). Nevertheless, the percentage of Florida's incoming students of color rose roughly 2%, with the population of incoming Black freshmen stagnating at 14% (*Diverse Issues in Higher Education*, 2005b; Robinson, 2003).

There are further implications of the Michigan decisions. Following the rulings on the University of Michigan cases and Governor Bush's new policies, the Florida Supreme Court ruled that the NAACP could challenge Governor Bush's removal of race and gender considerations in the admissions processes at state universities (*Black Issues in Higher Education*, 2003).

CRT as a Lens for Viewing Affirmative Action Discourse

Building on the discussion of White property rights in the last chapter, the work of Harris (1993) underscores the legitimating of Whiteness through visible and invisible privileges that maintain the present status quo and dominion over racial/ethnic minorities. In other words, exclusionary acts of denying anything that does not benefit oneself are universal to the value orientations and ideologies of White supremacy. This racialized reality is one of the unifying conceptual underpinnings of CRT. CRT presupposes that Whiteness as property is a socially constructed certainty, the structural inequalities of which are drawn across racial lines. The basic canon consists of the following six principles:

- CRT recognizes that racism is endemic to American life.
- CRT expresses skepticism toward dominant legal claims of neutrality, objectivity, colorblindness, and meritocracy.
- CRT challenges historicism and insists on a conceptual/historical analysis of the law. . . . Critical race theorists . . . adopt a stance that presumes that racism has contributed to all contemporary manifestations of group advantage and disadvantage.
- CRT insists on recognition of the experiential knowledge of people of color and our communities of origin in analyzing law and society.

- CRT is interdisciplinary.
- CRT works toward the end of eliminating racial oppression as part of the broader goal of ending all forms of oppression. (Matsuda, Lawrence, Delgado, & Crenshaw, 1993, p. 6).

The founding mothers and fathers of CRT scholarship established this framework of inquiry because of the perceived gap in Critical Legal Studies (CLS) for examining the role of race and racism in the civil rights discourse (Bell, 1987; Delgado, 1990; Ladson-Billings & Tate, 1995; Matsuda et al., 1993). CLS was critiqued for its color-blind, social justice message that propagated subordination, limited present or future civil rights gains, and maintained an imbalanced social order. Ladson-Billings and Tate (1995), Delgado and Stefancic (2001), as well as Parker and Lynn (2002), describe the unique narrative approach of CRT as an alternative method of legal analysis for unearthing inequities in education, politics, and economics because of the central role of race in society.

Equity and Education

In his historical review of the origins and implications of CRT, Tate (1997) suggested that the means by which individuals and institutions draw meaning from policy implementation that seeks to ensure equality are expansive and restrictive. The divergent constructions of equality and antidiscrimination laws that Tate references build on the work of Crenshaw's premise of intersectionality (Crenshaw, 1993; Crenshaw, Gotanda, Peller, & Thomas, 1995). Intersectionality is a conceptual framework for examining the interchange between race, gender, and class. It involves three constructs to analyze issues of race, gender, and/or class as related to domination that pervades laws and social policy discourse.

These constructs are (a) structural intersectionality, (b) political intersectionality, and (c) representational intersectionality. Structural intersectionality represents the overlap of vulnerability, oppression, and considerable subordination that African Americans (Black women in particular) are subject to; political intersectionality is the confluence of political practices in association with race and gender. Finally, representational intersectionality involves images of race and gender that interact to counter prevailing stereotypes (Crenshaw, 1993; Crenshaw et al., 1995; DeCulr & Dixson, 2004).

The contributions of Kimberly Crenshaw's views on intersectionality to the dialogue on the process of social change in education is quite relevant when considering CRT in relation to affirmative action. Structural and political intersectionality permeate mainstream, dominant groups' beliefs about affirmative action (especially race-conscious forms), resulting in a failure to acknowledge the institutionalized racism that still exists and the politics of identity. The statistics illustrate disparities in educational achievement gaps, wage differentials, and other types of practices that continue to unfairly disenfranchise people of color. Accordingly, the affirmative action debate includes politicized arguments asserting that opportunities abound for people of color while Whites are being robbed of inherent opportunities (Delgado, 1995). As such, people of color have to deal with the role model myth of assimilation, which reinforces the salience of race and the incessant encumbrance that people of color face when having to actively counteract negative images.

While affirmative action programs have been an interesting societal experiment aimed at engineering the social order of America toward obtaining and sustaining equitable outcomes for all citizens, a fallacy of homogeneity and a myth of monolithic identity exist that arise when American ideologies and objectives in the pursuit of fairness are discussed (Delgado, 1995; Stanfield, 1993). For this reason, among others, responses to affirmative action programs lack consensus, remain highly contested, and are constantly socially constructed and framed in contradictory and paradoxical manners. Dixson and Rousseau (2005), in their article "And We Are Still Not Saved: Critical Race Theory in Education Ten Years Later," found Harris's (1993) arguments about the property interest of Whiteness as well as the ideas on intersectionality forwarded by Crenshaw et al. (1995) very applicable to the previous and most recent challenges to affirmative action. The authors note:

> the plaintiffs in such cases do not challenge the admission of other white students with lower test scores and GPAs. Nor do they question admissions points given for other factors (legacy, high school quality, geographic location, etc.) that are more likely to benefit white applicants. Rather the action to file suit is based on racial discrimination, in essence served to protect the property value of whiteness by challenging opportunities provided to people of colour—opportunities that were perceived to threaten that which was due to whites. (p. 21)

The commonality of assumptions of inferiority that the dominant group attaches to potential beneficiaries of color has become almost unremarkable. Critics like Daniel McWhirter, Shelby Steele, and Abigail and Stephan Thernstrom suggest that affirmative action policy victimizes women and people of color, as they become tainted with self-doubt, poor self-worth, and guilt when they become the token admit or hire.

The Centrality of Race, Campus Climate, and Affirmative Action Attitudes

Race matters at institutions of higher learning, because it is an important factor in assessing campus climate (Gurin, Nagda, & Lopez, 2004; Milem, Chang, & Antonio, 2003; Yang, 1992). Research addressing the feelings and perceptions of the student body is needed to understand the campus climate (Yang, 1992). Campus climate can be defined as the daily sum of one's surrounding environment (Chang, 1999). Therefore, campus climate refers to the level of comfort experienced by majority students, students of color, faculty, administrators, and staff (Hurtado & Carter, 1997). Higher educational institutions should make concerted efforts to provide a campus community that is diverse and inclusive of students from all racial/ethnic groups (Hurtado, Engberg, Ponjuan, & Landreman, 2002; Rendón, Justiz, & Resta, 1988; Riordan, 1991).

The majority of students of color attend predominately White 2- and 4-year institutions where the campus climate is geared to the majority student (Chavous, 2005; Rendón et al., 1988; Riordan, 1991). The socialization and academic integration of students of color into a campus community that is seemingly foreign to them is difficult. The research has suggested that campus climate can have an impact on the adjustment and transition of students of color in higher education (Cabrera, Nora, Terenzini, Pascarella, & Hagedorn, 1999; Chavous, 2005; Hurtado, 2002; Hurtado & Carter, 1997). Riordan (1991) maintained that campus climate can positively or negatively affect student retention for students of color. In addressing overall campus climate it is critical for higher education to be concerned with the experience of students both in and out of the classroom.

Americans' beliefs about inequality illustrate a racial divide regarding policy implementation. A minute amount of research has investigated the extent to which campus climate and racial composition affect student attitudes toward diversity initiatives such as affirmative action. Chang (1996) examined whether the effects of racial diversity vary according to institutional characteristics (type, size, or selectivity), and whether they inform the debate concerning affirmative action in college admissions. The findings from his study were drawn from an analysis of the 1985 Cooperative Institutional Research Program database of college students and the 1989 follow-up survey. Two-year students were omitted from the analysis because of the small sample size. The results illustrated that institutional type was associated with racial diversity. Four-year colleges were found to be less racially heterogeneous than universities.

As universities have larger enrollments than 4-year colleges on average, the findings suggest that increases in racial diversity are consistent with larger enrollment sizes. The results did not provide evidence to support institutional selectivity being negatively associated with racial diversity. Chang asserted that selective institutions are no less successful at attracting underrepresented students of color than less-selective institutions. Furthermore, he contended that selective institutions are engaged in aggressive recruiting tactics and/or practice race-conscious admissions in diversifying enrollments.

Nosworthy, Lea, and Lindsay (1995) investigated the reactions of undergraduates to affirmative action programs benefiting African Americans. The findings suggested that students might object to affirmative action policy and program implementation when it pays special attention to African Americans. In questioning the predictive value of racial attitudes, negative racial affect resulted as the primary determinant of opposition to affirmative action (Nosworthy, Lea, & Lindsay). However, the negativity associated with student rejection of affirmative action may be because of misconceptions regarding the policy.

Smith (1998) acknowledged that the vast majority of available literature on affirmative action focuses on the oppositional attitudes of Whites toward these policy and program efforts. His study examined gender and racial/ethnic differences among college students as it related to support for affirmative action in higher education. Overall, the findings from his total net sample of 290 undergraduates illustrated that differences of opinion regarding affirmative action in higher education were more pronounced along racial/ethnic lines than gender lines. White and Asian American students expressed higher levels of opposition to affirmative action whereas African and Hispanic American students were most supportive. Similar to Nosworthy and colleagues (1995), Smith contends that negative racial affect, or what he refers to as *race-related orientations*, are shared among Asian Americans and Whites. More specifically, his results suggest that Asian Americans echo White race-related orientations, which predispose them to share the oppositional stance on affirmative action. By comparison, Smith holds that Hispanics shared similar race-related orientations with African Americans, which predisposed them to favoring affirmative action in higher education.

Meader (1998) conducted a cross-sectional study of six Midwest institutions in Illinois, Michigan, and Ohio examining student attitudes toward diversity and race-conscious policies. The survey findings revealed that African American and White students were more likely to oppose race-conscious policies when they perceived their institution as supportive of African American concerns. As a result of this finding, it was suggested that evaluating the need for race-conscious policies was based on the perceived level of institutional support to meet the needs of students of diverse backgrounds (Meader, 1998).

Consistent with Meader (1998), Sax and Arredondo (1999) assessed college student attitudes toward affirmative action. In a study of 277,850 college freshmen representing 709 U.S. colleges and universities, the study employed secondary data analysis of the 1996 Cooperative Institutional Research Program (CIRP) Freshman Survey; their study examined attitudes toward affirmative action in college admissions as it relates to gender, self-interest, political ideology, and prejudice/racism. The researchers concluded that first-year collegians might not understand the intentions of affirmative action. Right-wing conservatives may have mounted opposition to affirmative action, but resistance has sprung forth from a variety of citizens. The differences across and within racial/ethnic groups varied according to gender, racial background, socioeconomic status, academic preparation, political ideology, and attitudes concerning race. Students of color and women were generally more favorable toward affirmative action. Nonetheless, about 50% of college freshmen attending 4-year public institutions of higher learning responded in favor of abolishing the use of affirmative action in college admissions (Sax & Arredondo; Sax, Astin, Korn, & Mahoney, 1996).

In a mixed-methods study conducted by Knight and Hebl (2005), the researchers examined the reactions of 216 White undergraduates to the utilitarianism justification for affirmative action programs. The findings showed that highlighting utilitarianism as a benefit to minority and majority students increased levels of support for affirmative action. Taken as a whole, the study suggested that purposeful framing of affirmative action that explicitly accentuates the advantages of diversity to one's college experience would prompt those traditionally considered nonbeneficiaries to identify diversity as a compelling interest.

The Salience of College Choice, Institutional and Student Characteristics

Socioeconomics plays a significant role in college choice. Students from financially affluent families with a history of college attendance are likely to afford private institutions while low socioeconomic status [SES], first-generation students are likely to enroll in public colleges and universities (McDonough, 1994, 1997). Therefore, family finances and affordability are important considerations when students make decisions about college (Paulsen & St. John, 1997, 2002).

Literature examining the relationship between college choice and SES has addressed the role of financial aid in providing access and determining persistence rates at institutions of higher learning. Previous studies have noted that SES is a determinant in diminishing the educational aspirations of low-income students. Financial aid takes on increasing importance as students report major concerns regarding paying for college (Cress & Sax, 1998). SES has been found to relate to educational aspirations in addition to institutional choice (McDonough, 1994, 1997). It has been asserted that students of limited financial means less often attend their first-choice institution, which is particularly true for African American and Hispanic collegians (Hurtado, Inkelas, Briggs, & Rhee, 1997).

The institutional environment plays an important role in whether students earn baccalaureate degrees. Privately controlled institutions have been found to better foster student development, retention, and degree attainment (Astin, Tsui, & Avalos, 1996). There are about 100 historically Black colleges and universities (HBCUs) in the United States, making up 9% of the nation's baccalaureate-granting institutions, many of which are privately controlled (Trent, 1991b). Although 75% of African American students attend predominately White institutions (PWIs), HBCUs have consistently produced one-third of African American bachelor degree recipients (Chideya, 1995). Seifert, Drummond, and Pascarella (2006) assert that providing a richly supportive context for learning, social engagement, and growth is the unique mission of special population colleges. For that reason, there are significant differences in the educational outcomes for African American students at traditional Black colleges and universities versus PWIs (DeSousa & Kuh, 1996; Flowers, 2002; Jackson & Swan, 1991). Unfortunately, because of the costs of a private college education, many African American students cannot afford to attend these institutions that were founded specifically to foster their educational attainment. Although HBCUs and privately controlled, selective PWIs may be first-choice colleges for low-income and first-generation students, public 2- and 4-year state colleges are more often the routes taken toward the baccalaureate.

Capital Inequalities

Consistent with Marxist ideals of capitalism, the concept of capital describes an ability to generate wealth and promote means of production through social relationships. The birth of this nation exemplifies the use of relationships, particularly inequitable ties as a means of advancement through oppression, power, and ownership. In short, the United States built its economy and wealth on the so-called free enterprise of controlled free labor.

Karl Marx (1975) asserted that underlying capitalism are monopolies threatened by competition. The concept of capital and the system of capitalism are analogous to the reactions elicited in response to race-conscious and gender-specific forms of affirmative action. More plainly, it is the inequities in access and distribution of resources that have traditionally maintained the status quo and have allowed some groups the capital necessary to achieve upward mobility educationally, economically, politically, and socially. Therefore, the perceived threat experienced by many Whites is driven by a fear of losing control of resources and accessibility to various forms of capital that are critical to the current social order. Gordon (2001) discussed how the nature of capital has evolved. In accordance with the work of Blauner (1972), Becker (1975), Bourdieu (1986) and other theorists, capital includes nine types of assets that are necessary for participation in the full fold of society.

The first form of capital is *cultural capital*. Bourdieu (1986) states that cultural capital is everything one draws upon relative to knowledge, concepts, and ideas in participating in society. It embodies the views, techniques, and dispositions that are considered important in moving ahead. A second type of capital is *financial capital*, which refers to economic resources by means of income and wealth that an individual, family, or community possesses that may be used for education and further development. *Health capital* is the condition of the physical self; health matters can include the physical state as well as the emotional/mental, spiritual integrity of a person (Gordon, 2001). According to *human capital theory*, patterns of stratification and inequities along race/ethnic, gender, and class lines pertain to one's tacit knowledge, abilities, and social competence and other personal assets (Becker, 1975; Schultz, 1961).

Institutional capital refers to capital related to educational access, political acumen, and social networks. *Pedagogical capital* is the extent to which one has the appropriate educational background and experiences in relation to transferring and receiving knowledge with school, home, and community settings. The educational and career aspirations, disposition, and awareness of power and self-efficacy that individuals possess is called *personal capital*. *Polity capital* is the social concern and commitment shared by those who participate in a society relative to politics and economics. Finally, *social capital* is an individual's cultural norms, social beliefs, and value orientations that operate within particular networks or relationships (Gordon, 2001).

Given the unequal distribution of wealth and perceived scarcity of resources, it is obvious that every person does not have access to all the aforementioned kinds of capital. As it pertains to affirmative action discourse, not having access to particular capital restricts subsequent rights of entry, including educational disadvantaging and gender wage gaps. For this reason, opportunities for advancement are thwarted from the onset as U.S. society often reflects underlying racist, sexist, and classist principles in its democratic ideals. The code of ethics should ensure equal opportunities to self-actualize for its citizens. Similar to veteran's programs such as the GI Bill, components of affirmative action seek to develop and improve the skill base and lot in life of marginalized groups given the past perversions of American justice.

Note

1. See *Craig v. Boren* (1976) as the predecessor to *Mississippi University for Women v. Hogan* (1982). Also important in the consideration of gender classifications in affirmative action withstanding strict scrutiny is *Engineering Contractors Association of South Florida, Inc. v. Metropolitan Dade County* (1997).

4

FROM THE MARGINS

Community College Student Opinions on Affirmative Action

T he previous chapter explored the uneven custody of capital in its numerous forms. The disparate access to various types of capital is illustrated in the disproportionate numbers of students of color, women, individuals with disabilities, and low-income and first-generation students populating 2-year institutions in contrast to senior-level 4-year colleges and universities. Correspondingly, 2- and 4-year institutions of higher education, their roles, and admissions and enrollment policies are well documented (Adelman, 1999; Atwell, Melendez & Wilson, 2004; Cox & McCormick, 2003; Richardson & Bender, 1987; Townsend, 1999).

Community colleges provide routes to baccalaureate degrees by filling existing gaps in educational access for those who may not have other options for postsecondary attendance. Baccalaureate aspirants entering 2-year colleges often differ from students attending 4-year colleges or universities with regard to college readiness (Bragg, Loeb, Zamani, & Yoo, 2001; Burley & Butner, 2000; Dougherty, 1987; McJunkin, 2005; Perin, 2002; Richardson & Bender, 1987). Two-year institutions often enroll the majority of underprepared students attending college, many of which are members of underrepresented minority groups, are first-generation collegians, and come from economically disadvantaged backgrounds (Goldrick-Rab, 2006; Horn & Nuñez, 2000; Kocher & Pascarella, 1988; Richardson & Skinner, 1992; Thayer, 2000). Given the notable demographics, the following section seeks to describe the characteristics of community colleges and the students attending, and explore the role of affirmative action in 2-year institutional settings. Finally, this chapter examines the attitudes of community college students toward affirmative action in college admissions.

Two-Year Student Demographics and Institutional Environment

Rhoads (1999) asserts that institutions of higher learning illustrate the interconnectedness of culture, identity, and schooling. Not only does racial/ethnic cultural pluralism shape campus climates, but the heterogeneity of student characteristics such as gender, age, socioeconomic status, and enrollment level does as well. Contemporary community college student characteristics illustrate that the majority of college students enrolled, as well as subsequently earning associate degrees, are female (Phillippe & Gonzalez, 2005). Similar to people of color, however, women are overrepresented in 2-year institutions. Women also disproportionately attend institutions that are not their first-college choice (Jacobs, 1985, 1999).

Literature on the collegiate enrollment of women reports that a significant number of female students attend community colleges as part-time students, and many of them are not between the ages of 18 and 24, which is the traditional college-age range (Jacobs, 1999; McCormick & Carroll, 1997; Phillippe & Gonzalez, 2005). Transferring to a 4-year college or university within 5 years is less likely among part-time versus full-time community college students with baccalaureate degree aspirations, or for those from lower socioeconomic income levels (Goldrick-Rab, 2006; McCormick & Carroll, 1997).

In contrast to women, many African American and Hispanic students who are disproportionately concentrated at the 2-year level are positioned in urban areas, where they make up a significant percentage of the part-time student population (Maxwell, Hagedorn, & Cypers, 2003; Richardson & Bender, 1985). In addition, a study by Orfield (2001) concluded that issues of access and school choice for students of color are often based on their local residence. Frequently, institutions of higher learning that are within close proximity to where one lives and works, as well as within an individual's financial reach, are typically community colleges.

Given the nearness of 2-year institutions, studies have found that community colleges have a profound impact on student aspirations (Brint & Karabel, 1989a; Dougherty, 1994; Laanan, 2000; Pascarella, Edison, Nora, Hagedorn, & Terenzini, 1998; Richardson & Bender, 1985). Research indicates that there is an association between socioeconomic status, institutional proximity, and transfer behavior (McCormick & Carroll, 1997; Sewell & Shaw, 1967). For example, low SES students who begin their postsecondary education at a community college for reasons of cost and proximity are less likely to reach their goal of a baccalaureate. Among 2-year students with transfer intentions, 25% of low SES students transferred compared to 40% of middle SES, and 60% of high SES students.

Relative to location and institutional size, many urban community colleges boast large enrollments, and research has noted that the size and level of an institution can adversely impact student aspirations (Carter, 1999a). Attinasi (as cited in Carter, 1999b), suggests that irrespective of tier, large enrollments have been thought to hinder students from making sense of their institutional environments and in turn prevent them from self-actualizing. For students who look to 2-year institutions as the conduit to a bachelor's degree, critics contend that the community college is not the optimal environment for those seeking bachelor's degree completion (Brint & Karabel, 1989a, 1989b; Clark, 1960; Dougherty, 1987, 1994; Karabel, 1986; Pascarella et al., 1998; Whitaker & Pascarella, 1994). The racial/ethnic background, gender, and enrollment status of community college students bear some association to the campus climate, institutional culture, and orientation of those attending. Clearly issues revolving around race and gender affect the campus climate differently across institutional contexts given the unique student compositions at various colleges and universities.

Catalyst or Deterrent to Baccalaureate Education?

The profile of community college students is unique, as these collegians often differ from those at 4-year institutions in terms of having dependents, full-time employment, or lag time prior to enrollment, all of which are considered at-risk factors (Phillippe & Gonzalez, 2005). Consequently, the background characteristics of 2-year collegians are often thought to produce barriers to actualizing educational goals beyond the tier of postsecondary education they are enrolled in. Access to higher levels of education and subsequent degree completion has been strongly associated with economic, occupational, and social mobility, though differentially when considering race/ethnicity and gender (Averett & Dalessandro, 2001; Dougherty, 1992; London, 1992; Marcotte et al., 2005; Nordhaug, 1987; Pascarella & Terenzini, 1991; Paulsen & St. John, 2002).

There is some degree of return on investment for those enrolling and completing postsecondary education: a vocational certificate or associate degree at a community college. Close to half the students responding to the Community College Survey of Student Engagement (2005) stated that their primary goal was transferring to a 4-year institution of higher education. More recent estimates suggest around 75% intend to transfer to a 4-year institution and anticipate earning a bachelor's degree (Bradburn, Hurst, &

Peng, 2001; Hunter & Sheldon, 1980; Keener, 1994). While there are different ways to construct transfer success and various definitions of potential transfer, among beginning postsecondary students enrolled at public 2-year institutions during 1989–1990, 95% of those who expected to complete a bachelor's degree or higher transferred to 4-year institutions by spring 1994 (Floyd, 2004). For over three decades, there has been relatively little change in the overall transfer rate; roughly one-fourth of community college students transfer to 4-year institutions (Grubb, 1991, 2002). Conversely, only an estimated 20% to 25% of all students attending community colleges with baccalaureate degree aspirations earn one (Cohen & Sanchez, 1997; Piland, 1995; Pincus & Archer, 1989).

Currently more than 6.5 million credit-earning students attend community colleges (Phillippe & Gonzalez, 2005). Many students at community colleges enroll as a way of closing the gap to educational attainment at a 4-year institution. Close to two-fifths of first-time students attending community colleges during 1995–1996 reported transfer intentions, while little over three-fourths aspired to transfer to 4-year institutions to pursue a bachelor's degree (Keener, 1994; Phillippe & Gonzalez, 2005).

According to the U.S. Department of Education Community College Liaison Office, more than one-fifth of students at community colleges transfer directly into 4-year baccalaureate programs during their academic careers (Woods, 1997). The majority of students at 2-year institutions were enrolled in an academic program and enrolled continuously (Bradburn, Hurst, & Peng, 2001). As for community college attendance patterns examined through 1993–1994, an NCES report held that 20% completed an associate's degree while 78% transferred without earning any credential (McCormick & Carroll, 1997).

The term *transfer* can refer to numerous types of postsecondary transitions. Transfer can be horizontal and vertical (McCormick & Carroll, 1997). Horizontal refers to transferring between institutions on corresponding levels, for example, between two community colleges or from one 4-year to another 4-year college and university. Vertical transfer involves forward and reverse or upward and downward transfer. Forward transfer entails changing to a senior-level institution, while reverse transfer involves switching enrollment from a higher level college or university to a lesser institution (McCormick & Carroll).

Researchers have noted that one way community colleges can reaffirm their position in higher education is by reforming and/or restoring the transfer function within their home institutions (Bradburn et al., 2001; Laanan, 2000). According to enrollment trends, many community college entrants are vocational-technical students (Bragg, 2001; Prager, 1992). Notwithstanding, it has been estimated that as many as three-fourths of all vocational-technical students aspire to receive baccalaureate degrees (Hunter & Sheldon, 1980). In response, community colleges have initiated curricular reforms aimed at integrated academic and vocational-technical education (Bragg, Reger, & Thomas, 1997). However, the transferability of academic courses adapted or designed for career students has been problematic. Dougherty (1994) reported that the proportion of all community college transfers to 4-year colleges dropped about 8.5% during the 1980s, with vocational education cited as one contributing factor (Clark, 1960).

Transfer rates in regard to the number of students moving from 2-year to 4-year institutions have been unsteady over the past few decades (Bradburn et al., 2001; Prager, 1992). Still, students in applied associate degree programs, including those in business, health, technology, and service arenas, receive some training that qualifies them for baccalaureate pursuit. Subsequently, community colleges have begun to witness considerable growth in the rate of students enrolled in occupational and technical programs transferring to 4-year institutions for the baccalaureate degree (Bender, 1990; Bradburn et al., 2001; Bragg, 2001; Cohen & Brawer, 2003; Dougherty, 1992). Little research, however, has closely examined transfer with respect to vocational-technical enrollment exclusively.

The transfer function is critical to gaining admission to 4-year institutions for all students. However, program completion rates are low particularly for students of color and first-generation Whites (Brint & Karabel, 1989a; Horn & Nuñez, 2000; Pascarella, 2004; Thayer, 2000). The onus for low transfer rates usually falls upon community colleges, not 4-year institutions (Dougherty, 1992). Roughly 43% of students who began their collegiate careers at 2-year institutions transferred: 5% percent left to attend less than 2-year institutions, 15% left to attend another 2-year college, and 22% went on to 4-year colleges and universities (NCES, 1997). Consistent with the low rate of transfer is the low rate of conferral of bachelor's degrees among those that begin at community colleges. Pincus and Archer (1989) concluded that African American and Hispanic 2-year students were less likely to receive a baccalaureate degree than were White community college students. One way of addressing problematic transfer rates would be to develop admissions policies specifically targeting transfer students since many share defining characteristics including socioeconomic status, first-generation college student status, and belonging to an underrepresented group (Laanan, 2000). In sum, these findings suggest that issues of access for community college students beyond the 2-year context call for additional attention.

The Role of Affirmative Action in 2-Year Institutions

College attendance has become increasingly important for individuals to self-actualize personally and professionally. The demographic profile of community college students suggests many could potentially benefit from affirmative action initiatives. Affirmative action efforts to diversify colleges have been a contentious issue at many 4-year campuses. Given the open admissions of community colleges and the current retrenchment of diversity policies and programs, increasingly nontraditional students are looking to community colleges as a route to the baccalaureate. Accordingly, 2-year institutions offer educational access for those who may not have other immediate options for a postsecondary education and who eventually plan to pursue a baccalaureate.

Hiring and Contracting

Because community colleges do not typically use affirmative action in the student admissions process, issues surrounding the policy at these institutions have traditionally pertained to employment decisions (Johnston, 1997). One of the first and most significant suits to challenge affirmative action as violating Title VII of the Civil Rights Act of 1964, as well as the 5th and 14th Amendments, involved Cuyahoga Community College in Cleveland, Ohio. President Lyndon B. Johnson's administration had plans to provide federal support for developing the Cleveland area, and Cuyahoga Community College was to be on the receiving end of this support.[1] In the case of *Weiner v. Cuyahoga Community College* (1969), upon entertaining bids from contractors, the institution rejected the lowest estimate from Hyman R. Weiner. The president of Cuyahoga Community College based his decision not to hire Weiner on the contractor's actual bid proposal, which did not follow federal guidelines by neglecting to include a timetable and affirmative action goals outlining how many minorities would be employed on the project. Weiner's bid included a clause stating the ability to hire minorities was contingent upon availability from local unions. Weiner was unsuccessful in proving that he had no obligation to employ affirmative action standards and contended he was being mandated to give minorities preference in hiring for the sake of racial balance. Weiner's appeal to the Ohio Supreme Court rendered the same result, and the ruling against Weiner stood as law when a year later the U.S. Supreme Court declined to hear his case (Anderson, 2004).

Kelsey (1988) conducted a study that surveyed affirmative action/EEO officers at 175 public community colleges. In assessing whether those charged with fostering opportunities and equal access felt affirmative action was necessary, 62% felt that affirmative action should not be mandated. More specifically, the majority of 2-year professionals hired to sustain diversity thought institutions should elect to involve themselves instead of having to observe obligatory compliance. The results from this study typify the contradictory nature of this policy debate and the paradox that exists between espoused advocacies in theory versus actual practice.

Case study research that addressed the implementation of affirmative action and employment practices at one community college found that many department chairs and/or senior administrators made hiring decisions (Johnston, 1997). While little diversity among faculty and administrators existed at this 2-year institution, policies and practices illustrated a commitment from senior administrators to diversify the faculty through chosen compliance to affirmative action regulations. Among the recommendations forwarded from this policy analysis was to employ "grow your own" programs as a strategy to attract, retain, and promote greater participation at community colleges from professionals from racially/ethnically diverse backgrounds.

Maintaining and affirming diversity in employment has been especially cumbersome for public entities. After the passage of Proposition 209, Governor Pete Wilson petitioned the court to enable California's public community colleges to consider race/ethnicity and gender in employment decisions based on an existing statute that allowed gender- and race-conscious programs at 2-year institutions in the state. In December 1998 Proposition 209 was not overturned. Subsequently, in 2001 the California community college statute was struck down, ruling that the act was in breach of the tenets of Proposition 209 (Schmidt, 1998, 2001).

Affirmative Action in Admissions and Financial Aid

As noted above, there is little empirical research that addresses affirmative action in community colleges (Johnston, 1997; Kelsey, 1988; Zamani, 2003). Even less is known about student affirmative action in 2-year settings with regard to issues of access, given that community colleges do not have the traditionally closed system of admissions found in 4-year colleges and universities. One 1995 case, *Camarena v. San Bernardino Community College District*, involving the Pacific Legal Foundation, concerned a suit by Janice Camarena, a San Bernardino student (Caso & Corry, 1996). The suit, filed in U.S. District Court, alleged that the California college operated segregationist programs and challenged it on the basis of *Brown v. Board of Education* (1954). More specifically, Camarena charged she was locked out of a section of English 101 earmarked for the Bridge Transition Program because she was White. The purpose of the Bridge Transition Program and the Puente Project was to match students with mentors of the same racial background, provide additional support services, as well as seek to increase the transfer rates of students of African or Mexican descent (Rendón, 2002).

Caso and Corry (1996) contend that "community colleges have sacrificed the ideal of a prejudice-free society to an amorphous notion that the races are inherently different and need different treatment" (p. 44). The Camarena case was settled out of court. However, San Bernardino Community College maintained that Camarena's civil rights were not violated and that the open-door policy exists for all its course offerings. Because the majority of community colleges are open door, at least for most majors, race issues surrounding opposition to affirmative action may not be as evident in admissions as they are with 4-year institutions.[2] In community college settings, affirmative action tensions are more likely to manifest themselves through race issues within the curriculum, through the various course offerings, or in race-conscious scholarships (Rhoads & Valadez, 1996).

Concerns surrounding affirmative action at 2-year institutions have also extended to financial aid policies. Student financial aid is largely awarded to students who display monetary need. When assessing whether financial aid affects students' decisions to enter college, the answer is yes (Jackson, 1990). Many colleges and universities attempt to ensure that higher education remains affordable, particularly for high-achieving students who are members of underrepresented and/or disadvantaged groups, which are commonly racial/ethnic minorities. One technique for fostering minority participation in higher education is in the form of financial aid. Nevertheless, in recent years institutions of higher learning have been challenged for promoting race-conscious scholarships.

The assault on scholarships for students of color received great attention in *Podberesky v. Kirwan* (1994). Similarly, at the 2-year level, the multicampus of the Northern Virginia Community College (NVCC) faced a lawsuit for having a race-conscious merit scholarship (Barnes, 1996; Wright, 1997). Unlike the *Podberesky* case, which involved the University of Maryland's Banneker Scholarship funded with public money, the Leslie V. Forte Scholarship at NVCC is a race-conscious, privately funded award in the amount of $500. In his complaint filed with the Office of Civil Rights, Christopher Thompson cited the *Podberesky* case and contended that NVCC "discriminates against White male and female students by continuing to offer race and ethnicity-based scholarships that appear unconstitutional" (Wright, 1997, p. 14). The Fourth U.S. Circuit Court of Appeals that dismantled the

University of Maryland scholarship program for African Americans also has jurisdiction over Virginia. The Forte scholarship was one of two awards for students of color offered to five students per year at the college (Barnes, 1996).

The case at NVCC was particularly problematic prior to the court's determination that it is lawful to administer race-conscious scholarships if privately funded. According to Wright (1997), the coordinator of affirmative action, minority and legal affairs at NVCC felt that the suit regarding the Forte scholarship could have a negative effect on HBCUs. He stated, "The question is: If you can challenge this scholarship program, if it's illegal to administer these private funds, then the next step is to challenge funds like the United Negro College Fund and others who give money to Black colleges" (Wright, 1997, p. 14).

Whether an institution is a selective public university, state university or community college, the common thread within higher education is the pursuit of multiple missions. Research I and II universities promote a triple mission of research, teaching, and service (Carnegie Foundation for the Advancement of Teaching, 2001; Kerr, 1995). Comprehensive degree-granting institutions such as state universities focus on quality undergraduate and graduate programs and community relations, while liberal arts colleges and community colleges emphasize excellence in teaching and community service. Because of various factors, such as academic preparation, financial need, low SES, and family obligations, many students are locked out of attending 4-year institutions of higher learning, particularly disadvantaged and underrepresented students of color. Four-year colleges and universities may find it increasingly difficult to successfully admit students of color in large quantities (Gillett-Karam, Roueche, & Roueche, 1991; Lederman, 1997a; Rendón & Hope, 1996). Given the threat of ongoing affirmative action backlash in college admissions, community colleges may face the possibility of serving a larger segment of first-generation African American, Hispanic, and White students.

Community colleges have played a pivotal role in providing educational access to people of color and low-income students, as many of these students are dependent on 2-year institutions to advance their educational objectives (Kocher & Pascarella, 1988; Nora & Rendón, 1988, 1990, 1998; Richardson & Bender, 1987). When looking at racial/ethnic demographics of students at community colleges, roughly 58% of community college students enrolled is White, whereas 14% are Hispanic, and 13% are African American/Black. By comparison 6% of Asian American/Pacific Islanders make up the community college student body. Native Americans account for 1% of the

2-year student demographic, while 2% of those enrolled are nonresident aliens, and race/ethnicity is unknown for 6% of students (AACC, 2007). In fact, 47% of all African American collegians and well over half of all Native American and Hispanic students enrolled in college attend community colleges (Phillippe & Gonzalez, 2005). Fostering access and achievement in the education of the disadvantaged and underrepresented is a laudable contribution of community colleges. For many students of color, 2-year institutions serve as a viable alternative route to a 4-year college or university.

Conceptual Underpinnings

Social stratification in society is defined by its parameters or "any criterion implicit in the social distinctions people make in their social interaction" (Blau, 1975, p. 221). As applied, student background characteristics such as race/ethnicity, gender, age, parent's highest level of education, and annual family income illustrate the parameters that are thought to contribute to differentiation in social structure and have an effect on people's status attainment. This framework attempts to apply concepts of status attainment theory in explaining the odds of support or resistance of 2-year students toward affirmative action in college admissions.

Status attainment is a concept that explains adult attainment of select life outcomes based on systemic inequality (Karabel & Halsey, 1979). This approach to analyzing the occupational attainment and social mobility of adults argues that the occupational status of adults results from family origin and personal characteristics (Blau & Duncan, 1967; Duncan, Featherman, & Duncan, 1972; Grant, Horan, & Watts-Warren, 1994; Nordhaug, 1987; Sewell & Shaw, 1967). Status attainment research has been broadened to encompass the impact of social status on issues of college access and equity as well as on academic performance and educational attainment (McDonough & Antonio, 1996; Nordhaug, 1987; Sewell, Haller, & Portes, 1994; Sewell & Hauser, 1972; Sewell, Hauser, & Ohlendorf, 1970). Societal inequalities further perpetuate educational and occupational disparities and limit subsequent status attainment among marginalized groups (Persell, 1977). In this way, status attainment theory shares many of the basic tenets of social stratification and can be applied to determine whether community college students desiring a bachelor's degree (or higher) feel affirmative action in college admissions should be retained.

Given the paucity of inquiry regarding opinions of 2-year students on educational social policies, the following sections outline the aims and findings of an original study examining affirmative action views in association with the educational degree plans of students attending community colleges. This investigation is steered by two key research questions:

1. To what extent are student background characteristics, educational degree plans, self-interest, and racial beliefs associated with student attitudes toward affirmative action for each racial/ethnic group?
2. Among baccalaureate aspirants, to what degree do student background characteristics alone predict affirmative action attitudes; to what degree do educational degree plans, then self-interest followed by racial beliefs, add to the prediction of attitudes toward affirmative action in college admissions?

Significance and Implications

Traditionally, research has focused primarily on differences in the attitudes of African American and White 4-year students (Ayers, 1992; Doverspike & Arthur, 1995; Gurin, Nagda, & Lopez, 2004; Meader, 1998; Nacoste, 1994; Sax & Arredondo, 1999; Smith, 1998, 2006). However, the literature is lacking relative to how students attending community colleges (particularly those with baccalaureate or higher degree plans) respond to affirmative action in college admissions. The relevance of affirmative action in college admissions to students seeking to move from an open-door system to institutions with selective admissions criteria is unknown.

The study that is the focus of this chapter seeks to explore attitudes toward affirmative action by examining how a different segment of the student population responds to the policy as it relates to college admissions. The research questions posed may generate findings that clarify how affirmative action programming is perceived by a segment of higher education students overlooked in previous research.

Useful for theoretical and practical reasons, examining the affirmative action attitudes of students at the 2-year level could be useful to educators concerned with campus climate, in addition to being beneficial to researchers interested in issues surrounding access, participation rates, inclusion, transfer, and student support services. A better understanding of varied student views on affirmative action is cardinal, and would be useful in facilitating how college officials review, revise, and implement policies and programming geared toward promoting diversity.

Methodology

The Cooperative Institutional Research Program (CIRP) Freshman Survey (Sax, Astin, Korn, & Mahoney, 1996). served as the data source for the variables explored in this study.[3] The sample for this study was initially defined by selecting 2-year college students who first enrolled in 1996. The sample was further limited by restricting the analysis to include the three largest racial/ethnic groups: African American, Hispanic, and White 2-year students ($N = 20,339$) representing 73 2-year institutions.[4]

Variables and Procedures

Attitudes toward affirmative action in college admissions served as the dependent variable. "Affirmative action in college admissions should be abolished" was measured on a 4-point scale from $1 =$ disagree strongly to $4 =$ agree strongly. The dependent variable was recoded as a dichotomous variable ($0 =$ disagree, and $1 =$ agree) to conduct logistic regression analyses.

The independent variables selected for use in this study represented 4 constructs:

1. student background characteristics
2. educational degree plans
3. self-interest
4. racial beliefs

As stated previously, prior research has suggested that student background characteristics including race/ethnicity, gender, age, parents' highest level of education, annual family income, enrollment status, and political ideologies, bear some influence on differential educational access and subsequent educational degree attainment (Brint & Karabel, 1989a, 1989b; Carter, 1999a, 1999b; Grant et al., 1994; Nordhaug, 1987).

It was of primary interest to assess community college students' baccalaureate and beyond degree plans with their views about affirmative action in college admissions. Educational degree plans as characterized in this study correspond to the chances of getting a bachelor's degree, transferring to another college, and highest degree intentions. Collegians reporting "other" as their highest degree planned were retained for multivariate analyses to control the total number of cases rejected because of missing data. Additionally, students identifying "other" were also incorporated under the assumption that a degree was desired that may not be equivalent to the response options provided.

Conceptually, this study holds that self-interest may affect attitudes toward affirmative action in college admissions based on perceived benefit to oneself as well as the racial/ethnic or social group. In studying attitudes toward affirmative action in college admissions with 4-year CIRP Survey respondents, Sax and Arredondo (1999) operationalized constructs of self-interest using GPA and college choice. This study adapted that construct to

TABLE 3
1996 CIRP Participating Institutions by Norm Group, State, and Public or Private Control

Institution	Norm Group	State	Control
1. Abraham Baldwin Agricultural College	Yes	GA	Public
2. Adirondack Community College	Yes	NY	Public
3. Bainbridge College	Yes	GA	Public
4. Bronx Community College	No	NY	Public
5. Chattahoochee Valley State Community College	No	AL	Public
6. Chesapeake College	Yes	MD	Public
7. Citrus College	No	CA	Public
8. Community College of Denver	No	CO	Public
9. Coconino Community College	No	AZ	Public
10. College of the Canyons	No	CA	Public
11. College of the Sequoias	No	CA	Public
12. Dyersburg State Community College	No	TN	Public
13. Eastern Wyoming College	Yes	WY	Public
14. Floyd College	No	GA	Public
15. Fredrick Community College	No	MD	Public
16. Fresno City College	No	CA	Public
17. Harrisburg Area Community College	Yes	PA	Public
18. Hartnell Community College	Yes	CA	Public
19. Highland Community College	Yes	IL	Public
20. Independence Community College	Yes	KS	Public
21. James Sprunt Community College	Yes	NC	Public
22. Jefferson Community College	Yes	NY	Public
23. Kauai Community College	No	HI	Public

TABLE 3 (Continued)

Institution	Norm Group	State	Control
24. Lake City Community College	Yes	FL	Public
25. Los Angeles Valley College	No	CA	Public
26. Louisiana State University-Eunice	Yes	LA	Public
27. Massachusetts Bay Community College	No	MA	Public
28. Mid Michigan Community College	No	MI	Public
29. Minnesota West Community & Tech College-Worth	Yes	MN	Public
30. Monroe Community College	No	NY	Public
31. Mount Wachusetts Community College	Yes	MA	Public
32. North Shore Community College	No	MA	Public
33. Northeast Texas Community College	Yes	TX	Public
34. Northern Essex Community College	Yes	MA	Public
35. Northwest Arkansas Community College	Yes	AR	Public
36. Onondaga Community College	No	NY	Public
37. Quinebaug Valley Community & Technical College	No	CT	Public
38. Quinsigamond Community College	No	MA	Public
39. Rainy River Community College	No	MN	Public
40. San Diego City College	No	CA	Public
41. SUNY College of Technology-Alfred	Yes	NY	Public
42. SUNY College of Technology-Delhi	No	NY	Public
43. Tallahassee Community College	Yes	FL	Public
44. Texas State Tech College-Sweetwater	Yes	TX	Public
45. Texas State Tech College-Waco	Yes	TX	Public

	College		State	Type
46.	University of Pittsburgh-Greensburg	Yes	PA	Public
47.	University of Pittsburgh-Titusville	Yes	PA	Public
48.	University of South Carolina-Union	Yes	SC	Public
49.	University of Wisconsin-Centers	Yes	WI	Public
50.	Washtenaw Community College	No	MI	Public
51.	Andrew College	Yes	GA	Private
52.	Bethany Lutheran College	Yes	MN	Private
53.	Brevard College	Yes	NC	Private
54.	College of Aeronautics	Yes	NY	Private
55.	Dean College	Yes	MA	Private
56.	Emmanuel College	Yes	GA	Private
57.	Fisher College	Yes	MA	Private
58.	Florida College	Yes	FL	Private
59.	Holy Cross College	Yes	IN	Private
60.	MacCormac Junior College	Yes	IL	Private
61.	Manor Junior College	Yes	PA	Private
62.	Martin Methodist College	Yes	TN	Private
63.	Midway College	Yes	KY	Private
64.	Mount Saint Mary's College	Yes	CA	Private
65.	Newbury College	Yes	MA	Private
66.	Presentation College	Yes	SD	Private
67.	Springfield College	No	IL	Private
68.	St. Mary's College	Yes	NC	Private
69.	Suomi College	Yes	MI	Private
70.	Valley Forge Military College	Yes	PA	Private
71.	Villa Maria College of Buffalo	Yes	NY	Private
72.	Waldorf College	Yes	IA	Private
73.	Wisconsin Lutheran College	Yes	WI	Private

include the ability to finance education as a measure of self-interest as well, since it is thought to influence a student's agreement or disagreement with affirmative action in college admissions.

Other prior research examining attitudes toward affirmative action suggest that cross-racial interaction and racial beliefs have some correspondence with the policy stance of individuals (Bobo & Kluegel, 1993; Chang, Denson, Saenz, & Misa, 2006; Dietz-Uhler & Murrell, 1993; Dovidio et al., 2004). For this study, racial beliefs were measured by cross-race socialization, perception of racial discrimination, and promotion of racial understanding to reflect student attitudes toward other racial/ethnic groups.

Data Analysis

Preliminary analyses described 2-year student attitudes toward affirmative action and the other independent variables according to race/ethnicity. The following are descriptive statistics and cross-tabulations of affirmative action attitudes by racial/ethnic category, with each independent variable. The last set of analyses estimates odds ratios for each independent variable in determining support for abolishment of affirmative action in college admissions among baccalaureate-aspiring community college students.

A hierarchical logistic regression analysis was conducted with variables ordered in the equation according to temporal order. In determining the probability that 2-year students' favor the use of affirmative action in admissions rather than oppose it, based on all the independent variables of interest, the following logistic regression equation was estimated:

Let p_i be the probability of student support for abolishing affirmative action in college admission.

$$\log[p_i/(1-p_i)] = B_0 + B_1 Sc_i + B_2 Ea_i + B_3 Se_i + B_4 Ra_i + e^5$$

Where b_1 = the partial slope of attitude toward affirmative action in college admissions on student background variables while controlling for all other independent variables

b_2 = the partial slope of attitudes toward affirmative action in college admissions on educational aspiration variables while controlling for all other independent variables

b_3 = the partial slope of attitudes toward affirmative action in college admissions on self-interest variables while controlling for all other independent variables

TABLE 4
Dependent and Independent Variables of Interest in the CIRP Survey

Category/Variable	Scale/Coding
Affirmative Action in College Admissions Should Be Abolished (Dummy Variable)	*Recoded Into Dummy Variable 0 = Disagree; 1 = Agree*
Background Characteristics (Block I)	
Racial/Ethnic Identification	Created a series of dummy variables do if (race 2 = 2) compute as African American = 1 else compute African American = 0 do if (race 5 = 2 or race 6 = 2 or race 7 = 2 and race 2 = 1) compute as Hispanic, non-African American = 1 else compute Hispanic = 0 do if (race 1 = 2 and race 2 = 1 and race 5 = 1 and race 6 = 1 and race 7 = 1) compute as White, non-African American, non-Hispanic = 1 else compute White = 0
Gender	recoded 1 = 0 (Male) and 2 = 1 (Female)
Age	Recoded to three categories for descriptive analysis 1 = Under 18; 2 = 18 to 24; 3 = 25 and over; Recode to midpoints for multivariate analysis (1 = 16, 2 = 17, 3 = 18, 4 = 19, 5 = 20, 6 = 22.5, 7 = 27, 8 = 34.5, 9 = 47, 10 = 55)
Parents' Annual Income	Parents' income is measured on a 14-point scale from less than $6,000 to $200,000 or more. Recoded into four categories for descriptive analysis: 1 = $14,999 and under; 2 = $15,000 to $29,999; 3 = $30,000 to $59,999; 4 = $60,000 or more; Recoded to midpoints for multivariate analysis (1 = 3000, 2 = 7999, 3 = 12499, 4 = 17499, 5 = 22499, 6 = 27499, 7 = 34999, 8 = 44999, 9 = 54999, 10 = 67499, 11 = 87499, 12 = 124999, 13 = 174999, 14 = 200000)

TABLE 4 (Continued)

Category/Variable	Scale/Coding
Affirmative Action in College Admissions Should Be Abolished (Dummy Variable)	*Recoded Into Dummy Variable 0 = Disagree; 1 = Agree*
Parents' Educational Attainment	1 = grammar school or less, 2 = some high school, 3 = high school graduate, 4 = postsecondary other than college, 5 = some college, 6 = college degree, 7 = some graduate school, and 8 = graduate degree. Collapsed mother and father's education reflecting highest educational attainment of either parent and recoded into number of years of school to adjust intervals (1 = 8, 2 = 10, 3 = 12, 4 and 5 = 14, 6 = 16, 7 = 17, 8 = 18)
Enrollment Status	part-time = 0 and full-time = 1
Political Views	1 = far right; 2 = conservative; 3 = middle of the road; 4 = liberal; 5 = far left
Educational Aspirations (Block II)	
Get a bachelor's degree	1 = no chance; 2 = very little chance; 3 = some chance; 4 = very good chance
Transfer Intent	1 = no chance; 2 = very little chance; 3 = some chance; 4 = very good chance
Highest Degree Planned	Collapsed degrees and recoded into 0 = none; 1 = vocational certificate/associate; 1.5 = other; 2 = bachelor's or B.Div.; 3 = master's; 4 = LLB. or JD; 5 = PhD or EdD; 6 = MD, DO, DDS, DVM

Self-Interest (Block III)

Academic Preparedness $\quad$ 1 = D; 2 = C; 3 = C+; 4 = B−; 5 = B; 6 = B+; 7 = A−; 8 = A or A+.

College Choice $\quad$ 1 = first choice; 2 = second choice; 3 = third choice; 4 = less than third choice

Ability to Finance Education $\quad$ 1 = none; 2 = some; 3 = major

Racial Affect (Block IV)

Cross-race Socialization $\quad$ 3 = frequently; 2 = occasionally; 1 = not at all

Racial Discrimination $\quad$ 1 = disagree strongly; 2 = disagree somewhat; 3 = agree somewhat; 4 = agree strongly

Racial Understanding $\quad$ 1 = not important; 2 = somewhat important; 3 = very important; 4 = essential

Institutional Characteristics (Block V)

Institutional Race $\quad$ Recoded into 2 = 1 (Black) and 1 = 0 (White)

Institutional Control $\quad$ Created dummy variable 2 = 0 (private), 1 = 1 (public)

Institutional Size $\quad$ 1 = very low; 2 = low; 3 = medium; 4 = high; 5 = very high

Institutional Sex $\quad$ single sex = 1 and coeducational = 0

$b_4 =$ the partial slope of attitudes toward affirmative action in college admissions on racial affect variables while controlling for all other independent variables

$e =$ represents the portion of 2-year student attitudes toward affirmative action that cannot be accounted for by the independent variables proposed in the model

The above equation represents the final logistic model for analysis, whereby the notation represents the variables of interest with regard to conceptual grouping.

Findings

Descriptive Statistics

In providing a portrait of student participants in this sample, percentages are presented for the variables studied. Over three-fourths of the student sample was White ($n = 15,614$), 11.3% was Hispanic ($n = 2,300$), and about 12% ($n = 2,425$) was African American, representing a total sample size of 20,339. Overall, females represented the majority of the total sample, making up 55.4% of the sample.

With regard to students' age, 2% of students were under 18 years of age, with roughly 80% of students being of traditional college age: between 18 and 24 years old. Correspondingly, 17% of students reported being 25 years old or older. Self-reported measures of annual family income revealed 34.7% of families were between $30,000 and $59,999; 20% indicated annual family incomes between $15,000 and $29,999. Parents earning under $15,000 and those with incomes of $60,000 or more each accounted for 17% of the sample.

In addressing the highest educational attainment of their parents, 27.5% of students had one or both parents who were high school graduates, but roughly 13% of students' parents had educational attainment less than high school. About 23% of parents had completed some college, whereas 23.6% were college graduates and 11.5% of students reported parents' highest educational level as a graduate degree. In terms of their own enrollment in community colleges, the bulk of students (85%) indicated being full-time students. For the overall sample, 54% of students indicated being bipartisan in that they were in the "middle of the road" in reference to their political views. However, 20.5% reported being conservative, while 19.7% said they were liberal. Less than 2% of students stated their political ideologies as being far right, and about 4% referred to themselves as being far left.

In regard to educational degree plans, over 50% of students stated there was a very good chance they would get a bachelor's degree, with another 30.3% reporting some chance they would earn a bachelor's degree. In the CIRP Freshman Survey, students were asked if they intended to transfer to another college. Roughly 33% stated there was no chance that they would transfer, and almost 20% reported very little chance of transferring. Forty-seven percent of students indicated there was some to a very good chance they would transfer to another institution. Over two-thirds of the sample indicated attending their first choice college; hence, it is not surprising that roughly one-third of students stated they had no intentions to transfer to another two- or four-year institution.

Over half of students reported having high school GPAs in the B range, and over 67% reported academic preparedness of B minus or better. Reinforcing findings regarding their chances of getting a bachelor's degree, the vast majority of students aspired to attain degrees beyond the 2-year level. About one-third of them desired the baccalaureate as the highest degree, while another one-third planned to attain a master's degree, and almost 14% desired a doctoral or professional degree. Nearly one quarter of the students expressed a major concern about their ability to finance their education. Forty-five percent had some concerns over financing their education and 30.7% did not have any concerns regarding college costs.

With respect to racial beliefs, only 27% of the students felt it was not important to promote racial understanding. Thirty-nine percent thought promoting racial understanding was somewhat important, and roughly 34% of the students indicated that it was very important or essential. Fifty-five percent of the students frequently engaged in socializing with members of different racial/ethnic groups. Nevertheless, about 18% of the students agreed somewhat or strongly that racial discrimination was no longer a problem in society. Finally, there was overall support for affirmative action in college admissions, though greater percentages of students of color favored its use than White students (72% African American, 69% Hispanic, and 56% White were in favor).

Background Characteristics

Looking first at background characteristics, results illustrate that the degree of association between gender and support for abolishing affirmative action in college admissions was statistically significant for each racial/ethnic group (African Americans $\chi^2 = 10.697$, df = 1, $p = .001$; Hispanics $\chi^2 = 16.854$, df = 1, $p = .000$; and Whites $\chi^2 = 306.291$, df = 1, $p = .000$). Overall, fewer males in each racial/ethnic group supported retaining affirmative action in college admissions than women; the degree of association between age and attitudes toward affirmative action in college admissions was statistically significant for African Americans (χ^2 = 10.710, df = 2, p = .01) and Whites (χ^2 = 15.504, df = 2, p = .000), but not for Hispanics. For these two groups, support for affirmative action, including disagreement with abolishing affirmative action, increased with age.

The degree of association of parental educational attainment and attitudes toward affirmative action in college admissions was statistically significant for Whites only (χ^2 = 54.291, df = 6, p = .000). Interestingly, support for abolishing affirmative action among Whites was lowest among students who had parents with a grade school education or less, some high school, or high school diploma. Support for abolishing affirmative action among White students increased as their parental education increased.

There was variation in the number of students supporting the dismantling of affirmative action in college admissions by annual family income for the racial/ethnic groups. The degree of association between annual family income and attitudes toward affirmative action was statistically significant at the $p \leq$ .01 level for Whites (χ^2 = 47.886, df = 3, p = .000), but not other groups. Overall, lower-income White students were supportive of affirmative action more than affluent White students. Roughly one-half of White students from families with annual incomes of more than $30,000 disagreed with abolishing affirmative action in college admissions. By comparison, from two-thirds to three-fourths of African American students and about two-thirds of Hispanic students at each income level supported affirmative action.

The degree of association between enrollment status and abolishing affirmative action in college admissions was not statistically significant for any racial/ethnic group. As for the association of affirmative action and political views, a higher percentage of far-right and conservative White students favored abolishing affirmative action in college admissions than did far-left and liberal White students. White students' support for abolishing affirmative action in college admissions increased as political views became more conservative (χ^2 = 124.881, df = 4, p = .000). Among those who espoused conservative political views, less than one-half of White students (45.4%) favored affirmative action as compared to 73.6% of African American and 67% of Hispanic students. Although the association of political views with favoring the abolishment of affirmative action in college admissions was not statistically significant for Hispanic and African American students, far-right Hispanic students were slightly more likely to support abolishing affirmative action than conservative, middle-of-the-road, and more liberal Hispanics.

Educational Degree Plans

With regard to educational degree plans, Whites who stated there was some or a very good chance of getting a bachelor's degree were more likely to agree with abolishing affirmative action than were Whites who thought they had no chance or very little chance of getting a bachelor's degree. Chi-square analyses indicated statistically significant results for White students ($\chi^2 = 44.623$, df $= 3$, $p = .000$), implying students' outlook on obtaining a baccalaureate degree was associated with their attitude toward affirmative action in college admissions. There was no significant association between attitudes toward affirmative action in college admissions and planning to earn a bachelor's degree for Hispanic and African American students.

Large percentages of African American and Hispanic students favored affirmative action in college admissions regardless of transfer intentions. The chi-square test found the association of transfer intent and attitudes toward affirmative action in college admissions statistically significant for White students only ($\chi^2 = 51.552$, df $= 3$, $p = .000$). Approximately one-half of White students specifying some or very good chances of transferring supported affirmative action in college admissions, while a slightly larger percentage (57%) supported it when they indicated no chance of transfer. Similarly, the association between highest degree planned and attitudes toward affirmative action was statistically significant for White students only ($\chi^2 = 41.128$, df $= 6$, $p = .000$). Nearly 58% of White students who indicated vocational certificates or associate's degrees as their highest degree planned favored affirmative action in college admissions. White students planning to earn medical, law, or doctoral degrees were least supportive of affirmative action in college admissions.

Self-Interest

In examining the association of attitudes toward affirmative action with self-interest variables, statistically significant results were yielded for academic preparedness, including high school GPA, for African Americans ($\chi^2 = 36.420$, df $= 7$, $p = .000$) and Whites ($\chi^2 = 20.223$, df $= 7$, $p = .01$). The overall pattern of results suggests that White students with lower grades (B and below) favored affirmative action in college admissions slightly more than those with higher grades. Among African American students the reverse was true; students reporting GPAs of A and B were more favorable than those earning lower grades.

Attitude toward affirmative action was associated with college choice among White students ($\chi^2 = 17.235$, df $= 3$, $p = .001$), but not students of color. The percentage of White students who favored retaining affirmative action in college admissions tended to decrease as the student reported being at a lower-choice institution. Additionally, students reported their level of concern regarding ability to finance their college education, but no significant associations were found between concern about ability to finance education and attitudes toward affirmative action for any racial/ethnic group.

Racial Beliefs

Chi-square results show socialization outside of one's racial group was associated with attitudes toward affirmative action in college admissions for students in each racial/ethnic group. Students of color tended to support affirmative action more as they occasionally or frequently socialized with other racial/ethnic groups, but this finding was not statistically significant.

The degree of association between support for abolishing affirmative action and the belief that racial discrimination is no longer a problem was statistically significant within each racial/ethnic group (African Americans χ^2 = 90.790, df = 3, p = .000; Hispanics χ^2 = 63.336, df = 3, p = .000; and Whites χ^2 = 231.230, df = 3, p = .000). Thus, students who believed racial discrimination was still a problem favored use of affirmative action in college admissions. Connected to beliefs about racial discrimination, the majority of respondents indicated the importance of promoting racial understanding. For White students only, support of affirmative action increased along with students' views that promoting racial understanding was important (χ^2 = 36.237, df = 3, p = .000).

Logistic Regression

Logistic regression analysis was conducted to examine support for abolishing affirmative action in college admissions among students with degree plans to earn the baccalaureate or higher. Each of the following conditions had to be met for inclusion in this subgroup: some or very high chances of transfer, some or very high chances of getting a bachelor's degree, and highest degree plans for the baccalaureate degree or higher. Table 5 presents the hierarchical logistic regression results for 2-year baccalaureate aspirants using the block entry process.

With only student background characteristics in Model 1, nearly 60% of this sample was classified correctly as favoring or opposing affirmative action in college admissions. Chi-square analysis revealed that this block of variables was statistically significant in fit (χ^2 = 252.745, df = 8, p = .000).

TABLE 5
Predictors of Abolishing Affirmative Action in College Admissions for 2-Year Baccalaureate Aspirants

Variable	B	SE B	Wald[a]	Exp (B)
		Block I: Model 1		
Racial/Ethnic Identification				
African American	−.9983	.1269	61.9312**	.3685
Hispanic	−.6239	.1172	28.3623**	.5358
Gender				
Female	−.4962	.0623	63.3913**	.6088
Age Group	−.0064	.0070	.8356	.9936
Annual Family Income	.0289	.0111	6.7708**	1.0294
Parental Educational Attainment	.0014	.0135	.0114	1.0014
Enrollment Status	.0328	.0996	.1085	1.0333
Political Views	−.2465	.0398	38.2888**	.7816
		Blocks I & II: Model 2		
Racial/Ethnic Identification				
African American	−.9887	.1285	59.1849**	.3721
Hispanic	−.6104	.1182	26.6877**	.5431
Gender				
Female	−.5478	.0646	72.0000**	.5782
Age Group	−.0025	.0071	.1252	.9975
Annual Family Income	.0347	.0116	9.0076**	1.0353
Parental Educational Attainment	.0004	.0136	.0010	1.0004

TABLE 5 (Continued)

Variable	B	SE B	Wald[a]	Exp (B)
Blocks I & II: Model 2				
Enrollment Status	.0472	.0998	.2235	1.0483
Political Views	−.2388	.0401	35.3976**	.7875
Academic Preparedness (GPA)	.1736	.0538	10.4003**	1.1896
College Choice	.0642	.0327	3.8411	1.0663
Ability to Finance Education	.0709	.0450	2.4808	1.0735
Blocks I, II & III: Model 3				
Racial/Ethnic Identification				
African American	−.8407	.1314	40.9247**	.4314
Hispanic	−.5354	.1201	19.8782**	.5854
Gender				
Female	−.4889	.0656	55.4935**	.6133
Age Group	−.0005	.0071	.0047	.9995
Annual Family Income	.0359	.0116	9.5253**	1.0366
Parental Educational Attainment	.0016	.0137	.0136	1.0016
Enrollment Status	.0797	.1007	.6265	1.0830
Political Views	−.2118	.0407	27.0660**	.8091
Academic Preparedness (GPA)	.1609	.0542	8.8095**	1.1746
College Choice	.0650	.0330	3.8799	1.0672
Ability to Finance Education	.0888	.0456	3.7927	1.0928
Cross-Race Socialization	−.0067	.0540	.0153	.10067
Racial Discrimination	.2407	.0392	37.6672**	1.2722
Promoting Racial Understanding	−.0680	.0353	3.7177	.9343

Note. $n = 4447$; [a]$df = 1$; **$p \leq .01$

0 = disagree with abolishing affirmative action in college admissions; 1 = agree

Results of the logistic regression analysis for baccalaureate aspirants indicate that for the first block of Model 1, race/ethnicity, gender, family income, and political views were predictive of student attitudes toward affirmative action in college admissions. No significant differences in age, parental education, or student enrollment status resulted. The exponentiation of B in the first model illustrated African American and Hispanic students were less likely to agree with abolishing affirmative action in college. The odds of female support for affirmative action abolishment were .6088 times less than the odds for male baccalaureate aspirants. Specifically, women in pursuit of the baccalaureate were more favorable toward affirmative action in college admissions than their male counterparts. Additionally, the effect of increasing annual family income and more liberal political views was to reduce the odds of supporting abolishing affirmative action in college admissions.

Model 2 included block I variables and entered a second block of variables reflecting self-interest measures, including GPA, college choice, and concern about finances. The overall percentage classified correctly in favor or in opposition to dismantling affirmative action increased slightly to 60.13%. The addition of self-interest measures in the second model was statistically significant in improving overall model fit ($\chi^2 = 17.382$, df $= 3$, $p = .001$).

Similar to the first model, being a student of color, female, having a lower family income, and having more liberal political views lowered the odds of a student supporting the abolishment of affirmative action. Model 2 yielded significant differences in the impact of annual family income on affirmative action attitudes of baccalaureate aspirants as well. However, of the three self-interest variables, GPA was the only variable having a significant influence on attitudes toward affirmative action. As the GPA rose, the odds of supporting the abolishment of affirmative action in college admissions increased.

The last model added a third block of variables characterizing racial beliefs to the logistic regression equation. Racial beliefs variables measured the extent to which students socialize with different racial/ethnic groups, and how they view racial discrimination and rate the importance of promoting racial understanding. The overall percentage classified correctly rose slightly to 60.81% when block III was added to the last equation. The addition of racial beliefs measures enhanced the fit of Model 3 ($\chi^2 = 45.147$, df $= 3$, $p = .000$).

The addition of racial beliefs variables revealed that cross-race socialization and promoting racial understanding were not associated with the odds of abolishing affirmative action in college admissions among baccalaureate aspirants. However, the odds of agreeing with dismantling affirmative action were 1.272 times greater for students feeling racial discrimination was no longer a problem. In other words, each 1-point increase in this independent variable yielded a 27% increase in the odds of baccalaureate aspirants opposing affirmative action in college admissions. The final logistic regression equation for baccalaureate aspirants resulted in significant effects of race/ethnicity, gender, annual family income, political views, GPA, and views on racial discrimination on the odds of agreeing with abolishing affirmative action in college admissions.

Conclusions

Researchers have argued that opposition to affirmative action among Whites is largely because of aversive or symbolic racism (Bobo & Kluegel, 1993; Dovidio et al., 1989; Sears & Jessor, 1996). Past research has also examined attitudes toward race-conscious affirmative action among Whites, and to a lesser extent among people of color (Dovidio et al., 1994; Dovidio et al., 2004; Kluegel, 1990; Kluegel & Smith, 1983; Smith, 1993; Stanush, Arthur, & Doverspike, 1998; Zamani, 2002). In contrast, the literature on affirmative action contains modest inquiry on student attitudes toward affirmative action, principally in higher education and college admissions, with multiethnic samples (Amirkhan, Betancourt, Graham, Lopez, & Weiner, 1995; Knight & Hebl, 2005; Meader, 1998; Nosworthy et al., 1995; Pinel et al., 2005; Sax & Arredondo, 1999; Smith, 1998, 2006). Furthermore, studies on college students' attitudes toward affirmative action have exclusively examined 4-year student affirmative action attitudes.

Results of the study described in detail above, suggest that variables such as race/ethnicity, gender, political views, and promotion of racial understanding have an impact on the odds of supporting abolishing affirmative action among students enrolled in 2-year institutions. Specifically, when looking at the overall sample, students of color, women, liberals, and those placing importance on racial understanding had reduced odds of supporting abolishing affirmative action than other groups. Students' having higher income families, greater intentions of transferring, higher GPAs, lower college choice, and greater belief that racial discrimination is not a problem had greater odds for supporting affirmative action abolishment in college admissions. Consistent with Sax and Arredondo (1999), students espousing conservative political views had a greater likelihood of supporting abolishing affirmative action than students having more liberal political views.

Another conclusion drawn from this study pertains to race/ethnicity and gender bearing an influence on student attitudes toward affirmative action in college admissions. The findings illustrate that larger percentages of White students oppose affirmative action and have greater odds of supporting abolishing affirmative action consistent with previous studies addressing affirmative action attitudes (Bobo & Kluegel, 1993; Bobo et al., 1997; Bobo & Smith, 1994; Kluegel & Smith, 1983; Sax & Arredondo, 1999; Smith & Kluegel, 1984). However, despite the current period of affirmative action retrenchment in higher education, it appears from this study that there is widespread support for affirmative action in college admissions across each racial/ethnic group of community college students.

Interestingly, there were marked differences in levels of support for abolishing affirmative action between White males and females. White female students were less likely than White males to support abolishing affirmative action in college admissions. Consistent with Kravitz and Platania (1993), the effects of gender show that women evaluated affirmative action more positively than men. In previous research examining race-conscious affirmative action policies and gender (Smith, 1993; Zamani, 2002), a greater association between negative attitudes toward affirmative action and race-conscious White women was found. The present study could not discern whether attitudes toward affirmative action were associated with policies based on race, gender, or class, as CIRP data did not make such distinctions.

Similar to prior research, results revealed that African Americans and Hispanics approved of affirmative action at higher rates than did their White counterparts (Dovidio et al., 2004; Sax & Arredondo, 1999; Smith, 1998). However, in contrast to findings from Sax and Arredondo's (1999) study of 4-year collegians, there was no statistically significant effect of annual family income on Hispanic or African American 2-year student support for affirmative action in college admissions. Furthermore, previous research has noted African American support for affirmative action is more consistent, while Hispanic support is less cohesive and complex (Smith, 1998).

One of the original purposes of affirmative action was to eradicate the previous discrimination of African Americans and other disadvantaged groups (Crosby, 2006). As members of underrepresented groups, African American two-year students disagreed with abolishing affirmative action in college admissions slightly more than Hispanic collegians. Perhaps differences between African American and Hispanic support for affirmative action stem from the unique experiences of each group and the legacy of slavery endured by African Americans in contrast to the more recent disenfranchisement of voluntary Hispanic immigrants.

Prior research has stressed that affirmative action provides advantages to students of color in admissions through unfair exclusion of White students, leaving them to attend second- and third-choice institutions (D'Souza, 1992; Herrnstein & Murray, 1994; Raza, Anderson, & Custred, 1999). Yet, national data have suggested otherwise, as the percentage of 4-year students attending their first-choice institution was highest among White and Hispanic students (NCES, 1996). Confirming earlier results, this study revealed over two-thirds of White and Hispanic 2-year students were attending their first-choice college, whereas 59.5% of African Americans were at their first-choice institution. Still, college choice was not associated with or found to be a predictor of affirmative action attitudes for students affiliated with any of the racial/ethnic groups.

A subsample was drawn from the larger student sample to examine affirmative action attitudes of 2-year baccalaureate aspirants. While little research has examined student attitudes toward affirmative action in college admissions (Amirkhan et al., 1995; Sax & Arredondo, 1999), even less is known about 2-year student affirmative action attitudes, generally those students seeking to transfer in pursuit of a bachelor's degree. This study showed that race/ethnicity, gender, annual family income, political views, GPA, and views on racial discrimination influenced the odds of agreeing with abolishing affirmative action in college admissions.

Similar to earlier findings, logistic regression analyses for baccalaureate aspirants revealed that students of color and women were less likely to agree with abolishing affirmative action in comparison to Whites and males. Income and political views affected support for abolishing affirmative action, as higher income baccalaureate aspirants had greater odds of opposing affirmative action while more liberal students were more favorable toward retaining affirmative action in college admissions. Having a higher GPA also increased the odds of supporting affirmative action retrenchment in college admissions among baccalaureate aspirants. Finally, the belief that racial discrimination is no longer a problem revealed a decreased likelihood of affirmative action support in college admissions among baccalaureate aspirants.

What do we now know about attitudes toward affirmative action among community college baccalaureate aspirants—who represent an important segment of the higher education population and who have been previously neglected by researchers—that was not evident before? This study demonstrates that 2-year collegians have definite opinions regarding the use of affirmative action in college admissions that are associated with their personal backgrounds and political views. As many college students take the 2-year option, the community college makes sense for a growing number of students because it is often the most academically, geographically, and financially accessible to women and students of color (Townsend, 1999). Although the literature has indicated that entering a community college with baccalaureate aspirations reduces one's chances of obtaining a 4-year degree, a preponderance of 2-year college students do aspire to the baccalaureate degree. Consequently, it seems particularly relevant to consider the attitudes of baccalaureate-aspiring 2-year students toward affirmative action in college admissions. Additionally, with the growing resistance to affirmative action post–*Grutter v. Bollinger* (2003), community colleges may play an increased role in the postsecondary access of many underserved collegians, making them a viable alternate route to the baccalaureate, particularly in states such as California, Florida, Michigan, Texas, and Washington (Burdman, 2003; Roska, Grodsky & Hom, 2006).

Higher education administrators need to be aware of student attitudes toward affirmative action at 2- and 4-year institutions. More specifically, understanding 2-and 4-year students' views of affirmative action in college admissions may assist educational leaders in revising or reestablishing policies and programming efforts as tools for enhancing campus diversity. Also, as the central focus of this chapter is to share findings from an original study, it is important to note that the results reported stem solely from secondary analysis of CIRP data; absent from this investigation is the entire litany of factors that could have an impact on student attitudes toward affirmative action in college admissions. Consequently, the factors of interest in this study are not representative of the total number variables possible.

The findings from this study rely on cross-sectional data gathered at one point in time. Therefore, this study can only extend to time-bound inferences regarding 2-year student attitudes toward affirmative action in college admissions. Further research of a longitudinal nature is needed, which would be most interesting with a 2-year college student sample, because it would be possible to examine the transition to 4-year colleges and success at that level in correspondence to affirmative action attitudes/diversity beliefs. Future inquiry using qualitative methods would allow for a fuller understanding of 2-year student views on affirmative action in admissions. Additionally, examining the causal influences of affirmative action stance through path analytic approaches could inform our understanding of the role of student background characteristics, educational aspirations, self-interest, and racial affect in relation to college admissions, and examine whether there are interactions and combined effects of the variables.

Notes

1. Following Johnson's leadership in fostering opportunities for racial/ethnic minorities and because of some degree of success in Cleveland, goals for affirmative action evolved, resulting in the Philadelphia Plan, which aimed to produce minority group representation in all trades and phases of construction during the Richard M. Nixon administration (Anderson, 2004; Brunner, 2006a).

2. It is important to note that while the community college has an open door, many occupational programs, such as nursing and dental hygiene, have competitive admissions because of standing prerequisites, limited numbers, and the high cost of instructional delivery for more technical areas.

3. The Annual Freshmen Year Survey is a national study of first-year students in higher education attending U.S. colleges and universities. The annual survey was administered by the UCLA Higher Education Research Institute (HERI) in 1966 and is still administered by HERI at UCLA through the Cooperative Institutional Research Program (CIRP).

4. This study is delimited to the use of 1996 CIRP data, as it was the first and only time that UCLA's Higher Education Research Institute (HERI) included community colleges in the normative sample of the freshman year study. Subsequent years of data collection efforts failed to produce a representative sample that was as robust in the years to follow (i.e., from 1997 to 2003, roughly comprising little over 8,000 student respondents from 20–28 institutions). By contrast, the 1996 data is considered richer with nearly three times the number of participants and institutions. Consequently, HERI no longer collects two-year data for the national norms. The 2003 CIRP data was the last cycle for initiating data collection from community colleges. While the 1996 data set has limitations, it has a critical mass of participant responses and was collected at a key time in the policy debate over affirmative action (i.e., during the lobbying/passage of Proposition 209). For the purposes of examining community college student attitudes toward affirmative action in admissions, this is the best available data to date. Accordingly, there are limitations with this investigation.

5. In reference to the logistic regression equation Sc_i refers to student background characteristics; Ea_i refers to educational aspirations; Se_i refers to self-interest and Ra_i refers to racial affect.

ACCESS FOR STUDENTS
WITH DISABILITIES

Infusing Affirmative Action in ADA Compliance

Accerding to the U.S. Census Bureau (2005), 14% of all Americans age 5 and over in the civilian noninstitutionalized population have at least one disability. The 37.5 million people with disabilities in the United States reflect self-reported data available on disabilities; a larger percentage of the general population may be living with a disability. Many people with disabilities cannot fully participate in school, work, or other activities. Hence, much of the societal involvement of people with disabilities is contingent upon the extent of their disability and whether they are categorized as having a slight, moderate, or severe disability. However, often most limiting and pervasive are the negative attitudes regarding people with disabilities that continue to permeate society.

While the United States prides itself on its diversity, American employers have yet to keep pace in reflecting this diversity, especially as it pertains to marginalized groups, including Native Americans, African Americans, Hispanics, women, and people with disabilities (Katznelson, 2005). Although the cultural politics of race and gender have garnered continual consideration in the discourse examining access and equity, discussions about disability are a fairly contemporary social justice concern. Until now, minute attention has been paid to the centrality of disability within a cultural and sociopolitical context. Given the changing demographics racially, ethnically, and by gender as well as by ability, the U.S. workforce must become more diversified to include greater numbers of people from underrepresented groups in order to compete globally.

Traditionally, American institutions did not voluntarily seek diversity among their members/participants, as the vast majority of those with access to opportunity in education and the workplace are White middle-class males. As a consequence, federal mandates to equalize opportunities slowly began to transform access in the form of greater social, political, and economic mobility. Legislative actions prohibiting discrimination on the basis of race/ethnicity, national origin, gender, and disability were instituted, even though they sometimes contradicted ideas about American egalitarianism. These actions include the Civil Rights Act of 1964 (Title VII); Title IX of the Education Amendments of 1972; Section 504 of the Rehabilitation Act of 1973; Rehabilitation Act Amendments of 1978, 1986, and 1992; Education for All Handicapped Children Act (1975), also known as the Individuals with Disabilities Education Act (IDEA); Age Discrimination Act of 1975; Americans with Disabilities Act (ADA) of 1990; IDEA Amendments of 1997; and the IDEA Improvement Act of 2004. Historically, American culture has been resistant to social change even in light of glaring discrimination, oppression, and prejudice.

In attempting to alter the social, economic, and political disequilibrium, the U.S. federal government introduced policies to redress the lack of diversity and homogeneity of corporate workplaces and institutions of higher education. Affirmative action legislation was enacted as a means to correct long-standing prejudice against certain groups, first and foremost racial/ethnic minorities and women. To this end, affirmative action outlines measures and approaches that guarantee full consideration and equal opportunities for participation to interested and eligible citizens. In the same way, Section 504 of the Rehabilitation Act of 1973 was established to ensure that qualified individuals with disabilities are not discriminated against by being excluded from participation. Akin to underrepresented students of color and other disenfranchised collegians, the improvement of opportunities for students with disabilities calls for greater attention to postsecondary diversity initiatives in concert with the ADA.

The discord over promoting access for members of racial/ethnic minority groups via affirmative action has evolved into a controversial exchange of ideas surrounding how institutions of higher learning can best affirm diversity and encourages greater participation among underrepresented collegiate populations. However, virtually absent from the current discourse are the parallels between the ADA and affirmative action. Relatively little examination has addressed how the two policy agendas intersect in furthering the life chances for those facing inequality and who are commonly subjected to unfair treatment and shared uncertainties.

Given the lack of literature addressing the importance of affirmative action measures for enhancing opportunities for people with disabilities, this chapter focuses on the similar goals of affirmative action and the ADA in attempting to redress historical inequities of individuals who are members of stigmatized underrepresented groups in the United States. As such, this chapter pushes for reconceptualizing notions of diversity and reexamining antidiscrimination measures in protecting individuals with disabilities. This line of query is of theoretical and practical significance as it seeks to discuss the convergence of what is frequently considered divergent civil rights legislation in the United States.

Are affirmative action and the ADA parallel or mutually exclusive civil rights legislation? The line of reasoning offered in this chapter frames the nexus between affirmative action legislative efforts and social policies safeguarding full participation of students with disabilities. The central aim of this chapter is threefold:

1. to provide a portrait of people with disabilities
2. to discuss cultural identification beyond racial categorization and societal attitudes toward members of stigmatized groups
3. to link trends across different tiers of education to employability and right of entry into places of work for people with disabilities.

This chapter explores the ways in which issues of inclusion are not static but dynamic, relative to the far-reaching consequences of inaccessibility and inequality. More specifically, the importance of affirmative action as an antidiscrimination measure for enhancing opportunities for our nation's largest minority group, people with disabilities, is explored. Affirmative action in concert with the ADA could redress historical inequities of individuals with disabilities. Finally, in this chapter, the implications of infusing diversity initiatives with ADA compliance for policy, practice, and further research are offered.

Demographics on Disability and Participation in Education

When contrasting students with disabilities with the general school enrollment for students 6 through 21 years of age, there has been unparalleled growth. According to Wolanin and Steele (2004), students with disabilities have grown at a faster pace over the last decade, reaching nearly six million in the United States. As indicated in *To Assure the Free Appropriate Public Education of All Children With Disabilities: Twentieth Annual Report to Congress on the Implementation of the Individuals with Disabilities Education Act*

(U.S. Department of Education, 1998) the population of school-aged children with disabilities has grown. For example, children with disabilities ages 6 through 11 increased 25.3%, while those with disabilities between 12 and 17 years of age had risen by 30.7% and young adults between 18 to 21 grew by 14.7%. Additionally, the report noted that over 90% of the students served under IDEA in 1996–1997 were categorized into four general areas of disability: emotional disturbance, learning disabilities, mental retardation, and speech or language impairments. The greatest percentage irrespective of age group was classified as having a learning disability, ranging anywhere from a little over 41% for ages 6 through 11, 62.3% for ages 12–17, and slightly over half of students 18–21 years old.

The population growth among students with disabilities parallels the overall increase in secondary education graduation rates. Over the course of a 10-year period, the number of students earning high school diplomas rose by 31% between 1986 and 1996 (U.S. Department of Education, 1998). More exactly, the high school completion percentage of students with disabilities was 61% in 1986, and by 2001 78% of students with disabilities graduated from high school. In contrast, 91% of the general population of students without disabilities completed high school and among 1988 eighth graders who completed high school, 70% the percentage enrolled in postsecondary education by 1994 (NCES, 1999a, 1999b, 1999c; U.S. Department of Education, 2003; Wolanin & Steele, 2004). In short, there is a 13% gap in the conferral of high school diplomas between students with disabilities and their peers without disabilities.

The parity of educational experiences of students with or without disabilities is questionable. Although graduation rates have shown marked improvement, often a Pygmalion effect occurs when considering school-age children and adult learners with disabilities; in other words, to some degree you get what you expect. Traditionally, students with disabilities are found in special education and developmental/remedial courses and frequently have been subject to lower expectations from instructional staff (Heubert, 2002).

While well over half of students with disabilities graduate with diplomas and academic qualifications for college entry, granting access to postsecondary institutions is not mandatory, and students with disabilities do not matriculate to college in significant numbers (Wolanin & Steele, 2004). Students with disabilities at 2- and 4-year colleges and universities are primarily enrolled at medium- to large-sized publicly controlled postsecondary institutions. In fact, an estimated 428,280 students with disabilities attended public institutions of higher learning during the 1997–1998 academic year (NCES, 2000).

A stratification of educational attainment occurs among students with disabilities enrolled in higher education. Twelve percent of students without disabilities complete vocational certificates, while roughly 20% of students with disabilities do the same (Hurst & Smerdon, 2000). Additionally, little over half of students with disabilities persist in their chosen postsecondary programs with 18% earning associate degrees and 33% completing baccalaureate degrees. In contrast, nearly two-thirds of students without disabilities persist in postsecondary education, with 12% receiving vocational certificates, 7% awarded associate degrees, and just under half obtaining bachelor's degrees (Henderson, 2001; Hurst & Smerdon, 2000).

Access to Employment

Even though there is legislation geared at removing barriers and increasing access, an incredible divide exists between the haves and the have-nots. People with disabilities remain a disenfranchised, underrepresented group in higher education. The lack of participation as well as the retention and matriculation of students with disabilities adversely affects the labor market.

Despite the increase in high school graduates, a paucity of baccalaureate and higher degrees are being conferred to students with disabilities, and individuals with disabilities are underused in the workforce. About three-fourths of people with disabilities are unemployed, in large part, because of workplace discrimination (Blanck & Schartz, 2000; Unger, 2002). Given that people with disabilities are less likely to complete high school and college, it should be no surprise that their unemployment rate is five times the national average (Longmore, 2003). Longmore (2003) found that among those employed in the labor force, people with disabilities earned 20% less than their nondisabled counterparts, and poverty rates among individuals with disabilities are 50% to 300% higher than that of the general population.

The Policy Landscape of Social Justice: The ADA in Meeting the Needs of People With Disabilities

Like many racial/ethnic groups that have not been highly regarded in the United States, people with disabilities have a history of oppression and frequent mistreatment by society at large (Lombana, 1992; Shapiro, 2000). Akin to the perceived racial/ethnic threat Whites may experience, according

TABLE 6
Number/Percentage of Students Enrolled in Postsecondary Institutions by Level, Disability Status, and Select Student Characteristics, 2003–2004

Select Student Characteristics	Undergraduate			Graduate/Professional		
	All Students	Students with Disabilities	Students Without Disabilities	All Students	Students With Disabilities	Students Without Disabilities
Number (in thousands)	19,054	2,156	16,897	2,826	189	2,637
Gender						
Male	42.4%	42.1%	42.4%	41.9%	38.0%	42.2%
Female	57.6%	57.9%	57.6%	58.1%	62.0%	57.8%
Race/Ethnicity						
White, Non-Hispanic	63.1%	65.1%	62.9%	68.3%	67.0%	68.4%
Black, Non-Hispanic	14.0%	13.2%	14.1%	9.6%	12.5%	9.3%
Hispanic	12.7%	12.3%	12.8%	7.7%	7.9%	7.6%
Asian/PI	5.9%	3.8%	6.2%	11.0%	5.9%	11.3%
American Indian/AN	0.9%	1.2%	0.9%	0.6%	0.4%	0.6%
Other	3.3%	4.4%	3.2%	2.9%	6.3%	2.7%

Age						
15 to 23	56.8%	45.8%	58.2%	11.2%	8.5%	11.4%
24 to 29	17.3%	15.5%	17.5%	39.6%	33.9%	40.0%
30 or older	25.9%	38.7%	24.3%	49.2%	57.6%	48.6%
Attendance						
Full-time, Full Year	38.6%	33.5%	39.2%	32.7%	28.9%	32.9%
Part-time or Part Year	61.4%	66.5%	60.8%	67.3%	71.1%	67.1%
Veteran Status						
Veteran	3.4%	6.2%	3.0%	3.8%	2.7%	3.9%
Nonveteran	96.6%	93.8%	97.0%	96.2%	97.3%	96.1%

Note. PI = Pacific Islander; AN = Alaska Native. From National Center for Education Statistics (2006a). *Digest of Education Statistics*, 2005, Table 210. Retrieved May 12, 2008, from http://nces.ed.gov/programs/digest/d05/tables/dt05_210.asp?referrer = list to Rubin and Roessler (2001), people without disabilities perceive those with disabilities as threatening. Traditionally, people who had disabilities were segregated from society because of public worries. They were relegated to institutions designated for people with disabilities, as it was thought to be in their best interest. Therefore, individuals with disabilities were and continue to be stigmatized members of society who have been subjected to cruelty, as their civil rights and complete involvement in American life were considered questionable at best (Gollnick & Chinn, 2008; Rubin & Roessler, 2001).

While the Civil Rights Act of 1964 calls for antidifferentiation, whereby different treatment on the basis of race, sex, national origin, or religion is discriminatory and illegal, similar legislation as it relates to disability did not exist (Colker, 2005). Section 504 of the Rehabilitation Act of 1973 established that programs and facilities receiving federal funding would be in violation of federal law if such entities were *not* accessible to people with disabilities. Therefore, organizations and facilities *not* in receipt of federal monies were exempt from Section 504 and did not have to implement measures for non-discriminatory treatment of people with disabilities. As a result, the 1990 ADA legislation originated to further enforce the Rehabilitation Act of 1973. Signed into law on July 26, 1990, the ADA extended the legal rights of individuals with disabilities through instituting sanctions against American institutions for noncompliance, irrespective of federal dollars received.

As the civil rights of people with disabilities were limited prior to 1990, the ADA is considered landmark legislation that makes sure the civil liberties and rights of people with disabilities are not so easily encumbered by pervading stereotypes and barriers to full integration in American life. However, unlike the antidifferentiation notion associated with the Civil Rights Act of 1964, claims of discrimination, in accordance with the ADA, only qualify if the person's disability makes him or her a member of a historically disenfranchised group, which under the ADA is considered antisubordination (Colker, 2005).[1] According to Colker (2005), historical disenfranchisement is narrowly tailored, and the antisubordination approach would "disallow claims of discrimination by individuals with all types of physical or mental impairments" (p. 106). For example, antisubordination does not extend to people with diabetes, high blood pressure, hearing impairments, or monocular vision.

The ADA of 1990 has five titles. Title I focuses on employers and mandates that industry provide reasonable accommodations in all aspects of employment to protect the rights of people with disabilities. Title II turns attention to public services by requiring aids and services to individuals with disabilities by all local, state, and federal agencies, including the National

Railroad Passenger Corporation and commuter authorities. Title III addresses public accommodations and necessitates that all barriers to services in existing facilities be modified if not promptly removed and all new construction be fully accessible to persons with disabilities. Title IV places emphasis on telecommunications companies' services to provide telephone services and devices for the deaf. Finally, Title V contains provisions that prohibit retaliation, coercion, or threatening acts toward individuals with disabilities or advocates for the differently abled who champion their rights.

Affirmative "Acts" in Challenging the Status Quo

Traditionally, American society has been riddled with contrary opinions and values regarding diversity, as well as replete with examples of cross-cultural discord. Much of the friction surrounding issues of race/ethnicity, gender, and class are conflicts stemming from our long history of unevenly dealing with people who are not members of the dominant group (Nieto & Bode, 2008). Because of the disparity in treatment that existed between groups, affirmative action (Executive Order No. 11246) was implemented in 1965 to make certain that equality prevailed for underrepresented and disenfranchised groups, and that the eradication of the mistreatment endured by African Americans was supported (Crosby, 2006; Fleming et al., 1978). Affirmative action sought to remedy the wrongs against all historically disadvantaged racial/ethnic minorities and women. It later extended to prevent educational and employment disadvantaging of Vietnam veterans and people with disabilities (Mazel, 1998).

By 1971 adherence to Executive Order No. 11246, also known as affirmative action was also required of higher learning institutions just as with business and industry. Hence, the 1970s mark the period when the first affirmative action plans and programs were formulated at colleges and universities receiving federal funding (Fleming et al., 1978). Because of federal government intervention, affirmative action programs began to account for the disparate treatment of African American students and others who were not previously embraced by majority postsecondary institutions.

Mutually Distinct Yet Akin: Dilemma in Difference for the Underrepresented

Often there is an ideological departure from what constitutes or contributes to cultural diversity. Racial/ethnic communities are just one type of cultural group. There are distinctive cultural groups that are nonethnic (Nieto & Bode, 2008). Dominant culture values physical perfection, highly regards patriarchal ideals, and prefers what is closest to White (Grosz, 1989). For this reason, people with disabilities, women, and those from racial/ethnic groups are hindered from fitting in. This disdain makes becoming part of the larger community difficult. Therefore, diverse groups often become very distinctive communities unto themselves, also referred to as *subcultures* or *microcultures* (Gollnick & Chinn, 2008).

Researchers suggest that people of color and individuals with disabilities are caught between two or more cultural extremes and must be bicultural in order to successfully participate in education, be effective at work, and operate within their own respective communities (Gollnick & Chinn, 2008). Individuals who are competent in two or more cultures cross cultural borders that are politically derived. Therefore, disability, like race/ethnicity, is a social construct that brings with it discrepancies in group rights and varying obligations. For example, the identity of a low-income female of Latin decent who is vision impaired and from a Catholic family is based on five subcultural communities. Her interaction with dominant culture is shaped by her membership in each microcultural group. According to Gollnick and Chinn (2008), it is one's membership in microcultural groups that continuously interacts with and influences an individual's cultural identity. Furthermore, there is a vast amount of diversity within microcultures, and as such, certain microcultural memberships may shape an individual's identity more so than others, and might even shift in importance during different periods in life.

Shapiro (2000) maintains that disability is relative and culture bound, as legal definitions and cultural conceptualizations are made in reference to larger categories and not in reference to individual cases. Defining disability in this manner can compound the severity of hundreds of disabilities and how they are perceived. In terms of perception, negative attitudes toward various groups give license to oppression, and allow unequal treatment of people with disabilities to fester, mainly since the term disability is widely applied with no single accepted definition. Language has the power to harm, and attitudinal prejudice manifests in statements that illustrate stereotypic views of individuals with disabilities, including the following: People with disabilities are naturally inferior, people with mental illness are dangerous, or disability is something you can catch (Lombana, 1992; Shapiro, 2000). Stigmatized in the same fashion as racial/ethnic oppressed groups (Lombana, 1992), students with disabilities have not been fully integrated into postsecondary campus communities.

Reconceptualizing the Policy Context for Marginalized Groups

What is apparent in affirmative action and ADA policies but often regarded as separate are the analogous disparities endured by students with disabilities and those with racially/ethnically diverse backgrounds. Each group has been, and continues to be, devalued through perpetuation of negative labels, lower expectations, and antisentiment from the mainstream (Gollnick & Chinn, 2008; Lombana, 1992). This attitudinal prejudice directed toward people with disabilities has been referred to as *handicapism*, which refers to beliefs and practices that propagate inequality and differential treatment of people because of their apparent or assumed behavioral, mental, or physical differences (Gollnick & Chinn, 2008; Shapiro, 2000). In view of that, individuals with disabilities experience intolerance and bigotry, though not the same type of discrimination experienced by racial/ethnic minorities as differences-based discrimination varies across distinct cultural groups. Also noteworthy is that there is not a monolithic experience or history of mistreatment among people of color and individuals with disabilities. Though this point is not raised to endorse comparable suffering, it is extremely important to acknowledge the varying degrees of unfairness felt within and between different minority groups.

Are individuals with disabilities better off than African Americans or other marginalized groups? Research has noted that there is societal disregard and disdain in the form of stereotyping toward those perceived as self-evidently inferior, including people of color and those with disabilities (Ainlay et al., 1986; Gollnick & Chinn, 2008). However, with regard to prejudice and discrimination, Gliedman and Roth (1980) suggest that, to some degree, people with disabilities are worse off than African Americans and other groups because they lack the racial/ethnic pride that has been developed by some of these groups. On the other hand, individuals with disabilities are not necessarily subject to overt displays of racial hatred, discrimination, organized brutality, lynch mobs, or rallies by supremacists (Gliedman & Roth) as are African Americans. Hence, there are basic dignities that each group is stripped of that the other does not bear. Both groups, however, are rejected by the general public and are in the minority relative to the larger population.

Shapiro (2000) asserts that the minority group model is appropriate for viewing disability issues in terms of the rights of individuals as opposed to the medical paradigm, which focuses on physical and social inferiorities. Shapiro contends that the minority group model permits moving beyond depicting individuals with disabilities as charity cases for special services to viewing them more as oppressed minority group members. In this sense, affirmative action and the ADA are quite comparable in attempting to move American institutions to embrace and include all of its citizens. Interestingly, both affirmative action and ADA legislation are commonly interpreted to be compensatory measures for groups that, contrary to popular opinion, have been overlooked, excluded, underrepresented, and judged to be deficient in some capacity (Gollnick & Chinn, 2008; Grosz, 1989).

With regard to implementation, the ADA has not commonly infused issues of cultural diversity into compliance in hiring and admissions, nor has it satisfied affirmative action measures cognizant of ADA directives (Bruyere & Hoying, 1995). Changing demographics illustrate that nationally, one-third of all new employees hired in the United States are not White, and that women are participating in postsecondary education and the workplace in greater numbers (Bruyere & Hoying, 1995; Treloar, 1999). These trends, coupled with the 14% of Americans with a reported disability and the 31% increase in high school completion for students with disabilities, illustrate that homogenized college and work environments are slowly becoming a thing of the past (U.S. Census Bureau, 2005).

A heightened awareness of cultural diversity must surround the ADA, as considerations of race/ethnicity and gender should also include other nontraditional groups. As universities and employers grapple with the challenges of diversity, it is gravely important to extend our understanding of diversity to include individuals with disabilities as a diverse population with a cultural identity that is uniquely their own. As initiatives exist to remedy discriminatory imbalances and increase representation and participation of disadvantaged groups, affirmative action program efforts must recognize, target, and actively recruit people with disabilities (Pierce, 1990; Raskin, 1994).

Promoting Environments of Inclusion and Responsiveness: The Law and Accommodations in K–12 Education—ADA Meets IDEA

The ADA and IDEA are two important federal laws that have an impact on an organization's ability to provide accommodations in educational and employment settings for people with disabilities. Recognizing that school districts would incur higher costs in educating children with disabilities, the U.S. Congress vowed to contribute 40% of the average per-pupil expenditure when enacting the IDEA. However, like other federal policies, IDEA was another underfunded mandate and has not provided enough assistance to schools in covering the added expenses of educating students with disabilities (U.S. Department of Education, 1998). In spite of this lack of funding, proposals have been approved that allow school districts to allocate 20% of their IDEA funding increases for purposes other than education efforts for those with disabilities.

In addition to fiscal barriers, educating students with disabilities faces human resource challenges. Research by Lombana (1992) concluded that there are differences in educators' attitudes toward students with disabilities. Veteran teachers, defined as those with more than seven years of teaching experience, had less-favorable attitudes toward students with disabilities; in contrast, novice teachers exhibited less bias and had greater student-teacher interaction.

From K–12 Education to Postsecondary Access and Services

Although elementary and secondary schools must conform to IDEA requirements, many of the services and accommodations that exist in the K–12 environment are not necessarily available at the college level. Although institutional leaders purport to highly regard cultural pluralism, the campus climate is actually less supportive of practices that support the full participation of racial/ethnic minority students and collegians with disabilities. Studies have shown that when campus climate is inclusive of students of color and those with disabilities, their adjustment, matriculation, degree completion, and overall collegiate satisfaction is vastly improved (Nutter & Ringgenberg, 1993; Pacifici & McKinney, 1997). However, as greater proportions of students from oppressed groups attend 2- and 4-year institutions, the campus climate continues to be largely suited to the majority student (Dooley-Dickey et al., 1991).

The campus climate at 2- and 4-year institutions of higher learning differs as the demographics of students within divergent settings greatly shape the academic culture and social environment. Unlike senior institutions with some degree of selectivity, community colleges refrain from discriminatory practices regarding student admissions by virtue of their open-door policies. Given the open-door admissions of the community college, 2-year institutions enroll the overwhelming majority of underrepresented and disadvantaged students in higher education (London, 1992; Rhoads & Valadez, 1996). The student populace at community colleges comprises more first-generation, low-income, racial/ethnic minority, and female attendees than senior institutions. Adding to this rich diversity of collegians are individuals with disabilities.

The number of collegians with some disability is increasing, as an estimated one million students with disabilities were enrolled in American colleges, universities, and proprietary schools by the 1990s (Henderson, 2001).
Roughly 9% to 11% of college students have disabilities (Daddona, 2001).
According to Barnett and Li (1997), over half of students attending public
higher learning institutions are served by community colleges, and 71% of
students with disabilities are enrolled in 2-year institutions. Similarly, almost
half of all African American collegians and roughly two-thirds of Latino/
Latina students attend community colleges. Therefore, when considering the
postsecondary climate for students of color and individuals with disabilities,
most often the schools of choice are community colleges. Community colleges serve a much higher percentage of these students than do other higher
education institutions (Phillippe & Gonzalez, 2005).

The AACC reports that disability services increased between 1992 and
1995, with approximately 2% of all community college students requesting
disability services (Barnett, 1993; Barnett & Li, 1997; Phillippe & Gonzalez,
2005). In a study designed to increase educational opportunities for individuals with disabilities, about 14% of the 672 community colleges responding
reported that they do not maintain specific data on students with disabilities
(American Association of Community Colleges, n.d.). However, among the
institutions categorizing data by disability, learning disabilities led the group-
ings, with orthopedic or mobility disabilities and chronic illness or other disabilities following (Barnett, 1993).

Students with disabilities are frequently accommodated at institutions of
higher learning through a variety of support services that include one or
more of the following:

- adapted sports and extracurricular activities
- alternative exam formats
- counseling and transfer assistance
- disability-specific scholarships
- disability support services center and disability resources handbooks
- housing and community outreach
- learning labs and adaptive technology
- registration assistance
- taped texts, note takers, readers, interpreters, and tutors

This is not an exhaustive list of accommodations for individuals with disabilities in the college setting. It does represent, however, a range of services

that provide greater access within higher education to students with disabilities (Barnett & Li, 1997; Pacifici & McKinney, 1997). Institutions of higher learning (particularly 2-year institutions) are aiding students with disabilities by attempting to make the campus environment more conducive to their divergent learning styles, diverse interests, and improved collegiate satisfaction.

People With Disabilities and Workplace Opportunities

Interestingly, race and gender have protected status in the 14th Amendment to the U.S. Constitution, but the Equal Protection Clause does not include disability. It would appear that if the U.S. federal government was truly interested in equal application of the laws as related to civil rights, it would not be permissible for an individual with a disability to be prohibited from employment opportunities because of that disability under the 14th Amendment. Although people with disabilities are not fully protected from employment discrimination, the ADA, coupled with affirmative action measures, could serve as a stronger response to discrimination. Thus, affirmative action in the form of active recruitment and outreach, reasonable accommodations, personnel processes, and parity in salary and benefits is necessary in the hiring of qualified people with disabilities.

Research supports the fact that it is good business to hire individuals with disabilities. Additionally, people with disabilities (particularly persons of color with disabilities) could greatly benefit from ADA and affirmative action initiatives (Daddona, 2001; Pierce, 1990). The Mitsubishi Electric America Foundation has provided all-expense-paid grants to support students with disabilities at the Summer Institute for Public Policy at the University of California, Berkley (University of California, 1995). Also of note, each year the institute, in conjunction with the Woodrow Wilson Foundation, singles out outstanding students of color for graduate school and future employment with public sector government agencies.

Implications and Conclusions

There are notable differences between various segments of the educational pipeline in the level of support services provided to students with disabilities. While colleges and universities offer a wide range of services for students with disabilities, research has noted inconsistencies relative to how students were identified and served (Barnett, 1993; Satcher & Dooley-Dickey, 1990).

On college campuses faculty and student affairs administrators are not entirely aware of the needs of individuals with disabilities and commonly overlook this population of collegians. Correspondingly, students with disabilities often feel academically and socially misaligned with their peers because of the continual obstacles faced within postsecondary cultures limiting satisfactory engagement in the college setting (Dooley-Dickey et al., 1991; McCune, 2001; Michalko, 2002; Treloar, 1999).

Comparable to race/ethnicity and gender to some degree, disability is among those ascribed characteristics that bear influence on the educational and occupational attainment of collegians (Cummins, 1991). Inequalities still impede the progress of racially/ethnically diverse groups, persons with disabilities, and other disenfranchised members of society who continue to be underrepresented in K–12 education and in higher learning institutions.

Students with disabilities primarily attend community colleges where the dialogue regarding affirmative action in higher education is frequently relegated to employee hiring and promotion practices. Two-year students are generally disregarded in policy debates regarding diversity initiatives such as affirmative action in college admissions because of the open admissions policies of these 2-year institutions (Zamani, 2003; Zamani & Brown, 2003). Some research (Michalko, 2002) describes disability as a political act. For example, Snyder and Mitchell assert, "the formulation of a cultural model allows us to theorize a political act of renaming that designates disability as a site of resistance and a source of cultural agency previously suppressed" (2006, p. 10). However, there is a lack of inclusion of individuals with disabilities in the policy process from formation to implementation (Longmore, 2003). Accordingly, there are many dimensions to disability related to exclusion and inclusion and culture and civil rights, as played out in educational institutions and the larger society.

Although little literature has examined affirmative action in concert with ADA compliance, it is apparent that both policies and programs encourage nondiscriminatory practices against people with disabilities. Interestingly, gender and racial/ethnic information regarding students with disabilities has only recently been addressed and is not necessarily assessed by all institutional disability support services (American Association of Community Colleges, n.d.). Making college campus environments inclusive of people with disabilities should entail more than providing "reasonable access" to higher education by expanding diversity initiatives to incorporate students with disabilities and enhance their collegiate years (Bruyere & Hoying, 1995; Hauben, 1980; Nutter & Ringgenberg, 1993; Vickery & McClure, 1998). Greater collaboration and outreach activities are needed on behalf of these students, as on the whole, colleges and universities are doing very little to assess student outcomes or track students with disabilities upon exiting an institution.

In addition to increasing outreach efforts with external agencies to better meet the educational needs and career aspirations of students with disabilities, additional measures to track students via exit interviews, home visits, and/or follow-up surveys would greatly assist in measuring student outcomes (AACC, n.d.). Making strides in this direction would allow institutions to receive suggestions for improving disability support services and overall campus life, and determine if people with disabilities had a satisfactory college experience and whether they felt the institution sufficiently facilitated career placement. While K–12 and postsecondary institutions receiving federal financial assistance are expected to accommodate students with disabilities, a primary barrier to providing more effective services is funding or the lack thereof. A scarcity of resources and limited state government allocations make it increasingly difficult for learning institutions to maintain adequate disability support services and implement improvements, let alone sustain those improvements (Pacifici & McKinney, 1997).

Aside from monetary considerations, what also problematizes adequate responses to meeting the needs of people with disabilities is that this is not a monolithic group; this population comprises a rich diversity of races and ethnic groups. Longmore (2003) asserts that additional attention should be paid to disability culture and collective identity. For all diverse groups, especially people with disabilities, there is a multiplicity of identities. The discourse for future inquiry should include an examination of the importance of cultural identity in its impact on disability rights.

Human rights campaigns in the United States, including the movements for women's rights, disability rights, and gay-lesbian rights, were built on the back of the African American civil rights movement of the 1950s and 1960s. While numerous modern-day movements have been created to fully secure civil liberties for varying segments of society, historically there has been little recognition of how each of us have multiple identities that shift in importance given what we consider most salient at any particular time. Additionally, a convergence of our multiple group memberships must be acknowledged. The significant disregard of U.S. culture, and the highly racialized environment within many of its institutions, is yet another omission in contemporary disability research and scholarship on political activism. As such, nationally the United States is reflective of what Anderson (1991) refers to as an *imagined community* (p. 6). In other words, the politics of identity and political relations within and between groups are tempered by the frequent failure to accept cultural differences along lines of race/ethnicity, gender, disability, and income, among other factors.

Double, triple, or possibly quadruple jeopardy faces people of color with a disability given the interaction of race/ethnicity, gender, class, and disability which contribute to further marginalization. Students of color account for one-fifth of full-time college freshmen with disabilities and many have not been able to break into various career areas (such as engineering and science) because of institutional hurdles and pervasive stereotypes regarding ability (Henderson, 2001; National Science Foundation, 2004).

In conclusion, many of the historical dimensions of current group categorizations are considered mutually exclusive, just as affirmative action and ADA policies have not been viewed as complementary, parallel civil rights legislation. According to Bandura (2000), it is this sense of agency that validates people not only as products of social systems but as the producers as well. Having a sense of agency involves self-awareness of people's personal power and ownership of their actions whereby individuals conceive of themselves as their own best advocate and agent of change empowered to have an impact (Marcel, 2003). Therefore, it is important to underscore the context of cultural identity more broadly and endorse an agency perspective; having a sense of agency would allow people with disabilities to have a voice in the policy arena and feel that they can shape the discourse that affects their individual and shared realities.

There are many different ways of classifying groups of people. Many cultural groups in the United States can be described as voluntary and involuntary minorities, as there are discrete nuances regarding the historical experiences and initial incorporation of each into American society (Ogbu & Simons, 1998). It is this membership in one or more of these groups that shape the cultural lens and frames of reference for many living in the United States.

Among those who are involuntary minorities at the margins of full participation in the United States are individuals with disabilities. Unfortunately many students of color and people with disabilities in United States schools are too often subject to difficulties not experienced by their peers without disabilities, because of negative perceptions and views regarding their abilities. For that reason, as members of disadvantaged groups, people with disabilities and people of color continually have to overcome the stigma of cultural inheritance. Despite the fact that affirmative action and diversity have been largely framed as a "Black and White" dichotomy, issues underlying social oppression beyond race/ethnicity, gender, and class are often ignored. Therefore, efforts to improve early schooling and increase access to higher education in the United States may be achieved more swiftly if current policies are revisited, revamped, and used to accomplish social reform.

Note

1. The ADA is based on antisubordination (i.e., the notion of protected class status for individuals with disabilities), which differs from antidifferentiation, which is built on eradicating all discrimination based on race/ethnicity, gender, national origin, and religion. Hence, only people with disabilities can make claims of discrimination under the ADA in contrast to people of color or women having historically disadvantaged status and the ability to forward claims of gender and racial discrimination under the Civil Rights Act of 1964 (Colker, 2005).

6

SOCIAL JUSTICE, REMEDIATION, AND DISPUTES TO DIVERSITY

As educators and policy analysts, each of us has experienced a very interesting response to the term *diversity* when teaching cultural pluralism or conducting workshops. Quite often the knee-jerk reaction, usually of White males, when asked what readily comes to mind when they hear the word diversity is, "Oh, you mean that racial minority stuff," or "Here we go with the feminist agenda." Others quickly jump in and add descriptors including affirmative action and quotas. These responses illustrate how important it is to acknowledge the compendium of differences and to call for reconceptualizing the way diversity is so frequently viewed and misunderstood.

The Diversity Rationale: A Shifting Debate

In the 1990s higher education faced several affirmative action challenges. In particular, at the state-level, the *Gratz v. Bollinger* (2000) and *Grutter v. Bollinger* (2001) cases that were filed by CIR in 1997 (see pp. 58–59 in chapter 3) placed the University of Michigan's affirmative action admissions policies at the forefront of defending diversity. Many in the higher education community believed that Michigan was facing an uphill battle. In light of the fact that CIR successfully struck down the use of race in admissions decisions at the University of Texas School of Law in 1996 (*Hopwood v. State of Texas*), one year prior to filing the Michigan lawsuits, advocates of affirmative action were concerned about Michigan's chances of winning. CIR has antagonistically challenged affirmative action policies at the undergraduate, graduate, and professional levels, placing the democratic notions of pluralism, equal opportunity, and educational access for all on trial. However, the heart of these lawsuits, as well as others like them, reveal the system of privilege that is provided to those who attend the nation's elite public institutions.

The vast majority of collegians are not exposed to the opportunities and the level of educational resources or advancement possibilities available at schools such as the University of Michigan–Ann Arbor, the University of Texas–Austin, the University of California–Berkeley, or other highly selective, public institutions of higher learning. It is not difficult to discern that a low supply of admissions spots combined with extremely high public demand ignites many of the legal contests that surround affirmative action, educational access, and diversity. Given the mounting competition among prospective students and growing anti-affirmative-action litigation, the discourse has taken a strategic turn, transforming into a debate regarding racial/ ethnic diversity and its importance in higher education versus remediation for past discrimination and the need for social justice.

Anti–Affirmative Action Versus Remediation

Although the Michigan cases gained much attention during their six-year life cycle, the affirmative action debate with respect to educational access and the use of race as a factor in admissions to increase accessibility for underrepresented groups was all but a new phenomenon for higher education. As discussed in greater detail on pp. 130–133 in chapter 6, the landmark *Regents of the University of California v. Bakke* (1978) case, and the cases that preceded it, helped give opponents of affirmative action dominance in the debate, allowing their arguments for a color-blind system to gain much ground. Meanwhile, advocates of remediation and social justice–related arguments found it difficult to deflate the mounting opposition.

With a diverse set of stakeholders, including parents, prospective students, government officials, and conservative organizations, strongly voicing the opinion that admissions procedures should be merit based not race conscious, higher education leaders and supporters of affirmative action found the principles of fairness, meritocracy, equality, and opportunity at the center of the debate, though not on behalf of underrepresented groups. Those opposing affirmative action adamantly argue that race-conscious policies give an unfair advantage to minority applicants who do not deserve such a preference. But supporters of race-conscious admissions view these policies as simple attempts to equalize the playing field so White applicants do not accrue all the benefits. Amid the numerous positions that have been taken on both sides of the debate, two major opposing camps have emerged.

At one extreme is the anti-affirmative-action camp; its major position is that affirmative action is not required given the antidiscrimination laws presently on record. If these laws policed enforcement of affirmative action then the policy mandates would be moot. In other words, this camp acknowledges that racial discrimination exists but fails to provide any real solutions that could adequately address the legacy of racial discrimination in education or society at large.

The pro-affirmative-action camp aligns itself with issues of social justice and remediation policies. Its core position is that affirmative action is essential for addressing past and present-day discrimination across social arenas including education, employment, housing, and voting. Supporters of remediation argue that the historical legacy of racial discrimination in higher education warrants the need for race-conscious admissions policies in order to counterbalance the advantages that White applicants accrue. Given this imbalance, affirmative action serves to remedy racial/ethnic disparities in college admissions, largely at highly selective postsecondary institutions that have historically limited access to underrepresented minority students.

The courts, however, have dismissed the social justice argument, rendering it invalid in today's competitive marketplace where access to the top echelon of society is reserved for few Whites, and even fewer people of color. With the courts turning away from the social justice position as demonstrated in a string of court decisions regarding affirmative action in hiring and contracts, including *Adarand Contractors v. Pena* (1995), another camp has surfaced from within the ranks of higher education. This new camp does not promote the remediation argument or advance the anti-affirmative-action position but argues that racial/ethnic diversity is critical for maintaining educational excellence and democratic values. Before this diversity camp positions itself as a viable challenger, however, its members will need to canvass the landscape, as several critical organizations have gained momentum in their anti-affirmative-action campaigns by framing affirmative action policies as racial preferences.

The Anti-Racial-Preferences Argument

Although several interest groups have been involved in this debate, including the American Civil Liberties Union, the NAACP Legal Defense and Educational Fund, and the Mexican American Legal Defense and Education Fund, all of which support the use of racial preferences in admissions (Nieves, 1999; Schmidt, 1998), three key groups have been successful in advancing legal and political attacks against highly selective institutions that use racial preferences in admissions decisions. The three groups are CIR, the American Civil

Rights Institute (ACRI), and the Center for Equal Opportunity (Diaz, 1997; McQueen, 1999; Schmidt, 1998).

While the nonprofit public interest law firm CIR was discussed in chapter 3, its impact on the retrenchment agenda was not covered in great detail. To comprehend the unrelenting crusade to legally challenge affirmative action, one only needs to read CIR's mission:

> CIR's civil rights cases are designed to get the government out of the business of granting preferential treatment to members of favored racial groups. Just as the First Amendment prohibits the government from favoring the expression of certain points of view, the 14th Amendment prohibits the government from enforcing its laws, rules, and polices differently solely on account of the race of an individual. (CIR, 2005a, p. 4, para 1)

Because of CIR's aggressive tactics and legal challenges, the organization has evolved into a formidable affirmative action opponent.

In contrast to CIR, ACRI was created to educate the public regarding racial and gender preferences. The organization grew out of Ward Connerly's involvement in successfully leading the campaign to place Proposition 209 on the 1996 November ballot in California. According to Connerly:

> If U.C.L.A. would simply accept the will of the people that race should not be a factor, either explicitly or "under the table," abandon their foolish attempts to "level the playing field" based on race, and establish their credibility with the public as a fair and race-neutral entity, then they could admit whomever they want and carry the presumption of innocence about race that needs to become the model of the future for pluralistic societies. Anyone familiar with admissions and the U.C.L.A. experience for the 2007 academic year should certainly know that U.C.L.A. has somehow broken the law. (as cited by ACRI, 2007a)

Since the ACRI's formation in 1997, it has worked to assist "organizations in other states with their efforts to educate the public about racial and gender preferences" (ACRI, 2007b).

Roughly two years after CCRI was approved by a majority vote, ACRI claimed another victory against affirmative action. As a result of ACRI's involvement and Connerly's leadership, the Washington Civil Rights Initiative (WCRI) or Initiative 200, passed with a 59% majority vote supporting the banning of race as a consideration in education and employment (Healy, 1998c; St. John, 1998). Again, shortly after the *Grutter v. Bollinger* (2003) ruling affirmed that race could be considered as one factor among many in admissions decisions, Connerly launched the Michigan Civil Rights Initiative (MCRI) in the state of Michigan to bypass the U.S. Supreme Court's decision in *Grutter* by making the consideration of race/ethnicity, gender, and national origin illegal. With the passing of two state referendums to his credit, Connerly and ACRI continue to apply the racial preferences rhetoric.

The Center for Equal Opportunity (CEO), which was founded in 1995 by Linda Chavez, is a think tank with more of a research and policy analysis focus. As reported by the organization, "CEO supports colorblind public policies and seeks to block the expansion of racial preferences and to prevent their use in employment, education, and voting" (Center for Equal Opportunity, 2008a). CEO has been uniquely positioned to counter the divisive impact of race-conscious public policies. Chavez, who is also CEO president, has a broad reach with the press and in the political arena. As a former staff director of the U.S. Commission on Civil Rights, along with other prior government-appointed positions and a syndicated newspaper column, Chavez has led the organization to the forefront of the battle against race-conscious policies and positioned it as one of the most notable voices against affirmative action (Center for Equal Opportunity, 2008b; Chavez, 1998).

CEO's emphasis on research and policy analysis was produced through a series of reports that document the use of racial preferences in college admissions. In these reports, CEO targeted selective public institutions from across the country, including the University of Michigan (Center for Equal Opportunity, 2008c; McQueen, 1999; Schmidt, 1998). Additionally, CEO produced policy briefs, book reviews, amici curiae briefs, congressional testimonies, and monographs to inform the public, government officials, and its constituencies about affirmative action as a form of racial preferencing (CEO, 2008c). The proliferation of publications, especially the admissions reports, and its campaigner approach, positions CEO as another critical voice in the affirmative action debate that many institutions of higher education have had to respond to.

The three organizations profiled above can be viewed as having very different missions and purposes, even though all three have taken steps to abolish race-conscious policies (Healy, 1998c, 1998d, 1999a, 1999b; St. John, 1998). ACRI, CEO, and CIR are unified by their underlying values and interests (Coser, 1956) and by their focus on using higher education institutions as targets for legal and political attacks pertaining to racial preferences. The emergence of these organizations on the national scene has dictated the terms of the debate in a manner that was unforeseen by those who continue to fight for inclusion and against the lingering legacies of racial discrimination. Ironically the promotion of what these groups have termed *civil rights* is contemptible because essentially they have employed the same strategies and tactics used by historical civil rights groups, such as the NAACP, to undermine the inclusion of underrepresented groups, especially African Americans, these civil rights organizations fought so hard to include. By co-opting similar strategies and tactics, as well as civil rights language of the 1960s, the debate surrounding affirmative action has wallowed in a quagmire of arguments with similar terminology but changing definitions.

Although questioning the salience of race in the 21st century is central to the stance of the anti-racial-preferences camp, contesting, diminishing, and ignoring the importance of race/ethnicity in American society simply gives more credence to its notion of the color blindness principle. Members of this camp assert that if the notion of a color-blind society was accepted there would be little need for government intervention and policies that grant preferences to special groups. With their position that affirmative action is another venue for government to practice discrimination, CIR, CEO, ACRI, and other conservative activist organizations have adamantly expressed that such practices should be discontinued and outlawed by the courts, legislature, and executive branch.

Opponents of affirmative action claim that evidence of racial disparities in isolation is no longer a legitimate reason for the courts to justify the existence of racial discrimination against ethnic minorities. Discrimination has been framed in the context of racial preferences and is relegated to Black-White comparisons of GPAs and group averages on standardized tests. Their argument places great emphasis on the numerical average disparities that exist between these groups, and concludes that selective institutions are discriminating against White students when they admit minority students with lower grades and test scores.

According to the anti-racial-preferences camp, minority applicants are not required to work hard, meet standards of academic excellence, or adhere to the system of merit. They make the argument that race plays too much of a factor in admissions decisions and should not be considered. It is this so-called lowering of standards that adversaries suggest creates polarized campus communities of students who are perceived as deserving or undeserving of admission at top institutions. However, those institutions that admit White students with lower test scores/grades while rejecting underrepresented minority applicants with higher grade point averages and test performances are not accused of discrimination.

Social Justice and Remediation

The social justice and remediation argument begins with different assumptions regarding who truly suffers from discrimination and who is being treated unfairly in the admissions process at elite institutions. Those within this camp subscribe to the fact that race is a central aspect of American life and continues to significantly affect the economic and educational opportunities of underrepresented minorities, especially African Americans. In addition, the history and continued legacy of discrimination against African Americans and other groups are acknowledged and highlighted through research and reports that point out the disparities that still persist as a result of de facto and de jure segregation.

Higher education institutions are not exempt from the nation's history and legacy of discrimination. Through admission policies and common campus practices, discrimination aimed at marginalized groups is apparent but not appropriately confronted in the courts. Though the courts concede that societal discrimination exists and that economic and educational disparities persist along racial/ethnic lines, they refuse to incorporate the historical record of discrimination and its legacy. Many institutions would rather be vulnerable to lawsuits from African American plaintiffs than fall prey to the lawsuits with White plaintiffs that would result if this historical record was validated in the courts. The courts, however, do not seriously consider allegations of discrimination from Black plaintiffs and usually render them invalid (Bowen & Bok, 1998).

There is clearly bias in the system. Fairness is lacking and questionable when White students with lesser credentials than White plaintiffs are acceptable, but students of color with lesser credentials are suspect. Many in this camp would argue that SES has an impact on educational opportunities, however, race/ethnicity, to a great degree, dictates what opportunities are provided well before social class issues are evident.

Since traditional admissions qualifications correlate with factors that exclude rather than include racial groups, affirmative action access through implementation of race-conscious policies is needed to remedy the legacy of discrimination against African Americans and other groups that have been historically discriminated against. Inclusion rather than exclusion should be the aim. Arguing that race-neutral policies precipitate resegregation and greater exclusion among top selective institutions, many advocates of the social justice position interpret the diversity rationale of *Regents of the University of California v. Bakke* (1978) as a retreat from remedial solutions that are sorely needed to combat ongoing educational, economic, and social forms of discrimination.

The Diversity Argument

Finally, there's the diversity camp, one that has matured and gained a significant amount of support and prominence over the past six years. This camp is positioned toward the middle of the spectrum. While not claiming to address the legacy of racial discrimination, its argument focuses on the need to have a racially diverse student population to enhance educational outcomes and civic participation. The idea that diversity is integral to the mission of higher education is accepted by many. Having a diverse student body is critical to student learning, campus engagement, career development, and the leadership training that is required of emerging leaders in a democratic society.

With the *Hopwood v. State of Texas* (1996) decision, higher education was put on notice with respect to the diversity rationale. In *Hopwood* racial diversity was considered no more significant than eye color or other physical characteristics, leaving educators at a loss to justify why racial diversity was important (Hurtado et al., 2002). Dictates stemming from the *Hopwood* ruling undermined institutional autonomy and the value of racial diversity put forth in the *Regents of the University of California v. Bakke* (1978) decision. To combat conservative notions within the courts and right-wing activist organizations, during the latter half of the 1990s the AACC, the American Council on Education, the Association of American Colleges and Universities, the Association of American Universities, and the Education Commission of the States, in conjunction with other higher education associations and institutions, strongly expressed their stance on diversity and affirmative action. In these public declarations of support for diversity, the social justice argument recedes to the shadows while a narrowly focused conceptualization of diversity in higher education is espoused.

While reasserting their expertise and role as educators, presidents, and chancellors, members of the group noted that diverse student populations facilitate many interactions that are needed to enrich the educational experiences of students (Chang, 2002; Gurin, Nagda, & Lopez, 2004). The heterogeneity of students benefits all and prepares them for life in the 21st century and in an increasingly multicultural democratic society. Serving as the foundation for the diversity rationale is an acknowledgment that all admitted are qualified and bring a wealth of experiences that enhances cognitive and affective growth among students in the short term and over the long haul. While the previous statement demonstrates the individual benefits of diversity, the societal benefits that are gained include healthier social relations, strengthened communities and workplaces, and increasing global economic competitiveness (Gurin, Nagda, & Lopez, 2004).

Though some educational associations, colleges, and universities remain true to the premise that affirmative action is needed to facilitate equal opportunity, equal access, and inclusion, political maneuvering and litigation from the 1990s to the present have further marginalized the social justice position

from the discussion. With the emergence of supportive allies among prominent corporations and the U.S. military, the diversity rationale has gained
momentum and is no longer relegated to the education arena. General Motors (GM), for example, reiterated that racially and ethnically diverse student
bodies are undeniably vital for the nation's future economy and American
business (General Motors Corporation, 2003). The GM Brief further states
that diversity in higher education institutions is an important means for students to acquire the cognitive and human relation skills that are necessary
when working with a highly diverse clientele of customers, employees, and
worldwide business partners.

In addition to GM, 65 other leading businesses concurred that diversity
is a compelling interest and aids students in learning how to work with others from different backgrounds while placing an emphasis on leadership:

> Diversity in higher education is therefore a compelling government interest
> not only because of its positive effects on the educational environment it-
> self, but also because of the crucial role diversity in higher education plays
> in preparing students to be the leaders this country needs in business, law,
> and all other pursuits that affect the public interest. (*Fortune 500* Corpora-
> tions, 2003, p. 2)

A separate brief, filed by the military's elite, reinforced the diversity message by linking racial diversity to national security. More important, the military brief clearly affirms that "today, there is no race-neutral alternative that
will fulfill the military's, and thus the nation's compelling national security
need" (Retired Military Leaders, 2003, p. 10). Hence, there is a need to recruit, attract, and retain racially and ethnically diverse officers of the highest
quality in providing the best in protection for the U.S.

The aforementioned amicus briefs, along with several others, were cited
in the ruling by Justice Sandra Day O'Connor in the *Grutter v. Bollinger*
(2003) case to buttress the decision that race should be considered as one
factor among many in admissions decisions. Fortunately, the various corporate and government allies were not ignored by the high court. Although
each ally had a distinct view with respect to diversity and how it benefited
its organizational mission, the message was the same: racial diversity is a
compelling interest. Race-conscious policies are a means for institutions of
higher learning, industry, and society to achieve distinction in pursuing
excellence.

With all of the briefs filed, the media highlighted one in particular. It
was filed by the Bush administration (United States Executive Branch,

2003). Although President Bush characterized Michigan's policy as a quota system, he also acknowledged that racial diversity was important. The Bush administration suggested that diversity should be achieved by other means, referencing the Texas 10 Percent Plan that was instituted during his tenure as governor. Some applauded President Bush's stance, crediting him with providing a viable alternative; others voiced that the Texas 10 Percent Plan does not provide appropriate access to top-tier institutions for minority students. In spite of the demonstrated limitations of percent plans, they allow the Bush administration to denounce race-conscious policies under the guise of supporting racial diversity.

With the dawn of *Gratz v. Bollinger* (2003) and *Grutter v. Bollinger* (2003), "diversity as a compelling interest" serves as the primary justification for maintaining racial diversity—not social justice, equity, or remediation. The diversity rationale garners more support and credibility than the social justice and remediation position. Many voices from the higher education community, as well as from other segments of society, openly support this narrowly tailored position. Compared to the racial preferences rhetoric, it has its own language, which is heavily reliant upon diversity research and promotion of an inclusive democratic society. Rather than remaining in the zero-sum paradigm, diversity shifts the debate to a value-added framework that emphasizes the benefit to all members of campus and the larger community. With an emerging common language informed by a growing body of research, diversity versus equity as an institutional value is perceived as less threatening and receives greater support.

CIR completely denounced the use of racial preferences in admissions; however, as discussed earlier, other types of preferences were not ruled out by CIR. For example, students who are economically disadvantaged could be given additional consideration in the admissions process. CIR's assumption is that SES can place one at a disadvantage in the admissions process, but race does not necessarily do so. CIR does not take into account the disproportionately higher rate of low-income and of poverty status for people of color. Race/ethnicity does not provide insulation from limited access or mitigate the negative effects of being poor but instead intensifies them.

CIR argued that racial diversity should not be a contrived or forced outcome but that it should arise naturally as a result of factors aside from race/ethnicity. According to CIR, racial balancing among student populations should not be the goal.

CIR's interpretation of the University of Michigan's admissions processes conveys the organization's view that institutions attempt to engineer racially diverse—rather than intellectually diverse—student populations at the undergraduate and graduate/professional school levels. To CIR this is the same as instituting virtual quotas, which it sees as illegal. CIR and similar groups typically advocate for policies that are race neutral and color blind (Bonilla-Silva, 2002). They have characterized college leaders as promoting illegal admissions policies in a manner that is above the law in order to maintain political correctness through continued implementation of race-conscious policies.

The National Association of Scholars (NAS) also produced policy briefs, amicus briefs, and research studies addressing issues that arose in the University of Michigan lawsuits. The association, which claims itself to be "America's foremost higher education reform group, . . . [with] more than four thousand . . . members," in a report titled *Is Campus Racial Diversity Correlated With Educational Benefits?*, charged that the University of Michigan "misrepresented critical findings in order to defend its racially discriminatory admissions policies" (NAS press release, 2001).

NAS also produced a report that contested the logic of Justice Lewis F. Powell's diversity rationale. In a publication endorsed by NAS, Wood and Sherman (2001) concluded that race in higher education must be rejected given the lack of consensus among the justices on the *Bakke* (1978) case. Further, Wood and Sherman asserted that the University of Michigan's legal arguments and the research that used the *Bakke* opinion to substantiate its legal claims should be dismissed due to the Supreme Court failing to clarify the constitutionality of race as a factor in college admissions.

Diversity as a Compelling Interest of the State

CIR (1998) states that schools that are "serious about recruiting a diverse student body" should consider the following factors in the *absence* of race: "geographic origin, work experience, record of leadership, civic involvement, record of overcoming leadership, demonstrated maturity, grades, test scores, scholarly interests, and musical or special talent" (p. 7). Because CIR leans so heavily on the *Bakke* decision to stake its claim, it becomes important to highlight Justice Powell's decision. A portion of that decision reads as follows:

> In enjoining petitioner from ever considering the race of any applicant, however, the courts below failed to recognize that the State has a substantial interest that legitimately may be served by a properly devised admissions program involving the competitive consideration of race and ethnic

origin. (*Regents of the University of California v. Bakke*, 483 U.S. 265, 320, 1978)

It is also important to note that the court did rule racial quotas unconstitutional in *Bakke*. For the record though, oblivious to CIR, racial quotas are not the issue. The question remains: Can race, among several factors designated by CIR, contribute to the diversity of an institution of higher education? Not race as the sole factor but one factor in the admissions process. Once more, language becomes central to CIR's argument. The assumption is made that colleges admit students solely on the basis of race. This is inaccurate. In the most recent Michigan cases, race was not the single or deciding factor used in granting students admission to the university.

Under Michigan's old undergraduate system of admissions, a 150-point selection index was used, with 110 points being awarded for academic factors. An additional 20 points were allotted for persons meeting the following criteria: "a) underrepresented minorities and b) socioeconomically disadvantaged or who attend a high school that serves a predominately minority population, regardless of the student's race" (the 20 points were awarded only once for this category). Geographic diversity has also been considered important to the University of Michigan as students from Michigan's largely White Upper Peninsula earned an additional 16 points under the new system (University of Michigan, 2003). Outlined in an article by Tim Wise (2003) the points associated with meeting one of the above criteria could not be combined with the points allotted in the latter category, essentially preserving the latter category for Whites. In addition, 10 points were awarded to students who attended the best high schools in the state. A candidate for admission could also get an additional 8 points if he or she had a demanding advanced placement or honors schedule. In the state of Michigan, students attending the best schools with rigorous academic standards are White. Also, four points were given to children of Michigan alumni. In essence a White student could get up to 58 extra points compared to a student of color's possible 20. The ideology remains clear: as long as race goes unmentioned in policy, de facto White privilege is constitutionally legal.

CIR and the "Letter of the Law"

Returning to its handbook, CIR (1998) advises students on how to secure admissions criteria, interpret data, and seek counsel if they feel they have been discriminated against. Included in the reference guide is a brief definition of the constitutional value of strict scrutiny. Offering CIR's interpretation of the *Regents of the University of California v. Bakke* (1978) decision, an institution must have an admissions program "narrowly tailored" to pass strict scrutiny (CIR, 1998, p. 29).

Race, as a suspect category in the courts, is "strictly" scrutinized as a rationale to address past discrimination. Regarding compelling government interests, CIR notes that the courts do not consider goals such as achieving a particular racial mix of students or providing role models for students of color as "compelling" (CIR, 1998). Nevertheless, with courts deeming societal discrimination too amorphous to address, the rights of the individual are viewed as separate from historical discrimination. The Michigan cases were not about individual rights as much as they were about discrediting the use of race in college admissions. Returning to Justice Powell's decision, because none of the other eight Justices joined this portion of Powell's opinion or otherwise endorsed diversity as a compelling interest, Powell's diversity rationale is not the holding of the Court (CIR, 1997a, 1997b).

CIR continues to find fault with Powell's opinion regarding the use of race to achieve diversity. It argues that its lawsuit rests outside the Powell opinion because of University of Michigan's particular use of race in admissions. The 1998 CIR reference handbook states, "race cannot be systematically used to insulate the individual from comparison with all other candidates" (p. 32). CIR expresses that affirmative action is "still operating on a technicality, a window exists in that the court held using race in admissions is constitutionally legal if an individual institution can prove historical exclusion on the basis of race" (p. 32), though there was not consensus on its consideration. Quintessentially, CIR uses the Powell decision when convenient. If the language works at the time, it is admissible; if not, the group is quick to discredit the accepted opinion of the court.

A Narrow Escape

Although never stated in CIR literature, the underpinnings of its legal interpretations are clear: the rights of Whites have been violated through the use of race in college admissions. With regard to individual institutions, the concern is not whether Whites will be admitted to second- or third-tier schools. The concern regards the bastions of status quo—White privilege: the elite, flagship universities of the state.

State flagship institutions acquire significant research dollars while accounting for a significant amount of state expenditures. Plaintiffs, as "deserving" White taxpayers who fund the university, are suing for the rights provided to them by the constitution to attend said institution. People of color are stereotyped as undeserving and gaining admission through an illegal process. Systemic racism exists and any rationale developed to address it is too broad in scope, especially if it disrupts the status quo. In short, people of color can go wherever they please for college, as long as it's not at the expense of deserving Whites. This rationale is a new-age version of the *Plessey v. Ferguson* (1896) decision, in that flagship institutions should be reserved for Whites, but because everyone can access some form of postsecondary study, equality can be assumed.

The U.S. Supreme Court decision in the *Grutter v. Bollinger* (2003) case should be considered a narrow escape, with the future of affirmative action still in question. States have been given the authority to decide whether diversity remains a compelling interest. The political has become personal for many Michigan residents as affirmative action is thought to be a White man's burden, which is evidenced in the referendum that banned affirmative action in Michigan. Institutions like ACRI and CIR in particular, remain diligent in asserting the protection of White male privilege. Not helping matters, some people of color have begun to volunteer their services in support of conservative anti-affirmative-action agendas. Much work is necessary if access is to be affirmed and equal opportunity made a reality.

7

AFFIRMING ACTS FOR
INCREASING ACCESS

Considerations for Policy, Practice, and Future Inquiry

T he previous chapter paints a poignant picture of the dubious future of affirmative action in its various forms. In an effort to significantly revamp, and in some cases abolish, race-conscious or gender-specific affirmative action, states such as California, Florida, and Texas have adopted percentage plans. This chapter illustrates how percentage plans fall short of diversifying our campuses.

Percentage Plans: Not Making the Mark

Percentage plans fail to carry out four essential elements of Executive Order No. 11,246 (1965). First, the shift in White privilege and entitlement is meager given the stalemate and/or reduction experienced in participation of first-time, full-time racial/ethnic minority entrants at the undergraduate level and more dramatically in graduate and professional programs. Second, substituting percentage plans for the top 4%, 10%, or 20% of students still narrowly defines meritocracy by reducing it to strict numerical standards without allowing for other factors, including race, gender, and SES, in addition to class rank, GPA, and standardized test scores in admissions consideration. Third, percentage plans are not a panacea in guaranteeing equal access or outcomes, let alone fostering diversity as a compelling state interest. Finally, the initial goal of eradicating the previous discrimination of African Americans and other disadvantaged, underrepresented groups is of little consequence and minor importance under this alternative.

The U.S. Commission on Civil Rights (2000), under the leadership of former Chair Mary Frances Berry, conducted an assessment of percentage plans. The report concluded that percentage plans are harmful to promoting and increasing enrollment of students of color. For example, following the implementation of the Texas 10 Percent Plan, figures for incoming freshmen declined at the University of Texas at Austin, 4.3% for Hispanics, and 33.8% for African Americans. At Texas A&M, Hispanic enrollment fell by 12.6% and African American enrollment dropped by 29%. Additionally, in the case of Florida, the commission asserted that the state does not have a proviso for admitting students who are not in the top 20% of the graduating class yet are competitively qualified. As for California's Four Percent Plan, the UC system, especially UCLA and Berkeley, have not rebounded from the plummet of African American and Hispanic students in undergraduate and graduate admissions post–Proposition 209.

African American and Hispanic student enrollments were expected to drop by more than 50% following implementation of Proposition 209 (Alim, 1996). According to *Diverse Issues in Higher Education* (2005a), the 2005 fall enrollment statistics of racial/ethnic minority students in the UC system were distressing. At Berkeley only 129 freshmen were African Americans, out of a total enrollment of 4,000. At Berkeley's School of Law, only 9 of 268 incoming students were African American. Not as dramatic, but of concern nonetheless, was that Hispanics accounted for only 11% of students in the entire UC system, even though Hispanics represent 30% of the California population. Florida, like California, has a large population of people of color, Latinos/Latinas in particular. The Florida 20 Percent Plan that Governor Jeb Bush promoted and lobbied for has been in effect for more than five years. Like California and Texas, Florida is experiencing steep drops in African American enrollment (Eckes, 2004).

Advocates and opponents of affirmative action debate whether percentage plans are an appropriate response to equalizing postsecondary access. Unfortunately, the 2003 University of Michigan decisions in the cases of *Gratz v. Bollinger* and *Grutter v. Bollinger* do not provide a definitive direction for diversity initiatives. Some institutions are cheering the U.S. Supreme Court ruling that race could be one of many factors considered in college admissions, as their campus culture and climate already support affirmative action. Other institutions are holding firm abolitionist positions on affirmative action (Springer, 2005). *Black Issues in Higher Education* (2004c) reported that, in spite of the University of Michigan rulings, Texas A&M University officials announced that preferences would not be an issue as race no longer would be considered in admissions. Texas A&M President Robert Gates stated:

We all have a toolbox. The choice of which tools you use doesn't have to be the same at every university. Every student here will have been admitted based on personal merit. This is the best course for us. (p. 10)

Texas A&M University has been referred to as "an enclave for the education of White students" (*Black Issues in Higher Education*, 2004c), given that well over four-fifths of undergraduates are White. The fall 2004 class was 9% Hispanic, 3% Asian American, and 2% African American (*Black Issues in Higher Education*, 2004c, 2004d, 2005).

Like Texas A&M, the University of Washington intends to continue prohibiting race-conscious policies and programming. The University of Washington is held by the continued observance of Initiative 200, which abolished consideration of race/ethnicity, gender, color, and/or national origin in public employment, education, and contracting in the state in 1998. The state of Washington's policies regarding race have not wavered in light of the 2003 University of Michigan decisions. Senate Bill 6268 was introduced at the governor's request to allow Washington public institutions of higher education to use race as one of many factors in admissions decisions. However, the bill, which sought to repeal Initiative 200 banning affirmative action, did not have enough favorable votes in the House Higher Education Committee to pass (Trick, 2004; University of Washington, 1999).

It is apparent from the extant literature that so-called color-blind policies in Washington and percentage plans in California, Florida, and Texas do not increase minority student participation in higher education. More specifically, research has illustrated that need-based forms of affirmative action have not produced a critical mass of talented racially/ethnically diverse students (Eckes, 2004; Feinberg, 1996; Orfield, 2001; Rendón, 2005). We have a long way to go in achieving diversity in higher education, especially at elite institutions. Institutions of higher education need much guidance to navigate the logistics of carrying out diversity initiatives amid coercive tactics to rid public entities of affirmative action programs.

Michiganders and the Next Act in Affirming Access

I think about the Michigan Militia and its sister organizations, some with their militant white supremacy. In the past two years I've struggled to understand better that peril which America faces, first working as Special Counsel to President Clinton, managing the White House review of affirmative action, and then writing this. The peril is that the many sharp differences between the races, expressed along hardened political and social battle lines, may be precursors for an escalating racial conflict and, ultimately, conflagration. This process is already at work, and accelerating. (Edley, 1996 p. 3)

In 2003 the U.S. Supreme Court decision of *Grutter v. Bollinger* affirmed access for all students. Through amicus briefs, expert witnesses and friends of the court examined and explained trends in (a) historical patterns and legacies, (b) demographic data, (c) University of Michigan survey data, (d) personal reflections, and (e) longitudinal data on the consequences of considering race in college and university admissions. In spite of the decision's definitive explication of a review process that, at its core, valued individualized consideration and took into account all pertinent factors including race/ethnicity, opponents, who span the entire spectrum of higher education, have attempted to thwart affirmative access for all.

From 1997 to 2003 the *Gratz v. Bollinger* and *Grutter v. Bollinger* litigation brought to the forefront a unified voice from the higher education community, the U.S. military, and major American corporations asserting that racial diversity is important to classrooms, educational institutions, college campuses, and society. Whereas before the Michigan litigation the debate primarily juxtaposed the social justice camp against the racial preferences camp (Eckes, 2004; Graca, 2005; Ogletree, 2004), after Michigan, the social justice rhetoric has largely disappeared, while the diversity argument has become more prominent.

Diversity as an institutional value is less threatening and garners broad support because diversity is said to benefit all students. In the end, there is a resounding recognition that racial diversity is important to education and other areas of American life. With this profound recognition among education, business, and political leaders, campus administrations have opportunities to advocate or advance the institutional values of affirmative access, diversity, and inclusion on their campuses but not without substantial opposition or conflict.

Ward Connerly, who was instrumental in leading the charge to pass Proposition 209 in California, is spearheading a referendum campaign in the state of Michigan (and a few other states) to eliminate the consideration of race/ethnicity in admissions (*The Chronicle of Higher Education*, 2006; University of Michigan, 2005). Only a few weeks following the Supreme Court's 2003 decisions on the Michigan cases, Connerly announced a campaign to remove "preferences" in the state of Michigan, referring to this effort as the Michigan Civil Rights Initiative (MCRI). In July 2003, in a speech at the University of Michigan, Connerly expressed that as a Black man he was embittered by the misplaced pity shown in the need for racial preferences. He said that equality is devalued and we are obligated to support anti-affirmative-action measures to comply with the true ideals of justice that the Civil Rights Act of 1964 sought to preserve (Connerly, 2003). While Connerly and his oppositional entourage failed to produce enough signatures to make the 2004 ballot, over 500,000 signatures were collected and later submitted.

The MCRI appeared on the November 2006 ballot (DeBose, 2006; MCRI, 2005). Noted as Proposal 2, the referendum called for adding a section to Article I to amend Michigan's constitution to forbid the use of race/ethnicity, gender, national origin, or color from consideration in public contracting, education, and employment by state government and all of its subdivisions, including any county, city, school district, or public college/university. Among the considerations Michigan voters contended with were: Would the MCRI improve or harm the quality of education? Would Proposal 2 assist or set back minorities and women? Could the MCRI enhance social cohesion and cross-racial socialization or retard progress in public relations? (Page & Suhay, 2006).

O'Brien (2006) asserts that the MCRI provided a sense of poetic justice among many conservatives. Since opponents continue to move the affirmative access battle from the legal to the political realm, what has the higher education community truly gained from the *Grutter v. Bollinger* (2003) and *Gratz v. Bollinger* (2003) decisions? Apparently legal precedent has not been set despite the U.S. Supreme Court rulings in those cases.

Taking Sides: The Complex Political Backdrop of Michigan

It is not coincidental that the poor economic landscape of Michigan symbolically shaped perceptions of public policy and swayed voters in supporting the MCRI agenda. Unlike other states, Michigan's economy is heavily dependent on the Big Three automobile manufacturers: General Motors, Ford, and Chrysler.[1] The American auto industry, which has primarily been concentrated in Michigan, has endured a sharp decrease in manufacturing jobs. Michigan's annual job growth has declined by about 11,000 jobs each year because of the declining share of the national automobile industry held by the Big Three. This loss in market share has created a negative impact to the tune of 6,000 existing jobs lost each year, with a total deterioration of about 17,000 jobs (Bartik, Erickcek, Huang, & Watts, 2006). The decreases in auto job creation, coupled with job declines and the multiple effects on other Michigan auto-related industries, amounts to a decrease of nearly 85,000 jobs per year.

Generational Transmission

Education is the key to opportunities. . . . these jobs at Ford aren't heredi-
tary; you can't pass your job down to your kid. The auto plant jobs can no
longer be passed on because those jobs are moving on.

—Steve Harvey[2]

The above comment, made in jest by actor/comedian Steve Harvey, has
sobering implications. The transmission of capital in the form of family resources to secure gainful employment in Michigan manufacturing has fizzled
out. As a consequence, the prior cues and messages about the role of educational attainment must shift in order to encourage diversification of the
state's economy.

A study from the W. E. Upjohn Institute for Employment Research
(Bartik et al., 2006) confirmed that regional economies with greater proportions of college graduates are more successful. Michigan is above average in
terms of high school graduates residing in the state, but below average relative to its share of college completers. Michigan residents were 3.3% below
the national average for college degree attainment at 24.4%. Michigan Governor Jennifer Granholm has been very vocal about the need to increase the
average years of education among state residents in order to be less dependent on the auto industry for economic sustenance and growth. Having
more educated Michigan citizens is considered necessary in attracting new
industries to the state. One example of the state administration's attempt
to make Michigan more educationally and economically competitive is the
revamping of the secondary education curriculum to be more rigorous and
by encouraging postsecondary attainment, as cited in the Cherry Commission (2004) and witnessed in Granholm's 21st Century Jobs Fund, which
capitalizes on tobacco settlement money to finance the state's new high
school reforms that were implemented in 2007. Another initiative that can
greatly affect higher education in Michigan appeared on the 2006 November
ballot. The K–16 Coalition for Michigan's Future acquired enough signatures to petition a referendum requiring the state to increase monies to public schools and colleges minimally at a rate consistent with the rate of
inflation (*The Chronicle of Higher Education*, 2006).

Return On Investment, Perceived Threat, and Advancing All Michiganders

By investing in the education of young people and by creating more strin-
gent minimum standards for high school completion, politicians are hopeful

that over time residents will be highly skilled, poised to make significant contributions to the overall educational attainment in Michigan, and able to garner greater attention from businesses that could assist in expanding the state's economy. Return on investment (ROI), as applied to education, is a theoretical perspective that holds that there are positive individual and social rates of return associated with more years of schooling. Increasing the number of college-educated residents in Michigan would provide a social rate of return in attracting new industries seeking a highly capable, skilled workforce that is technologically competent and culturally diverse. The difficulty in framing a discussion of Michigan's positionality, and the nebulous future of affirmative action within the context of ROI, lies in the lack of consensus regarding the social versus individual ROIs when considering diversity as a compelling state interest, particularly at a time of scarce resources.

Of course, there are individual ROIs for more educated people. The literature has illustrated that greater levels of education are associated with higher wages and/or occupational prestige. At the individual level, though, the societal benefit of increasing the number of racial/ethnic minorities and women in postsecondary education and the workplace may not be easily seen or accepted in Michigan, when working-class Whites feel threatened by the possibility of a massive layoff and/or possess a sense of entitlement with regard to college access and degree attainment. Given the connection between the global economy and local/regional economies, Michigan residents should understand that improving gaps in educational attainment based on gender and race/ethnicity could potentially benefit everyone by providing a greater tax base and employment growth, among other things. The depressed economic picture coupled with the exporting of talented college graduates because of a poor climate for career advancement should prompt Michigan citizens to rally in support of promoting access and optimal opportunities for higher education attendance and completion.

An economic turnaround in Michigan calls for a variety of approaches, including introduction of major tax changes that could assist the state in being more financially stable and educationally competitive. The overall state and local taxes per dollar for personal income in Michigan are 5% below the national average, while the state is 12% below the U.S. average for state and local business taxes per dollar of private gross state product. The state and local business taxes for new businesses are 19% under the national norm (Bartik et al., 2006). The bleak economic conditions in the State of Michigan remain with tax and spending reforms among the top of Governor Jennifer Granholm's priorities. In fact, the state's per capita income is now five percent below the national average (i.e., the lowest since 1933). Michigan ranked last among states in 2007 for the index of economic momentum which charts quarterly changes in personal income, employment, and population. Additionally, domestic auto sales of Chrysler, Ford, and General Motors continue to fall with domestic share predicted to drop to 45.2% by 2011 from 73.7% in 1993 (*Michigan's Defining Moment: Report of the Emergency Financial Advisory Panel,* 2007).

The future of access policies and diversity initiatives in the state of Michigan is frightening. Some supporters of the MCRI contend that banning affirmative action policies is a necessary step, as they fault affirmative action policies for the despondent financial condition of Michigan (Cottman, 2006). Proposal 2 and the issue of racial/ethnic and/or gender-conscious affirmative action have direct ramifications for Michigan residents and repercussions across public sectors countrywide. With the fall 2006 midterm elections, political ads from earlier that spring picked up pace during the GOP primary and intensified during the days leading up to election day.

Citizens for a United Michigan, the National Association for Women Business Owners, the Presidents Council of State Universities of Michigan, the American Association of University Women, the American Civil Liberties Union, the Urban League, NAACP, and the Michigan Women's Commission initiated local and regional grassroots efforts to educate citizens about the benefits of affirmative action (*Black Issues in Higher Education,* 2004e). Democrats have been open about their disfavor for the MCRI (Michigan Civil Rights Commission, 2005). Additionally, a federal lawsuit was filed that maintained the MCRI illegally obtained signatures of Black voters through confusing double-talk by telling them the ballot initiative would uphold civil rights. The suit, filed in June 2006, by Detroit Mayor Kwame Kilpatrick, two labor unions, Operation King's Dream (Operation King's Dream is a civil rights campaign launched by Michigan By Any Means Necessary [BAMN] for the purpose of defeating the Proposal 2, anti-affirmative action ballot initiative), and numerous registered Black voters, received support from Governor Jennifer Granholm, who filed an amicus brief on behalf of the plaintiffs in August of 2006 (Gray, 2006). Critics of the governor suggest that her lack of support for the MCRI is a tactic to maintain the critical Black vote that she captured when first elected to office.[3]

The dynamics in that gubernatorial race were attention grabbing. Dick DeVos, the republican challenging Jennifer Granholm, disappointed many neoconservatives when he stated, "Until I feel comfortable with the system we have in place today, I will support affirmative action." Additionally, the Republican candidate for the Michigan State Senate, Mike Bouchard, opposed the MCRI, commenting, "Any time there's an effort to amend and change the constitution, it always gives me pause. . . . this language would be a constitutional hurdle for same sex public schools, which I believe are not only worthwhile but valuable" (O'Brien, 2006).

Although the leading Republican candidates for the Senate and governor were not your typical right-wing conservatives, arch neoconservative Terrence Pell, president of CIR, was described in *The Detroit News* as being agitated by the federal voting rights lawsuit filed by BAMN, a multiethnic student activist group (Pell, 2006). In an opinion piece with an apparent play on words and distraction tactics, Pell (2006) called the suit "frivolous . . . filed to keep the Michigan Civil Rights Initiative off the November ballot." His tirade follows:

> The initiative asks voters to decide whether "affirmative action" means judging individuals by merit, regardless of race, or whether it means that the state can grant preferential treatment to individuals based on color. So while there's no denying that the term "affirmative action" means different things to different people, the solution to this problem is to let the voters of Michigan go ahead and decide what this term will mean in Michigan. BAMN's effort to inject the federal Voting Rights Act into this debate is a thinly disguised effort to prevent the voters from ever getting to settle the question of what affirmative action really means.

Perhaps Pell's statements reflected nervousness, as the polling figures leading up to Election Day measuring support and disfavor for the MCRI were too close to call. In late summer 2006 a *Detroit Free Press* poll showed Michigan voters nearly split on Proposal 2, with 48% stating they were not likely to support a ban on affirmative action, and 43% favoring the MCRI. Additional polls leading up to the election estimated that from 9% to 15% of voters were undecided (Chapman, 2006; *The Chronicle of Higher Education*, 2006). The projected outcome showed Proposal 2 as a "dead heat issue" (Chapman, 2006).

Rock the Vote

With the use of affirmative action in admissions, hiring, and contracts at stake, it was anyone's guess which side would have the final say in affirming or derailing access. Of related interest, the Voting Rights Act (VRA) of 1965 was up for renewal in 2005. Unfortunately, stall tactics were employed, and the renewal decision was pulled from the U.S. House of Representatives' legislative calendar in July 2006 because of a petition by Representative Lynn Westmoreland of Georgia.[4] As the first policy to prohibit discriminatory practices in voting had expired, backers of Westmoreland's amendment insisted that their states needed more time to look at their voting rules to discern if the VRA unfairly singles out certain southern states with greater scrutiny relative to requesting permission to change their voting rules prior to VRA renewal approval (Arnwine, 2006; *Jet Magazine*, 2006;). Nonetheless, protection of voting access prevails (though only for another 25 years) as President Bush signed the bill to renew the VRA on July 27, 2006 (Cano, 2006).

The Importance of Voter Turnout and Proposal 2

A *Time* magazine feature titled "America by the Numbers" (2004) examined how we vote in the United States and revealed the alarming fact that only 35% of American adults are registered and regularly vote. According to the article, "About three-quarters of voting-age Americans are registered to vote, but many don't bother on Election Day" (p. 46). Detroit Mayor Kilpatrick was quoted, saying, "There will be affirmative action today. . . . there will be affirmative action here tomorrow and there will be affirmative action in our state forever" (as cited in O'Brien, 2006). The mayor, along with other liberal activists, seemed unconcerned about the intermittent/rare voting patterns of nearly two-fifths of adult Americans, in addition to the 22% who are not registered to vote at all (*Time*, 2006).

Early indicators showed support for Connerly's MCRI, patterned after Proposition 209 in California 10 years earlier. Many harmful effects in California followed the passage of Proposition 209 in 1996, including the following:

- The American Indian Early Childhood Education Program was prohibited.
- College preparation programs and educational outreach initiatives for students of color, such as the Student Opportunity and Access Program under the Student Aid Commission, were barred.
- Minority college admissions witnessed a significant decline, and initiatives to curb underrepresentation of women in male-dominated fields were banned.
- Employment and contracting opportunities for women and minorities were eliminated, and 33 state affirmative action programs were expelled, adversely affecting $4 billion in annual contracts.
- Governor Pete Wilson disqualified affirmative action initiatives in recruitment, appointment, training and career development, promotion, and transfer, which frequently encouraged greater participation

among underrepresented groups—particularly African Americans and Hispanics (Doss, 2006; Kaufmann, 2006; Stovall, 2001).

Similarly, Initiative 200, which was on the November 1998 ballot in Washington state, passed with 58% of the vote. The number of minority students at the University of Washington and Washington State University decreased by 30% following implementation of Initiative 200. Within four years of its passage, the number of Seattle public works contracts awarded to minority and/or women-owned businesses decreased by 25%. Additionally, only 1.1% of contracts awarded went to African American firms in 2001, in contrast to 2.3% awarded in 1998 (Doss, 2006).

Just as Proposition 209 and Initiative 200 passed with flying colors, so too did Proposal 2 in Michigan's midterm elections. Detroit has been notorious for being racially polarized in terms of residential patterns and race relations. Many advocates of affirmative action felt that MCRI's campaign purposefully confused voters, especially older African American Detroit residents (Gray, 2006). One could argue that there could be some margin of error among Michigan voters, based on the language of the ballot and personal framing of affirmative action. Nonetheless, the constitutional amendment to ban affirmative action programs in the state of Michigan received overwhelming support, as only three out of 83 counties voted no to abolishing affirmative action (Michigan Department of State, 2006).

In taking a closer look at the general election results, Table 7 highlights the county, the percentage of registered voters, how they voted on Proposal 2, and the percentage of White residents who are 18 years and older. Not surprisingly, the three counties (in boldface) that advocated for affirmative action to remain in Michigan were Ingham County, home to Michigan State University; Washtenaw County, where the University of Michigan resides; and Wayne County, home of Detroit's Wayne State University. Sixty-three percent of rural, 64% of suburban, and 41% of urban dwellers supported prohibiting affirmative action. Also noteworthy is that, while Detroit is a city that has a minority majority and women are the majority of Michiganders, these two groups were unable to stop the banning of affirmative action. With women and people of color combining to represent the majority of individuals residing in Michigan, it would appear that affirmative action is not a minority issue but a majority concern. So, how is it that this ballot measure passed?

Eighty percent of the U.S. population lives in metropolitan areas, and the vast majority of people of color reside in urban areas (*Time*, 2006). However, with the majority of Detroiters being people of color, Whites in the

TABLE 7
County Election Results—Michigan Proposal 2: Constitutional Amendment to Ban Affirmative Action Programs

County, Code/Name	Total by County	% Yes Votes for Proposal 2	% No Votes for Proposal 2	% of Registered Voters	% of White Population, 18 Years or Older
1 ALCONA	5,211	67.3	32.7	53.2	98.5
2 ALGER	3,608	72.0	28.0	50.2	87.8
3 ALLEGAN	43,428	65.6	34.4	57.1	94.4
4 ALPENA	11,607	61.1	38.9	49.0	98.5
5 ANTRIM	11,175	66.0	34.0	59.7	97.6
6 ARENAC	6,462	65.0	35.0	52.7	95.4
7 BARAGA	3,106	59.0	41.0	53.0	80.2
8 BARRY	24,726	66.2	33.8	57.7	97.4
9 BAY	45,436	62.7	37.3	55.9	96.0
10 BENZIE	8,052	58.9	41.1	60.2	96.9
11 BERRIEN	50,509	68.2	31.8	42.2	82.8
12 BRANCH	13,844	66.5	33.5	44.5	93.0
13 CALHOUN	26,245	60.9	39.1	25.9	86.1
14 CASS	15,813	67.8	32.2	42.4	90.6
15 CHARLEVOIX	10,997	67.3	32.7	53.0	97.0
16 CHEBOYGAN	11,244	64.2	35.8	54.1	95.9
17 CHIPPEWA	12,845	61.7	38.3	46.9	78.3
18 CLARE	11,302	63.6	36.4	48.8	97.8
19 CLINTON	30,247	64.8	35.2	62.1	97.1
20 CRAWFORD	5,643	63.3	36.7	49.7	96.3

TABLE 7 (Continued)

County, Code/Name	Total by County	% Yes Votes for Proposal 2	% No Votes for Proposal 2	% of Registered Voters	% of White Population, 18 Years or Older
21 DELTA	14,263	64.1	35.9	50.9	96.7
22 DICKINSON	9,377	74.2	25.8	46.5	98.5
23 EATON	44,812	62.1	37.9	57.0	91.4
24 EMMET	13,513	64.6	35.4	53.3	95.1
25 GENESEE	160,562	57.9	42.1	46.7	78.2
26 GLADWIN	10,560	67.4	32.6	48.4	98.0
27 GOGEBIC	5,921	70.0	30.0	44.1	94.8
28 GD. TRAVERSE	35,303	87.8	12.2	55.9	97.1
29 GRATIOT	14,698	63.1	36.9	56.2	91.6
30 HILLSDALE	15,262	72.4	27.6	45.7	98.0
31 HOUGHTON	11,422	59.6	40.4	48.7	95.5
32 HURON	13,702	66.1	33.9	53.4	98.5
33 INGHAM	**102,762**	**48.2**	**51.8**	**50.3**	**82.2**
34 IONIA	21,930	66.7	33.3	53.4	90.7
35 IOSCO	10,864	65.0	35.0	47.8	97.4
36 IRON	4,635	69.0	31.0	48.9	96.7
37 ISABELLA	18,395	53.6	46.4	46.6	92.5
38 JACKSON	55,370	61.9	38.1	49.2	89.5
39 KALAMAZOO	91,989	52.7	47.3	51.5	86.9
40 KALKASKA	6,352	67.8	32.2	46.9	98.0

	NAME					
41	KENT	234,889	60.2	38.9	57.9	85.5
42	KEWEENAW	1,138	64.5	35.5	61.9	97.2
43	LAKE	4,343	61.7	38.3	50.7	86.2
44	LAPEER	35,439	71.1	28.9	54.8	96.4
45	LEELANAU	11,863	57.4	42.6	65.0	95.1
46	LENAWEE	33,497	73.1	26.9	47.5	93.4
47	LIVINGSTON	76,086	72.7	27.3	59.4	97.5
48	LUCE	2,221	64.5	35.5	49.0	82.3
49	MACKINAC	5,306	58.7	41.3	55.9	83.8
50	MACOMB	306,893	68.3	31.7	52.4	93.5
51	MANISTEE	10,329	60.5	39.5	53.9	94.6
52	MARQUETTE	23,347	66.1	33.9	46.9	95.5
53	MASON	11,813	60.1	39.9	54.5	96.6
54	MECOSTA	14,511	65.8	34.2	55.0	93.2
55	MENOMINEE	7,325	65.2	34.8	41.2	97.3
56	MIDLAND	33,799	62.8	37.2	53.7	96.0
57	MISSAUKEE	6,007	64.5	35.5	56.1	97.8
58	MONROE	53,902	71.0	29.0	48.1	96.2
59	MONTCALM	21,973	66.2	33.8	53.9	94.7
60	MONTMORENCY	4,434	66.5	33.5	55.7	98.5
61	MUSKEGON	61,887	55.7	44.3	48.8	83.7
62	NEWAYGO	18,475	65.7	34.3	53.5	95.7
63	OAKLAND	498,631	57.1	42.9	56.1	83.9
64	OCEANA	10,110	63.7	36.3	53.3	92.4
65	OGEMAW	8,391	64.9	35.1	49.5	97.9
66	ONTONAGON	2,972	68.7	31.3	46.4	97.9

TABLE 7 (Continued)

County, Code/Name	Total by County	% Yes Votes for Proposal 2	% No Votes for Proposal 2	% of Registered Voters	% of White Population, 18 Years or Older
67 OSCEOLA	9,130	66.8	33.2	54.2	98.0
68 OSCODA	3,455	68.3	31.7	51.4	98.0
69 OTSEGO	10,012	66.7	33.3	50.9	98.0
70 OTTAWA	106,365	68.8	31.2	63.7	92.9
71 PRESQUE ISLE	6,193	65.7	34.3	54.9	98.5
72 ROSCOMMON	11,410	68.1	31.9	51.8	98.4
73 SAGINAW	78,567	54.6	45.4	49.8	78.8
74 ST. CLAIR	61,223	67.1	32.9	51.2	95.8
75 ST. JOSEPH	18,472	64.6	35.4	43.4	94.4
76 SANILAC	16,007	64.0	36.0	51.6	97.5
77 SCHOOLCRAFT	3,265	67.1	32.9	53.3	90.3
78 SHIAWASSEE	28,773	67.3	32.7	54.4	97.8
79 TUSCOLA	21,946	67.0	33.0	51.1	96.7
80 VAN BUREN	25,519	63.2	36.8	47.4	89.8
81 **WASHTENAW**	**131,210**	**42.5**	**57.5**	**52.3**	**78.8**
82 **WAYNE**	**620,614**	**41.0**	**59.0**	**43.9**	**54.9**
83 WEXFORD	11,802	66.0	34.0	49.4	97.7
Total	3,676,736 (100%)	2,131,096 (58%)	1,545,640 (42%)		

Note. Michigan Department of State (2006). *State Proposal—06–2: Constitutional Amendment: Ban Affirmative Action Programs.* Bureau of Elections. Retrieved on June 2, 2007, from http://miboecfr.nicusa.com/election/results/06GEN/90000002.html

metropolitan area live mainly on the fringes of southeastern Michigan's suburbia. Racial homogeneity in Michigan neighborhoods is not uncommon and racially segregated school contexts are the norm (Chang et al., 2006; Gurin, Lehman, & Lewis, 2004; Gurin, Nagda, & Lopez, 2004). The failures of successful integration in Michigan are apparent in the 2006 postelection findings that illustrate a schism between those casting ballots. Detroit residents largely voted against Proposal 2, while suburban dwellers and residents in the overwhelmingly White Upper Peninsula of Michigan, crushingly favored banning affirmative action (Chapman, 2006). Detroit Mayor Kilpatrick referred to Proposal 2 as the "single biggest election issue," and declared that the banning of affirmative action "bodes poorly for Detroit residents, more than 80% of whom are Black, a third of them unemployed" (as cited in Chapman, 2006).

If you disaggregate the data by voter characteristics, it is clear that White men oppose affirmative action. However, while affirmative action benefits White women, White women, as a group, did not vote against Proposal 2 (CNN, 2006). Any uncertainty relative to the 2006 Michigan voting patterns can be addressed by looking at the CNN exit poll results of 1,955 respondents on the Proposal 2 ballot measure. Although women still find workplace progress difficult, and although White women have benefited most from affirmative action initiatives, they are still wary of the devalued status that is often associated with those who benefit from affirmative action. For example, 64% of Whites, 70% of White men, and 59% of White women voted yes to Proposal 2, while 14% of African Americans supported the ballot measure. Although Hispanics, Asian Americans, and others combined for an exit poll total of 4%, only 30% of non-White men and 18% of non-White women voted in favor of banning affirmative action (CNN, 2006).

While economic inequality is quite pronounced in the United States, the only people who were at least half in favor of affirmative action were those earning between $15,000 and $30,000 and those making between $150,000 and $200,000 annually. Two-thirds of those who stated they were getting ahead financially wished to dismantle affirmative action; 54% who said they had just enough to get by, and 48% of those who indicated they were financially falling behind supported Proposal 2 (CNN, 2006). Given that SES is exacerbated by gender and race/ethnicity, one could hypothesize that the disproportionately high number of people of color who are low income, earning between $15,000 and $30,000, may see benefits in approaches that encompass race-conscious and economic-based components. Additionally, the 50% who earn $150,000 and higher may support affirmative action because they see the utility of the social and redistributive justice aspects of the policies. Having said that, however, it is important to remember that exit poll data is not the most reliable, as there are often discrepancies.

The exit poll also inquired about the overall financial health of each family. Sixty-six percent of those who said they were getting ahead supported abolishing affirmative action; 54% of those who felt they had just enough voted yes on Proposal 2. By comparison, less than half the individuals who reported they were falling behind financially backed the dismantling of affirmative action (accounting for 20% of the total net sample). For this reason, it is fair to assume that financial disparities, coupled with the disproportionately higher poverty rates along racial/ethnic and gender lines, lead to lower-income people valuing affirmative action, and those who are more affluent seeking to protect their position and maintain the status quo.

Voting participation is said to be strongly associated with attitudes, beliefs, and community ties that generally increase with age and income (*Time*, 2006). In trying to determine if there were variations by age in voting yes to Proposal 2, there was not much divergence, as 55% to 60% across age groups supported the ballot measure abolishing affirmative action. Moreover, given the heavily unionized employment environment in Michigan, greater support for banning affirmative action was exhibited by nonunion members. Hence, efforts to defeat Proposal 2 by the United Auto Workers (UAW) and the American Arab Chamber of Commerce did not persuade Michigan's workers to see the benefits of diversity. Furthermore, the vote by education illustrates virtually no difference between those with no college degree and college graduates.

Theoretically, with more years of education individuals should exhibit more democratic dispositions. However, in regard to political affiliation, Michigan could be described as not actually red (Republican) or blue (Democratic) but purple (*Time*, 2006). Two-fifths of those who describe their political ideology as liberal, voted in favor of Proposal 2's goal to abolish affirmative action. Despite the U.S. Conference of Catholic Bishops' taking a strong stand against Proposal 2 in support of the pro-affirmative-action stance of the Michigan Catholic Conference, as well as support from the Michigan Jewish Conference, affirmative action has not translated into a socially conscious, moral issue for many. There was little deviation in voting patterns by religious affiliation and church attendance when examining yes votes on Proposal 2 (CNN, 2006).

Much of the reaction to affirmative action is related to the idea that resources are scarce and many people are fearful of losing them. Therefore, many Michiganders who disfavor affirmative action, simultaneously assert egalitarian values but are afraid of their tentative personal positioning in a

TABLE 8
Ballot Measures—Michigan Proposal 2 Exit Poll Data

Voter Characteristics	Percent Total	Percent Yes to Proposal 2	Percent No to Proposal 2
Vote by Gender			
Male	49	64	36
Female	51	52	48
Vote by Race & Gender			
White Men	42	70	30
White Women	42	59	41
Non-White Men	7	30	70
Non-White Women	8	18	82
Vote by Race/Ethnicity			
White	85	64	36
African American	12	14	86
Latino	2	*	*
Asian	1	*	*
Other	1	*	*
Vote by Age			
18–29	16	59	41
30–44	28	60	40
45–59	31	57	43
60 and older	25	55	45
Vote by Income			
Under $15,000	6	58	42
$15,000–30,000	15	50	50
$30,000–50,000	21	57	43
$50,000–75,000	24	59	41
$75,000–100,000	15	61	39
$100,000–150,000	14	64	36
$150,000–200,000	3	50	50
$200,000 or more	2	*	*
Vote by Education			
No College Degree	58	55	45
College Graduate	42	56	44
Vote by Union Membership			
Union Member	22	50	50
Non-Union	78	57	43

TABLE 8 (Continued)

Voter Characteristics	Percent Total	Percent Yes to Proposal 2	Percent No to Proposal 2
Vote by Political Affiliation			
Democrat	39	40	60
Republican	34	78	22
Independent	28	59	41
Vote by Political Ideology			
Liberal	21	40	60
Moderate	47	53	47
Conservative	32	76	24
Vote by Religious Affiliation			
Protestant	53	57	43
Catholic	27	64	36
Jewish	1	*	*
Other	7	42	58
Vote by Church Attendance			
Weekly	44	59	41
Occasionally	37	55	45
Never	14	55	45
State Economy			
Excellent or Good	14	58	42
Not Good or Poor	84	53	47
Job Situation in Your Area			
Better	6	56	44
Worse	62	52	48
About the Same	29	54	46
Family's Financial Situation			
Getting Ahead	19	66	34
Have Just Enough	57	54	46
Falling Behind	20	48	52
Vote by Size of Community			
Urban	26	41	59
Suburban	52	64	36
Rural	21	63	37

Note. (N = 1,955). Cable Network News. (2006, November). *Ballot measures/Michigan Proposition 2 exit poll.* Retrieved May 24, 2008, from http://www.cnn.com/ELECTION/ 2006//pages/results/states/MI/I/01/epolls.o.html fledgling economy that is entirely too reliant on the automobile industry. According to the CNN (2006) exit poll data, 53% of those who supported the ban on affirmative action also felt that the state economy was not good or poor. Those who responded in this fashion were the overwhelming majority of those polled, accounting for 84% of the total net sample of 1,642.

There has been a steep shrinkage in manufacturing jobs as well as in white-collar positions in the state of Michigan, given that the majority of employment opportunities have traditionally originated in the Big Three auto makers. In response to these developments and the passage of Proposal 2, the Pontiac division of General Motors announced that it would no longer use hiring quotas (Egan as cited in Citizens Research Council of Michigan, 2006). In exploring the linkage between endorsing Proposal 2 and perceptions of employment circumstances, support for ending affirmative action was clear, irrespective of whether participants in the CNN (2006) exit poll felt that their job prospects were better (117), worse (1,212), or about the same (567).

Theoretical Perspectives and Access Policy Research

The politics of identity comes into play when examining Proposal 2 voting patterns and their correspondence to individuals' ascribed characteristics. Identity politics and issues of access represent the sweeping changes that have occurred in civil rights over the years, which are far from settled as evidenced in the recent VRA reauthorization and MCRI referendum. In *Freedom Is Not Enough: The Opening of the American Workplace*, Lipsitz asserts, "Most white voters in the North, Democrats and Republicans alike, came to think of policies that privileged them and excluded Blacks as fair entitlements" (as cited in MacLean, 2006, p. 17). We have discussed White male hegemony throughout this book. However, the relationship between access and feminism hasn't been fully explored. Has feminism reached a point of full affinity with women of color? More often than not, White women are primarily concerned with sexism, and race/ethnicity is not considered salient. This is clearly evident in the *Gratz v. Bollinger* (2003) and *Grutter v. Bollinger* (2003) cases whereby the quid pro quo of White women materialized in their leading the anti-affirmative-action charge, claiming racial preferences. Would the suits have been filed had the plaintiffs felt they enjoyed the benefits of gender-targeted policies and programming?

White women often fail to recognize that the racial prejudice that leads to discrimination in the form of institutionalized power is very different from underrepresentation that exists solely along gender lines. To be sure, there is systemic discrimination in the treatment of group members because of sex bias, but this is organically dissimilar to the limited access to opportunities that arises from racialized discrimination.

If the women at the center of the double University of Michigan litigation really recognized the multiple oppression and the magnified marginalization that occurs when race and gender are combined, the current national conversation around affirmative action would be altered. The here and now climate surrounding personal liberties and access is not that different from the Bush-Regan era when *Blacklash* was acceptable and women were to remember their proper place. During George W. Bush's two terms in office, again, there has been a trend toward appeasing traditional yet contradictory American ideologies of justice for all, while subordination, hegemony, individualism, and competitive self-interest are all in heavy rotation. Since assuming the presidency, Bush attempted to project the "compassionate conservative" image of being so-called pro–affirmative action but antipreferences. His replacement for the chair of the U.S. Civil Rights Commission, Gerald Reynolds, was previously counsel for the Center for Educational Opportunity, a conservative think tank. Reynolds replaced Mary Frances Berry, who served for over two decades on the U.S. Civil Rights Commission and was considered by many to be a staunch advocate for social justice, unlike Reynolds who is more interested in perpetuating individual rights and competitive self-interest.

President Bush was precise, if not strategic, in swinging the pendulum of opportunity in a counterproductive fashion. This is evident in his political appointments from Reynolds to U.S. attorney general John Ashcroft. Accordingly, it is essential that more studies weigh the costs and benefits of access policies such as ADA, Title IX, and especially affirmative action. In considering the continuum of access and difference, it is central that research addresses how oppression occurs in the form of selective, unequal access (as per our discussion on Critical Race Theory (CRT) in chapter 3, pp. 62–65) and fully analyzes how power and privilege operate in educational institutions as microcosms of society in general.

Tate (1997) suggests that when studying the politics of education at the intersection of the color line, it is incumbent upon researchers to "find theoretical frameworks that allow for an expansive examination of race that moves beyond those associated with the inferiority paradigm"(p. 236). Various themes, messages, and potential findings emerge when considering access policies alongside state politics and social inquiry. Taking into account new directions for research on access policies, similar though very different from CRT, the following theoretical frameworks illustrate the need for voice and the necessity of deconstructing White patriarchal hegemony and the presumed authority and entitlement of the dominant culture.

Aside from the social stratification theory and status attainment theory discussed in chapter 4, the conceptual underpinnings of the following perspectives have received little, if any, attention relative to studies on affirmative action. Thus, there may be some heuristic value in shaping, as well as scrutinizing, the research tradition to date through an alternate lens that could see how social oppression is perpetuated by policies, procedures, programs, and practices that are based on race/ethnicity, gender, and class, along with other cultural categories.

Political Culture Theory

Fowler (2008) provides a theoretical perspective on the political nature of culture that is very suitable for educational researchers interested in social inquiry on access policy. For a little over 40 years, affirmative action has been a political issue. National opinion polls and social scientific studies have attempted to gauge the country's stance on public policies such as affirmative action as well as on other political subjects, including busing, abortion, welfare, and the death penalty. Fowler states that political culture is the way one's beliefs about proper policy and appropriate action merge into a collective response and way of viewing politics and the political process. The three indispensable political cultures found in the U.S. are (a) traditionalistic, (b) moralistic, and (c) individualistic.

Fowler describes the traditionalistic culture as one that seeks to maintain the current social order and not seek change as it interrupts the established status quo. Conservative government is viewed positively by this culture. The traditionalistic culture flourishes in conservative pockets of the United States, including the states of Alabama, Florida, Georgia, Louisiana, Mississippi, Texas, and Virginia. It is no coincidence that the aforementioned states have a political culture with documented histories of discriminatory practices in education, employment, housing, and voting.

The moralistic political culture appreciates active participation in politics and considers impartial implementation of public policies favorable. The government is viewed as a body that should seek to improve American life and uphold egalitarian American ideologies (Fowler, 2008). In association with affirmative action, the moralistic culture has been under attack in the 25 plus years since *Regents of the University of California v. Bakke* (1978) rendered race as one of several factors acceptable in admissions. States exhibiting a moralistic political culture are those with institutions of higher education that have been under the most scrutiny for their activities in attempting to affirm access for all state residents, including California, Michigan, and Washington.

The third political tradition is the individualistic culture. This political culture runs parallel to the paradoxical nature of America to promote individualism yet cling to democratic ideals of egalitarianism, which exemplifies the contradiction in theory and practice. Alaska, Hawaii, and Nevada are examples of this culture. At the root of an individualistic culture is capitalism at its best and the belief that the function of government and the role of politics are primarily to serve individual economic gain. Affirming access is not considered the role of government, as there should be little, if any, intervention on behalf of securing access; individuals need to pull themselves up by the boot strap and attain some level of personal success themselves.

Concerns Theory

Frances Fuller (1969) created an area of research she referred to as *teacher concerns*, whereby she proposed three phases of concern: preteaching, early teaching, and late teaching phase. The preteaching phase is marked by little, if any, concern with the specifics or involvement in teaching. The early teaching phase is a self-absorbed period concerned with teaching preparedness, adequacy, and disciplinary control. Conversely, the late teaching stage is characteristic of master teachers whose main concern is their students' actualization and the exchange of teaching and learning.

From Fuller's work regarding experienced and inexperienced teachers, the Concerns-Based Adoption Model (CBAM) evolved (Hall, Wallace, & Dossett, 1973). This model sought to more fully understand and describe the process of change in educational settings. More specifically, the model offered diagnostic tools to assess where people in the organization stood in relationship to adopting change or innovation.

Hypothetically, the CBAM should assist leaders in the diffusion of innovation by ascertaining the interventions necessary to facilitate change efforts. Hall, George, and Rutherford (1998) built on Fuller's CBAM, forwarding the Stages of Concern About Innovations. In essence, they argued that "depending on one's closeness to and involvement with an innovation, one's concerns will be different in type as well as in intensity" (p. 5).

With regard to access policies, for example, affirmative action is the innovation to address inequities in access. Individual's perceptions regarding affirmative action stimulate their level of concern, mental anguish, or worry about the personal impact of the policy. Often, everyday people experience varying concerns that differ in intensity because of their frame of reference.

This frame of reference may not mirror the reality of affirmative action, resulting in an individual's inability to mentally contend with race-conscious and gender-specific initiatives.

Liberal Egalitarian Theory

Connected to liberal egalitarian theory is the concept of valuing and upholding democracy in a manner that is indicative of equal access and opportunities (Dworkin, 2000; Howe, 1997). This conceptual base holds that the compensatory nature of education is a mandatory means of achieving social justice and eradicating past discrimination. Hence, from a liberal egalitarian theoretical perspective, until victims of previous racial/ethnic discriminatory acts and behavior have been compensated, affirmative action is necessary.

This conceptual framework would be helpful in examining the social utility of affirmative action, as it is a mechanism for realizing a representative democratic system. A theory such as this counters dehumanizing conceptualizations of people of color and women by offering to remedy the damage inflicted by the status quo in the workplace and in education. The intentions of affirmative action policies within the context of the liberal egalitarian theoretical perspective would explicitly call neoconservatives' political agendas into question, with their racial injustices and the participatory idea of equal access not being realized.

Restorative Justice Theory

Present social conditions call for critical examination of the sociopolitical context with regard to ethical and moral dimensions that have been absent in American race relations. If we had a true American democracy, the vestiges of discrimination would not continue to surface, nor would the need for cultural restitution to restore justice. As a framework to address the intent of affirmative action, the theory of restorative justice is a viable option in conceptualizing the compulsory, obligatory reassurance and reparation that mainstream organizations should embrace in affirming diversity.

Restorative justice is "fundamentally concerned with restoring relationships, with establishing or re-establishing social equality in relationships" (Leung, 1999, p. 1). The concept of restorative justice originated from aboriginal justice teachings, faith communities, prison abolition, and alternative dispute movements (Leung, 1999; Zehr, 1990). A criminal law perspective describes the aims of restorative justice as identifying the needs of individuals and turning wrongdoings into solutions for healing the harm done, however unintentional.

At the root of restorative justice is an acceptance of the wrongdoing and/ or acknowledgment of the harm endured. Within the context of White privilege and entitlement, race-conscious affirmative acts tend to engender blame shifting, as America's ugly truths regarding inequality and oppression are secondary to the personal social injury of feeling less empowered. Triandis, Bontempo, and Villareal (1988) describe what they term *individualist* and *collectivist cultures*. Individualist cultures, including those of European descent, carry more of a retributive lens and an adversarial battle mode in dialogues on affirmative action. The imposition of feeling ignored or victimized as a White person is not considered normative in this society. There has never been a collective denunciation of the harm that slavery inflicted and its continued effects, nor do White contemporaries feel any responsibility for resolution. According to its critics, affirmative action is not restitution but another social injury that is fragmenting America to put group rights ahead, or in place of, individual rights (Lopez-Vasquez, 2005).

In understanding restorative justice as a framework to assess White attitudinal opposition to affirmative action, it is not surprising that few are satisfied with a system that is expanding to empower those most alienated when competitive and individualistic values have been the norm. By searching for processes that aim to reconcile the scar of race in U.S. society, mainstream America assumes win-lose outcomes as opposed to seeing greater balance in the social order. As collectivist cultures, generally speaking, people of color have a central need for social injuries to be repaired, for Whites to acknowledge that they have the complexion for protection from being ignored and/ or oppressed, and that they hold some partial responsibility in restoring race relations.

The communalism of many racial/ethnic minorities is also spiritual in nature, in its coalescence with the reality that a community has been hurt. According to Ross (1996), the spiritual connection of restorative justice and the law is illustrated in the term *shalom*, which biblically refers to feeling a sense of peace, wholeness, and overall well-being. Traditional aboriginal teachings explain that there are varying perceptions of truth and events. When it comes to matters of truth, what is deemed fact or fiction is more often an individual's reaction to and sense of involvement with what is in question (Ross, 1996); therefore, what is considered true and real to one person is unfounded information to the next. The conversations brewing, as they relate to affirmative action, speak to the advocates and opponents of diversity initiatives not reaching a bipartisan compromise—the former, wanting to maintain and affirm formal legal safeguards for equalizing opportunities; the latter, confused about the legal processes and perceiving affirmative action as a reverse form of discrimination carried out in the name of diversity.

Acknowledging and Promoting the Panorama of Access

There are sound reasons why diversity is a compelling interest, and why public institutions need to be proactive in affirming access for a diverse group of students, workers, and society at large. In a global service economy with shrinkage in manufacturing markets, such as Michigan and the auto industry, failure to pay attention to the evolving demographic changes could be a socioeconomic and geopolitical disaster over the long haul. It is very clear from listening to the political campaign ads for the November 2006 elections in the state of Michigan that diversity is a powerful agitator that stirs up a major commotion in the policy discourse.

The generational career path of many Michiganders, which involves seeking employment within the auto industry in lieu of postsecondary enrollment, no longer equates to getting ahead or to a better life. Instead, this path provokes fears of an uncertain future and increased skepticism regarding employment prospects in an age of affirmative action. An endorsement of policy prescriptions is needed to affirm access for marginalized groups' post–*Gratz v. Bollinger* (2003) and *Grutter v. Bollinger* (2003). Questions that *should* be pressing for college/university leaders, company CEOs, and politicians alike are:

- How do we reverse the misconception that growing diversity is a problem and reframe the conversation from tokenism/preferences to accommodating diverse student learners who will enter a multicultural workforce?
- What can be done at the front end to maximize the potential of people of color, women, or people with disabilities?
- What can we do to create benchmarks of success for assisting people (particularly White males) in appreciating cultural differences as value added, and not exaggerate the intent of affirmative action or perceive non-White people as threatening to the dominant culture?
- How can we become leaders in this area by establishing organizational cultures that have a high regard for affirming access and not for just merely managing diversity?

Diversity at School and Work

The truth of the matter is that today's world contains more people of color, more women, larger numbers of older employees, and more individuals with disabilities than ever before. Strategic leaders acknowledge the need to employ activist leadership to affirm access and foster opportunities for the underserved. Change agents, who lead by example, must provide direction from the top, the middle, or the so-called bottom of the ladder of influence to affirmatively recruit and develop openings that can begin to establish parity in prospects for divergent groups.

The 21st century has witnessed dramatic changes in the perception of self and group positioning, the family unit, the structuring of work, and the role of education and technology in the global knowledge economy. In acknowledging cultural pluralism, accountability for challenging the socially stratified hierarchies that exist in American institutions is key to our survival and growth in a global community. Activist leaders must capture diversity as a compelling interest through institutional values and commitment to inclusion across a range of cultural group differences. Whether it is industry or the educational arena, leaders should be cognizant of the impact of diversity, or the lack thereof, on student outcomes, democratic citizenship, and profit margins. The means by which diversity is promoted and affirmed are the source of conflict for various stakeholders. The next chapter couches the affirmative action debate within conflict theory, proposing alternate strategies for taking action as well as new directions in race/gender relations that are relevant to maintaining diversity as a compelling interest.

Notes

1. General Motors, Ford, and Chrysler are commonly referred to as the "Big Three" for the automobile industry in the state of Michigan, though these rankings no longer apply. Toyota ranks number one, having surpassed each of the Big Three in sales and profits.

2. Quote from Steve Harvey during a live broadcast of the *Steve Harvey Morning Show* from Detroit, MI, on 92.3 FM, October 13, 2006.

3. According to the U.S. Census Bureau (2004), well over fourth-fifths of Detroit residents are African American/Black. There are about 700,000 registered Black voters in the state of Michigan; an estimated 611,000 of Michigan's Black registered voters reside in the city of Detroit. According to Montemurri, Arellano, Christoff, and McGraw (2000), Detroit's voting trend has become increasingly Democratic in correspondence with the large Black demographic. However, less than 50% of registered Detroiters voted in the 2000 and 2004 presidential elections, compared to 62% for the rest of the state's registered voters. On average, voter turnout is higher during national elections. Fewer Detroit and other Michigan residents cast votes during midterm elections, such as the November 2006 race, which had

the MCRI at the center of discourse (Lopez, Marcelo, & Sagoff, 2006). However, the percentage of Michigan midterm ballots cast varied by age. For example, the voter turnout for those 18 to 29 dropped from 25% in 1998 to 22% for 2002, whereas for voters 30 and over, voter turnout increased during the same period from 52% to 57%.

4. While African Americans had been prevented from voting in northern and southern territories, states such as Alabama, Alaska, Arizona, Georgia, Louisiana, Mississippi, South Carolina, Texas, and Virginia, the southern states, are among those with documented histories of discrimination that may indeed warrant additional dissection.

8

CONFLICT, DIVERSITY, AND ACTIVIST LEADERSHIP

C onflict is an inevitable and essential part of organizational life. According to Pondy, if an organization does not experience conflict, then it will essentially lose its ability to adapt to its changing environment (as cited in Holton, 1995a). Higher education institutions are not exempt from this conflict, which is pandemic to organizational culture across institutional types in academia. "In the late 1960s conflict emerged in its more violent forms and, although there has since been a marked recession in the resort to overt violence, there is little doubt that conflict remains a daily part of academic life" (Leslie, 1972, p. 702).

In spite of conflict being a common occurrence in higher education, and its potential for initiating positive change, the implicit or explicit norm is to ignore, minimize, or eliminate the presence of conflict in academe or to hope that conflict will miraculously disappear (Holton, 1995a; Leslie, 1972). There seems to be an incongruent relationship between individuals' treatment of conflict and the presence of conflict within higher education institutions. Although benefits may emerge from conflict situations, the norm is to essentially avoid it.

Philosophical Approaches to Conflict and Conflict Management

According to the classical view of organizational theory, conflict was initially treated and perceived as a phenomenon detrimental to organizations and their mode of production (Rahim, 1992). Given this assumption, managers were inclined to eradicate conflict. Certain organizational structures or controls, such as policies, were put in place within organizations to increase harmony, cooperation, and eliminate conflict. "In the 1950s, the organizational perspective on conflict was altered to the behavioral approach, which saw conflict as natural and which encouraged people to accept conflict as an inevitable part of working together" (Holton, 1995b, p. 7). The assumption that conflict was harmful and needed elimination still remained; however, individuals were expected to change their behaviors in order to handle episodes of conflict.

The modern view of conflict has departed from the original assumption that all conflict is detrimental to an organization and therefore is essentially a negative phenomenon. At present, the view of conflict is grounded in scholarship that underscores the need for conflict in organizations. Conflict provides a positive, irreplaceable social function for the organization; without it, the organization could not thrive, change, or survive (Holton, 1995b; Leslie, 1972; Rahim, 1992). Therefore, managers are encouraged to confront conflict and in some cases elicit it (De Dreu & Van De Vliert, 1997).

Although this evolution has taken place both in theory and in practice, higher education remains in the classical era. "Some within higher education are beginning to acknowledge the importance of this principled approach. Yet, in their perception of conflict, and the ways of managing it, many people are stuck in the pre-1950s traditional approach" (Holton, 1995b, p. 7).

Governance Models, Leadership, and Perceptions of Conflict

Negative perceptions and attitudes toward conflict are linked to notions of institutional governance models and leadership styles. In particular, three governance models are relevant: collegial, bureaucratic, and political. In Baldridge's *Power and Conflict in the University,* he "identifies . . . three models of university governance based on attitudes toward conflict" (as cited in Tucker, 1993, p. 400). According to the collegial model, conflict is not allowed and is considered abnormal. Individuals are expected to respect each other's humanity and to rationally approach disagreements as fellow scholars. Under this model, conflict is something that individuals attempt to eliminate. Ultimately, faculty view themselves as scholars who avoid engaging in behaviors that negate consensus building and a sense of community (Tucker, 1993).

The bureaucratic model, unlike the collegial model, does not seek to eliminate conflict but to control it. Conflict is perceived as abnormal, but if conflict emerges, allowances are made for it. Through policies and formalized organizational relationships, conflict is kept to a minimal and controllable level. For instance, large institutions and multicampus systems often employ bargaining tactics, where guides to organizational behavior are increasingly codified to fit the bureaucratic model (Tucker, 1993).

In the political model, conflict is considered normal and is an essential element of organizational life. Contrary to the community of like minds in the collegial model, diversity and heterogeneity are the norm. Parties are expected to experience conflict episodes before structural changes are made. The balance of power is constantly challenged by the forming and reforming of coalitions and interest groups. Hence, "effective bargaining is contingent upon having the political capital necessary to strategically negotiate and influence institutional decision making and policy agenda" (Tucker, 1993, p. 400).

In spite of the political model's application to higher education institutions, traditionally, various members of the higher education community, specifically faculty, have rarely engaged in political activity, such as lobbying or coalition building, either within or outside their respective institutions (Cook, 1998). Although higher education associations have increasingly engaged in political strategies and tactics to acquire government funding at both state and federal levels, college presidents and faculty continue to view politics as something "dirty" that runs counter to the codes of education (Cook, 1998). Therefore, in spite of the appropriateness of the political model, the prevailing norms and negative perceptions of political activity held by the higher education community hinder greater implementation of this particular governance model, which indirectly limits conflict. That is, if the political governance model is the only model that supports conflict as a normative behavior, then the tendency to eschew this model will also promote the avoidance of conflict.

Conflict—Principles, Process, and Strategies

One contentious issue in higher education is affirmative action. Institutions of higher learning have waffled back and forth on diversity initiatives based on the ebb and flow of societal opinion. The fact remains that higher education has been the battleground for struggles waged by opponents who wish to eliminate any form of opportunity targeting underrepresented minority students. More important, the debate over practices and policies that use race and/or gender in admissions, as well as for scholarships, student services programming, and faculty/staff hiring, demonstrates that affirmative action initiatives in higher education elicit strong disagreements to intractable value conflicts (McPherson, 1983; Steele & Green, 1976). Both popular and scholarly writings have asserted this tension (Edley, 1996; Tierney, 1997; Witt, 1990). Given the natural adversarial connection that arises when issues of racial diversity in higher education are addressed, campus leaders would be well served to better understand the nature of conflict, its process, and response strategies.

Toward a Definition of Conflict

"The term conflict has no single clear meaning" (Rahim, 1992, p. 15). Since conflict has been studied in a variety of disciplines, including sociology and psychology, the term has lacked precision. According to the definitions cited in the conflict literature, conflict can be a struggle, a situation, or a process. Donohue and Kolt (1992) described the interference of goal attainment by interdependent people seeking to satisfy their own needs and self-interests. Both Thomas (1976) and Tucker (1993) defined conflict in terms of a process whereby one party attempts to hinder or prevent the other party from fulfilling its needs or accomplishing its objectives. For the purpose of this discussion, as it pertains to affirmative action in higher education, we rely on the definition forwarded by Rahim (1992), "Conflict is defined as an interactive process manifested in incompatibility, disagreement, or dissonance within or between social entities, including individuals, groups, and organizations" (p. 16).

Conflict Levels, Strategies, and Processes

Different concepts posed in the conflict management literature provide useful frameworks that aid leaders in understanding the anatomy of a conflict scenario. In particular, Filley's six-element model of conflict (Holton, 1995a, p. 82), Blake and Mouton's (1970) conflict management grid, and Donohue and Kolt's (1992) seven levels of conflict and tension all bring to light different aspects and perspectives of the conflict process.

   Donohue and Kolt's (1992) levels of conflict and tension are a) no conflict, b) latent conflict, c) problems to solve, d) dispute, e) help, f) fight/flight and g) intractable. Given the characteristics that Donohue and Kolt ascribe to these seven levels, they all characterize the various levels of conflict and tension that leaders face when advocating for change pertaining to racial diversity and inclusion. In particular, at the fight/flight level of conflict, parties' "emotions intensify because, by the time the conflict has reached this level, personal needs, important values, or major principles have become the exclusive focus of the conflict" (Donohue & Kolt, 1992, p. 16). Although intensified emotions may not be exhibited by institutional leaders, the institution's values and principles are expected to play a central role in sustaining or terminating the conflict. Subsequent to intensified emotions, battle is declared, strategies for winning are developed, and the assistance of others is requested (Holton, 1995b).

Intractable conflict is essentially the level where "parties involved see themselves as 'doing the right thing.' Their cause is to bring justice to the situation, not just to defeat the enemy. Each side, of course, sees his or hers as the 'just' one" (Holton, 1995a, p. 88). In connecting this level of conflict to affirmative action, parties engage in responses that include negative speech, speaking to the press, and other activities that make public their pro- or anti-sentiments as a means of soliciting others to share their views (Donohue & Kolt, 1992; Holton, 1995a). Given the public nature of the debate regarding the *Gratz v. Bollinger* (2003) and *Grutter v. Bollinger* (2003) cases, along with other affirmative action challenges, educational leaders need to become more aware of the levels of conflict that continually emerge from strongly advocating diversity and inclusion on their campuses.

Contrary to identifying levels of conflict, Blake and Mouton (1970) developed a 2 x 2 conflict management grid that outlines five primary strategies for managing conflict. The five strategies are avoidance, compromise, confrontation, cajolery, and problem-solving (Blake & Mouton, 1970). An avoidance response is exhibited if parties remain neutral or withdraw in order not to provoke conflict. If winning is the major goal, a confrontational response is exhibited when parties wish to fight it out and/or have a third-party arbitrate (Blake & Mouton, 1970). A compromise strategy is exhibited when parties bargain for what they want but are willing to make concessions. Essentially, cajolery is a smoothing over of the offending issue so that harmony and accord can exist (Blake & Mouton, 1970). Often previously held positions are recanted with this strategy. Problem solving is considered the optimal response because stakeholders are allowed to agree to disagree while still attempting to find middle ground through fact finding or binding arbitration. According to Blake & Mouton (1970):

> Whenever a man meets a situation of conflict, he has at least two basic considerations in mind. One of these is the people with whom he is in disagreement. Another is production of results, or getting a resolution to the disagreement. It is the amount and kind of emphasis he places on various combinations of each of these elements that determine his thinking in dealing with conflict. (p. 417)

After the development of Blake and Mouton's grid, subsequent conflict research provided different "names and conceptualizations" that stemmed "most directly from the work of Blake and his colleagues" (Thomas, 1976, p. 900). The revised conflict responses are enclosed in parentheses in Figure 2 (Holton, 1995a; Thomas, 1976). Potentially all five strategies of the grid may be operating in a university setting in order to advance diversity and affirmative action.

Filley's six-element model of conflict outlines the conflict process as consisting of the following:

1. antecedent conditions
2. perceived conflict
3. felt conflict
4. manifest behavior
5. conflict resolution or suppression
6. resolution aftermath (as cited in Holton, 1995a, 1995b)

FIGURE 2
Blake and Mouton's 2 x 2 Grid With Revised Conflict Strategies

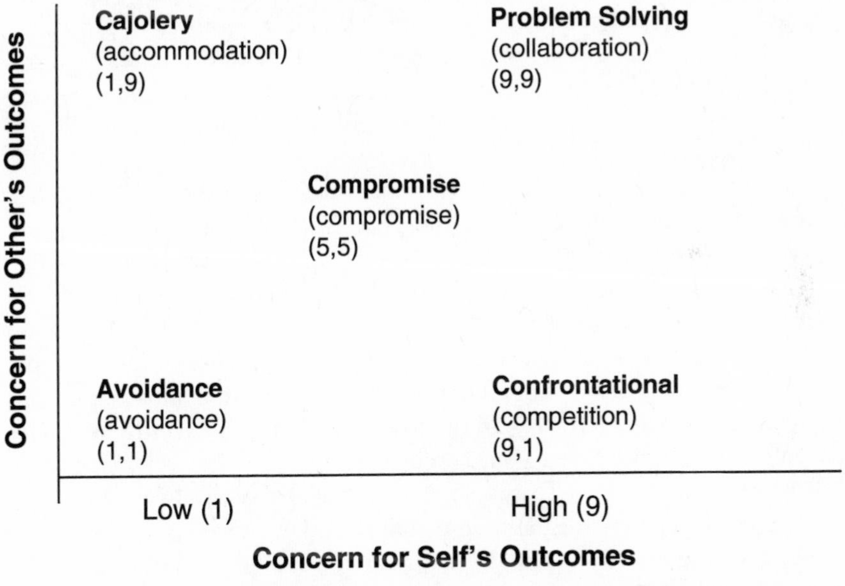

Cajolery (accommodation) (1,9)	**Problem Solving** (collaboration) (9,9)
	Compromise (compromise) (5,5)
Avoidance (avoidance) (1,1)	**Confrontational** (competition) (9,1)

Concern for Other's Outcomes

Low (1)   High (9)

Concern for Self's Outcomes

From "The Fifth Achievement" by R. R. Blake and J. S. Mouton, 1970, *The Journal of Applied Behavioral Science, 6*(4), pp. 413–442. Also from "Conflict and conflict management" by K. Thomas, 1976, In M. D. Dunnette (Ed.), *Handbook of industrial and organizational psychology* (pp. 889–935). Chicago: Rand McNally College Publishing.

However, conflict does not occur in a vacuum. The causal antecedents most prevalent in the post–civil rights debates are the issue and social context. In terms of the issue, arguments over affirmative action have manifested because of antecedent conditions that reflected a social context that countered the push for equity time after time. Subsequently, conflict emerged and over time escalated, over the fight for human and civil rights.

Filley "defined perceived conflict as a logically and impersonally recognized set of conditions that are conflictive to the parties; on a parallel track is felt conflict, personalized conflict relationship, expressed in feelings of threat, hostility, fear, and mistrust" (as cited in Holton, 1995a, p. 81). Similarly, the heightened perceived threat surrounding affirmative action is a conflict both perceived and real. As discussed earlier, Blake and Mouton (1970) provided five distinct responses to conflict, one of which is conflict resolution or suppression, whereby the appropriate resolution is sought or the conflict is suppressed (Holton, 1995a, 1995b). Please note that the conflict over diversity initiatives has ebbed and flowed but has yet to be contained, let alone be resolved. On both sides of the affirmative action dispute, the behavior exhibited is simply the action exhibited in response to the conflict. For example, the ballot initiatives in California, Washington, and most recently in Michigan portray reasoned action and planned behavior in response to protecting or abolishing affirmative action. The ensuing aftermath of the referendums to abolish affirmative action at a state level, has generated unintended outcomes that show positive and negative consequences as a result of the discord and conflict over diversity.

The conflict literature clearly provides several concepts that can assist educational leaders in navigating the post–*Gratz v. Bollinger* (2003) and *Grutter v. Bollinger* (2003) climate, while seeking to achieve access, celebrate diversity, and promote inclusion within their educational communities. In particular, Donohue and Kolt's (1992) seven levels of conflict and Blake and Mouton's (1970) conflict management grid detail responses to conflicts that require third-party arbitration. They propose that being combative, declaring war, determining how to gain the advantage, and soliciting the assistance of others are clearly linked with conflicts that need third-party arbitration (Blake & Mouton, 1970; Donohue & Kolt, 1992). Politically astute leaders will respond actively in negotiating conflict as they affirm diversity amid the adversarial litigious climate of affirmative action in higher education.

Activist Leadership: An Introduction

Armed with a better understanding of the conflict process and the acknowledgment that conflict is an important and integral aspect of the process of institutional change, an activist leadership paradigm is the frame that leaders must adopt to adequately confront the politics of affirmative access (equity and educational access).

Gratz v. Bollinger (2003) and *Grutter v. Bollinger* (2003) demonstrate that executive college leadership must be willing to confront divisive issues that threaten diversity, specifically racial/ethnic diversity, on its campuses, and not allow the press or activist opponents, such as CIR and CEO, to dictate practices and policies. Executive leaders have seen how students, faculty, administrators, board members, and external constituencies can easily become divided on issues that pertain to race and gender in higher education (Green, 2004a, 2004b).

As advocates of diversity, institutions must be clearly defined and maintained in light of the divisive issues. Retreating from a former position that is challenged or avoiding a conflict allows the opposition to gain ground and place the executive leadership on the defensive instead of the offensive. Unfortunately, some college leaders do not address diversity until a crisis or conflict has occurred, and then only by installing a committee or task force to commission a report (Green & Trent, 2005). Afterward, a program is added or a new position is created to oversee diversity-related matters. In the long term, these reactions can be helpful, but only if they are part of a larger campuswide effort and commitment.

Given the steady stream of lawsuits in the 1990s that challenged the constitutionality of affirmative action admissions policies in higher education, and the resolve of the country's affirmative action opponents to continue their campaign to eradicate any means of achieving equity and access for underrepresented minority students, it is crucial that executive officers and middle management understand the need for activist leadership to strategically steer their institution in a direction that best achieves diversity, affirmative access, and institutional change.

Responses to the Michigan cases, as well as other affirmative action challenges, have demonstrated varied approaches to defending affirmative access. Some institutions retreated from using race-conscious policies because of state referenda, successful legal challenges, or successful legal threats. Retreating did not force these institutions to give up on racial diversity as an important value; nevertheless, alternative strategies that required revising institutional policies often did not achieve the same level of racial diversity. Other institutions have stayed on course because they maintain an open admissions policy. And finally, institutions as defendants fought to maintain their right to employ race-conscious policies to achieve a racially diverse student body (Green, 2004a).

Steps Toward Activist Leadership

Activist leadership moves beyond simply stating that there is a commitment to equity, educational access, racial/ethnic diversity, and gender participation. It is a form of leadership that demonstrates through active engagement, within and outside the campus community, the importance and vital nature of building an inclusive community. To execute this form of activist leadership to affirm diversity, the following six steps are necessary:

Take a Clear Diversity Stance

Taking a clear position, followed by deliberate action, is the first step. Many have weighed in on the national debate on affirmative action, racial preferences, and equity in higher education (Chang, 2002; Edley, 1996; Green, 2004a; Zamani & Brown, 2003). Among those who have taken a stance, their perceptions and notions of racism, discrimination, justice, equal opportunity, and educational access dictate their positions, which influence the policies and practices they recommend for institutions. Those using a remediation or social justice lens argue that higher education institutions need to address the inequities that have resulted from institutional practices of discrimination and exclusion, which have systematically harmed underrepresented minority students (Feinberg, 1996; Green, 2004b). Ignoring the salience of race in dictating educational opportunity in today's society, opponents using the racial preferences lens argue that all policies and practices should be race neutral (Green, 2004a, 2004b; Rendón, 2005).

In light of these conflicting camps, it is crucial for college and university leaders to remain explicit in their language about the factors that shape the current landscape of higher education. The litany of affirmative access court cases has resulted in a wholesale retreat of the use of race, gender, and class inequality and equity in mission statements. Explicit use of such language demands accountability to students and the community at large. Providing an example of what this could potentially look like, the mission of the San Francisco State University, Institute for Civic and Community Engagement (n.d.), while not reflective of the entire university community, has drafted a statement that speaks to these concerns:

> Our mission is to bring faculty, students and specialized technical assistance from our premier urban university together with city and county agencies, nonprofit service providers, policy makers, other educational institutions, neighborhood residents and planning groups to address the

most critical social justice issues of San Francisco and the Bay Area: equitable access to education, economic and community development, affordable housing, nutrition and health, workforce analysis and preparation, urban environmental issues, welfare reform, poverty, homelessness, disability and violence. (para. 3)

As most university mission statements would not read this explicitly, it is imperative that the framework is graphic in describing institutional responsibility and commitment in meeting the needs and concerns of the larger community.

Craft and Articulate a Clear Message to Campus Constituents

With a stance taken, an activist leader should craft a clear message regarding the importance of the institutional values of diversity, equity, and educational access, followed by delivery of the message to the campus community and external stakeholders. The message should be informed by the emerging diversity research and complemented by the institutional mission statement and discussions regarding the implications for institutional responsibility in a democratic society. Nancy Cantor, president and chancellor of Syracuse University, sends a strong message regarding the importance of engaged scholarship at the university level. From the university's homepage, Cantor (n.d.) communicates the following statement to campus, as well as external, constituencies:

Syracuse University encourages *scholarship in action*. On campus and off, our students and faculty are deeply engaged with practitioners in the field and with communities at home and abroad, addressing vital issues and making discoveries that can change the world.

Other leaders have also articulated a clear diversity message to their respective campus communities. At the 2006 State of the University Address and through subsequent e-mail communication to the entire University of Nebraska-Lincoln (UNL) community, Chancellor Harvey Perlman (2006) articulated his diversity message and communicated that diversity is a campus community endeavor.

Slowly but surely this campus is beginning to look more like the people we serve. We have exceeded the average of our peers in the percentage of women faculty. Our recent recruitment efforts have demonstrated that this campus can be an attractive place for undergraduate students of color.

These successes should give us confidence and renewed energy to focus on our continuing shortcomings: recruitment and retention of faculty of color in all disciplines, increasing the number of women and faculty of color in those disciplines in which they are under represented, addressing the particular difficulty of attracting graduate students to many of the science and engineering based disciplines.

The most important ingredient for success in achieving diversity is the commitment of decision-makers to make it happen. Consistent with our efforts in strategic planning, a new proposed diversity plan for the campus has been crafted and it will be made available for your comments with the hope we can arrive at a common set of objectives and priorities. The campus leadership, with the assistance of the deans, will also be reexamining how we use those funds available to us to support diversity with the hope that we can make our efforts even more effective. (p. 4)

According to Perlman, the message is clear. An assessment of diversity reveals successes and shortcomings at UNL; hence UNL has not reached its potential with respect to racial/ethnic and gender diversity. However, these shortcomings provide teachable moments as opportunities for decision makers and the broader campus community to stay the course in terms of their commitment to realize diversity's benefits. Cantor and Perlman demonstrate that executive leaders should not shy away from crafting and articulating messages that describe the institution's purpose as well as serve as a call to action.

Educate the Press/Media

An activist leader proactively approaches the press/media regarding the importance of racial diversity. By approaching the press rather than defensively responding to awkward inquiries, terms of the debate or story line can potentially be dictated by the institutional leader versus the journalist who needs to create a story. However, leaders must not assume that one encounter with journalists, editors, or media personalities will guarantee that the institution's diversity, access, or equity message is heard. Hence, the media should be approached on multiple occasions to educate journalists and help them understand the issues and importance of the institutions' diversity initiatives.

One example of engaging the media could come in the form of extending an open invitation to the press for any open meeting or discussion on issues of racial diversity, class, or gender. Where some would view this as having the potential for the spread of negative publicity, it can be seen as the contrary. Such invitations would quell the issue of the institutional leader worrying about responding to negative inquiries. Instead, the open invitation serves as a preemptive measure that has the ability to change how diversity arguments are framed. Coupled with an explicit stance on diversity, the press could be used as a potential ally. Furthermore, the internal public relations staff should be educated and knowledgeable of diversity issues and concerns to assist the institution in spreading its diversity message. Debriefing public relations staff on a regular basis and requiring a senior-level public affairs administrator to coordinate communication between executive officials and public affairs units regarding diversity and related story lines are key strategies for educating the press/media.

Encourage and Participate in Ongoing Dialogues

Unfortunately, discussions on tough topics that concern minority students and other disenfranchised student populations arise from adversarial situations requiring ongoing dialogues structured to improve campus climate. If executive leaders would encourage their respective campuses to engage in ongoing diversity dialogues through semiannual Web casts, annual conferences, or retreats, and provide funding to support such activities, then students, faculty, and staff would have opportunities to voice their multiple viewpoints on issues that affect the entire community in a safe setting. The ongoing dialogue, while creating a forum for proactive solutions, provides students, faculty, and the administration an arena to identify issues before they reach crisis level. If dialogues are maintained and supported through underwriting by university units, the university community develops a culture to address diversity issues of immediate and long-term concern.

Along with underwriting diversity dialogues, activist leaders should participate as well. Given that participation entails listening to the various perspectives of one's campus constituencies, ongoing dialogues should provide leaders with an intimate knowledge of their campus's strengths, needs, and shortcomings with respect to building a more inclusive community.

Use a Leadership Team Approach

Oftentimes the president, chancellor, or dean is designated as the executive leader. However, in spite of this natural designation, a team approach toward activist leadership will provide more benefits. For those leaders committed to enforcing affirmative access, diversity, and inclusion, enlisting the assistance of others to help manage campus diversity makes the enterprise achievable. Such approaches ensure the fact that issues of diversity are not passed on to "diversity committees" or benign university administrative units that become isolated, marginalized, or ghettoized by university bureaucratic structures.

The leadership team approach has been used to implement the 5-year diversity plan (2001–2005) for the College of Education at Ohio State University. More specifically, the college has a system in which each school has a diversity committee and a diversity school coordinator (Hodge, S., personal communication, May 25, 2006). The diversity school coordinator serves as a member of the collegewide diversity team. Additional support for the college's diversity implementation policies bolsters this team approach, including direct support from the dean's office and faculty involvement. The salient point to be made, however, is that the college instituted a system that does not leave diversity and equity to chance but has built them into the organizational structure of the college as a means of carrying out the diversity plan.

Revise or Correct Failed Practices

Institutional leaders have relied on age-old standard policies and practices to address the divergent needs and interests of a changing student body. These policies, programs, and problem-solving approaches of the past do not address the contemporary issues and conflicts of a diverse, inclusive campus. Leadership must revise or correct failed policies and practices, including those surrounding financial aid and admissions, to advance the institution's diversity effort. Even private schools have changed a few policies. For example, Harvard and Princeton eliminated their early admissions programs because it gave an unfair edge to students who are advantaged.

Maintaining a biannual audit of campus programs and their impact on campus climate can aid leaders in correcting poor practices and redirecting resources to foster a campus environment that values everyone in the community. Such audits should include interviews with staff and student employees responsible for diversity initiatives. Interview and survey data that assess student, faculty, and staff's campus experiences should also be incorporated. Last, and most important after each audit, university units responsible for diversity initiatives should be responsible for creating an action plan to correct failed strategies.

Practical Policy Recommendations for Affirming Access

The U.S. Supreme Court upheld diversity as a compelling interest, and it should be a priority of every state to bring the best and most talented into their institutions of higher learning and into their public employment sector.

Diversity is here to stay, so American institutions need to ensure that all their citizens are brought into the full fold of participation; that means the first-generation, poor Hispanic migrant student with the artistic eye; the young White honor roll student, with aspirations to be an equestrian, who is bused from a low-income rural community to a magnet school; and the African American veteran with a disability who still doesn't get fair consideration from potential employers. We can all seek to better understand the very tangible reasons why cultural pluralism should be one of our top priorities. Meaningful diversity is a strength not a weakness.

Institutional strategies should focus on upholding diversity and defending affirmative action, as opposed to cultivating homogenization in education and the workplace. Educators should seek a more complete understanding of the relationship between affirmative action, diversity, and student outcomes. Gurin, Nagda, and Lopez (2004) maintain that it is through a diverse student body that all students experience a real education, one that can only come from cross-racial socialization and heterogeneous intergroup contact. The following policy and program recommendations are for the activist leader committed to affirming diversity at institutions of higher learning:

- **Deal With Precollege Factors**—Address college readiness with underserved groups, as there is a disproportionately high placement of African American and Hispanic students in special education and in need of remediation at the postsecondary level.
- **Step Up Outreach Initiatives**—Encourage people of color, women, and people with disabilities to apply for admission or employment at your institution. Place less emphasis on ACT and SAT scores, highlighting how narrowly merit is defined in terms of strict numerical standards without considering a wide range of other factors.
- **Intensify Recruitment Efforts**—Target potential students as early as the middle grades in racially/ethnically diverse communities. Partner with local K–12 districts and community colleges, capitalizing on the sizable number of transfer students to facilitate greater participation from underrepresented students across disciplines.
- **Scholarships**—Seek guidance and take note of the University of Michigan (*Gratz v. Bollinger*, 2003; *Grutter v. Bollinger*, 2003) cases by exploring diversity-conscious forms of financial assistance. Keep in mind, however, that the programs should be configured to stand strict scrutiny and be narrowly tailored. For example, several institutions

have made commitments to provide financial assistance to promising
students who have been admitted but have very little financial means.

- **Mentoring Approaches**—Infuse service-learning activities in the curriculum and volunteerism through student affairs to reach out to students from disenfranchised groups within disciplinary areas or along
other interests. With a small commitment, prospective students will
be more apt to feel an affinity for attending college and affirmed in
their decision to pursue higher education.
- **Look Abroad**—Affirmative action doesn't exist in a vacuum. Investigate what other countries are doing to adequately reflect the distribution of their societies across groups. Though the past discrimination
and histories of oppression may not align, insights could be drawn
from a comparative perspective of how higher education and industry
outside of a Western context seek to affirm diversity.

There are important implications for failing to accept differences in race/
ethnicity, gender, class, and other cultural group characteristics, including
color, national origin, language, disability, religion, and sexual orientation.
We can all derive maximum value from the rich cultural pluralism that exists
when diversity is affirmed. The institutional environment can foster optimal
outcomes for students and employees when there is a consideration of diverse viewpoints and a structure in place that can uphold cultural values that
are pluralistic.

Challenges to Activist Leadership

Acknowledging that diversity can be defined in many ways, fostering an inclusive campus culture that embraces all forms of diversity can be difficult.
But because of *Gratz v. Bollinger* (2003) and *Grutter v. Bollinger* (2003), there
is more political and public support affirming the importance of diversity
in education. Given increased support for access and diversity, an activist
leadership style can capitalize on the present sentiment to establish or revisit
a strategic plan geared toward developing an inclusive institutional culture.

Since taking on an activist leadership style is likely to engender conflicts
rather than deter them, several higher education scholars and former executive officers have proposed that individuals in designated leadership roles
should learn to understand, analyze, manage, and use conflict (Shaw, 1988;
Tucker, 1993). Understanding the nature of conflict and how it operates is a
basic first step toward responsible conflict management. One's attitude must
also incorporate the positive aspects of conflict and recognize that conflict is

necessary for organizational change, especially in the context of diversity (Shaw). "Social institutions, at least in diverse societies, thrive on conflict, and a wise leader recognizes this" (Shaw, p. 54).

Although institutions have gradually added more programs and policies to handle conflict, including offices of diversity, campus diversity commissions, and hate crime policies, the classical perception of conflict still remains (Holton, 1995a). Individuals continue to view conflict primarily as a negative phenomenon that causes hurt feelings, havoc, and irreversible harm to units, groups, and organizations (Holton, 1995a, 1995b; Rubin, Pruitt, & Kim, 1994). Conflict is also considered "divisive, destructive, a time and energy waster, and more importantly, a destroyer of effectiveness" (Tucker, 1993, p. 397). In light of these negative attributes, what evidence is there to demonstrate that conflict is beneficial?

Positive conflict conditions and behaviors entail three essential elements: (a) the type of conflict, (b) the type of task being performed, and (c) behaviors in response to the conflict or conflict style behaviors. First, conflict has two important dimensions: cognitive and affective. Cognitive conflict is linked with cognitive disagreements related to performing a decision-making task. Affective conflict involves "personalized disagreement or individual disaffection" (Amason & Schweiger, 1997, p. 106). Cognitive conflict is beneficial, while affective conflict is negative. If a group is performing a problem-solving or decision-making task, then cognitive conflict will assist with the exploration of the diverse alternatives needed prior to making a decision or choosing a solution.

Second, the types of task groups or units should engage in are complex and nonroutine in nature (Jehn, 1995, 1997). These types of tasks complement cognitive conflict so that a positive relationship is likely to exist in order to generate a beneficial outcome or performance. Third, conflict styles of avoidance and suppression keep at bay potentially good ideas while the problem-solving approach elicits all ideas that may address the problem (De Dreu, 1997). In the higher education literature, Tucker (1993) and others (Feltner & Goodell, 1972) emphasize that the department chair, dean, president, or other academic leaders should aim to transform the conflict situation into a problem-solving task.

Finally, an environment of trust and openness must be established so that members of the unit, group, or organization feel free to engage in cognitive conflict without repercussions. The higher education literature echoes this sentiment. Leaders should establish trust and openness by actively listening (Holton, 1995a; Tucker, 1993). Amason and Schweiger (1997) stated that "management of conflict . . . must be exercised before decision making begins, through the establishment of a context that encourages open, frank and even critical disagreement but holds in check the natural tendency for disagreement to arouse personal animosity. . . . the critical responsibility for creating such conditions must fall disproportionately on the formal leader" (p. 110). Clearly, the leader is expected to create a safe environment for positive conflict to foster.

Activism and the Next Stage in the Battle for Civil Rights

> You do not wipe away the scars of centuries by saying: "now, you are free to go where you want, do as you desire, and choose the leaders you please." You do not take a man who for years has been hobbled by chains, liberate him, bring him to the starting line of a race, saying, "you are free to compete with all the others," and still justly believe you have been completely fair. . . . This is the next and more profound stage of the battle for civil rights. We seek not just freedom but opportunity—not just legal equity but human ability—not just equality as a right and a theory, but equality as a fact and as a result. (President Lyndon B. Johnson, June 4, 1965)

In delivering the commencement address at Howard University in the summer of 1965, President Johnson captured how race relations is a major source of conflict, articulating the necessity of legal and social remedies for stomping out discrimination and affirming access (Brunner, 2006a). Will leaders of the 21st century also unapologetically embrace and uphold diversity? The complexities of the problems associated with affirmative action are appreciable, and activist leaders must multiply their efforts in being responsive to the post–civil rights crisis. In an effort to sustain opportunities and access during the millennium, a paradigm shift is necessary. Activist leaders acknowledge that affirmative action is not a temporary measure but a requisite policy agenda for the foreseeable future because of the changing demographics in the educational, economic, social, political, and legal realities of persistent unevenness. Business leaders and college and university administrators will have to be highly creative in repositioning policies and programs that will produce consistency in equal opportunities and rates of success provided to diverse populations.

While the elusive goal of having a color-blind society is utopian, in actuality the banner of preference has historically and contemporarily been held by Whites (males in particular), not racial/ethnic minorities or women. The outcome of the 2006 midterm election in Michigan is bound to have profound ramifications for race and gender relations in the state, as the average annual income for African Americans is $35,536 in contrast to $56,320 for Whites. Nationally, women earn 77 cents for every dollar earned by men, but in Michigan women earn 67 cents for every dollar that men make (Chapman, 2006). When national data are disaggregated, the wage gap illustrates that White women earn more on every dollar than women of color. Annual earnings by race and sex for 2006 show African American women making 64 cents for every dollar earned by White men, and Latinas earning 52 cents for every dollar earned by White men (U.S. Census Bureau, 2007). When considering the gender gap nationally and in the state of Michigan, there are within-group differences for males by race/ethnicity, as African American males earn 72 cents, and Latino men make 58 cents for every dollar earned by White men.

The above data highlighting the wage gap by gender and race/ethnicity illustrates how women maintain a subordinated status in American society, though they outnumber males. Across the country and in the state of Michigan women and people of color live in poverty at disproportionately higher percentages than the White populace. For example, in Michigan roughly one-third of African Americans in Michigan live below the poverty line.

The examination of gender and race exposes various social, political, and financial disparities and inequities. It is crucial as the numerical majority, that women achieve parity. It is through the continuation of affirmative action programs in education and employment that females can be encouraged to consider academic majors in traditionally male-dominated fields, enter nontraditional occupations, challenge pay inequities, and crack the glass ceiling. Also imperative as the United States moves toward a new majority composed of people of color over the next three to four decades is additional dialogue regarding affirmative action relative to the public and private good as a viable investment whereby the country as a whole reaps the benefits of equity.

Although there are payoffs in terms of individual and societal rates of return for breaking down barriers for talented females to compete, the progress of racial/ethnic minorities could reach a stalemate if institutions do not demonstrate a commitment to ensure access for those ready to vie for educational and professional opportunities. For a little over 40 years, despite the tumultuous climate surrounding affirmative action, hindrances to advancement were lessened for many African Americans and Hispanics. Nonetheless, a lag in participation and access in many educational and professional areas is still prevalent, as representation proportionate to the numbers of racial/ethnic minorities within the larger population is evident of modest growth and in some cases stagnation. In higher education in particular many students of color are not considered equal and are often separate, experiencing isolation by being subjected to malicious stereotyping and harmful harassment. This treatment further reinforces the abysmal state of cultural wounds and fractured race relations.

Michigan race relations have worsened since the passage of Proposal 2. In fact, business major John Andrews, a senior at the University of Michigan was met with racial antipathy one week following the election. Racial slurs were hurled at him via his Facebook.com account in reaction to his photo profile that featured a map of Michigan with "No on 2" printed across the picture in bold red font. The message posted to his Facebook account read, "No on 2 eh??? I'm a WOMAN and I say YES on 2!!!!! You must be a nigger" (Dziadosz, 2006). As told to *The Michigan Dailey* staff writer Alex Dziadosz, Andrews said the profile of the woman who instigated such ugly remarks confirmed that she is an employee of Rock Financial, Michigan's largest mortgage company. Andrews stated "I was taken aback. . . . it took me a few minutes just to work through those emotions. People see situations in history textbooks, but they aren't aware that this still happens now, all around them. It's not the first time I've been called the n-word, and I'm sure it won't be the last." Andrews forwarded an e-mail with the subject line "Messages of Hate" through the University of Michigan Business School's mass e-mail system to find that members of the African American community were not shocked as others revealed comparable hate messages. Sharon Vaughters, assistant to the dean of students, verified that within a week of the passage of Proposal 2, several complaints of maltreatment were reported, noting, "The passage of Proposal 2 has simply lent a new edge to the harassment that already exists on campus" (Dziadosz, 2006).

It is not surprising that forms of individual and institutionalized racism surface when considering the support base of proponents of Proposal 2. In soliciting support for Proposal 2, Ward Connerly courted White supremacist groups and encouraged political extremism. He was seen posing and shaking hands in a photograph with John Raterink while visiting Grand Rapids, Michigan. Raterink is the chair of the Michigan chapter of the Council of Conservative Citizens and a subscriber to the neo-Nazi newsletter produced by the National Alliance, which also supported Proposal 2. Connerly appears comfortable with wooing groups with racist ideologies and White supremacist agendas.

In an opinion column in Michigan State University's paper *The State News*, Notman (2006) opened with:

Imagine a group of people who promote white supremacy, anti-Semitism, racism, anti-Catholicism, homophobia and nativism. A group that outwardly hates blacks, Hispanics, Latino/as, Arabs, immigrants and homosexuals. A group that opposed the Civil Rights Act and desegregation. A group that has used violence, terror and intimidation to spread their evil message. You don't have to imagine, because the group exists. I'm sure you've heard of this racist organization I'm referring to—the Ku Klux Klan, or KKK.

Clearly Connerly was not exaggerating when he held that he would "accept support banning affirmative action wherever he finds it." He specifically avowed, "If the Ku Klux Klan thinks that equality is right, God bless them. Thank them for finally reaching the point where logic and reason are being applied, instead of hate."

Extra Steps in Sustaining Diversity

Immediately following the election, BAMN and other plaintiffs filed a suit on November 8, 2006, to challenge the scope of Proposal 2 and establish a new constitutional amendment to invalidate race/ethnic and gender classifications at the state level (i.e., *Coalition to Defend Affirmative Action By Any Means Necessary (BAMN), et al., v. Governor Jennifer Granholm, University of Michigan, Michigan State University, Wayne State University, et al.*, 2007). Proposal 2 had virtually the same ballot language as California's Proposition 209. It stated that affirmative action programs that served a compelling state interest could be contested and extinguished if not required by federal law. In other words, the state could lose federal funding if it did not enact affirmative action. However, numerous federal programs are specifically earmarked for women and racial/ethnic minorities, including the Summer Science and Technology Academy and the Registered Nurse Education Program, that require compliance as remedies to prior discrimination but were revamped or altogether dismissed in California following Proposition 209 (see *Connerly v. State Personnel Board*, 2001; *Coral Construction, Inc. v. City & County of San Francisco*, 2004; *Kidd v. State of California*, 1998; *High Voltage Wire Works v. City of San Jose*, 2000).

With supporters of Proposal 2 enjoying the passage of the state referendum to end affirmative action, Michigan's three largest public universities, the University of Michigan-Ann Arbor, Michigan State University, and Wayne State University, filed briefs with the federal appeals court during the first half of December 2006 to seek a delay of implementing the ban on affirmative action (Bell, 2006); the legal documents filed by these institutions were perceived as a "strategy to thwart the wishes of Michigan voters" according to Attorney General Mike Cox (Bell, 2006). Additionally, in trying to extend the time to implement Proposal 2, BAMN filed a request claiming that the measure would be in violation of the U.S. Constitution's equal protection clause.

Proposal 2 was slated to become effective on December 22, 2006, unless overturned in court. On December 19, 2006, David Lawson, a U.S. district judge in Detroit, found that in review of the pertinent issues, the universities should be permitted to delay instituting the ban on affirmative action until July 1, 2007, following the current admissions cycle (Wisely, 2006). However, in another motion of the legal contestation surrounding affirmative action, Eric Russell, a prospective applicant to the University of Michigan Law School, filed a complaint asking the appeals court to overturn Lawson's ruling to allow Michigan universities to delay implementation of Proposal 2. Also of note, the MCRI filed a brief requesting that Lawson's decision be halted in order to make all public institutions comply with the constitutional amendment to abolish affirmative action as approved by voters.

In an interesting turn of events, on December 29, 2006, an order from a three-member panel of the U.S. Sixth Circuit Court of Appeals in Cincinnati expressed that there was no plausible cause to delay the enforcement of Proposal 2 on the grounds of federal law (Patton, 2006). In its order, the Sixth Circuit rescinded the standing agreement made by Granholm, Cox, and Lawson on December 19, 2006, to permit admissions practices to remain unaffected until July 1, 2007. The briefs filed by the universities asserted that the immediate ban on affirmative action would have harmful effects to their current applicant pool, as their applications would be subject to a different set of rules than the ones that existed at the time of application. According to Patton (2006), the appellate court contended that it was inappropriate for any decision on the ban to come from the federal bench as opposed to working through the state courts. The undergraduate affirmative action procedures had already been altered following the *Gratz v. Bollinger* (2003) ruling to incorporate more comprehensive reviews, devoting greater attention to every application filed. For that reason, the University of Michigan employed additional admissions reviewers to copiously appraise all dossiers across a myriad of factors. In short, the University of Michigan's admissions staff poised themselves to alter their selection process midstream, as they had begun rendering thousands of admissions decisions and financial aid awards based on affirmative action programs that were forbidden from operation following passage of Proposal 2 (Williams, Schmidt, & Schmidt, 2007).

New Chapters in Race/Gender Awareness: The High Court Rules Again

The fight over the future of affirmative action will continue to have an impact on employment as well as on elementary, secondary, and postsecondary education. Another legal attack on educational diversity, filed in June of 2006, illustrates the ongoing nature of this battle. In the case of *Meredith v. Jefferson County Board of Education* (2006), America's K–12 system was effectively put on notice. The case was accepted on appeal as one of two cases (the other one being *Parents Involved in Community Schools v. Seattle School District*, 2006) that were slated to go before the U.S. Supreme Court. At the heart of each case was the question of whether diversity would still rule at the federal level, post–*Gratz v. Bollinger* (2003) and *Grutter v. Bollinger* (2003). The two cases challenged the use of racial guidelines in public school assignment in the absence of a desegregation mandate for the purposes of student integration by school districts in Louisville, Kentucky, and Seattle, Washington (Rawe, 2006; Schmidt, 2006). The *Gratz* and *Grutter* decisions will inevitably be revisited when determining whether racial classification serves as a compelling state interest in the diversification of schools to prevent patterns of resegregation (Schmidt, 2006; Tatum, 2007). However, with the anti-affirmative-action campaign still going strong, and the absence of liberal Justice Sandra Day O'Connor, it has been difficult to determine what the Supreme Court will rule, particularly in cases like *Crawford v. Huntington Beach Union High School District* (2002), which upheld legally required desegregation plans but found proactive measures to ensure integration unlawful if not mandated by law.

In late December 2006, final arguments were wrapped up in the *Meredith v. Jefferson County Board of Education* (2006) and *Parents Involved in Community Schools v. Seattle School District* (2006) cases. Advocates for affirmative action were hopeful that Justices Stephen Breyer, Ruth Bader Ginsburg, David Souter, and/or John Paul Stevens would maintain their resolve in affirming diversity as they did in the *Grutter* case, with Justice Anthony M. Kennedy as the projected wild card (Schmidt, 2006). However, the tide has continued to change as foes of affirmative action on the bench, including Chief Justice John G. Roberts, and Justices Antonin Scalia and Clarence Thomas, were projected to maintain that schools avoid considering race at all costs. On June 28, 2007, the Supreme Court in what is considered the most significant ruling on the use of race as a factor in education since *Grutter v. Bollinger* (2003), which upheld the consideration of race in college admissions, overruled Seattle's and Louisville's school desegregation programs that created racial targets for school admissions in a split 5–4 decision (Schwartz, 2007). The dissenting opinions that have come from *Meredith* and *Parents Involved in Community Schools* are primed to extend considerations of the benefits of racially diverse student bodies in K–12 and postsecondary education, while advancing race-conscious admissions in higher education.

Strictly for the Brothas

While race-conscious programs and policies are vulnerable at the state level, the susceptibility of current Black male initiatives that are gender-specific is also noteworthy. The knee-jerk reaction to gender-specific programming pointedly addresses female issues of participation, access, and outcomes. A grave concern has emerged in recent years at the intersection of gender and race regarding the status of African American males. As a result, there are new discussions about gender equity and its relationship to Black male masculinities in school contexts and educational outcomes. Zamani-Gallaher and Callaway (2006) emphasize that when looking at the participation figures for Black males in education, the workplace, the political landscape, health care, and other areas of social life, opportunities equal to those of their White male counterparts are not readily reflected.

The preponderance of research examining the nexus between gender identity, race, and schooling, with a focus on African American males, has been produced by Black scholars (Akbar, 1991; Boykin 1994; Brown & Davis, 2000; Cuyjet, 1997; Ferguson, 2000; Gibbs, 1988; Polite & Davis, 1999). These studies have stressed that Black boys and men are faced with severe issues that call for additional attention in the form of special programming and policy efforts. The research indicates that the situation is even direr for them than it is for their female counterparts. Many colleges and universities have sponsored forums, workshops, and conferences that seek to raise awareness about the unique circumstances facing Black males in the academy and society, including Eastern Michigan University's 2006 summit on The State of the African American Male in Michigan and the Empowerment Symposium: Investing in the Black Male, sponsored by the Indiana Commission on the Social Status of Black Males (2006).

Research and practical programs that seek to address the participation and outcomes of African American males in K–12 and postsecondary education acknowledge that Black male students are more often plagued by considerable at-risk factors, including low income, poverty, and lack of educational and economic mobility, than their White and Asian male counterparts (Akbar, 1991; Boykin, 1994; Brown & Davis, 2000; Cuyjet, 1997;

Polite & Davis, 1999; Zamani-Gallaher & Callaway, 2006). A significant percentage of non-Asian minority men are vulnerable to high unemployment rates, crime, being a victim of violence, alienation, teen pregnancy and incarceration, and young Black males are a considerable portion of this group. The aforementioned risk factors explain the less than desirable outcomes for Black males. One of the reasons often cited for the achievement gap and inconsistent school success of this group is the shortage of African American teachers in K–12, which, sadly, is often a result of the risk factors mentioned above.

Call Me Mister is a federally funded collaborative teaching scholarship program that involves public elementary schools with Benedict College, Claflin University, and Morris College, HBCUs in South.Carolina working in conjunction with Clemson University (Lewis, 2006). The program was enacted to tackle the problematic shortage of Black male teachers. The overall aims of the program include recruiting, attracting, training, certifying, and placing African American males in South Carolina's public elementary schools. The program emphasizes the role of mentorship and service learning in assisting participants to become civic-minded teacher leaders.

Other similar initiatives have emerged to mentor Black men and draw them into teaching careers, including Brother 2 Brother Program, Real Men Teach, and the Black Collegian Teaching Scholarship Program in states such as South Carolina, North Carolina, and Texas. Alternative teaching certification programs have also surfaced. Georgia's Troops-to-Teachers is a unique program that recruits military personnel seeking a career change or retirement from the military (Roach, 2003). It is the contention of advocates that special initiatives intended for Black males employ methods that challenge the traditional teacher education programs to be more inclusive by bringing in perspectives that are more encompassing of race and gender. New types of teaching personnel can rejuvenate the curriculum, breathe life into the conventional canon, and provide creativity in mentoring and facilitating enriching extracurricular activities. In effect, Black Male Initiatives (BMIs) can assist in lowering attrition rates, increasing high school completion rates, and persuading young Black male students to stay in school longer and pursue collegiate endeavors.

With headlines in the media such as "Missing: Black Men" and "Black Males an Endangered Species," it is remarkable that there would be less than favorable public support for efforts designed to increase the participation and educational outcomes of African American males (Ferguson, 2000; Gibbs, 1988). For example, Meyers (2008) contends that government is contradictory in stating support for the desegregation decision of *Brown v. Board of*

Education (1954) while reinforcing separate treatment and considers BMIs to perpetuate racial and gender stereotyping. Although there has been some modest government assistance to BMIs under George W. Bush's administration, it is arguable that programs such as these equate to fiscal mismanagement of public resources or create an even larger gulf in racial and gender divide.

In critiquing Bush's fiscal spending, de Rugy (2004) questioned whether Bush has really placed "hard caps" on federal spending. Moreover, de Rugy suggests that Congress does not employ exceptional budgeting restraint, citing irritation that Congress is still spending $250,000 to fund programs like Call Me Mister at Clemson University.

In October of 2005 National Public Radio (NPR) covered the Millions More Movement March, which was organized to garner greater attention for challenges such as high school dropout and incarceration rates among young Black men in America, and to provide a forum for solutions to these problems. However, other news media are not as interested in publicizing such events. In *The Washington Post*, columnist Michael Myers (2006) called for an end to "Black-Only Treatment," as BMIs are merely "race fads" aimed at saving Blacks from themselves by providing "special and separate attention." He states:

> Many black leaders in and outside academia seem to have no objection to these figurative black-only signs over certain doorways at America's colleges. Not surprisingly, this racial identity ferment—aka self-determination—is proudly endorsed by white liberals disturbed by the dwindling numbers of black men on campus, as well as by many black female students for whom interracial dating is either taboo or impracticable.
>
> Hence, college presidents are listening to their black students and to their officials for diversity and affirmative action or minority affairs and they are setting up BMIs as a way of making life on campus more comfortable for black students. And black faculty has a new source of grants to apply for, from foundations that urge the study of the black male problem and experimentation with intervention techniques. No educator rebukes such offerings with the hard, nonstatistical truth that there is no such thing as "the black male," just as there never was such a thing as "the Negro." (p. A21)

While Meyer's comments refer to BMIs at the postsecondary level, similar programs have targeted Black boys in K–12 settings including private Afrocentric male academies and public charter schools for African American boys. For many reasons, the basis for BMIs is arguable, as these efforts are seen by some as separatist agendas that segregate Black males. Others believe the mission of these programs reflects quality of intent to better serve this segment of learners.

As a spin-off of affirmative action, BMIs are being legally challenged. Schmidt (2006) reported in *The Chronicle of Higher Education* that a federal complaint was filed against the City University of New York (CUNY) by a New York civil rights group. The suit sought to block a BMI being proposed by CUNY's Brooklyn-based Medgar Evers College, asserting that it was in violation of Title VI of the Civil Rights Act of 1964 (Schmidt, 2006), prohibiting racial discrimination, as well as being in breach of Title IX of the Education Amendments of 1972 (Schmidt, 2006), forbidding sex discrimination by institutions of higher learning that receive federal assistance. Features of the BMI have already taken shape at CUNY's Queensborough Community College in the form of tailored academic advising, tutorials, and career services. Additionally, until a couple of years ago, CUNY's Hunter College hosted planning conferences that invited only African American male students (Meyers, 2008). The complaint filed against CUNY challenges that the planned efforts at Medgar Evers College to assist Black male students are discriminatory in nature and that they should be blocked prior to the formation of multiple programs throughout the university system and prior to mass replication in other university systems (Schmidt, 2006).

CUNY sought to implement a variety of programs targeting various campuses in support of its BMI. Medgar Evers College wanted to embark on this endeavor because of its staggering statistics of less than one-fourth of the student body consisting of Black males when over 90% of its student body is Black (Biorski, 2005). Similarly, at CUNY, York College, a mere 305 African American males are students in a student body that is over 50% male. The commitment of the university to increase the participation and completion rates for African American males was evident in the system's pledge to spend over $2 million on the program (Biorski). It is interesting to note as well that Black male students were not the only group that CUNY sought to assist. In September 2005 a cooperative program with Mexico was established to increase Mexican student attendance.

What's It Going to Be—Cellmate or Classmate?

The future of African American and Hispanic males requires attention. To ignore the sobering trends would be irresponsible. A social and financial contract must be drawn to ensure that the future of Black and Latino males is in classrooms and not in cell blocks. Smiles (2002) reports that incarcerating minority men costs two to three times more than educating them. Hence, a necessary redirection must occur to steer Black and Hispanic males toward postsecondary education.

Cottman (2005), writer for Black America Web, outlined the aims of the National Commission on the Black Male, established by the National Urban League to explore racial disparities in sentencing and other social trends that have an adverse impact on Black men. According to the National Urban League's 2005 report on criminal justice, four Black men are imprisoned for every three who attend college. The findings also reported that one in 20 Black men are incarcerated, compared with one in 155 White men; for Black males born in 2005, 29% can expect to spend some time in jail, and 1 in 14 Black children has a parent behind bars.

The National Center on Institutions and Alternatives (NCIA), a liberal policy think tank, released a report titled "Masking the Divide: How Officially Reported Prison Statistics Distort the Racial and Ethnic Realities of Prison Growth," arguing that there is an overuse of incarceration that is wreaking disproportionate harm on particular segments of American society (Holman, 2001). In examining incarceration rates from 1985 to 1997, the NCIA found that the prison population more than doubled in the United States with 70% of the growth stemming from convictions of racial/ethnic minorities in state and federal jails. More specifically, the 12-year study proved that while there was a 102% rate of increase for Whites put in prison during this period, the number of African American and Hispanic inmates rose by 180%. Also noted were the suspect techniques used by the government to estimate the inmate rates by race/ethnicity (Holman, 2001). For instance, data for Hispanic imprisonment was not disaggregated from non-Hispanic Whites, making the Black-White incarceration gap appear considerably smaller than it was actually. Whites are 9.1 times less likely than Blacks to spend time behind bars, and with the figures teased out Hispanics are 3.7 times more likely than Whites to be imprisoned.

National figures for 1997 reflect that Asians tend to be imprisoned the least of all major groups, while Hispanics made up 16% of the adult prison population; non-Hispanic Whites composed 34.8% of the prisoners, and African Americans were 46.9% of those jailed (Holman, 2001). Available 2005 figures on the racial dynamics in jailing from The Sentencing Project (2006) reveal that in seven states African Americans are incarcerated at more than 10 times the rate of Whites (Iowa, 13.6; Vermont, 12.5; New Jersey, 12.4; Connecticut, 12.0; Wisconsin, 10.7; North Dakota, 10.1; and South Dakota,

10.0). Also noted was that the lowest Black incarceration rate of 851 in Hawaii still outnumbers the highest White rate of 740 in Oklahoma.

The emergence of mandatory minimum sentencing in the 1990s worsened the already disparate and uneven rate of imprisonment. One result of mandatory minimum sentencing is the 93% higher average sentence for Blacks than Whites (Jones, 1994). By 2005 African American males were being imprisoned at more than six times the rate of White males and Hispanic males at double the rate (The Sentencing Project: Research and Advocacy for Reform, 2006). The negative consequences of one million plus Black males being under the thumb of the criminal justice system include but are not limited to revocation of voting rights, increasing single-female heads of households, and absentee parenting. Some might even argue that the plan of the power elite in constructing more prisons was to ensure Blacks cannot fully participate in society.

As the jail sentences thrown at Black males increase, the creation of additional social programs and public policies aimed at male offenders would be a laudable contribution in the effort to reduce recidivism rates. One way of curtailing repeat offenses is the presence of psychological counseling in prisons, in addition to educational training both during and after inmates' time served. In considering the important backdrop of Michigan to the national discussion on affirmative action, consider this fact: even though African Americans make up 15% of the population in the state of Michigan, they account for 56% of Michigan's prison population (Cottman, 2005).

In an article titled "Bar None: Extending Affirmative Action to Higher Education in Prison," Torre and Fine (2005) identify how the multiple forms of marginalization in higher education also exist in correctional facilities with regard to differential access to learning opportunities. As the original intent of affirmative action was to equalize and increase life chances for disenfranchised groups, the authors assert that affirmative action should be extended to prison populations. In their mixed-method study of the impact of college in prison, Torre and Fine surveyed prison faculty and interviewed inmates participating in the college program, former inmates, and the children of inmates, jail officials, and corrections officers. Additionally, the researchers conducted secondary data analysis of available recidivism rates. The overall findings from their study suggest that when prisons offer broad-based educational access for inmates that include psychosocial counseling, the results include lower crime-related activities, less psychological stress, and academic enrichment that positively affects the individual, the family, the community, and the larger society.

Access, Immigration, and Contemporary Civil Rights Concerns

Racial and ethnic realities fuel the growth of the prison industry as evidenced in the marked increases of African American and Hispanic men incarcerated. While the figures for African American men are the most discouraging, the growth rate of Hispanic men jailed is also troubling, given the shifting demographic landscape in the United States. As of July 1, 2004, according Bernstein (2005), the U.S. Census Bureau national estimates by race revealed that the Hispanic population numbered 41.3 million. In fact, Latinos/Latinas experienced close to a 4% population increase over a one-year period, three times the growth of the entire population. Over three-fourths of the estimated 11 million illegal immigrants in the United States are from Mexico or other Latin American countries (*Time*, 2006; Horwedel, 2006). This Hispanic population explosion has heightened negative racial affect through responses to affirmative action as well as recent immigration debates.

Barry (2005) offers that immigration restrictionists are seeking to influence public policy with ideological anti-immigration rhetoric, while others believe that immigration should not be stringently regulated. The Senate passed the new immigration reform bill on May 25, 2006, by a 62 to 36 vote, the Comprehensive Immigration Reform Act of 2006 (CIRA), which outlines the extent to which undocumented immigrants may seek employment and citizenship in the United States. Critics suggest that the provisions laid out in the new bill will present barriers to those attempting to become legal U.S. citizens (Barry, 2005).

Among the barriers to advancement for Hispanic immigrants are work and residence requirements. Thornburgh (2007) argues that amnesty is the "pariah term of the immigration debate," but contends that legalizing the illegals can work politically, will not further burden social service agencies, does not undermine the law, won't make illegal immigration rise, and will not depress American wages (p. 38). In discussing the challenges of illegal immigration in a small town in Illinois, Thornburgh states, "When Beardstown opened a bilingual program for all the kids in the elementary school, Hispanic parents were as worried as White parents about missing out on an English-only education. Assimilation is slow, but it is inevitable" (p. 39).

Immigration issues are also presenting obstacles to equal access that spill over into K–12 education for children of migrant workers. Additionally, debates swirl over whether undocumented students have a right to American higher education. The right to access higher learning, coupled with the high attrition rates at the secondary level for this steadily growing population, is problematic. By 2015, the undergraduate enrollment for Hispanics is anticipated to increase across the country by one million (Lane, 2001).

Perez (2002) reported that the largest drop in ACT scores was among Puerto Rican, Cuban, and other Hispanic test takers (from 19.4 to 18.8 points out of 36), and this drop was twice that of Mexican American students, the second largest group. The author suggests that there may be some correlation between the educational gap of Hispanic students and whether their parents are non-English speakers. Perez also mentions the need to raise academic expectations for school-age Latinos/Latinas. Latinos/Latinas who do find their way into academia, often enroll in community colleges. States such as Arizona, California, Florida, New York and Texas are expected to witness an increase of 1.4 million students, with nearly half the predicted growth coming from Hispanic populations (Lane, 2001). Hispanic community college students are two times less likely to go on to complete a bachelor's degree than their White counterparts (Horwedel, 2006). California has the highest percentage of Hispanic collegians (37%), followed by Texas (17%), Florida (8%), New York (7%), and Illinois (5%). The remaining 26% of Hispanics enrolled in college are spread out across all other states (Horwedel, 2006).

Immigration policies have been in desperate need of reform, however, some of the restrictions of the new policies penalize students who have spent the majority of their growing years in the United States, treating them like international students because of their undocumented status. One example of this is the argument over in-state versus out-of-state tuition. Nine states, including California, Illinois, Kansas, New Mexico, New York, Oklahoma, Texas, Utah, and Washington, have active laws that provide in-state tuition benefits to undocumented students, while other states, such as Alabama, Alaska, Florida, Mississippi, and North Carolina, have proposed legislation to deny in-state tuition benefits for undocumented students (Horwedel, 2006).

Perhaps the bipartisan Development, Relief and Education of Alien Minors (DREAM) Act will eventually become federal legislation as an amendment to the new immigration reform, or as another separate piece of related legislation (National Immigration Law Center, 2006b). On November 21, 2005, U.S. Senator Richard Durbin, a Democrat from Illinois, along with Senator Chuck Hagel, a Republican from Nebraska, and Republican Senator Richard Lugar, from Indiana, reintroduced this 2003 bill originally forwarded by Republican Senator Orrin Hatch of Utah. On March 27, 2006, the Senate passed the DREAM Act (S.2205) with little debate. Advocates of the bill claim that present laws are prohibitive and punitive for young people raised in the United States who attend American elementary and secondary schools but have no recourse for attaining citizenship given their parents illegal residency. Subsequently, they are then cast into limbo and considered immigrants because of their undocumented status. DREAM seeks to provide a mechanism to obtain legal residency for those who meet the following conditions:

- lived in the United States for five years or more
- moved to the U.S. at the age of 15 or younger
- graduated from a U.S. high school
- had no previous trouble with the law

For all of those meeting the above criteria, under the DREAM Act they would be permitted to apply for legal, conditional permanent residency (Horwedel, 2006; National Immigration Law Center, 2006b). In spite of the remarkable reform promised by the DREAM Act, the Senate Judiciary Committee stopped the proposed legislation in its tracks by a 52–44 vote on October 24, 2007, eight votes short of a filibuster.

On the battlefield of the immigration wars stands a rival proposal to the DREAM Act, which is the Border Protection, Antiterrorism, and Illegal Immigration Control Act of 2005. Also known as HR 4437, this proposed anti-immigrant legislation features measures that seek to further hinder the progress of undocumented people seeking citizenship and impede access to employment and schooling. On December 16, 2005, the U.S. House of Representatives passed HR 4437, which would make felons of any immigrants who are undocumented; according to regulations under HR 4437, direct violation of the immigration laws is punishable by a fine and one-year imprisonment. Those in jeopardy of becoming felons include (a) infants/children brought to the United States without a visa, (b) college/university honor students who fall short of maintaining the requisite course load as required by their student visas, (c) foreign business executives who do not notify the Department of Homeland Security of a change of address in writing within 10 days, and (d) hospitalized tourists with expired visas (National Immigration Law Center, 2006b).

In June 2007 the proposed Comprehensive Immigration Reform Act of 2007, or under its full name, the Secure Borders, Economic Opportunity and Immigration Reform Act of 2007 (Senate Bill 1348 and related Senate Bill 1639 titled, a bill to provide for comprehensive immigration reform and for other purposes), was initially designed to tighten border security and impose regulatory measures surrounding the use of migrant or temporary workers; it reached a standstill as the measure fell short of the required 60 votes needed to become a bill (Hirschfeld, 2007; Sullivan, 2007). Bush's support for Senate Bill 1348 as a compromise between legalization of illegal immigrants and increased border enforcement has caused it to be dubbed the "President's Immigration Bill." Had the bill passed, it would separate illegal immigrants into three categories:

1. those who have been in the United States more than five years could work for six years and apply for legal permanent residency without having to leave the country;
2. illegal immigrants who have been in the United States for two to five years would have to return to border entry points within three years but could immediately return as temporary workers; and
3. individuals in the United States less than two years would have to leave and wait in line for visas to return (Hirschfeld, 2007; Sullivan, 2007).

The DREAM Act (2007) would enact needed reforms, while HR 4437 (2005) could potentially undermine the goals of the proposed restructuring by imposing mandatory detention for certain illegal immigrants and forced deportation for those who have been here two years or less. The great absurdity of the anti-immigration movement and retrenchment on affirmative action is the nomenclature that highlights core American democratic values, when what is really being presented is counteregalitarian. As far as seeking a slice of the American pie, by the numbers Latinos/Latinas are a far larger force to be reckoned with when considering those most prominently affected by immigration issues; however, less obvious to the general public are White illegal immigrants who do not enter the country by crossing the borders clandestinely but enter legally without any intentions of returning following the expiration of their visas. Irish immigrants are one of the largest groups in this category. There has been a crackdown on this trend, however. One example was cited by columnist Kevin Cullen (2007) of the *Boston Globe*:

> A couple of months ago, David Knox and his girlfriend, Elaine, threw in the towel. After seven years in the Boston area, they were tired of looking over their shoulders, tired of being told there was no way they could become legal residents, and so they decided to move back to Ireland. (p. 1)

By comparison, Asian and Black immigration is receiving little attention in the news media and policy briefs. What is unmistakably existent, though plagued by inattentiveness, is the interaction of race/ethnicity and the immigration debates. Haitians and other groups seeking to flee dire circumstances in their homelands are all but turned around, treated as socially less desirable foreigners, and subsequently rendered invisible in immigration rights matters. As told to Charisse Jones (2006) in *Essence Magazine*, Mirdiane Chery immigrated to the United States from Haiti at the age of 10, and ponders why more African Americans are not involved in the debate on immigration, with the belief that more "faces like mine need to be represented too." The 19-year-old stated:

> I was speaking to an American friend who is of Haitian descent. He's a construction worker, and he was angry that illegal immigrants were doing his job for less money. So I understand to some extent why Americans are mad. But when immigrants are denied human rights—such as a livable wage—it has a ripple effect on all of us. (p. 164)

Immigrant status among people of color poses serious considerations regarding the goals of diversity, the purpose of affirmative action, and issues of access. In *Diverse Issues in Higher Education*, Banerji (2007) reported that data from the National Longitudinal Survey of Freshmen revealed that over 40% of Black students at elite Ivy League institutions are first- or second-generation immigrants; whereas Black U.S. natives constituted 13% of the overall Black student population at these selective universities. Little over 7% were of Latin decent, just fewer than 29% were from Africa, and over two-fifths of the Blacks of immigrant origin surveyed were Caribbean. However, most students were Jamaican (20%) and Nigerian (17.3%). The findings concluded that the attendance and outcome disparities between Black natives and Black immigrants were, in part, because of variations in parental educational attainment, religion, standardized test performance, and value orientation toward schooling (Banerji).

Policy Merger Anyone? Linking Immigration and Affirmative Action

In previous chapters of this book, it was noted that the earliest objectives of affirmative action were to eradicate the previous discrimination directed against African Americans, women and other racial/ethnic minorities. Very little notice has been given in the public discourse to the idea of amalgamating features of affirmative action with immigration reform to remove obstacles to advancement. Although affirmative action programs aim to counter pay inequity and increase employment and educational opportunities, discussions of addressing the limitations facing many immigrants (especially

Latinos/Latinas) via affirmative action programs are few and far between. Additionally, the frequent framing of affirmative action in Black and White implies that other people of color and women have not benefited from the policy. However, affirmative action has been very successful in facilitating the progress of all racial/ethnic minorities and women. Nonetheless, according to the National Asian Pacific American Legal Consortium, White men, who make up less than half of the U.S. college-educated workforce, continue to hold over 80% of the top positions in academia, contracting, corporations, government, law, and media (as cited by AffirmativeActionAdvocacy.com (n.d.). Hence, with the continued growth of immigrant populations, chiefly Hispanics, followed by Asians, public policies that address access and educational achievement for underrepresented multiethnic populations is critical if the United States is to remain globally competitive.

Graham (2001) emphasizes that affirmative action and immigration should not be treated as distinct, unrelated policies but instead should be linked. He further contends that major studies, such as the 1997 New Americans Study conducted by the National Research Council, examine immigration issues, yet steer clear of introducing a conversation that includes affirmative action policies and programs. In chapter 5 we discussed the parallels between affirmative action and ADA as two key pieces of civil rights legislation. Similarly, policy pundits have begun to find that the Civil Rights Act of 1964 corresponds with the 1965 Immigration and Nationality Act (Graham, 2001). There has been unanticipated convergence and unintended consequences of affirmative action and immigration policy since the mid-1960s (Skrentny, 2001). Moreover Graham notes, "The unique moral force of affirmative action's original public rationale, as a temporary remedy to compensate for the lingering, institutionalized effects of past discrimination against the descendants of slaves, was eroded when preferences were extended to newly arrived immigrants from Latin America and Asia" (p. 67).

While the literature to date includes numerous studies that investigate the attitudes of Whites toward affirmative action, as well as a body of work focusing on the views of African Americans, Asians, and Hispanics, as the intended beneficiaries, toward affirmative action programming, little inquiry has sought to disaggregate the views of Whites or people of color by citizenship status. Kravitz and Klineberg (2000) examined how affirmative action plans are perceived in the Houston area. The researchers surveyed 392 African Americans and 414 Whites. Additionally, the study evaluated the response of Hispanics to affirmative action as assessed in two groups: American-born Hispanics (162) and Hispanic immigrants (177).

Each of the groups in the Kravitz and Klineberg study were questioned regarding their views on traditional affirmative action plans that sought to increase diversity among the underrepresented. They were also asked about affirmative action practices that were framed as tiebreakers, which are conditionally applied when equal qualifications and underrepresentation are present. Their findings illustrated that African Americans and Hispanics were more supportive of traditional forms of affirmative action, while Whites showed a preference for the tiebreak model, because of differing beliefs about the procedural fairness of affirmative action. Additionally, the subjects in this sample varied in terms of their political leanings and perceptions of workplace discrimination. Particularly interesting among the results was perceived fairness being a predictor of support for traditional and tiebreak forms of affirmative action for all American-born respondents. The conclusions of the study suggest that in adequately determining the factors that predict attitudes toward affirmative action, separate analyses of each racial/ethnic group should be conducted.

Final Thoughts

In this multiracial society, a new ethnic order has emerged in the United States. What must be considered a thing of the past is the Black-White dichotomy; with the growing number of Latinos and Asians, this binary frame of reference does not accurately depict today's global community. Wu and Kidder (2006) shed light on how affirmative action has been largely framed as a Black and White issue stating:

> Yet like all Americans, Asian immigrants and their native-born children benefit from the modest efforts to include everyone in the American Dream. The misleading claims about Asian Americans are quite common. For example, in the 2003 Supreme Court cases involving the University of Michigan, even though the plaintiffs were White, their legal counsel obtained class action status to represent Asian Americans as well. They asserted that affirmative action harmed not only their Caucasian clients but "especially Asian Americans." (p. 48)

The authors argue that Whites benefit from a form of affirmative action that perpetuates a tradition of policies/practices that give an advantage to Whites while not seeking to achieve a critical mass of historically underserved African Americans and Latino. In addition, "White affirmative action" harms Asian Americans by treating them in a differential manner that holds them to a higher standard than Whites with similar qualifications (Wu & Kidder, 2006).

Revisiting public policies while being cognizant of social justice remains a challenge for mainstream Americans. Converging in the post–civil rights movement are highly loaded, heated controversies that span multiple access-policy agendas. It is hoped that this text prompted you to reexamine affirmative action and how it is framed.

The quest for equity in American society continues unabated. Unfortunately, the implementation of affirmative action programs has resulted in a tumultuous journey, with a great deal of controversy surrounding these efforts. Redressing discrimination while affirming diversity does not have to be a zero-sum game as many opponents of affirmative action maintain. And while the playing field is still not level, many members of the dominant group fail to see that the past, which shapes the present for descendants of European immigrants, is quite different from the reality that exists for the descendants of enslaved Africans and other immigrant groups of color. As stated more plainly by historian Roger Wilkins, "Blacks have a 375 year history on this continent: 245 involving slavery, 100 involving discrimination, and only 30 involving anything else" (as cited in Brunner, 2006a).

Commonly unrecognized by mainstream society are the unique paths various groups have traveled to be in the United States. Culture counts, and as our demographics continue to change, the axiology of many Whites still reflects a conflict between their concerted efforts to be egalitarian and their underlying social biases that are not embracing of a diverse democracy. Apple (2006) in his work titled "Interrupting the Right: On Doing Critical Educational Work in Conservative Times" refers to the gulf between rhetoric, reason, and ritual as evidence of a "false consciousness" (p. 27) that stems from a new hegemonic bloc consisting of various rightist factions. There is great paradox between the espoused axiology of the right wing (values and beliefs regarding equity) and its altered ontology (perceptions of reality) in terms of understanding the systemic incongruence of certain laws/rules when applied to minorities.

Earlier discussions in this volume pointing to competitive self-interest and individualism in contrast to collectivist cultures make it seem plausible that the various exclusions based on difference would be sufficient enough to topple the pervasive surface-level democratic ideals of affirmative action foes who actually harbor a "closed openness" (Asher, 2007, p. 69). Epistemologically, from a CRT point of reference, the source of truth is grounded in an ethic of ameliorating race relations via acknowledgment of Whites' historical possession of protection, and the distinctly different opportunities provided to individuals along the color line (Scheurich & Young, 1997). The lack of recognition regarding the very different experiences of voluntary versus forced immigration is one of the reasons that special population colleges including HBCUs, Hispanic-Serving Institutions, and Tribal Colleges, were called into existence. In a post–civil rights retrenchment era, community colleges and special population-serving institutions for students of color are gravely important. The pendulum is swinging away from affirmative action and toward the literal promotion of ivory towers and traditionally closed systems of higher education (Garibaldi, Dawson, & English, 2001; Laden, 2001; Sternberg, 2005; Townsend, 1999). Nonetheless, the institutional leadership across all college types can sustain diversity on campuses by being activist leaders who illustrate their commitment to affirming access. As in the case of the University of Michigan lawsuits, only when dedication to diversity starts from the top can it permeate the various campus units, surrounding community, and higher education at large.

Administrative leaders (especially those in states that have banned affirmative action and those who have been put on notice for upcoming referendums to abolish affirmative action) must be creative in finding federal grants to market/recruit in diverse communities by race/ethnicity and income. For instance, the strategic use of TRIO programs[1] such as Gear Up, McNair Postbaccalaureate Achievement, Upward Bound, Talent Search, Educational Opportunity Centers and Student Support Services could prove useful in circumventing the state-level retrenchment on affirmative action. Also, leaders should continue to institute mentoring programs, promote retention, partner with secondary schools, and make use of the transfer function and articulation initiatives at community colleges. The University of Michigan-Ann Arbor announced in March 2006 that as part of the university's diversity efforts, it would begin to target poor, moderate-income, high-achieving community college students (Gershman, 2006). With the passage of Proposal 2 in Michigan, surely the university will seek to multiply purposeful efforts to meet the challenge of maintaining a world-class multiethnic campus environment.

With the shift in momentum favoring the anti-affirmative-action camp, business and educational leaders will need to maintain their resolve to affirm diversity through initiating and participating in grassroots efforts to increase community awareness about the benefits of diversity and how it improves the educational experience for majority and minority students. This is especially important as the right-wing American Civil Rights Coalition announced on the heels of helping defeat affirmative action in Michigan its plans to expand efforts for the 2008 elections. The group formed committees to explore introducing referendums to ban affirmative action in eight other states, including Arizona, Colorado, Missouri, Nebraska, Nevada, Oregon, South Dakota, and Utah (Martin, 2006). However, as of May 2008, campaigns to collect enough signatures to have anti-affirmative action referendums on the November 2008 ballots continued in Nebraska and Arizona, while sufficient signatures secured the ACRI ballot initiative in Colorado. Advocates of affirmative action successfully blocked the ACRI's efforts to have referendums in Missouri and Oklahoma for the November 2008 elections (Jaschik, 2008). Also encouraging is evidence of pockets of activist leadership emerging in states such as Illinois[2] and Wisconsin, despite the anti-affirmative-action movements sweeping the nation. The discussion on affirmative action is sure to continue, with strong voices on both sides of the debate urging Congress to take a stronger stand. However, the platform for civil rights is replete with many other concerning social issues, such as health care, immigration, Social Security, and livable wages (Berry, 2006).

The triad of conflict, diversity, and activist leadership is inevitable for higher education in the 21st century. Proclamations of affirmative access for all will be useless without the aggressive leadership that is required to keep institutions on task and accountable to their constituencies of prospective students. Understandably, education in the 21st century is more important than ever for mobility, economic advancement, and citizenship. As a result, student activism will become more pronounced as various groups jockey for position to gain access to their first-choice institution. In the wake of post–*Grutter v. Bollinger* (2003) strife, deserving groups, including people of color, women, and people with disabilities, will be left behind without a compendium of diversity initiatives that actively affirm access, equity, and continued opportunities for advancement.

Notes

1. Federal TRIO Programs were established as a result of the first reauthorization of the Higher Education Act in 1968 to assist disadvantaged students. The moniker of "TRIO" is still used in reference to the original three programs: Upward Bound, Talent Search, and Student Support Services.

2. The Southern Illinois University Faculty Senate backed the administration in continued support of three graduate fellowships earmarked for women and minorities following a letter of dispute addressed to the U.S. Justice Department (*Diverse Issues in Higher Education*, 2006). The University of Wisconsin Board of Regents approved an overhaul of the system's admissions policies, voting 16 to 0 in favor of requiring all campuses to take into account race/ethnicity of an applicant among other factors being considered (Schmidt, 2007b).

WHERE DO WE FIND THE CASE FOR AFFIRMATIVE ACTION IN HIGHER EDUCATION?

Look to Seminal Civil Rights Cases of Yesterday and Classrooms of Today

Charles J. Ogletree, Jr. and Susan Eaton

The roots of the civil rights movement stretch deep into institutions of higher education. In fact, it was equal opportunity desegregation cases at the higher education level that laid the crucial groundwork for the legal progenitor of the civil rights movement, *Brown v. Board of Education*, in 1954. Looking back today at the theories underlying the most important pre-*Brown* cases—cases constructed in part by Charles Hamilton Houston, the man for whom the Charles Hamilton Houston Institute for Race and Justice Ogletree founded and directs is named—one is struck by their contemporary relevance. In fact, it's in yesterday's mostly forgotten cases, and too, in the persistent inequities at the K–12 level, where we might find the most compelling modern arguments for continuing affirmative action efforts on college campuses today.

Back in the late 1940s, expert witnesses at the trial level in the case *Sweatt v. Painter*, which Thurgood Marshall argued in federal courts in Texas and later at the U.S. Supreme Court, testified in favor of admitting a Black man, Hemann Sweatt, to a law school he'd been rejected from because of his skin color. In order to avoid admitting Sweatt, the state of Texas had proposed construction of a one-man law school solely for him, its one Black student. While the days of explicitly barring applicants on strictly racial grounds might be long past, the arguments put forth in this six-decades-old case apply to our modern challenges too.

In *Sweatt*, expert witnesses gathered by NAACP lawyer Thurgood Marshall spoke about the often immeasurable components necessary to a good education and, too, about the priceless component of what we might define today as *diversity*. For example, Earl Harrison, dean at the University of Pennsylvania Law School, testified for the NAACP's plaintiffs in *Sweatt* that "it isn't enough to have a good professor. It is equally essential that there be a well-rounded, representative group of students in the classroom to participate in the . . . discussion" (as cited in Kluger, 1976, p. 264).

Similarly, Thurgood Marshall's star witness, Robert Redfield, head of social sciences at the University of Chicago, testified in *Sweatt* that segregation, "prevents the student from the full, effective and economical coming to understand the nature and capacity of the group from which he is segregated." Redfield continued: "segregation intensifies suspicion and distrust between Negroes and whites, and suspicion and distrust are not favorable conditions either for the acquisition and conduct of an education or for the discharge of the duties of a citizen" (Kluger, 1976, p. 264).

Hemann Sweatt lost in Texas's federal courts but in 1950 won admittance to the University of Texas Law School after a unanimous decision by the U.S. Supreme Court, written by Chief Justice Fred M. Vinson. This marked the first time the high court ordered that a Black student be admitted to a White school. In *McLaurin v. Oklahoma State Regents for Higher Education*, another of Thurgood Marshall's cases that was decided at the same time as *Sweatt*, the court ruled that a Black man could not be separated from his White classmates at the University of Oklahoma.

The key arguments here are that the necessary ingredients of a quality education are often subtle and immeasurable. They are directly related to a student's ability to interact freely in a setting that provides practice in an approximation of the society a student wishes to join in the future. This argument applied to Black students such as Sweatt and McLaurin, who were denied such opportunity before *Brown* was even brought before the high court. It also would apply today to Black and Latino children in high-poverty, segregated schools who are cut off from mainstream opportunity and provided no firsthand knowledge of life and experience outside their neighborhoods. And it applies more than ever these days to White students, who surely would be handicapped and lacking in a quality education if their classroom discussions and interactions failed to include the perspective of and exposure to people of varying backgrounds, races, and ethnicities who make up the larger society. After all, let's remember that by the year 2050, Whites will be the minority.

These higher education cases of 1950 were vitally important victories in their own right. But they were also constructed deliberately as building blocks for a case to overturn *Plessey v. Ferguson* (1896) and outlaw segregation and its inherent inequalities in public schools at the K–12 level. Thus, *Brown* and the civil rights movement it made possible were built on the backs of these higher education cases. Sadly, though, *Brown* has now, more than a half century later, lost much of its power and reach. It may be fully extinguished by the U.S. Supreme Court, which, in a pair of cases, *Parents Involved in Community Schools v. Seattle* (2006) and *Meredith v. Jefferson County Board of Education* (2006) is scheduled to rule on the question of whether school districts may even employ minimally race-conscious means to achieve racially diverse classrooms. What's more, the nation's schools and its most impoverished neighborhoods are becoming more, not less, segregated. According to the Civil Rights Project at Harvard, schools in poor communities are more segregated now than at any time in the last three decades. We've been left with few, if any, legal mechanisms for reversing this troubling trend. Research shows too that college preparatory courses are less likely to be offered in schools of concentrated poverty that enroll disproportionate shares of African American and Latino students. Similarly, such schools are more likely to employ less-qualified and less-experienced teachers who could prepare students adequately for college.

The state of public education for students of color today brings to mind the stirring dissent penned by Thurgood Marshall more than three decades ago in the 1974 case *Milliken v. Bradley*, which eviscerated *Brown* by making it impermissible for racially segregating urban districts to include their suburbs in desegregation plans. These vast, persistent inequalities in public education—inequalities that disproportionately affect children of color—should be a mandate for maintaining strong affirmative action programs and policies intended to create and maintain racial and ethnic diversity on campus. The inequities at the K–12 level and the lack of redress for them, makes the task of creating and maintaining diversity in higher education more important and more difficult.

Affirmative action in higher education has been more or less upheld on legal grounds in a period when efforts to desegregate K–12 education have been thwarted; this clearly increases the responsibility for university-level educators and administrators to consider race as one of many factors in admissions. Colleges and universities that are not doing so already might consider new programs that would, for example, target their recruitment from highly segregated schools and school districts that serve disproportionate shares of children of color. Obviously, the earlier educators associated with institutions of higher education begin working with children at the K–12 level—either through directed mentoring programs or concentrated preparation—the better. Partnerships between K–12 educators and college and university officials that might help better prepare young people of color for college are more vital now, perhaps than they have ever been.

In the affirmative action case *Grutter vs. Bollinger* (2003), Justice Sandra Day O'Connor presented a robust endorsement of the principle of diversity as a factor in university admissions. She noted in the 25 years since the court first ruled on affirmative action in *Regents of the University of California v. Bakke* (1978), the number of racial minority applicants with high scholastic scores has increased, and that in another 25 years the use of racial preferences may no longer be required in order to further the general interests of diversity.

Our reading of the data, however, says we are most certainly a long way from reaching a place where we need not consider race in order to achieve diversity on campuses. O'Connor's 25-year sunset clause on diversity can properly be viewed as a challenge to institutions of higher education. On the other hand, her sunset provision can be viewed as aspirational because it forces civil rights advocates and others to use her call as a mandate to focus their work on structural changes in our society. Civil rights advocates must regard O'Connor's 25 years not as a deadline but as a call to arms—a mandate to attack the pervasive societal discrimination that has made affirmative action a dirty word in the 21st century.

In the meantime, if our society is sincere in trying to reach O'Connor's mandate, we will see universities and colleges—fairly or not—playing a larger role in ameliorating disparities at lower educational levels. It wasn't supposed to end up this way, of course. But until we can provide truly equal educational opportunities for children and teenagers of color in elementary, middle, and high school classrooms, access to campuses will remain closed for far too many and generations will never reach their full potential.

REFERENCES

Adarand Contractors, Inc. v. Pena, 115 S. Ct. 2097 (1995).

Adelman, C. (1999). *Answers in the tool box: Academic intensity, attendance patterns, and bachelor's degree attainment.* DC: U.S. Department of Education.

AffirmativeActionAdvocacy.com (n.d.). *Talking point E: Race and gender matter.* Retrieved May 27, 2008, from http://affirmativeactionadvocacy.com/pdf/talking pointE.pdf

Age Discrimination Act of 1975, 42 U.S.C. Sections 6101–6107 (1975).

Ainlay, S. C., Becker, G., & Coleman, L. M. (1986). *The dilemma of difference: A multidisciplinary view of stigma.* New York: Plenum Press.

Akbar, N. (1991). *Visions of black men.* Nashville: Winston-Derek Publications.

Alim, F. (1996, October 31). California faces a watershed election issue. *Black Issues in Higher Education, 13,* 16–18.

Allen, W. R. (May/June, 2004). E-racing history: America's struggle with diversity, race, and affirmative action in higher education. *Academe,* 1–8.

Almonte v. Pierce, 666 F. Supp. 517, 527 (S.D.N.Y. 1987).

Amar, A. R., & Katyal, N. K. (1996). Bakke's fate. *UCLA Law Review, 43,* 1745–1780.

Amason, A., & Schweiger, D. (1997). The effects of conflict on strategic decision making effectiveness and organizational performance. In C. De Dreu & E. Van De Vliert (Eds.), *Using conflict in organizations* (pp. 101–115). London: Sage.

America by the Numbers. (2004, October 30). *Time,* 41–54.

American Association of Community Colleges. (n.d.). *Disability support services national survey.* Retrieved October 14, 2000, from http://199.75.76.25/initiatives/ DISSRVCS/survey.htm

American Association of Community Colleges. (2007, January). *About community colleges: Fast facts.* Retrieved September 6, 2007, from http://www2.aacc.nche .edu/research/index.htm

American Civil Rights Institute. (2007a, October 5). *College admissions: Let's not break the law, Chairman's message.* Retrieved June 1, 2008 from http://www.acri .org/chairman.html

American Civil Rights Institute. (2007b). *About the American civil rights institute.* Retrieved June 1, 2008 from http://www.acri.org/about.html

Americans with Disabilities Act of 1990, Pub. L. No. 101–336, §2, 104 Stat. 328 (1991).

Amirkhan, J., Betancourt, H., Graham, S., Lopez, S. R., & Weiner, B. (1995). Reflection on affirmative action goals in psychology admissions. *Psychological Science, 6,* 140–148.

Anderson, B. (1991). *Imagined communities*. London: Verso.

Anderson, T. (2004). *The pursuit of fairness: A history of affirmative action*. New York: Oxford University Press.

Apple, M. W. (2006). Interrupting the right: On doing critical educational work in conservative times. In G. Ladson-Billings and W. F. Tate (Eds.), *Education Research in the Public Interest: Social justice, action and policy* (pp. 27–45). New York: Teachers College Press.

Aragon, S. R., & Zamani, E. M. (2002). Promoting access and equity through minority-serving institutions. In M. C. Brown and K. Freeman (Eds.), *Equity and access in higher education: New perspectives for the new millennium* (Readings on Equal Education, Volume 18, pp. 23–50). New York: AMS Press.

Arnwine, B. (2006, June 27). Protect democracy by renewing the Voting Rights Act. *Philadelphia Tribune*. Retrieved October 12, 2006, from http://www.votingrights act.org/inthenews/6.27.06.html

Asher, N. (2007, March). Made in the (multicultural) U.S.A.: Unpacking tensions of race, culture, gender, and sexuality in education. *Educational Researcher, 36*(2), 65–73.

Ashmore, R. D., & Del Boca, F. K. (1981). Conceptual approaches to stereotypes and stereotyping. In D. L. Hamilton (Ed.), *Cognitive processes in stereotyping and intergroup behavior* (pp. 1–35). Hillsdale, NJ: Lawrence Erlbaum.

Astin, A. W., Tsui, L., & Avalos, J. (1996). *Degree attainment rates at American colleges and universities: Effects of race, gender, and institutional type*. Los Angeles: Higher Education Research Institute, University of California, Los Angeles.

Atwell, R. H., Melendez, S., & Wilson, R. (2004). *Reflections on 20 years of minorities in higher education and the ACE Annual Status Report*. Washington, DC: American Council on Education.

Averett, S., & Dalessandro, S. (2001). Racial and gender differences in the returns to 2-year and 4-year degrees. *Education Economics, 9*(3), 281–292.

Ayers, L. R. (1992). Perceptions of affirmative action among its beneficiaries. *Social Justice Research, 5*, 223–238.

Bandura, A. (2000). Social cognitive theory: An agentic perspective. *Annual Review of Psychology, 52*, 1–26.

Banerji, S. (2007, February 22). Black immigrant study puts spotlight back on affirmative action debate. *Diverse Issues in Higher Education, 24*(1), 24–25.

Barnes, E. (1996). Community college becomes battleground for complaint about privately funded scholarship. *Black Issues in Higher Education, 13*(16), 8–10.

Barnett, L. (1993). *Services for students with disabilities in community colleges: Final report*. Washington, DC: American Association of Community Colleges. (ERIC Document Reproduction Service No. ED364308)

Barnett, L., & Li, Y. (1997). *Disability support services in community colleges: Research brief* (ACC-RB-97-1). Washington, DC: American Association of Community Colleges.

Barry, T. (2005, June_17). *Immigration debate: Politics, ideologies of antiimmigration forces*. Retrieved January 1, 2007 from http://www.civilrights.org/press_room/

press-releases/immigration-debate-politics-ideologies-of-anti-immigration-forces .html

Bartik, T. J., Erickcek, G., Huang, W., and Watts, B. (2006, August 11). *Michigan's economic competitiveness and public policy.* Kalamazoo, MI: W. E. Upjohn Institute for Employment Research.

Becker, G. S. (1975). *Human capital* (2nd ed.). Chicago: University of Chicago Press.

Becker, G., & Arnold, R. (1986). Stigma as a social and cultural construct. In S. C. Ainlay, G. Becker, & L. M. Coleman (Eds.), *The dilemma of difference: A multidisciplinary view of stigma* (pp. 39–58). New York: Plenum.

Bell, D. (1987). *And we are not saved: The elusive quest for racial justice.* New York: Basic Books.

Bell, D. (1992). *Faces at the bottom of the well: The permanence of racism.* New York: Basic Books.

Bell, D. (1995a). Brown v. Board of Education and the interest convergence dilemma. In K. Crenshaw, N. Gotanda, G. Peller, & K. Thomas (Eds.), *Critical race theory: The key writings that formed the movement* (pp. 20–29). New York: The New Press.

Bell, D. (1995b). Racial realism. In K. Crenshaw, N. Gotanda, G. Peller, & K. Thomas, (Eds.), *Critical race theory: The key writings that formed the movement* (pp. 303–312). New York: The New Press.

Bell, D. (2000). *Race, racism and American law.* Boston: Little, Brown.

Bell, D. (2001). Love's labor lost? Why racial fairness is a threat to many White Americans. In L. Guinier & S. Sturm (Eds.), *Who's qualified?* (pp. 42–48). Boston, MA: Beacon Press.

Bell, D. (2006, December 15). Cox warns universities not to dawdle on Proposal 2: Colleges have sought more time. *Detroit Free Press.* Retrieved May 27, 2008, from http://www.redorbit.com/news/education/768702/cox_warns_universities_not _to_dawdle_on_proposal_2_colleges/index.html

Bender, L. W. (1990). *Spotlight on the transfer function: A national study of state policies and practices.* Washington, DC: American Association of Community and Junior Colleges.

Bergmann, B. R. (1999). The continuing need for affirmative action. *Quarterly Review of Economics and Finance, 39,* 757–768.

Bernstein, R. (2005, July 9). *Hispanic population passes 40 million, Census Bureau reports.* Retrieved on June 2, 2007 from http://www.census.gov/PressRelease/ www/releases/archives/population/ 005164.html

Berry, D. B. (December 31, 2006). Rights groups to seek action on profiling, elections. *Gannett News Service.* Retrieved December 31, 2006, from http://www .freep.com/apps/pbcs.dll/article?AID = 2006612310530

Biorski, G. (2005, December 12). Black male college enrollment in decline. *The Ticker.* Retrieved December 31, 2006, from http://www.theticker.org/media/stor age/paper909/news/2005/12/12/News/Black.Male.College.Enrollment.In.Decline -1781450.shtml?norewrite200701020854&sourcedomain = www.theticker.org

Black Issues in Higher Education. (2003, December 18). Florida court says NAACP can challenge anti-affirmative action measures, *20*(22), 11.

Black Issues in Higher Education. (2004a, September 9). Know your enemy: The assault on diversity, *21*(15), 32.

Black Issues in Higher Education. (2004b, April 8). New report finds Berkeley admitting more minorities than predicted, *21*(4), 8–9.

Black Issues in Higher Education. (2004c, January 1). Texas A&M to leave race out of admissions decisions, *20*(23), 10–11.

Black Issues in Higher Education. (2004d, July 15). Texas minority groups seek continuation of admissions policy, *21*(11), 13.

Black Issues in Higher Education. (2004e, September 23). Women's groups speak out against Michigan 2006 affirmative action measure, *21*(16), 14.

Black Issues in Higher Education. (2005, February 10). Texas 10 percent plan has not improved minority representation, republican leader says, *21*(26), 14.

Blaine, B., Crocker, J., & Major, B. (1995). The unintended negative consequences of sympathy for the stigmatized. *Journal of Applied Social Psychology, 25,* 889–905.

Blake, R. R., & Mouton, J. S. (1970). The fifth achievement. *The Journal of Applied Behavioral Science,* 6(4), 413–442.

Blalock, H. M. (1967). *Toward a theory of minority-group relations.* New York: Wiley.

Blanck, P. D., & Schartz, H. A. (2000). *Towards researching a national employment policy for persons with disabilities: A report for the 22nd Mary Switzer Memorial Seminar.* Retrieved May 24. 2008, from http://disability.law.uiowa.edu/lhpdc/publications/documents/blancketaldocs/Switzer_draft_MS011701.doc

Blau, P. M. (Ed.) (1975). *Approaches to the study of social structure.* New York: The Free Press.

Blau, P. M., & Duncan, O. D. (1967). *The American occupational structure.* New York: Wiley.

Blauner, R. (1972). *Racial oppression in America.* New York: Harper and Row.

Bobo, L. (2000). Race and beliefs about affirmative action. In D. O. Sears, J. Sidanius, & L. Bobo (Eds.), *Racialized politics: The debate about racism in America* (pp. 137–165). Chicago: University of Chicago Press.

Bobo, L., & Kluegel, J. R. (1993). Opposition to race-targeting: Self-interest, stratification ideology, or racial attitudes? *American Sociological Review, 58,* 443–464.

Bobo, L., Kluegel, J. R., & Smith, R. A. (1997). Laissez-faire racism: The crystallization of a kinder, gentler, antiblack ideology. In S. A. Tuch & J. K. Martin (Eds.), *Racial attitudes in the 1990s: Continuity and change* (pp. 15–42). Westport, CT: Praeger.

Bobo, L., & Smith, R. A. (1994). Antipoverty policy, affirmative action, and racial attitudes. In S. H. Danziger, G. D. Sandefur, and D. H. Weinberg (Eds.), *Confronting poverty: Prescriptions for change* (pp. 365–395). New York: Russell Sage.

Bonacich, E. (1975). Abolition, the extension of slavery, and the position of free blacks: A study of split labor markets in the United States, 1830–1863. *American Journal of Sociology, 81,* 601–628.

Bonacich, E. (1989). Inequality in America: The failure of the American system for people of color. *Sociological Spectrum, 9,* 77–101.

Bonilla-Silva, E. (2001). *White supremacy and racism in the post–civil rights era.* Boulder, CO: Lynne Rienner.

Bonilla-Silva, E. (2002). The linguistics of color blind racism: How to talk nasty about blacks without sounding "racist." *Critical Sociology, 28,* 41–64.

Border Protection, Antiterrorism, and Illegal Immigration Control Act of 2005 (H.R. 4437).

Boris, E. (1998). Fair employment and the origins of affirmative action. *National Women's Studies Association Journal, 10*(3), 142–151.

Bourdieu, P. (1986). The forms of capital. In J. Richardson (Ed.), *Handbook of theory and research for the sociology of education* (pp. 241–258). Westport, CT: Greenwood.

Bowen, W. G., & Bok, D. (1998). *The shape of the river: Long-term consequences of considering race in college and university admissions.* Princeton, NJ: Princeton University Press.

Bowen, W. G., Kurzweil, M. A., Tobin, E. M., & Pichler, S. C. (2005). *Equity and excellence in American higher education.* Charlottesville, VA: University of Virginia Press.

Boykin, A. W. (1994). Reformulating educational reform. Toward the proactive schooling of African American children. In R. J. Rossi (Ed.), *Educational reforms and students at risk* (pp. 116–138). New York: Teachers College Press.

Bradburn, E. M., Hurst, D. G., & Peng, S. (2001). *Community college transfer rates to 4-year institutions using alternative definitions of transfer.* Washington, DC: National Center for Education Statistics.

Bragg, D. D. (2001). The past, present, and future of federal vocational legislation in U.S. community colleges. *Journal of Applied Research in the Community College, 9*(1), 57–76.

Bragg, D. D., Loeb, J., Zamani, E. M., & Yoo, J. S. (2001, November). *Ready or not, here they come! College readiness among tech prep participants and non-participants in four disparate settings.* Paper presented at the annual meeting of the Association for the Study of Higher Education, Richmond, VA.

Bragg, D. D., Reger, W., & Thomas, S. H. (1997). *Integration of academic and occupational education in the Illinois community college system.* Springfield: Illinois Community College Board.

Brint, S., & Karabel, J. (1989a). American education, meritocratic ideology, and the legitimization of inequality: The community college and the problem of American exceptionalism. *Higher Education, 18,* 725–735.

Brint, S., & Karabel, J. (1989b). *The diverted dream: Community colleges and the promise of educational opportunity in America, 1900–1985.* New York: Oxford University Press.

Brown, M. C. (1999). *The quest to define collegiate desegregation: Black colleges, Title VI compliance, and post-Adams litigation.* Westport, CT: Bergin & Garvey.

Brown v. Board of Education, 347 U.S. 483, 98 L. Ed. 873 (74 S. Ct. 686. 1954).

Brown, M. C., & Davis, J. E. (2000). *Black sons to mothers: Compliments, critiques, and challenges for cultural workers in education.* New York: Peter Lang.

Brunner, B. (2006a). *Affirmative action history: A history and timeline of affirmative action.* Retrieved December 21, 2006, from http://www.infoplease.com/spot/affirmative1.html?mail-12–18

Brunner, B. (2006b). *Timeline of affirmative action milestones.* Retrieved December 21, 2006, from http://www.infoplease.com/spot/affirmativetimeline1.html?mail-12–18

Brunner, B., & Haney, E. (2006). *Civil rights timeline: Milestones in the modern civil rights movement.* Retrieved December 22, 2006, from http://www.infoplease.com/spot/civilrightstimeline1.html

Bruyere, S. M., & Hoying, J. (1995). *Cultural diversity and the ADA: Implementing the Americans With Disabilities Act.* Washington, DC: National Institute on Disability and Rehabilitation Research. (ERIC Document Reproduction Service No. ED418513)

Bryd, C.M. (1999, April 24). An interview With Ward Connerly. *Interracial Voice.* Retrieved on May 28, 2008 from http://198.66.252.234/interv6.html

Burdman, P. (2003). Taking an alternative route. *Black Issues in Higher Education, 20*(14), 32–35.

Bureau of Labor Statistics. (2005). *Women in the labor force: A data book.* Washington, DC: U.S. Department of Labor.

Burley, H. E., & Butner, B. K. (2000). Should Student Affairs offer remedial education? *Community College Journal of Research and Practice, 24*(3), 193–295.

Busenberg, B. E., & Smith D. G. (1997). Affirmative action and beyond: The woman's perspective. In M. Garcia (Ed.), *Affirmative action's testament of hope: Strategies for a new era in higher education* (pp. 149–180). Albany, NY: SUNY Press.

Cable Network News. (2004, February 17). *Women a minority of tenured faculty and administrators.* Retrieved January 25, 2005, from www.cnn.com/2004/EDUCATION/02/17/women.on.campus.ap/

Cable Network News. (2006, November). *Ballot measures/Michigan Proposition 2 exit poll.* Retrieved May 24, 2008, from http://www.cnn.com/ELECTION/2006//pages/results/states/MI/I/01/epolls.0.html

Cabrera, A. F., Nora, A., Terenzini, P.T., Pascarella, E., & Hagedorn, L.S. (1999).

Camarena v. San Bernardino Community College District, No. CIV-S-95–589 (1995). Campus racial climate and adjustment of student to college: A comparison between white students and African-American students. *Journal of Higher Education, 70,* 134–160.

Cano, M. (2006, July 27). *Civil rights coalition celebrates renewal of landmark Voting Rights Act.* Retrieved October 12, 2006, from http://renewthevra.civilrights.org/vra_news/details.cfm?id = 45845

Cantor, N. (n.d.). *University of Syracuse welcome message.* Retrieved October 26, 2006, from http://www.syr.edu/chancellor/

Carnegie Foundation for the Advancement of Teaching. (2001). *The Carnegie classification for institutions of higher education: 2000 edition.* Menlo, CA: Carnegie Foundation for the Advancement of Teaching.

Carter, D. F. (1999a, November). *College students' degree aspirations: A theoretical model and literature review with a focus on African American and Latino students.* Paper presented at the annual meeting of the Association for the Study of Higher Education, San Antonio, Texas.

Carter, D. F. (1999b). The impact of institutional choice and environments on African American and white students' degree expectations. *Research in Higher Education, 40,* 17–41.

Carter, S. L. (1991). *Reflections of an affirmative action baby.* New York: Basic Books.

Caso, A. T. & Corry, R. J. (1996). Whites need not apply: The conservative Pacific Legal Foundation challenges college classes designed exclusively for minorities. *California Lawyer, 16*(9), 42–45.

Center for Equal Opportunity. (2008a). *About CEO.* Retrieved May 29, 2008, from http://www.ceousa.org/content/view/40/52/

Center for Equal Opportunity. (2008b). *Meet our staff: Linda Chavez, chairman.* Retrieved May 30, 2008, from http://www.ceousa.org/content/view/506/122/

Center for Equal Opportunity. (2008c). *Our focus areas: Affirmative action.* Retrieved May 29, 2008 from, http://www.ceousa.org/content/blogsection/11/83/

Center for Individual Rights. (1997a). *CIR files second lawsuit against University of Michigan.* Retrieved May 24, 2008, from http://www.cir-usa.org/releases/24.html

Center for Individual Rights. (1997b). *CIR sues to end use of racial preferences by University of Michigan.* Retrieved May 24, 2008 from http://www.cir-usa.org/releases/20html

Center for Individual Rights. (1998). *Racial preferences in higher education: The rights of college students.* Washington DC: Center for Individual Rights. Retrieved June 1, 2008 from http://www.cir-usa.org/student_web.pdf

Center for Individual Rights. (2005a). *Civil rights today.* Retrieved June 1, 2008 from http://www.cir-usa.org/civil_rights_theme.html

Center for Individual Rights. (2005b, July 29). *CIR's mission: Fighting for individual rights, The clients.* Retrieved April 20, 2006 from http://www.cir-usa.org/mission_new.html

Chacko, T. I. (1982). Women and equal employment opportunity: Some unintended effects. *Journal of Applied Psychology, 67,* 119–123.

Chang, M. J. (1996). *Racial diversity in higher education: Does a racially mixed student population affect educational outcomes?* Unpublished doctoral dissertation, University of California, Los Angeles.

Chang, M. J. (2002). The impact of an undergraduate diversity course requirement on students' racial views and attitudes. *Journal of General Education, 51*(1), 21–42.

Chang, M. J., Denson, N., Saenz, V., & Misa, K. (2006). The educational benefits of cross-racial interaction among undergraduates. *Journal of Higher Education, 77*(3), 430–455.

Chapman, M. (November 8, 2006). *Affirmative Action nixed in Michigan.* Retrieved December 21, 2006, from http://www.bet.com/News/WARDCONNERLY AFFIRMATIVEACTION.htm

Chavez, L. (1998). *The color bind: California's battle to end affirmative action.* Berkeley, CA: University of California Press.

Chavous, T. M. (2005). An intergroup contact-theory framework for evaluating racial climate on predominantly white college campuses. *American Journal of Community Psychology, 36*(3–4), 239–257.

Cherry Commission. (2004). *Final report of the Lt. Governor's Commission on Higher Education and Economic Growth.* Lansing, MI: Cherry Commission.

Chiang, S. (1998). UCLA feeder program takes sting out of anti-affirmative action policies. *Black Issues in Higher Education, 15*(16), 12–13.

Chideya, F. (1995). *Don't believe the hype: Fighting cultural misinformation about African Americans.* New York: Penguin.

Chideya, F. (1999). *The color of our future.* New York: William Morrow.

Citizens Research Council of Michigan. (2006, September). *Statewide issues on the November general election ballot Proposal 2006–02: Michigan civil rights initiative.* Retrieved June 5, 2008 from http://www.crcmich.org/PUBLICAT/2000s/2006/ rpt343.pdf

City of Richmond v. Cronson, 488 U.S. 469 (1989).

Civil Rights Act of 1866, 14 Stat. 27 (1866).

Civil Rights Act of 1964, 78 Stat. 252; 42 U.S.C. 2000d (1964).

Civil Rights Act of 1964, Title VII, Pub. L. 88–352 (1964).

Clark, B. (1960). The "cooling out" function in higher education. *American Journal of Sociology, 65*, 569–576.

Clegg, R. (2004). African Americans should oppose racial preferences. *Black Issues in Higher Education, 20*(25), 74.

Coalition to Defend Affirmative Action By Any Means Necessary (BAMN), et al., v. Governor Jennifer Granholm, University of Michigan, Michigan State University, Wayne State University, et al., US Dist Court Case No. 06–15024 (2007).

Cohen, A. M., & Brawer, F. B. (2003). *The American community college* (4th ed.). San Francisco: Jossey-Bass.

Cohen, A., & Sanchez, J. (1997). The transfer rate: A model of consistency. *Community College Journal, 68*(2), 24–26.

Cohen, G. L., & Steele, C. M. (2002). A barrier of mistrust: How negative stereotypes affect cross-race mentoring. In J. Aronson (Ed.), *Improving academic achievement: Impact of psychological factors on education* (pp. 303–327). San Diego, CA: Academic Press.

Colker, R. (1986). Anti-subordination above all: Sex, race, and equal protection. *New York University Law Review, 61*, 1003–1066.

Colker, R. (2005). *The disability pendulum: The first decade of the Americans with Disabilities Act.* New York: New York University Press.

Collison, M. N. K. (1992). Young people found pessimistic about relations between the races. *The Chronicle of Higher Education, 38*(29), A1–32.

Collison, M. N. K. (1999, October, 14). Georgia reaffirms affirmative action: University of Georgia admission policy. *Issues in Higher Education.* Retrieved May 20, 2008, from http://findarticles.com/p/articles/mi_moDXK/is_17_16/ai_57745861

Community College Survey of Student Engagement. (2005). *Final report.* Retrieved November 22, 2006, from http://www.ccsse.org/publications/CCSSE_report final2005.pdf

Comprehensive Immigration Reform Act of 2006 (CIRA) S.2611. S.2611 (2006)

Connerly v. State Personnel Board, C032042 Cal. Ct. App. (2001).

Connerly, W. (2003, July 4). The cloudy vision of a race-free America. *The Chronicle of Higher Education.* Retrieved July 21, 2004, from, http://chronicle.com/weekly/v49/i43/43b01201.htm

Cook, C. (1998). *Lobbying for higher education: How colleges and universities influence federal policy.* Nashville, TN: Vanderbilt University Press.

Copage, E. V. (1996). *Black pearls—Book of love: Romantic meditations and inspirations for African Americans.* NY: William Morrow and Company.

Coral Construction, Inc. v. City & County of San Francisco, 116 Cal. Ct. App. (2004).

Cose, E. (1993). *The rage of a privileged class: Why do prosperous Blacks still have the blues?* New York: HarperCollins.

Coser, L. (1956). *The functions of social conflict.* New York: The Free Press.

Cottman, M. H. (2005, March 27). *National Urban League targeting plight of jailed black men.* Retrieved December 30, 2006 from http://www.blackamericaweb.com/site.aspx/bawnews/nul328

Cottman, M. H. (2006). *Voters urged to reject deceptively-named initiative ending affirmative action.* Retrieved October 27, 2006, from http://www.blackamerica web.com/site.aspx/bawnews/affirmativeaction104

Cox, R. D., & McCormick, A. C. (2003). Classification in practice: Applying five proposed classification models to a sample of two-year colleges. In A.C. McCormick & R. D. Cox (Eds.), *Classification systems for two-year colleges* (pp. 103–121). *New Directions for Community Colleges, 122.* San Francisco: Jossey-Bass.

Craig v. Boren, 429 U.S. 190 (1976).

Crawford v. Huntington Beach Union High School District, 98 Cal. App. 4th 1275 (2002).

Crenshaw, K. W. (1993). Beyond racism and misogyny: Black feminism and 2 Live Crew. In M. J. Matsuda, C. R. Lawrence, R. Delgado, & K. W. Crenshaw (Eds.), *Words that wound: Critical race theory, assaultive speech and the First Amendment* (pp. 111–132). Boulder, CO: Westview Press.

Crenshaw, K. W. (2003, January 17). *The preference of white privilege: In opposing affirmative action, President Bush resurrects Jim Crow.* Retrieved on December 18, 2006, from http://aapf.org/resourcelibrary/aarl/?post_id = 27

Crenshaw, K., Gotanda, N., Peller, G., & Thomas, K. (1995). *Critical race theory: The key writings that formed the movement.* New York: The New Press.

Cress, C. M., & Sax, L. J. (1998). Campus climate issues to consider for the next decade. *New Directions for Institutional Research, 98,* 65–79.

Crocker, J., & Lutsky, N. (1986). Stigma, stereotyping, and attitudes. In G. Becker, L. M. Coleman, & S. Ainlay (Eds.), *Stigma: A multidisciplinary approach.* New York: Plenum.

Crocker, J., & Major, B. (1989). Social stigma and self-esteem: The self-protective properties of stigma. *Psychological Review, 96,* 608–630.

Crosby, F. J. (2006). Understanding affirmative action. *Annual Review of Psychology, 57,* 585–611.

Cross, T. (1999). African-American opportunities in higher education: What are the racial goals of the center for individual rights? *The Journal of Blacks in Higher Education, 23,* 94–99.

Cross, T., & Slater, R. B. (1999). Only the onset of affirmative action explains the explosive growth in black enrollments in higher education. *The Journal of Blacks in Higher Education, 23,* 110–115.

Cross, W. E. (1978). The Thomas and Cross models of psychological nigrescence: A review. *The Journal of Black Psychology, 5*(1), 13–31.

Cullen, K. (2007, March 8). Boom times, crackdown slow emerald wave. *The Boston Globe.* Retrieved April 14, 2007, from http://www.boston.com/news/local/articles/2007/03/18/boom_times_crackdown...slow_emerald_wave/

Cummins, J. (1991, May). *Empowering culturally and linguistically diverse students with learning problems.* ERIC Digest #E500. Reston, VA: ERIC Clearinghouse on Handicapped and Gifted Children. Retrieved May 27, 2008 from http://eric.ed.gov/ERICDocs/data/ericdocs2sql/content_storage_01/0000019b/80/23/0a/56.pdf

Cuyjet, M. J. (1997). African American men on college campuses: Their needs and their perceptions. *New Directions for Student Services, 80,* 5–16.

D'Souza, D. (1992). *Illiberal education: The politics of race and sex on campus.* New York: Vintage.

Daddona, M. F. (2001). Hiring student affairs staff with disabilities. *College Student Affairs Journal, 21,* 73–81.

Davis, L. E. (2003, July 29). *A gender gap in black and white: Explaining why African-American boys lag in school—and deciding what to do about it.* Retrieved from http://www.post-gazette.com/forum/comm/20030729davis0729p1.asp

DeBose, B. (2006, May 28). Group seeks affirmative action vote. *Washington Times.* Retrieved August 12, 2006, from http://www.michigancivilrights.org/washington times_052806.html

DeCulr, J. T., & Dixson, A. D. (2004, June/July). "So when it comes out come, they aren't that surprised that it is there": Using critical race theory as a tool of analysis of race and racism in education. *Educational Researcher, 33*(5), 26–31.

De Dreu, C. (1997). Productive conflict: The importance of conflict management and conflict issue. In C. De Dreu & E. Van De Vliert (Eds.), *Using conflict in organizations* (pp. 87–100). London: Sage.

De Dreu, C. &. Van De Vliert, E. (Eds.). (1997). *Using conflict in organizations.* London: Sage.

DeFunis v. Odegaard, 416 U.S. 312 (1974).

Delgado, R. (1990). When a story is just a story: Does voice really matter? *Virginia Law Review, 76*, 95–111.

Delgado, R. (1995). Affirmative action as a majoritarian devise: Or, do you really want to be a role model? In R. Delgado (Ed.), *Critical race theory: The cutting edge* (pp. 355–361). Philadelphia, PA: Temple University Press.

Delgado, R., & Stefancic, J. (2001). *Critical race theory: An introduction.* New York: New York University Press.

Delpit, L. (1995). *Other people's children: Cultural conflict in the classroom.* New York: The New Press.

DeRonde v. Regents of the University, 28 Cal. 3d 875; 625 P.2d 220 (1981).

de Rugy, V. (2004). *Budget Busting Bushies: Overspending is not fiscal responsibility.* National Review Online. Retrieved May 3, 2007 from, http://www.cato.org/pub_display.php?pub_id=5645

DeSousa, D., & Kuh, G. D. (1996). Does institutional racial composition make a difference in what black students gain from college? *Journal of College Student Development, 37*, 257–267.

Diaz, I. M. (1997). Mischief makers: The men behind all those anti-affirmative action lawsuits. *Black Issues in Higher Education, 14*(22), 14–19.

Dietz-Uhler, B., & Murrell, A. J. (1993). Resistance to affirmative action: A test of four explanatory models. *Journal of College Student Development, 34*, 352–357.

Diverse Issues in Higher Education. (2005a, October 6). Blacks remain an extreme minority at University of California Campuses, *22*(17), 9.

Diverse Issues in Higher Education. (2005b, October 6). Falling black college enrollment in Florida puts heat on Gov. Bush's policy, *22*(17), 14.

Diverse Issues in Higher Education. (2006, January 12). Southern Illinois University faculty senate backs minority fellowships, *22*(24), 8.

Dixson, A. D., & Rousseau, C. K. (2005). And we are still not saved: Critical race theory in education ten years later. *Race, Ethnicity, and Education, 8*(1), 7–27.

Donohue, W. A., & Kolt, R. (1992). *Managing interpersonal conflict.* Newbury Park, CA: Sage.

Dooley-Dickey, K., & colleagues. (1991). Understanding the college LD student: A qualitative approach. *College Student Affairs Journal, 11*(2), 25–33.

Doss, J. (2006, October). Ending affirmative action would mean . . . *Connections: National Association of Social Workers-Michigan Chapter Newsletter, 30*(8), 12–13.

Dougherty, K. (1987). The effects of community colleges: Aid or hindrance to socio-economic attainment? *Sociology of Education, 60*, 86–103.

Dougherty, K. J. (1992). Community colleges and baccalaureate attainment. *The Journal of Higher Education, 63*, 188–214.

Dougherty, K. J. (1994). *The contradictory college: The conflicting origins, impacts, and future of the community college.* Albany, New York: SUNY Press.

Doverspike, D., & Arthur, W., Jr. (1995). Race and sex differences in reactions to simulated selection decision involving race-based affirmative action. *Journal of Black Psychology, 21*, 181–200.

Dovidio, J. F., Gaertner, S. L., & Murrell, A. J. (1994). *Why people resist affirmative action.* Paper presented at the 102nd Annual Convention of the American Psychological Association, Los Angeles, CA.

Dovidio, J., Gaertner, S., Stewart, T., Esses, T., ten Vergert, M., & Hodson, G. (2004). From intervention to outcome: Processes in the reduction of bias. In W. G. Stephan & W. P. Vogt (Eds.), *Education programs for improving intergroup relations* (pp. 243–279). New York: Teachers College Press.

Dovidio, J. F., Mann, J. A., & Gaertner, S. L. (1989). Resistance to affirmative action: The implication of aversive racism. In F. A. Blanchard & F. J. Crosby (Eds.), *Affirmative action in perspective* (pp. 83–102). New York: Springer-Verlag.

DREAM Act, S.2205 (2007).

Dred Scott v. Sandford, 60 U.S. 393 (1857).

Duncan, O. D., Featherman, D. L., & Duncan B. (1972). *Socioeconomic background and achievement.* New York: Seminar Press.

Dutt, D. (1997). How much gender disparity exists in salary? A profile of graduates of a major public university. *Research in Higher Education, 38*(6), 631–646.

Dworkin, R. (2000). Affirmative action: Is it fair? *Journal of Blacks in Higher Education, 28,* 79–88.

Dziadosz, A. (2006, November 17). Face book racial slur targets foe of Prop 2: Increase in campus racial harassment reported after Proposal 2's passage. *Michigan Daily.* Retrieved December 6, 2006, from, http://media.www.michigandaily .com/media/storage/paper851/news/2006/11/17/CampusLife/Facebook.Racial .Slur.Targets.Foe.Of.Prop.2–2467096.shtml

Eastern Michigan University. (2006). *The state of the African American male in Michigan: A courageous conversation.* Retrieved July 23, 2006, from http://www .emich.edu/coe/summit/index.php

Eckes, S. E. (2004). Race-conscious admissions programs: Where do universities go from Gratz and Grutter? *Journal of Law & Education, 33,* 21–62.

Edley, C., Jr. (1996). *Not all black and white: Affirmative action and American values.* New York: Hill & Wang.

Education for All Handicapped Children Act, Public Law 94–142 (S. 6) (1975).

Engineering Contractors Association of South Florida, Inc. v. Metropolitan Dade County, 122 F.3d 895, 910 (11th Cir. 1997).

Exec. Order No. 9981, 13 FR 59 (1948).

Exec. Order No. 10925, 66 FR 8497 (1961).

Exec. Order No. 11246, 30 FR 12319 (1965).

Exec. Order No. 11375, 32 FR 14303 (1967).

Falcon, A. (1988). Black and Latino politics in New York City: Race and ethnicity in a changing urban context. In F. C. Garcia (Ed.), *Latinos and the political system* (pp. 171–194). Notre Dame, IN: University of Notre Dame Press.

Feagin, J. R., & O'Brien, E. (2004). *White men on race: Power, privilege, and the shaping of cultural consciousness.* Boston, MA: Beacon Press.

Feinberg, W. (1996). Affirmative action and beyond: A case for a backward looking gender- and race-based policy. *Teachers College Record, 97,* 362–399.

Feldman, S., & Zaller, J. (1992). The political culture of ambivalence: Ideological responses to the welfare state. *American Journal of Political Science, 36,* 268–307.

Feltner, B., & Goodell, D. (1972). The academic dean and conflict management. *Journal of Higher Education, 43*(9), 692–701.

Ferguson, A. A. (2000). *Bad boys: Public schools and the making of Black masculinity (law meaning and violence).* Ann Arbor: University of Michigan Press.

Fleming, J. (1984). *Blacks in college.* San Francisco: Jossey-Bass.

Fleming, J. (2000). Affirmative action and standardized test scores. *Journal of Negro Education, 69,* 27–37.

Fleming, J. E., Gill, G. R., & Swinton, D. H. (1978). *The case for affirmative action for Blacks in higher education.* (Washington, DC: Howard University Press).

Florida ex.rel. Hawkins v. Board of Control, 350 U.S. 413 (1956).

Flowers, L. (2002). The impacts of college racial composition on African American students' academic and social gains: Additional evidence. *Journal of College Student Development, 43,* 401–410.

Floyd, M. F. (2004). Race, ethnicity and culture—implications for resource management: An overview and synthesis. In M. Manfredo, J. Vaske, B. Bruyere, D. Field, & P. Brown (Eds.), *Society and natural resources: A summary of knowledge* (pp. 71–92). Jefferson City, MO: Modern Litho.

Fortune 500 Corporations. (2003, February 18). *Brief for amici curiae 65 leading American businesses in support of respondents, Grutter v. Bollinger,* 123 S. Ct. 2325 (2003) (Nos. 02–241 and 02–516). Retrieved May 28, 2008 from http://supreme .lp.findlaw.com/supreme_court/briefs/02–241/02–241.mer.ami.sixtyfive.pdf

Fowler, F. C. (2008). *Policy studies for educational leaders: an introduction* (3rd ed.). Upper Saddle River, NJ: Allyn & Bacon/Pearson Education.

Fraga, L. R., Meier, K. J., & England, R. E. (1988). Hispanic Americans and educational policy: Limits to equal access. In F. C. Garcia (Ed.), *Latinos and the political system* (pp. 385–410). Notre Dame, IN: University of Notre Dame Press.

Freeman, C. E. (2005, November). Trends in educational equity of girls and women, 2004. (Crosscutting statistics). *Educational Statistics Quarterly, 6*(4). Retrieved November 29, 2006 from http://nces.ed.gov/programs/quarterly/vol_6/6_4/8_1.asp

Fuller, F. F. (1969). Concerns of teachers: A developmental conceptualization. *American Educational Research Journal, 6*(2), 207–226.

Fullilove v. Klutznick, 448 U.S. 448 (1980).

Garcia, J. A. (1986). The Voting Rights Act and Hispanic political representation in the Southwest. *Publius: The Journal of Federalism, 16*(4), 49–66.

Garibaldi, A. M., Dawson, H. G., & English, R. A. (2001). The continuing and expanding roles of historically black colleges and universities in an era of affirmative action and diversity in higher education. In B. Lindsay & M. J. Justiz (Eds.), *The quest for equity in higher education: Toward new paradigms in an evolving affirmative action era* (pp. 183–205). NY: SUNY Press.

Gaston-Gayles, J. L. (2004). Examining academic and athletic motivation among student athletes at a Division I university. *Journal of College Student Development, 45*, 75–83.

General Motors Corporation. (2003, February). Brief for Amicus Curiae General Motors Corporation in Support of Respondents, *Grutter v. Bollinger*, 123 S. Ct. 2325 (2003) (Nos. 02–241 and 02–516). Retrieved May 27, 2008, from http://supreme.lp.findlaw.com/supreme_court/briefs/02–241/02–241.mer.ami.gm. pdf

Gershman, D. (2006, March 6). U-M wants transfer students: Poor, moderate-income community college grads to be sought. *The Ann Arbor News*, B1.

Gibbs, J. (1988). *Young, Black, and males in America: An endangered species.* Dover, MA: Auburn House.

Gillett-Karam, R., Roueche, S., & Roueche, J. (1991).*Underrepresentation and the question of diversity: Women and minorities in the community college.* Washington, DC: Community College Press.

Glazer, N. (1999, September 27). The end of meritocracy: Should the SAT account for race? *The New Republic, 221*(12), 26.

Gliedman, J., & Roth, W. (1980). *The unexpected minority.* New York: Harcourt Brace Jovanovich.

Goffman, E. (1963). *Stigma: Notes on the management of spoiled identity.* Englewood Cliffs, NJ: Prentice-Hall.

Goldrick-Rab, S. (2006). Following their every move: An investigation of social-class differences in college pathways. *Sociology of Education, 79*, 61–79.

Gollnick, D. M., & Chinn, P. C. (2008). *Multicultural education in a pluralistic society* (7th ed.). Upper Saddle River, NJ: Pearson Merrill Prentice Hall.

Gordon, E. W. (2001). *Affirmative development of academic abilities.* New York: Teachers College, Columbia University Institute for Urban and Minority Education.

Gordon, E. W., & Bridglall, B. L. (2007). *Affirmative development: Cultivating academic ability.* Lanham, MD: Rowman & Littlefield Publishers, Inc.

Graca, T. J. (2005). Diversity-conscious financial aid after Gratz and Grutter. *Journal of Law & Education, 34*(4), 519–532.

Graham, H. D. (2001). Affirmative action for immigrants? The unintended consequences of reform. In J. D. Skrentny (Ed.), *Color lines: Affirmative action, immigration and civil rights options for America* (pp. 53–70). Chicago, IL: University of Chicago Press.

Grahnke, L. (1999, July 5). Group threatens race bias suit: Objects to local universities' affirmative action programs. *Chicago Sun-Times*, p. 13.

Grant, C. A. (2006). Multiculturalism, race, and the public interest: Hanging on to great-great-granddaddy's legacy. In G. Ladson-Billings and W. F. Tate (Eds.), *Education in the public interest: Social justice, action and policy* (pp. 158–172). New York: Teachers College Press.

Grant, L., Horan, P. M., & Watts-Warren, B. (1994). Theoretical diversity in the analysis of gender and education. In A. M. Pallas (Ed.), *Research in sociology of education and socialization* (pp. 71–110). Greenwich, CT: JAI Press.

Gratz v. Bollinger, 122 F. Supp. 2d 811. (E.D. Mich. 2000).

Gratz v. Bollinger, (02–516) 539 U.S. 244 (2003).

Gray, K. (2006, August 16). Granholm joins civil rights ballot suit: Critics say move is ploy to get votes. *Detroit Free Press*. Retrieved August 22, 2006, from http://www.accessmylibrary.com/coms2/summary_0286–16398776_ITM

Green, D. O. (2004a). Fighting the battle for racial diversity: A case study of Michigan's institutional responses to Gratz and Grutter. *Educational Policy, 18*(5), 733–755.

Green, D. O. (2004b). Justice and diversity: Michigan's response to Gratz, Grutter, and the affirmative action debate. *Urban Education, 39*(4), 374–393.

Green, D. O., & Trent, W. (2005). The public good and a racially diverse democracy. In A. Kezar, T. Chambers, & J. Burkhardt (Eds.), *Higher education for the public good: Emerging voices from a national movement* (pp. 102–123). San Francisco: Jossey-Bass.

Grosz, K. S. (1989). Meeting the needs of the disabled. *CAPED Journal, 5*, 20–25.

Grubb, W. N. (1991). The decline of community college transfer rates: Evidence from national longitudinal surveys. *Journal of Higher Education, 62*(2), 194–222.

Grubb, W. N. (2002). Learning and earning in the middle. Part I: National studies of pre-baccalaureate education. *Economics of Education Review, 21*(4), 299–321.

Grutter v. Bollinger, 137 F. Supp. 2d 821. (E.D. Mich. 2001).

Grutter v. Bollinger, 539 U.S. 306 (2003).

Gurin, P., Lehman, J. S, & Lewis, E. (2004). *Defending diversity: Affirmative action at the University of Michigan* (with E. L. Dey, G. Gurin, and S. Hurtado). Ann Arbor: University of Michigan Press.

Gurin, P., Nagda, B. A., & Lopez, G. (2004). The benefits of diversity in education for democratic citizenship. *Journal of Social Issues, 60*(1), 17–34.

Hall, G. E., George, A. A., & Rutherford, W. A. (1998). *Measuring stages of concern about the innovation: A manual for use of the SoC Questionnaire*. Austin, TX: Southwest Educational Development Laboratory.

Hall, G. E., Wallace, R. C., Jr., & Dossett, W. A. (1973). *A developmental conceptualization of the adoption process within education institutions*. Austin: Research and Development Center for Teacher Education, University of Texas.

Hamilton, D. (1981). *Cognitive processes in stereotyping intergroup behavior*. Hillsdale, NJ: Lawrence Erlbaum.

Haney Lopez, I. F. (1996). *White by law: The legal construction of race*. New York: New York University Press.

Harris, C. I. (1993). Whiteness as property. *Harvard Law Review, 106*(8), 1709–1791. Retrieved on May 14, 2007 from http://www.lexisnexis.com.ezproxy.emich.edu/us/lnacademic/results/docview/docview.do?risb = 21_T3779249171&treeMax = true&sort = BOOLEAN&docNo = 5&format = GNBFULL&startDocNo = 1& treeWidth = 0&nodeDisplayName = &cisb = 22_T3779249175&reloadPage = false

Hartigan, J., Jr. (1999). *Racial situations: Class predicaments of whiteness in Detroit*. Princeton, NJ: Princeton University Press.

Hartmann, H., & Whittaker, J. (1998). *The male-female wage gap: Lifetime earnings losses.* Washington, DC: Institute for Women's Policy Research.

Harvey, W. B., & Anderson, E. L. (2005). *Minorities in higher education 2003–2004: Twenty-first annual status report.* Washington, DC: American Council on Education.

Hauben, R. B. (1980). A campus handicap? Disabled students and the right to higher education—Southeastern Community College v. Davis. *New York University Review of Law and Social Change, 9*(2), 163–198.

Healy, P. (1998a, April 3). Admissions law changes the equations for students and colleges in Texas. *The Chronicle of Higher Education, 44*(30), A29–A31.

Healy, P. (1998b, October 30). Foes of preferences try a referendum in Washington State. *The Chronicle of Higher Education, 45*(10), A34–A35.

Healy, P. (1998c, May 8). Texas attorney general declines to appeal Hopwood ruling. *The Chronicle of Higher Education,* A41.

Healy, P. (1998d, December 4). U.S. appeals court ruling may imperil university defenses for affirmative action. *The Chronicle of Higher Education, 45*(15), A29.

Healy, P. (1999a, February 5). A group attacking affirmative action seeks help from trustees and students. *The Chronicle of Higher Education, 45*(22), A36.

Healy, P. (1999b, March 5). University of Massachusetts limits racial preferences, despite vow to increase minority enrollment. *The Chronicle of Higher Education,* A30–31.

Hecker, D. E. (1998). Earnings of college graduates: Women compared with men. *Monthly Labor Review, 121*(3), 62–71.

Heilman, M. E., Simon, M. C., & Repper, D. P. (1987). Intentionally favored, unintentionally harmed? The impact of sex-based preferential selection on self-perceptions and self-evaluations. *Journal of Applied Psychology, 72,* 62–68.

Helms, J. E. (1993). *Black and white racial identity: Theory research, and practice.* Westport, CT: Praeger.

Henderson, C. (2001). *College freshmen with disabilities: A biennial statistical profile.* Washington, DC: American Council on Education, HEATH Resource Center.

Herrnstein, R. J., & Murray, C. (1994). *The bell curve: Intelligence and class structure in American life.* New York, NY: The Free Press.

Heubert, J. P. (2002). *Disability, race, and high-stakes testing of students.* CAST Universal Design for Learning. Retrieved December 29, 2004, from, http://www.cast.org/publications/ncac/ncac_disability.html

High Voltage Wire Works v. City of San Jose, 24 Cal. App. 4th 537 (2000).

Higher Education Act, P.L. 89–329 (1965).

Higher Education Act Amendments of 1968, P.L. 90–575 (1968).

Hinich, M., & Munger, M. (1994). *Ideology and the theory of political choice.* Ann Arbor: University of Michigan Press.

Hirschfeld, J. D. (2007, June 12). Bush presses Senate GOP on immigration. *USA Today.* Retrieved May 28, 2008, from http://www.usatoday.com/money/economy/2007–06–12–4186101087_x.htm

Holman, B. (2001). Masking the divide: How officially reported prison statistics distort the racial and ethnic realities of prison growth. *National Center on Institutions and Alternatives*. Retrieved January 1, 2007, from http://66.165.94.98/stories/maskdivo501.pdf

Holton, S. (1995a). And now . . . the answers! How to deal with conflict in higher education. In S. Holton (Ed.), *Conflict management in higher education* (Vol. 92, pp. 79–89). San Francisco: Jossey-Bass.

Holton, S. (1995b). Conflict 101. In S. Holton (Ed.), *Conflict management in higher education* (Vol. 92, pp. 5–10). San Francisco: Jossey-Bass.

Hopwood v. State of Texas, S.C. 95–1773 (1996).

Horn, L., & Nuñez, A. M. (2000). *Mapping the road to college: First-generation students' math track, planning strategies, and context of support* (NCES 2000–153). Washington, DC: National Center for Education Statistics.

Horwedel, D. M. (2006, May 4). For illegal college students, an uncertain future. *Diverse, 23*(6), 22–26.

Howard, J. R. (1997). Affirmative action in historical perspective. In M. Garcia (Ed.), *Affirmative action's testament of hope: Strategies for a new era in higher education* (pp. 19–45). Albany, NY: SUNY Press.

Howe, K. R. (1997). *Understanding equal educational opportunity: Social justice, democracy, and schooling.* New York: Teachers College Press.

Hudson, J. B. (1999). Affirmative action and American racism in historical perspective. *Journal of Negro History, 84*(3), 260–274.

Hunter, R., & Sheldon, S. M. (1980). *Statewide longitudinal study: Report on academic year 1978–1979. Part II—Spring Results 1978–1979.* Woodland Hills, CA: Pierce College.

Hurst, D., & Smerdon, B. (2000). *Postsecondary students with disabilities: Enrollment, services, and persistence.* Washington, DC: National Center for Education Statistics.

Hurtado, S. (2002). Creating a climate of inclusion: Understanding Latina/o college students. In W. A. Smith, P. G. Altbach, & K. Lomotey (Eds.), *The racial crisis in American higher education: Continuing challenges to the twenty-first century* (pp. 121–137). Albany, NY: SUNY Press.

Hurtado, S., & Carter, D. F. (1997). Effects of college transition and perceptions of the campus climate on Latino college students' sense of belonging. *Sociology of Education, 70,* 324–345.

Hurtado, S., Engberg, M. E., Ponjuan, L., & Landreman, L. (2002). Students' pre-college preparation for participation in a diverse democracy. *Research in Higher Education, 43*(2), 163–186.

Hurtado, S., Inkelas, K. K., Briggs, C., & Rhee, B. (1997). Differences in college access and choice among racial/ethnic groups: Identifying continuing barriers. *Research in Higher Education, 38,* 43–75.

IDEA Amendments of 1997, Pub. L. No. 105–17, 111 Stat. 37 (1997).

IDEA Improvement Act of 2004, Pub. L. No. 108–446, 118 Stat. 2647 (2004).

Indiana Commission on the Social Status of Black Males. (2006). *About us.* Retrieved May 30, 2008, from http://www.in.gov/fssa/dfr/6485.htm

Individuals with Disabilities Education Act (IDEA), Pub. L. No. 101–476, 104 Stat. 1142 (1990).

Jackman, M. R. (1996). Individualism, self-interest, and white racism. *Social Science Quarterly, 77*(4), 760–767.

Jackson, G. A. (1990). Financial aid, college entry, and affirmative action. *American Journal of Education, 98*(4) 523–550.

Jackson, K. W., & Swan, L. A. (1991). Institutional and individual factors affecting black undergraduate student performance: Campus race and student gender. In W. R. Allen, E. G. Epps, & N. Z. Haniff (Eds.), *College in black and white: African American students in predominantly white and in historically black public universities* (pp. 127–141). Albany, New York: SUNY Press.

Jacobs, J. A. (1985). Sex segregation in American higher education. In L. Larwood, A. H. Stromberg, & B. Gutek (Eds.), *Women and work: An annual review* (pp. 191–214). Beverly Hills, CA: Sage.

Jacobs, J. A. (1999). Gender and the stratification of colleges. *The Journal of Higher Education, 70*(2), 161–187.

Jaschik, S. (2008, May 6). No so super Tuesday. Retrieved on May 15, 2008 from http://www.insidehighered.com/news/2008/05/06/affirm

Jehn, K. (1995). A multimethod examination of the benefits and detriments of intragroup conflict. *Administrative Science Quarterly, 40,* 256–282.

Jehn, K. (1997). Affective and cognitive conflict in work groups: Increasing performance through value-based intragroup conflict. In C. De Dreu & E. Van De Vliert (Eds.), *Using conflict in organizations* (pp. 87–100). London: Sage.

Jet Magazine. (2006, July 10). Decision to renew Voting Rights Act delayed in Washington, 7–8.

Johnson, L. B. (1965, June 4). *Commencement Address at Howard University.* Retrieved on February 15, 2008 from http://wps.prenhall.com/wps/media/objects/173/177665/28_lbjho.htm

Johnson v. Board of Regents of the University of Georgia, 32 F. Supp. 2d 1370 (S.D. Ga. 1999).

Johnson v. Board of Regents of University of Georgia, 263 F.3d 1234 (11th Cir. 2001).

Johnston, G. H. (1997). *Piecing together the mosaic called diversity: One community college's on-going experience with hiring a more diverse faculty.* Unpublished doctoral dissertation, University of Illinois, Urbana-Champaign.

Jones, C. (2006, September). Walking an immigrant's path: Where are the African Americans in the debate? *Essence,* 164.

Jones, E. E., Farina, A., Hastrof, A. H., Markus, H., Miller, D. T., & Scott, R. A. (1984). *Social stigma: The psychology of marked relationships.* New York: Freeman.

Jones, N. R. (1994). For Black males and American society—The unbalanced scales of justice: A costly disconnect *23 Cap. U.L. Rev. 1,* 13–20.

Karabel, J. (1986). Community colleges and social stratification in the 1980s. *New Directions for Community Colleges, 54,* 13–30.

Karabel, J., & Halsey, A. J. (1979). Educational research: A review and interpretation. In J. Karabel & A. Halsey (Eds.), *Power and ideology in education*. New York: Oxford University Press.

Katznelson, I. (2005). *When affirmative action was white: An untold history of racial inequality in twentieth-century America*. New York: Norton.

Kaufmann, S. W. (2006). *The potential impact of the Michigan Civil Rights Initiative on employment, education and contracting*. Ann Arbor: Center for the Education of Women, University of Michigan.

Keener, B. J. (1994). Capturing the community college market. *Currents, 20*(5), 38–43.

Kelly, J. (1996). Who benefits from affirmative action? *Black Issues in Higher Education, 13*(7), 78.

Kelsey, W. M. (1988). Affirmative action in public two-year colleges. *CUPA, 39*(4), 35–39.

Kerlinger, F. N. (1984). *Liberalism and conservatism: The nature and structure of social attitudes*. Hillsdale, NJ: Lawrence Erlbaum.

Kerr, C. (1995). *The uses of the university* (4th ed.). Cambridge, MA: Harvard University Press.

KewalRamani, A., Gilbertson, L., Fox, M. A., & Provasnik, S. (2007, September). *Status and Trends in the Education of Racial and Ethnic Minorities*. Washington, DC: U.S. Department of Education, National Center for Education Statistics (NCES 2007–039).

Kidd v. State of California, 62 Cal. App. 4th 386 (1998).

Kinder, D. R., & Sanders, L. M. (1996). *Divided by color: Racial politics and democratic ideals*. Chicago: University of Chicago Press.

Kinder, D. R., & Sears, D. O. (1981). Prejudice and politics: Symbolic racism versus racial threat to the good life. *Journal of Personality and Social Psychology, 40*(3), 414–431.

King, M. L. Jr. (1963, August, 28). I have a dream—Address at March on Washington. Retrieved on May 20, 2008 from http://www.mlkonline.net/dream.html

King, M. L., Jr. (1964). *Why we can't wait*. New York: New American Library, Signet Books.

Kingdon, J. W. (2003). *Agendas, alternatives, and public policies* (2nd ed.). New York: Longman/Pearson Education.

Kluegel, J. R. (1990). Trends in whites' explanation of the black-white gap in socio-economic status, 1977–1989. *American Sociological Review, 55*, 512–525.

Kluegel, J. R., & Smith, E. R. (1983). Affirmative action attitudes: Effects of self interest, racial affect, and stratification beliefs on whites' views. *Social Forces, 61*, 796–824.

Kluegel, J. R., & Smith, E. R. (1986). *Beliefs about inequality: Americans' views of what is and what ought to be*. New York: Aldine deGruyter.

Kluger, R. (1976). *Simple justice: The history of Brown v. Board of Education and Black America's struggle for equality*. New York: Knopf.

Knight, J. L., & Hebl, M. R. (2005). Affirmative reaction: The influence of type of justification on nonbeneficiary attitudes toward affirmative action plans in higher education. *Journal of Social Issues, 61*(3), 547–568.

Kocher, E., & Pascarella, E. (1988). *The effects of institutional transfer on status attainment.* Paper presented at the annual meeting of the American Educational Research Association, New Orleans, LA.

Kravitz, D. A., & Klineberg, S. L. (2000). Reactions to two versions of affirmative action among whites, blacks, and Hispanics. *Journal of Applied Psychology, 85*(4), 597–611.

Kravitz, D. A. & Myer, B. (1995). *Reactions of Hispanics to affirmative action plans directed at Hispanics.* Poster session accepted for presentation at the 1996 annual meeting of the Society for Industrial and Organizational Psychology.

Kravitz, D. A., & Platania, J. (1993). Attitudes and beliefs about affirmative action: Effects of target and of respondent sex and ethnicity. *Journal of Applied Psychology, 78,* 928–938.

Krysan, M. (2000). Prejudice, politics, and public opinion: Understanding the sources of racial policy attitudes. *Annual Review of Sociology, 26,* 135–168.

Laanan, F. S. (2000). Community college students' career and educational goals. *New Directions for Community Colleges, 112,* 19–33.

Laden, B. V. (2001). Hispanic-serving institutions: Myths and realities. *Peabody Journal of Education, 76,* 73–92.

Ladson-Billings, G., & Tate, W. (1995). Toward a critical race theory of education. *Teachers College Record, 97,* 47–68.

Lane, K. (2001, September 27). Educating a growing community. *Black Issues in Higher Education, 18*(16), 28–31.

Lederman, D. (1997a, October 24). New briefs to high court take opposing views on key affirmative action case. *The Chronicle of Higher Education,* A28.

Lederman, D. (1997b, October 24). Suit challenges affirmative action in admissions at University of Michigan. *The Chronicle of Higher Education,* A27.

Leo, J. (2000, April 17). Jeb Bush's college try. *U.S. News & World Report, 128*(15), 15.

Lerman, R. I. (1997). *Meritocracy without rising inequality? Wage rate differences are widening by education and narrowing by gender and race.* Washington, DC: Urban Institute.

Leslie, D. (1972). Conflict management in the academy: An exploration of the issues. *Journal of Higher Education, 43*(9), 702–719.

Leung, M. (1999). *The origins of restorative justice.* Retrieved July 28, 2003, from http://www.cfcj-fcjc.org/full-text/leung.htm

Lewis, C. W. (2006). African American male teachers in public schools: An examination of three urban school districts. *Teachers College Record, 108*(2), 224.

Lombana, J. H. (1992). *Guidance for students with disabilities* (2nd ed.). Springfield, IL: Charles C. Thomas.

London, H. B. (1992). Transformations: Cultural challenges faced by first generation students. *New Directions for Community Colleges, 80,* 5–12.

Longmore, P. (2003). *Why I burned my book and other essays on disability*. Philadelphia, PA: Temple University Press.

Lopez, M. H., Marcelo, K. B., & Sagoff, J. (2006). *Quick facts about young voters in Michigan: The midterm election year 2006*. Center for Information and Research on Civic Learning and Engagement. Retrieved October 27, 2006, from, http://www.civicyouth.org/PopUps/FactSheets/FS_FastFacts2006/michigan_final.pdf

Lopez-Vasquez, A. (2005). Affirmative action in the name of restitution, equity, diversity and cultural democracy. *Diverse Issues in Higher Education, 22*(16), 38.

MacLean, N. (1999). The hidden history of affirmative action. *Feminist Studies*, 25, 42–78.

MacLean, N. (2006). *Freedom is not enough: The opening of the American workplace*. Cambridge, MA: Harvard University Press and the Russell Sage Foundation.

Major, B., Feinstein, J., & Crocker, J. (1994). Attributional ambiguity of affirmative action. *Basic and Applied Social Psychology, 15*, 113–141.

Marcel, A. (2003). The sense of agency: Awareness and ownership in action. In J. Roessler & N. Eilan (Eds.), *Consciousness and self-consciousness: Agency and self-awareness. Issues in philosophy and psychology*. New York: Oxford University Press.

Marcotte, D. E., Bailey, T., Borkoski, C., & Kienzl, G. S. (2005). The returns of a community college education: Evidence from the National Education Longitudinal Survey. *Educational Evaluation and Policy Analysis, 27*(2), 157–177.

Martin, T. (2006, December 13). Anti-affirmative action group looking at 8 more states. *Detroit Free Press*. Retrieved December 21, 2006 from http://www.freep.com/apps/pbcs.dll/article?AID = 20066121301 5&template = print art

Marx, K. (1975). *Early writings*. London: Pelican Books.

Matsuda, M., Lawrence, C., Delgado, R., & Crenshaw, K. (1993). *Words that wound: Critical race theory, assaultive speech and the First Amendment*. Boulder, CO: Westview Press.

Maxwell, W., Hagedorn, L. S., & Cypers, S. (2003). Community and diversity in urban community colleges course taking among entering students. *Community College Review, 30*(4), 21–46.

Mazel, E. (1998). *"And don't call me a racist!" A treasury of quotes on the past, present, and future of the color line in America*. Lexington, MA: Argonaut Press.

McConahay, J. B. (1986). Modern racism, ambivalence, and the modern racism scale. In J. F. Dovidio & S. F. Gaertner (Eds.), *Prejudice, discrimination, and racism* (pp. 91–125). Orlando, FL: Academic Press.

McCormick, A. C., & Carroll, C. D. (1997). *Transfer behavior among beginning postsecondary students: 1989–94*. Washington, DC: U.S. Department of Education, National Center for Educational Statistics.

McCune, P. (2001). What do disabilities have to do with diversity? *About Campus, 6*(2), 5–12.

McDonough, P. M. (1994). Buying and selling higher education: The social construction of the college applicant. *Journal of Higher Education, 65*(4), 427–446.

McDonough, P. M. (1997). *Choosing colleges: How social class and schools structure opportunity.* Albany, NY: SUNY Press.

McDonough, P. M., & Antonio, A. L. (1996, April). *Ethnic and racial differences in selectivity of college choice.* Paper presented at the annual meeting of the American Educational Research Association, New York, NY.

McJunkin, K. S. (2005). African-Americans in community colleges. *Community College Journal of Research and Practice, 29*(2), 251–256.

McLaurin v. Oklahoma State Regents, 339 U.S. 637; 70 S. Ct. 851; 94 L. Ed. 1149 (1950).

McPherson, M. (1983). Value conflicts in American higher education. *Journal of Higher Education, 54*(3), 243–278.

McQueen, A. (1999). Conservatives attack affirmative action. *Community College Week, 11*(15), 3–4.

Meader, E. W. (1998, November). *College student attitudes toward diversity and race-based policies.* Paper presented at the annual meeting of the Association for the Study of Higher Education, Miami, Florida.

Meredith v. Jefferson County Board of Education, 05–915 (2006).

Meyers, M. (2008, February 5). *CUNY schemes around civil rights law.* New York: Center for the American University, Manhattan Institute. Retrieved February 8, 2008 from http://www.mindingthecampus.com/originals/2008/02/at_a_recent_manhattan_institut.html

Michalko, R. (2002). *The difference that disability makes.* Philadelphia, PA: Temple University.

Michigan Civil Rights Commission. (2005). Michigan Civil Rights Commission adopts resolution opposing Michigan Civil Rights Initiative. Retrieved December 20, 2005, from http://www.michigan.gov/documents/aarelease3_86196_7.pdf

Michigan Civil Rights Initiative (MCRI). (2005). Ballot language. Retrieved November 22, 2005 from, http://www.michigancivilrights.org/ballotlanguage.html.

Michigan's Defining Moment: Report of the Emergency Financial Advisory Panel. (2007, February 2). Retrieved on September 6, 2007 from http://www.michigan-.gov/documents/gov/Emergency_Financial_Advisory_Panel Report185781_7.pdf

Michigan Department of State. (2006, November 13). *State Proposal—06–2: Constitutional amendment: Ban affirmative action programs.* Bureau of Elections. Retrieved November 17, 2006, from http://miboecfr.nicusa.com/election/results/06GEN/90000002.html

Milem, J. F., Chang, M. J., & Antonio, A. L. (2003). *Making diversity work on campus: A research based perspective.* Washington, DC: Association of American Colleges and Universities.

Mississippi University for Women v. Hogan, 458 U.S. 718 (1982).

Montemurri, P., Arellano, A., Christoff, C., & McGraw, B. (2000, November 10). Detroit helps Democrats triumph in Michigan. *Detroit Free Press,* 1B.

Monterey Mechanical Co. v. Wilson, 125 F.3d 702, 211 (9th Cir. 1997).

Moore, J. (2005). Why isn't eligibility part of the affirmative action debate? *Diverse Issues in Higher Education, 22*(18), 39.

Myers, M. (2006, May 26). Stop the black-only treatment. *The Washington Post*, A21.

Nacoste, R. W. (1994). If empowerment is the goal: Affirmative action and social interaction. *Basic and Applied Psychology, 15*, 87–112.

Nacoste, R. W. (1987). But do they care about fairness? The dynamics of preferential treatment and minority interest. *Basic and Applied Social Psychology, 8*, 177–191.

National Advisory Committee on Black Higher Education and Black Colleges and Universities. (1979). *Access of black Americans to higher education: How open is the door?* Washington, DC: U.S. Department of Health, Education and Welfare.

National Association of Scholars. (2001, April 5). *NAS releases study refuting University of Michigan diversity theory.* Retrieved September 25, 2002 from http://mela net.com/uncut/forums/messages/23/1169.html?TuesdaySeptember1120010727am

National Center for Education Statistics. (1996). *Common core of data survey.* Washington, DC: U.S. Department of Education.

National Center for Education Statistics. (1997). *Transfer behavior among beginning postsecondary students: 1989–94.* Washington, DC: U.S. Department of Education, Office of Educational Research and Improvement.

National Center for Educational Statistics. (1999a). *Integrated postsecondary education data system (IPEDS) fall enrollment survey.* Washington, DC: U.S. Department of Education.

National Center for Educational Statistics. (1999b). *National postsecondary student aid survey: 1995–96 (NPSAS: 96) Data analysis system.* Washington, DC: U.S. Department of Education.

National Center for Education Statistics. (1999c). *Students with disabilities in postsecondary education: A profile of preparation, participation, and outcomes.* Washington, DC: U.S. Department of Education.

National Center for Education Statistics. (2006a). *Digest of Education Statistics, 2005,* Table 210. Retrieved May 12, 2008 from http://nces.ed.gov/programs/digest/do5/tables/dt05_210.asp?referrer=list

National Center for Education Statistics. (2006b). *Profile of undergraduates in U.S. postsecondary institutions: 2003–2004, with special analysis of community college students.* NCES 2006–184. Washington, DC: NCES.

National Center for Education Statistics. (2007, September). *Status and trends in the education of racial and ethnic minorities,* Table 25.1. Retrieved May 12, 2008 from http://nces.ed.gov/pubs2007/minoritytrends/tables/table_25_1.asp?referrer =report

National Immigration Law Center. (2006a, March 28). DREAM Act passes Senate Judiciary Committee. Retrieved January 2, 2007, from http://www.nilc.org/imm lawpolicy/DREAM/Dream004.htm

National Immigration Law Center. (2006b, February). How HR 4437 would criminalize immigrants. Retrieved January 2, 2007, from http://www.nilc.org/imm lawpolicy/CIR/ciro03.htm

National Labor Relations Act of 1935, 29 U.S.C. §§ 151–169 (1935).

National Postsecondary Aid Study. (2000, March). *Low-income students: Who they are and how they pay for their education*. NCES Number: 2000169. Washington, DC: NCES.

National Public Radio. (2005, October 20). Challenges facing young black men. *News & Notes*. Retrieved December 30, 2006 from http://www.npr.org/tem plates/story/story.php?storyId=4966879

National Science Foundation. (2004, May). *Women, minorities, and persons with disabilities in science and engineering: 2004*. Washington, DC: NSF, Division of Science Resources Statistics.

Naturalization Act of 1790, 1_Stat._103 (1790).

Nieto, S., & Bode, P. (2008). *Affirming diversity: The sociopolitical context of multicultural education* (5th ed). Boston/NY: Allyn & Bacon/Longman.

Nieves, E. (1999, February 3). Civil rights groups suing Berkeley over admissions policy. *The New York Times on the Web*. Retrieved June 6, 2008 from http://www.ny times.com/library/national/020399berkeley-bias-suit.html.

Nora, A., & Rendón, L. I. (1988). Hispanic students in community colleges: Reconciling access with outcomes. In L. Weis (Ed.), *Class, race and gender in U.S. education* (pp. 126–143). New York: State University of New York Press.

Nora, A., & Rendón, L. (1990). Determinants of predisposition to transfer among community college students. *Research in Higher Education, 31*, 235–255.

Nora, A., & Rendón, L. (1998). *Quantitative outcomes of student progress*. Report prepared for the Ford Foundation. New York: Ford Foundation.

Nordhaug, O. (1987). Outcomes from adult education: Economic and sociological approaches. *Scandinavian Journal of Education, 31*(3), 113–122.

Northcraft, G. B., & Martin, J. (1982). Double jeopardy: Resistance to affirmative action from potential beneficiaries. In B. Gutek (Ed.), *Sex role stereotyping and affirmative action policy* (pp. 81–130). Los Angeles: University of California, Institute of Industrial Relations.

Nosworthy, G. J., Lea, J. A., & Lindsay, C. L. (1995). Opposition to affirmative action: Racial affect and traditional value predictors across four programs. *Journal of Applied Social Psychology, 25*, 314–337.

Notman, V. (2006, November 15). Only open endorsement of Prop. 2 came from hate group. *The State News*. Retrieved December 12, 2006, from http://www.statenews.com/index.php/article/2006/11/only_open_endorsement

Nutter, K. J., & Ringgenberg, L. J. (1993). Creating positive outcomes for students with disabilities. *New Directions for Student Services, 64*, 45–58.

O'Brien, M. (2006, June 14). Preferences preferred: Michigan Republicans line up to oppose the MCRI. *National Review Online*, Retrieved August 22, 2006, from http://article.nationalreview.com/?q=NWNjMDMoZmFmMzYyYjk3ZjBiOG ZlYjc2YWRlOTkiNTI=

Ogbu, J. U., & Simons, H. D. (1998). Voluntary and involuntary minorities: A cultural ecological theory of school performance with some implications for education. *Anthropology and Education Quarterly, 29*(2), 155–188.

Ogletree, C. J. (2004). *All deliberate speed: Reflections on the first half-century of Brown v. Board of Education*. New York: Norton.

Orfield, G. (2001). *Diversity challenged: Evidence on the impact of affirmative action*. Cambridge, MA: Harvard Education Publishing Group.

Pacifici, T., & McKinney, K. (1997). *Disability support services for community college students*. Los Angeles: ERIC Digest. Retrieved May 28, 2006 from http://www.eric.ed.gov/ERICDocs/data/ericdocs2sql/content_storage_01/0000 0 19b/80/16/c7/b8.pdf

Padron, E. J. (1992). The challenge of first-generation college students: A Miami-Dade perspective. *New Directions for Community Colleges, 80*, 71–80.

Page, S. E., & Suhay, E. (2006). *A decision making guide to the Michigan Civil Rights Initiative*. Retrieved October 3, 2006 from http://www.cscs.umich.edu/~spage/diversity_files/MCRI.pdf

Parents Involved in Community Schools v. Seattle School District, 05–908 (2006).

Parker, C. P., Baltes, B. B., & Christiansen, N. D. (1997). Support for affirmative action, justice perceptions, and work attitudes: A study of gender and racial-ethnic group differences. *Journal of Applied Psychology, 82*(3), 376–389.

Parker, L., & Lynn, M. (2002). What's race got to do with it? Critical race theory's conflicts with and connections to qualitative research methodology and epistemology. *Qualitative Inquiry, 8*, 7–22.

Pascarella, E. (2004, May/June). First generation college students. *The Journal of Higher Education, 75*(3), 249–284.

Pascarella, E. T., Edison, M., Nora, A., Hagedorn, L. S., & Terenzini, P. T. (1998). Does community college attendance versus four-year college attendance influence students' educational plans? *Journal of College Student Development, 39*(2), 179–193.

Pascarella, E. T., & Terenzini, P. T. (1991). *How college affects students: Findings and insights from twenty years of research*. San Francisco: Jossey-Bass.

Patton, N. R. (2006, December 30). U.S. panel rejects a delay for Prop 2: Affirmative action ban is upheld. *The Detroit Free Press*. Retrieved December 30, 2006, from http://mathforum.org/kb/plaintext.jspa?messageID = 5462899

Paulsen, M. B., & St. John, E. (1997). The financial nexus between college choice and persistence. *New Directions for Institutional Research, 95*, 65–84.

Paulsen, M. B., & St. John, E. (2002). Social class and college costs: Examining the financial nexus between college choice and persistence. *Journal of Higher Education, 73*(2), 189–236.

Pell, T. J. (2006, August 31). By Any Means Necessary: A federal judge plays politics in Michigan. *The Wall Street Journal*. Retrieved May 20, 2008, from http://www.michigancivilrights.org/

Peller, G. (1995). Race-consciousness. In Crenshaw K., Gotanda, N., Peller, G., & Thomas, K. (Eds). *Critical race theory: The key writings that formed the movement* (pp. 127–158). New York: The New Press.

Perez, A. (September 26, 2002). Hispanics must raise the bar. *Black Issues in Higher Education, 19*(16), 37.

Perin, D. P. (2002). The location of developmental education in community colleges: A discussion of the merits of mainstreaming vs. centralization. *Community College Review, 30*, 27–44.

Perlman, H. (2006, September 7). *University of Nebraska-Lincoln state of the university address.* Retrieved October 27, 2006, from http://www.unl.edu/ucomm/chancllr/sua2006/sua2006_4.shtml

Persell, C. H. (1977). *Education and inequality: A theoretical and empirical synthesis.* New York: The Free Press.

Phillippe, K. A., & Gonzalez, L. (2005). *National profile of community colleges: Trends and statistics* (4th ed.). Washington, DC: Community College Press.

Pierce, P. A. (1990). Access to employment: People with disabilities. *The Journal of Intergroup Relations, 16*(3/4), 37–40.

Piland, W. E. (1995). Community college transfer students who earn bachelor's degrees. *Community College Review, 23*(3), 35–44.

Pincus, F., & Archer, E. (1989). *Bridges to opportunity: Are community colleges meeting the transfer needs of minority students?* New York: Academy for Educational Development and College Entrance Examination Board.

Pinel, E. C., Warner, L. R., & Chua, P. (2005). Getting there is only half the battle: Stigma consciousness and maintaining diversity in higher education. *Journal of Social Issues, 61*(3), 481–506.

Plessy v. Ferguson, 163 U.S. 537; 16 S. Ct. 1138; 41 L. Ed. 256 (1896).

Podberesky v. Kirwan, 38 F.3d 147 (1994).

Polite, V., & Davis, J. E. (1999). *African American males in school and society: Policy and practice for effective education.* New York: Teachers College Press.

Prager, C. (1992). Accreditation and transfer: Mitigating elitism. *New Directions for Community Colleges, 78*, 45–61.

Proposition 209. (1996). Retrieved May 24, 2008 from http://vote96.ss.ca.gov/Vote96/html/BP/209.htm.

Rahim, M. A. (1992). *Managing conflict in organizations* (2nd ed.). Westport, CT: Praeger.

Raskin, C. (1994). Employment equity for the disabled in Canada. *International Labour Review, 133*, 75–88.

Rawe, J. (2006, December 4). When public schools aren't color-blind. *Time*, 54–56.

Raza, M. A., Anderson, A. J., & Custred, H. G. (1999). *The ups and downs of affirmative action preferences.* Westport, CT: Praeger.

Regents of the University of California v. Bakke, 438 U.S. 265 (1978).

Rehabilitation Act of 1973, 29 U.S.C. § 794 (1973).

Rehabilitation Act Amendments of 1978, Pub. L. No. 95–602, 92 Stat. 2955 (1978).

Rehabilitation Act Amendments of 1986, Pub. L. No. 99–506, 100 Stat. 1807 (1986).

Rehabilitation Act Amendments of 1992, Pub. L. No. 12–569 (1992).

Rendón, L. I. (2002). Community college Puente: A validating model of education. *Educational Policy, 16*(4), 642–667.

Rendón, L. I. (2005). Testing race-neutral admissions models: Lessons from California State University-Long Beach. *The Review of Higher Education, 28*(2), 221–243.

Rendón, L. I., & Garza, H. (1996). Closing the gap between two- and four-year institutions. In L. I. Rendón & R. O. Hope (Eds.), *Educating a new majority: Transforming American's educational system for diversity* (pp. 289–308). San Francisco: Jossey-Bass.

Rendón, L. I. & Hope, R. O. (1996). *Educating a new majority: Transforming American's educational system for diversity.* San Francisco: Jossey-Bass.

Rendón, L. I., Justiz, M., & Resta, P. (1988). *Transfer education in southwest community colleges.* Columbia: University of South Carolina Press.

Rendón, L. I., & Matthews, T. B. (1994). Success of community college students: Current Issues. In J. L. Ratcliff, S. Schwarz, & L. H. Ebbers (Eds.), *Community Colleges: ASHE Reader Series* (pp. 343–353). Needham Heights, MA: Simon & Schuster Custom Publishing.

Retired Military Leaders. (2003, February 19). *Consolidated brief of Lt. Gen. Julius W. Becton, Jr., et al., as amici curiae in support of respondents, Grutter v. Bollinger,* 123 S. Ct. 2325 (2003) (No. 02–241 and 02–516). Retrieved May 28, 2008, from http://supreme.lp.findlaw.com/supreme_court/briefs/02–241/02–241.mer.ami.military.pdf

Rhoads, R. A. (1999). The politics of culture and identity: Contrasting images of multiculturalism and monoculturalism. In K. M. Shaw, J. R. Valadez, & R. A. Rhoads (Eds.), *Community colleges as cultural texts: Qualitative explorations of organizational student culture* (pp. 103–124). Albany, New York: SUNY Press.

Rhoads, R. A., & Valadez, J. R. (1996). *Democracy, multiculturalism, and the community college.* New York: Garland.

Richardson, R. C., & Bender, L. W. (1985). *Students in urban settings: Achieving the baccalaureate degree.* ASHE-ERIC Higher Education Report No. 6, 1985. Washington, DC: ASHE-ERIC Clearinghouse on Higher Education.

Richardson, R. C., & Bender, L. W. (1987). *Fostering minority access and achievement in higher education: The role of urban community colleges and universities.* San Francisco: Jossey-Bass.

Richardson, R. C., & Skinner, E. F. (1992). Helping first-generation minority students achieve degrees. *New Directions for Community Colleges, 80,* 29–43.

Riordan, C. A. (1991). *The campus climate for minorities at the University of Missouri-Rolla.* Rolla: University of Missouri-Rolla Press.

Roach, R. (2003, October 23). Georgia on the mind. The state's higher education system puts research, policy focus on Black males. *Black Issues in Higher Education.* Retrieved December 30, 2006, from http://www.findarticles.com/cf_dls/moDXK/18_20/110619171/print.jhtml

Robinson, D. K. (2003, December 4). More implications of the Michigan decisions. *Black Issues in Higher Education, 20*(21), back cover.

Roelofs, T. (2006, October 24). Photo shows Proposal 2's extremist ties, say critics. *Grand Rapids Press.* Retrieved December 12, 2006, from http://www.mlive.com/news/grpress/index.ssf?/base/news-32/1161701 173225720.xml &coll = 6

Rosen, J. (1996, April 22). The day quotas died. *The New Republic,* 21–27.

Roska, J., Grodsky, E., & Hom, W. (2006, October). *The role of community colleges in promoting student diversity in California.* Paper presented at the Equal Opportunity in Higher Education: Proposition 209—Past and Future Conference, University of California, Berkeley.

Ross, R. (1996). *Returning to the teachings: Exploring aboriginal justice.* Toronto, Ontario, Canada: Penguin Books.

Rubin, J., Pruitt, D., & Kim, S. (1994). *Social conflict: Escalation, stalemate, and settlement* (2nd ed.). New York: McGraw-Hill.

Rubin, S. E., & Roessler, R. T. (2001). *Foundations of the vocational rehabilitation process* (5th ed.). Austin, TX: Pro-Ed.

Rubio, P. F. (2001). *A history of affirmative action 1619–2000.* Jackson: University Press of Mississippi.

Sable, J., & Stennett, J. (1998). The educational progress of Hispanic students. In *The U.S. Department of Education, the condition of education 1998* (pp. 11–19). Washington, DC: U.S. Department of Education.

Salinas, M. F. (2003). *The politics of stereotype: Affirmative action and psychology.* Westport, CT: Praeger.

San Francisco State University, Institute of Civic and Community Engagement (n.d.) *Mission and goals.* Retrieved October 26, 2006, from http://www.sfsu.edu/~icce/about

Satcher, J., & Dooley-Dickey, K. (1990). Services for learning disabled students at community colleges. *College Student Affairs Journal, 10*(1), 29–35.

Sax, L. J., & Arredondo, M. (1999). Student attitudes toward affirmative action in college admissions. *Research in Higher Education, 40*(4), 439–459.

Sax, L. J., Astin, A. W., Korn, W. S., & Mahoney, K. (1996). *The American freshman: National norms for fall 1996.* Los Angeles: Higher Education Research Institute, University of California, Los Angeles.

Scheurich, J. J., & Young, M. D. (1997). Coloring epistemologies: Are our research epistemologies racially biased? *Educational Researcher, 26*(4), 4–16.

Schmidt, P. (1998, December 11). California judge upholds law allowing 2-year college to use hiring preferences. *The Chronicle of Higher Education, 45*(16), A52.

Schmidt, P. (2001, September 14). California court strikes down minority-hiring goals for community college. *The Chronicle of Higher Education, 48*(3), A29.

Schmidt, P. (2002, May 24). Next stop, Supreme Court? Appeals court upholds affirmative action at University of Michigan Law School. *The Chronicle of Higher Education, 48*(37), A24–28.

Schmidt, P. (2003, July 9). Foes of affirmative action in Michigan plan to take their battle to the ballot. *The Chronicle of Higher Education Daily News.* Retrieved October 13, 2003 from http://chronicle.com/daily/2003/07/2003070901.htm

Schmidt, P. (2006, December 15). Supreme court shows increased skepticism toward affirmative action. *The Chronicle of Higher Education, 53*(17), 1.

Schmidt, P. (2007a, September 28). At the elite colleges—dim white kids. *The Boston Globe.* Retrieved December 7, 2007, from http://www.boston.com/news/

globe/editorial_opinion/oped/articles/2007/09/28/at_the_elite_collegesdim_white
_kids/

Schmidt, P. (2007b, February 23). Regents' diversity vote means trouble for U. of
Wisconsin: The university may pay a price for directing its campuses to consider
applicants' race. *The Chronicle of Higher Education, 53*(25), 25a. Retrieved March
1, 2007, from http://chronicle.com/weekly/v53/i25/25a01701.htm

Schultz, T. W. (1961). Investment in human capital. *American Economic Review, 51*,
1–17.

Schwartz, E. (2007, June 28). Court school ruling isn't the last word. *U.S. News
and World Report.* Retrieved December 7, 2007, from http://www.usnews.com/
usnews/news/articles/070628/28court.htm

Sears, D. O., Henry, P. J., & Kosterman, R. (2000). Egalitarian values and contemporary racial politics. In D. O. Sears, J. Sidanius, & L. Bobo (Eds.), *Racialized
politics: The debate about racism in America* (pp. 75–117). Chicago: University of
Chicago Press.

Sears, D. O., & Jessor, T. (1996). Whites' racial policy attitudes: The role of white
racism. *Social Science Quarterly, 77*(4), 751–759.

Sears, D. O., & Kinder, D. R. (1985). White opposition to busing: On conceptualizing and operationalizing group conflict. *Journal of Personality and Social Psychology, 48*, 1141–1147.

Secure Borders, Economic Opportunity and Immigration Reform Act of 2007 (S.
1348) (2007).

Seifert, T. A., Drummond, J., & Pascarella, E. T. (2006). African American students' experiences of good practices: A comparison of institutional type. *Journal
of College Student Development, 47*, 185–205.

Senate Bill 1348 (the Senate Comprehensive Immigration Reform Bill), AILA Doc.
No. 05072440 (2007).

Senate Bill S.1639 (2007).

Sewell, W., & Hauser, R. (1972). Causes and consequences of higher education:
Models of the status attainment process. *American Journal of Agricultural Economics, 54*, 851–861.

Sewell, W., Hauser, R., & Ohlendorf, G. (1970). The educational and early occupational attainment process: Replications and revisions. *American Sociological Review, 35*, 1014–1027.

Sewell, W. H., Haller, A. O., & Portes, A. (1994). The educational and early occupational attainment process. In D. B. Grusky (Ed.), *Class, race, and gender: Social
stratification in sociological perspective* (pp. 336–346). Boulder, CO: Westview
Press.

Sewell, W. H., & Shaw, V. P. (1967). Socioeconomic status, intelligence, and the
attainment of higher education. *Sociology of Education, 40*(1), 1–23.

Shapiro, A. (2000). *Everybody belongs: Changing negative attitudes toward classmates
with disabilities.* New York: Routledge Falmer.

Shapiro, J. P. (1995, February 13). How much is enough? *U.S. News and World Report, 118*(6), 38.

Shaw, K. (1988). Making conflict work for you. In J. Fisher & M. Tack (Eds.), *Leaders on leadership: The college presidency* (Vol. 61, pp. 53–58). San Francisco: Jossey-Bass.

Shingles, R. D. (1992). Minority consciousness and political action: A comparative approach. In A. M. Messina, L. R. Fraga, L. A. Rhodebeck, & F. D. Wright (Eds.), *Ethnic minorities in advanced industrial democracies* (pp. 161–184). New York: Greenwood Press.

Shulman, J. L., & Bowen, W. G. (2001). *The game of life: College sports and educational values.* Princeton, NJ: Princeton University Press.

Sidanius, J., Singh, P., Hetts, J. J., & Federico, C. (2000). It's not the affirmative action, it's the African Americans: The continuing relevance of race in attitudes toward race-targeted policies. In J. Sidanius, D. Sears, & L. Bobo (Eds.), *Racialized politics: The debate about racism in America* (pp. 191–235). Chicago: University of Chicago Press.

Sigelman, L., & Welch, S. (1991). *Black Americans' views of racial inequality: The dream deferred.* Cambridge, MA: Harvard University Press.

Sipuel v. Board of Regents, 332 U.S. 631; 68 S. Ct. 299; 92 L. Ed. 247 (1948).

Skrentny, J. D. (1996). *The ironies of affirmative action: Policy, culture, and justice in America.* Chicago: University of Chicago Press.

Skrentny, J. D. (2001). *Color lines: Affirmative action, immigration and civil rights options for America.* Chicago: University of Chicago Press.

Smiles, R. V. (2002, October 10). Calling all potential Misters: South Carolina's teacher-training program "Call Me Mister" seeks to put Black males at the front of the class. *Black Issues in Higher Education.* Retrieved December 30, 2006, from http://www.findarticles.com/cf_dls/moDXK/17_19/92800207/print.jhtml

Smith, E. R., & Kluegel, J. R. (1984). Beliefs and attitudes about women's opportunity: Comparisons with beliefs about blacks and a general perspective. *Social Psychology Quarterly, 47*, 81–95.

Smith, K. M. (1993, May). *The impact of college on white students' racial attitudes.* Paper presented at the Association for Institutional Research (AIR) Annual Forum in Chicago, Illinois. (ERIC Document Reproduction Service No. ED360923).

Smith v. University of Washington Law School, No. 9935348 (1997).

Smith, W. A. (1998). Gender and racial/ethnic differences in the affirmative action attitudes of U.S. college students. *Journal of Negro Education, 67*(2), 127–141.

Smith, W. A. (2006). Racial ideology and affirmative action support in a diverse college student population. *Journal of Negro Education, 75*(4), 589–605.

Sniderman, P. M. (1991). *Reasoning and choice: Explorations in political psychology.* New York: Cambridge University Press.

Sniderman, P. M. (1993a). *Prejudice, politics, and the American dilemma.* Stanford, CA: Stanford University Press.

Sniderman, P. M. (1993b). *The scar of race.* Cambridge, MA: Belknap Press of Harvard University Press.

Snyder, S. L., & Mitchell, D. T. (2006). *Cultural locations of disability*. Chicago: University of Chicago Press.

Sokol, J. (2006). *There goes my everything: White Southerners in the age of civil rights, 1945–1975*. New York: Knopf.

Sowell, T. (2004). *Affirmative action around the world: An empirical study*. New Haven, CT: Yale University Press.

Spann, G. A. (2000). *The law of affirmative action: Twenty-five years of Supreme Court decisions on race and remedies*. New York: New York University Press.

Spring, J. (2006). *Deculturalization and the struggle for equality: A brief history of the education of dominated cultures in the Unites States* (5th ed.). New York: McGraw-Hill.

Springer, A. D. (January, 2005). Diversity and affirmative action update: Update on affirmative action in higher education: A current legal overview. *American Association of University Professors* Retrieved May 28, 2008, from http://www.aaup .org/AAUP/protect/legal/topics/aff-ac-update.htm

Springer, A. D., & Baez, B. (2002). Affirmative action is not discrimination. *The Chronicle of Higher Education, 49*(15), B17.

Stanfield, J. H. (1993). Epistemological considerations. In J. H. Stanfield and R. M. Dennis (Eds.), *Race and ethnicity in research methods* (pp. 16–36). Newbury Park, CA: Sage.

Stanush, P., Arthur, W., Jr., & Doverspike, D. (1998). Hispanic and African American reactions to a simulated race-based affirmative action scenario. *Hispanic Journal of Behavioral Sciences, 20*, 3–16.

Steele, C. M. (2000). Expert testimony in defense of affirmative action. In F. J. Crosby & C. VanDeVeer (Eds.), *Sex, race, & merit: Debating affirmative action in education and employment* (pp. 124–133). Ann Arbor: University of Michigan Press.

Steele, C. M. (2001). Understanding the performance gap. In L. Guinier & S. Sturm (Eds.), *Who's qualified?* (pp. 60–67). Boston, MA: Beacon Press.

Steele, C. M., & Aronson, J. (1995). Stereotype threat and the intellectual test performance of African Americans. *Journal of Personality and Social Psychology, 69*(5), 797–811.

Steele, C. M., & Green, S. G. (1976). Affirmative action and academic hiring: A case study of a value conflict. *Journal of Higher Education, 47*(4), 413–435.

Sternberg, R. J. (2005, January/February). Accomplishing the goals of affirmative action—with or without affirmative action. *Change, 1*, 6–13.

Sternberg, R. J. (2006). The Rainbow Project: Enhancing the SAT through assessments of analytical, practical, and creative skills. *Intelligence, 34*, 321–350.

St. John, E. (1998). Taking the initiative. *Black Issues in Higher Education, 15*(20), 12–15.

Stoker, L. (1996). Understanding differences in white's opinions across racial policies. *Social Science Quarterly, 77*(4), 768–777.

Stovall, D. O. (2001). *Possessive investment: California, 209 and the reconstruction of racist educational policy.* Unpublished dissertation, University of Illinois at Urbana-Champaign.

Sullivan, W. (2007, June 12). Bush tests clout on immigration bill. *U.S. News and World Report.* Retrieved June 12, 2007, from http://www.usnews.com/usnews/news/articles/070612/12immigration.htm

Sweatt v. Painter, 339 U.S. 629; 70 S. Ct. 848; 94 L. Ed. 1114 (1950).

Synder, S. L., & Mitchell, D. T. (2006). *Cultural locations of disabilities.* Chicago, IL: University of Chicago Press.

Tate, W. F. (1997). Critical race theory and education: History, theory, and implications. *Review of Research in Education, 22,* 195–247.

Tatum, B. D. (2003). *Why are all the black kids sitting together in the cafeteria? A psychologist explains the development of racial identity* (rev. ed.). New York: Basic Books.

Tatum, B. D. (2007). *Can we talk about race? And other conversations in an era of school resegregation.* Boston: Beacon Press.

Taylor-Carter, M. A., Doverspike, D., & Cook, K. D. (1996). The effects of affirmative action on the female beneficiary. *Human Resource Development Quarterly, 7,* 31–54.

Terry, W. (1998, May 31). Racial preferences are outdated. *Parade Magazine,* 4–5.

Tharp, M. (1998, November 9). Copying California. *U.S. News & World Report,* 34.

Thayer, P. B. (2000, May 2–8). *Retention of students from first generation and low income backgrounds. Opportunity Outlook.* (ERIC Document Reproduction Service No. ED446633).

The Chronicle of Higher Education (2006, August 25). The almanac issue, 2006–07.

The Chronicle of Higher Education (2008, August 29). The almanac issue, 2008–9. Degrees conferred by racial and ethnic group, 2005–6, p. 20.

The Sentencing Project: Research and Advocacy for Reform. (2006, May). *New incarceration figures: Thirty-three consecutive years of growth.* Retrieved January 1, 2007, from http://www.sentencingproject.org/pdfs/1044.pdf

Thernstrom, A. (1999, September 27). The end of meritocracy: Should the SAT account for race? No. *The New Republic, 221*(13), 27, 29.

Think Progress. (2006, November 4). Leader of Michigan initiative to end affirmative action welcomes Ku Klux Klan support. Retrieved December 12, 2006 from http://thinkprogress.org/2006/11/04/connerly-ku-klux-klan/

Thomas, K. (1976). Conflict and conflict management. In M. D. Dunnette (Ed.), *Handbook of industrial and organizational psychology* (pp. 889–935). Chicago: Rand McNally College Publishing.

Thornburgh, N. (2007, June 18). The case for amnesty. *Time, 169*(25), 38–42.

Tierney, W. G. (1997). The parameters of affirmative action: Equity and excellence in the academy. *Review of Educational Research, 67*(2), 165–196.

Time (2006, October 30). An in-depth view of America by the numbers, *168*(18), 41–54.

Title I—Employment of the American with Disabilities Act of 1990 (42 USC §§ 12111–12117; 29 CFR Parts 1630, 1602) (1990).

Title II—State and Local Government (Part A) of the Americans with Disabilities Act of 1990 (42 USC §§ 12131–12134; 28 CFR Part 35) (1990).

Title II—Public Services and Public Transportation (Part B) of the Americans with Disabilities Act of 1990 (42 USC §§ 12141–12165; 49 CFR_Parts 37, 38) (1990).

Title III—Public Accommodations (and Commercial Facilities) of the Americans with Disabilities Act of 1990, (42 USC §§ 12181–12189; 28 CFR Part 36) (1990).

Title IV—Telecommunications of the Americans with Disabilities Act of 1990 (47 USC § 225, 611; 47 CFR 64.601 et seq.) (1990).

Title V—Miscellaneous Provisions of the Americans with Disabilities Act of 1990 (42 U.S.C. 12115) (1990).

Title IX, Education Amendments of 1972, 20 U.S.C. §§ 1681 – 1688 (1972).

Torre, M. E., & Fine, M. (2005). Bar none: Extending affirmative action to higher education in prison. *Journal of Social Issues, 61*(33), 569–594.

Townsend, B. (1999). *Two-year colleges for women and minorities: Enabling access to the baccalaureate.* New York: Falmer Press.

Treloar, L. L. (1999). Lessons on disability and the rights of students. *Community College Review, 27,* 30–40.

Trent, W. T. (1991a). Student affirmative action in higher education: Addressing underrepresentation. In P. Altbach & K. Lomotey (Eds.), *The racial crisis in American higher education* (pp. 107–132). New York: University of New York.

Trent, W. T. (1991b). Focus on equity: Race and gender differences in degree attainment, 1975–76; 1980–81. In W. R. Allen, E. G. Epps, & N. Z. Haniff (Eds.), *College in black and white: African American students in predominantly white and in historically black public universities* (pp. 41–60). Albany: SUNY Press.

Triandis, H. C., Bontempo, R., & Villareal, M. J. (1988). Individualism and collectivism: Cross-cultural perspectives on self-in-group relationships. *Journal of Personality and Social Psychology, 54*(2), 323–338.

Trick, R. (2004, February 6). Race bill unlikely to see action. *The UW Daily Online.* Retrieved May 6, 2006 from http://www.adversity.net/washington/1200_news.htm

Trower, C. A. (2002, June). *What do we have to hide? Data and diversity.* Paper presented at the Association for Institutional Research (AIR) Annual Forum, Toronto, Ontario, Canada. (ERIC Document Reproduction Service No. ED473075)

Tuch, S. A., & Hughes, M. (1996a). Whites' opposition to race-targeted policies: One cause or many? *Social Science Quarterly, 77*(4), 778–788.

Tuch, S. A., & Hughes, M. (1996b). Whites' racial policy attitudes. *Social Science Quarterly, 77*(4), 723–745.

Tuch, T., & Sigelman, L. (1997). Race, class, and black-white differences in social policy views. In B. Norrander & C. Wilcox (Eds.), *Understanding public opinion* (pp. 37–54). Washington, DC: Congressional Quarterly Press.

Tucker, A. (1993). *Chairing the academic department: Leadership among peers* (3rd ed.). Phoenix, AZ: Oryx Press.

Turner, M. E., & Pratkanis, A. R. (1994). Affirmative action as help: A review of recipient reactions to preferential selection and affirmative action. *Basic and Applied Social Psychology, 15,* 43–69.

Unger, D. D. (2002). Employers' attitudes toward persons with disabilities in the workforce: Myths or realities? *Focus on Autism and Other Developmental Disabilities, 17*(1). Retrieved April 25, 2004, from http://www.worksupport.com/Main/proed17.asp

United States Executive Branch. (2003, January). *Brief for United States as amicus curiae supporting petitioner, Grutter v. Bollinger, 123 S. Ct. 2325 (2003)* (No. 02–241). Retrieved May 28, 2008, from http://supreme.lp.findlaw.com/supreme_court/briefs/02-241/02-241.mer.ami.usa.pdf

United States v. Paradise, 480 U.S. 149 (1987).

University of California. (1995, February 8). *Mitsubishi grants support students with disabilities. Berkeley: Regents of the University of California.* Retrieved September 3, 2002, from http://berkeley.edu/news/berkeleyan/1995/0208/mitsubishi.html

University of Illinois. (1997). *Affirmative action programs to advance minority student success in higher education.* Urbana: University of Illinois at Urbana-Champaign.

University of Michigan. (1998). Fact Sheet. Retrieved July 30, 1999, from http://www.umich.edu/~ure/admissions

University of Michigan. (2003, February 23). *Why Michigan's former admissions systems comply with Bakke and are not quotas.* Retrieved June 1, 2008, from http://www.vpcomm.umich.edu/admissions/archivedocs/comply.html

University of Michigan. (2005, January 5). *U.S. Supreme Court rules on University of Michigan cases.* Retrieved April 19, 2005, from http://www.umich.edu/news/Releases/2003/Jun03/supremecourt.html

University of Washington. (1999, May). *Maintaining diversity at the University of Washington after Initiative 200.* Retrieved May 28, 2008 from http://www.lib.washington.edu/specialcoll/collections/uarchives/mccormick/mccormick142.pdf

U.S. Census Bureau. (2000). Race for the population 18 years and over. *American Fact Finder.* Retrieved November 17, 2006, from http://factfinder.census.gov/servlet/SAFFFacts

U.S. Census Bureau. (2004). *U.S. interim projections by age, sex, race, and Hispanic origin: 2000–2050.* Retrieved October 3, 2007 from http://www.census.gov/ipc/www/usinterimproj/

U.S. Census Bureau. (2005, July). *Facts for features: 15th Anniversary of Americans with Disabilities Act: July 26, 2005.* Retrieved January 10, 2006, from, http://www.census.gov/Press-Release/www/releases/archives/facts_for_features_special_editions/004998.html

U.S. Census Bureau (2006, May 6). *Nation's population one-third minority.* Retrieved June 4, 2006 from http://www.census.gov/Press-Release/www/releases/archives/population/006808.html

U.S. Census Bureau. (2007). *Current population survey, annual social and economic supplement.* Washington, DC: U.S. Census Bureau.

U.S. Commission on Civil Rights. (2000, April). *Toward an understanding of percentage plans in higher education: Are they effective substitutes for affirmative action?* Washington, DC: U.S. Commission on Civil Rights.

U.S. Department of Education. (1998). *To assure the free appropriate public education of all children with disabilities: Twentieth annual report to Congress on the implementation of the Individuals with Disabilities Education Act.* Retrieved June 28, 2005, from http://www.ed.gov/offices/OSERS/OSEP/Research/OSEP98AnlRpt/index.html

U.S. Department of Education. (2000). *Beginning Postsecondary Students Longitudinal Study First Follow-up 1996–98 (BPS:96/98) Methodology Report, NCES 2000–157.* Washington, DC: National Center for Education Statistics.

U.S. Department of Education. (2003, March). *Race-neutral alternatives in postsecondary education: Innovative approaches to diversity.* Washington, DC: U.S. Department of Education, Office for Civil Rights.

Van Dyke, V. (1995). *Ideology and political choice: The search for freedom, justice, and virtue.* Chatham, NJ: Chatham House Publishers.

Velez, W. (1985). Finishing college: The effects of college type. *Sociology of Education, 58,* 191–200.

Vickery, L. J., & McClure, M. D. (1998, March). *The 4 p's of accessibility in postsecondary education: Philosophy, policy, procedures, and programs.* Paper presented at the annual meeting of California State University–Northridge (ERIC Document Reproduction Service No. ED421825).

Voting Rights Act of 1965, Pub. L. No. 89–110, 79 Stat. 437 (1965).

Webster, B. H., & Bishaw, A. (2007, August). *American Community Survey Reports, ACS-08, Income, Earnings, and Poverty Data from the 2006 American Community Survey.* Washington, DC: U.S. Government Printing Office.

Weiner v. Cuyahoga Community College, 19 Ohio St.2d 35, 249 N.E.2d 907, 908, 910 (1969).

West, C. (1986, July 16–23). Unmasking the black conservatives. *Christian Century,* 644. Retrieved May 23, 2008 from http://www.religion-online.org/show article.asp?title = 1046

Whitaker, D. G., & Pascarella, E. T. (1994). Two-year college attendance and socioeconomic attainment. *Journal of Higher Education, 65*(2), 194–210.

Williams, A., Schmidt, J. & Schmidt, P. (2007, January 12). Court tells Michigan universities to comply immediately with preference ban. *The Chronicle of Higher Education, 53*(19), 1.

Williamson, J. (2003). *Black power on campus: The University of Illinois 1965–1975.* Champaign: University of Illinois Press.

Wilson, R. (2001). The threatened future of affirmative action and the search for alternatives. In B. Lindsay and M. J. Justiz (Eds.), *The quest for equity in higher education: Toward new paradigms in an evolving affirmative action era* (pp. 129–139). Buffalo, NY: SUNY Press.

Wilson, W. J. (1987). *When work disappears: The world of the new urban poor.* New York: Knopf.

Wise, T. (2003). Misleading the dream: Color-blindness and the distortion of Martin Luther King Jr. Retrieved May 31, 2008 from http://www.lipmagazine.org/~timwise/misreadingdream.html

Wisely, J. (2006, December 29). Granholm backs delay on Prop 2: Group challenges admissions ruling. *Detroit Free Press.* Retrieved December 29, 2006 from http://www.freep.com/apps/pbcs.dll/article?AID=2006612290301

Witt, S. L. (1990). Affirmative action and job satisfaction: Self-interested v. public spirited perspectives on social equity—some sobering findings from the academic workplace. *Review of Public Personnel Administration, 10*(3), 73–93.

Wolanin, T. R., & Steele, P. E. (2004). *Higher education opportunities for students with disabilities: A primer for policymakers.* Washington, DC: Institute for Higher Education Policy. (ERIC Document Reproduction Service No. ED485430). Retrieved June 7, 2008 from http://www.eric.ed.gov/ERICDocs/data/ericdocs2sql/content_storage_01/0000 0 19b/80/1b/aa/6b.pdf

Wood, T. E., & Sherman, M. J. (2001). Is campus racial diversity correlated with educational benefits? *Academic Questions, 14*(3), 72–88.

Woods, J. E. (Ed.). (1997). *Investing in quality, affordable education for all Americans: A new look at community colleges.* Washington, DC: Community College Liaison Office, Office of Vocational and Adult Education.

Wright, S. W. (1997). Private scholarships for minorities challenged. *Black Issues in Higher Education, 14*(5), 14–16.

Wu, F. H. (2002). *Yellow: Race in America beyond black and white.* New York: Basic Books.

Wu, F. H., & Kidder, W. (2006, October 5). Asian Americans aren't White folks' "racial mascots." *Diverse Issues in Higher Education, 23*(17), 48.

Wygant v. Jackson Board of Education, 476 U.S. 267 (1986).

Yang, J. (1992). *Chilly campus climate: A qualitative study on white racial identity.* Washington, DC: U.S. Department of Education, Office of Educational Research and Improvement.

Zamani, E. M. (2002). Exploring racial policy views of college-age white Americans: Implications for campus climate. In R. Moore (Ed.), *The quality and quantity of contact between black and white collegians* (pp. 160–185). New York: Mellen Press.

Zamani, E. M. (2003). Affirmative action attitudes of African American community college students: The impact of educational aspirations, self interest and racial affect. In C. Camp Yeakey, R. D. Henderson, & M. Shujaa (Eds.), *Research on African American education: Vol. 2. Surmounting all odds: Education, opportunity, and society in the new millennium* (pp. 595–619). Greenwich, CT: Information Age Publishing.

Zamani, E. M. (2006). African American student affairs professionals in community college settings: A commentary for future research. In B. K. Townsend, D. D. Bragg, K. Dougherty, & F. S. Laanan (Eds.), *ASHE reader on community colleges* (3rd ed., pp. 173–180). Boston, MA: Pearson Publications.

Zamani, E. M., & Brown, M. C. (2003). Affirmative action in postsecondary educational settings: The historic nexus of meritocracy and access. *Higher Education Policy, 16,* 27–38.

Zamani-Gallaher, E. M., & Callaway, Y. (2006, June). *The challenge and call for cultural adjustments in educating African American males: Implications for school counselors and leaders.* White paper presented at the summit on The State of the African American Male in Michigan: A Courageous Conversation, Eastern Michigan University, College of Education, Ypsilanti.

Zehr, H. (1990). *Changing lenses: A new focus for crime and justice.* Waterloo, Ontario: Herald Press.

Zuniga, X., Williams, E. A., & Berger, J. B. (2005). Action-oriented democratic outcomes: The impact of student involvement with campus diversity. *Journal of College Student Development, 46*(6), 660–678.

Timeline of Affirmative Action Legislative and Judicial Developments

1788   U.S. Constitution as ratified is drafted including Article I, Section 2, to include the "Three-Fifths Compromise," which originally counted each African American slave as three-fifths of a person.

1863   The Emancipation Proclamation is issued ending slavery in the Confederate States.

1865   The 13th Amendment is added to the U.S. Constitution abolishing slavery throughout the nation.

1868   The 14th Amendment is added to the U.S. Constitution guaranteeing equal protection under the law.

The 15th Amendment is added to the U.S. Constitution extending the right to vote to all male citizens.

The Morrill Act establishes 16 higher education institutions specifically dedicated to the education of African Americans.

1896   In *Plessy v. Ferguson* (163 U.S. 537; 16 S. Ct. 1138; 41 L. Ed. 256; 1896 U.S. LEXIS 3390), the U.S. Supreme Court establishes the doctrine of "separate but equal" helping to promote segregationist laws and policies.

President Harry S. Truman issues Executive Order No. 9981, which ends segregation in the U.S. Armed Forces.

1948/1950   In two separate cases, the U.S. Supreme Court requires the state of Oklahoma to change its approach to the higher education of African Americans. In *Sipuel v. Board of Regents* (332 U.S. 631; 68 S. Ct. 299; 92 L. Ed. 247; 1948 U.S. LEXIS 2645), the court ordered the University of Oklahoma to admit an African American law student because the state did not provide a separate law school for African Americans. In *McLaurin v. Oklahoma State Regents* (339 U.S. 637; 70 S. Ct. 851; 94 L. Ed. 1149; 1950 U.S. LEXIS 1810), the court ruled that it was unconstitutional for an African American student to be physically segregated from other students because of his race.

In *Sweatt v. Painter* (339 U.S. 629; 70 S. Ct. 848; 94 L. Ed. 1114; 1950 U.S. LEXIS 1809), ruled that the state of Texas's newly established law school for African Americans did not provide separate but equal facilities. As such, it was not good enough to deny the petitioner the right to attend the University of Texas Law School.

1954   Focusing on elementary and secondary education, the U.S. Supreme Court reverses its doctrine of "separate but equal" established in *Plessy v. Ferguson*. In *Brown v. Board of Education* 347 U.S. 483, 98 L. Ed. 873 (74 S. Ct. 686, 1954), the court held that state laws mandating or permitting segregation are unconstitutional under the Equal Protection Clause of the 14th Amendment.

1961   The first reference to affirmative action is made by President John F. Kennedy via Executive Order No. 10925, which installs the EEOC and mandates that projects financed with federal funds "take affirmative action" in removing racial bias and ensuring fair hiring and employment practices.

1964   Civil Rights Act of 1964 signed by President Lyndon B. Johnson. This legislation included Title VI, which prohibits public and private institutions receiving public funds from discriminating on the basis of "race, color, religion, sex, or national origin" and provided for the establishment of the EEOC.

1965   President Lyndon B. Johnson issues Executive Orders No. 11246 and No. 11375 requiring organizations that receive federal contracts of $50,000 or more and have 50 or more employees to develop affirmative action plans. The OFCCP is developed to monitor compliance with these regulations.

1969   President Richard Nixon delivers the "Philadelphia Order," also known as the most forceful affirmative action plan to date in guaranteeing fair hiring practices in construction by requiring federal contractors to show affirmative action in meeting the goals of increasing minority employment.

1972   Title IX of the Education Amendments of 1972 prohibits gender-based discrimination in the programs and employment practices of federally funded organizations.

1978   In *Regents of the University of California v. Bakke* 438 U.S. 265 (1978), a White student sued on the basis of reverse discrimination. Resolving the case, the U.S. Supreme Court ruled that UC-Davis Medical School's special admissions program designed to recruit more disadvantaged students established a quota and was therefore unlawful. At the same time, the court also ruled that the type of program UC-Davis Medical School attempted to implement is only lawful when properly devised in a manner that race could factor into admissions' decisions without serving as the sole determinant.

1980   *Fullilove* v. *Klutznick*, 448 U.S. 448 (1980) was a key case following the striking down of strict quotas in *Bakke*, as the Supreme Court ruled that some modest quotas were permissible. Additionally, in *Fullilove*, the court upheld a federal law requiring that 15% of funds for public works be set aside for qualified minority contractors.

1981   In another reverse discrimination case, *DeRonde v. Regents of the University* (28 Cal. 3d 875; 625 P.2d 220; 1981 Cal. LEXIS 119), the Supreme Court of California ruled that the affirmative action plan in place at the UC-Davis Law School violated the Equal Protection Clause of the Fourteenth Amendment.

1986   In *Wygant v. Jackson Board of Education*, 476 U.S. 267 (1986) the U.S. Supreme Court held that the school board's plan to consider race in laying off teachers violated the Equal Protection Clause of the 14th Amendment. In this case, the court also established the "strict scrutiny" test (i.e., affirmative action programs fulfilled a "compelling governmental interest"), which contends that race-based decision making is lawful only when it is a compelling interest of the state and the procedures for enacting it are narrowly tailored for that specific purpose.

1987   In *United States v. Paradise*, 480 U.S. 149 (1987) the use of numerical quotas was challenged in Alabama relative to the hiring of Black state troopers in response to the 1970 federal mandate to implement specific racial quotas after it was found that the state of Alabama's Department of Public Safety systematically discriminated against Blacks; there had never been a Black trooper hired in the 37-year history of the patrol. However, the Supreme Court upheld the use of strict quotas in this case.

1989   *City of Richmond v. Croson*, 488 U.S. 469 (1989) is important, as the precedent of meeting strict scrutiny and unconstitutionality without proof of widespread racial discrimination emerged. The case involved challenging affirmative action set-aside programs at the state and local levels. Thirty percent of city construction funds were reserved for Black-owned firms. However, the Supreme Court ruled that an "amorphous claim that there has been past discrimination in a particular industry cannot justify the use of an unyielding racial quota." The court maintained that the strict scrutiny test would ensure that the means chosen "fit" diversity via numerical goals and that no suspect motives would be employed in rendering illegitimate racial prejudice.

1992   In an effort to resolve affirmative action controversy, the U.S. Department of Education and the University of California, Berkeley, established an agreement ending the admissions practice of placing applicants in separate pools on the basis of race.

1994   In *Podberesky v. Kirwan*, 38 F.3d 147 (1994) the U.S. Circuit Court of Appeals for the Fourth Circuit held that the University of Maryland's Banneker Scholarship Program unlawfully violated the Equal Protection Clause of the 14th Amendment. Applying the strict scrutiny test, the Fourth Circuit ruled that the scholarship program did not satisfy the first element of the test. The case was remanded to the U.S. District Court for the District of Maryland for further review and resolution.

In the case of *Hopwood v. State of Texas* (861 F. Supp. 551; 1994 U.S. Dist. LEXIS 11870), the U.S. District Court for the Western District of Texas held that the admissions policy of the University of Texas School of Law established an unlawful quota system.

1995   In the case of *Adarand Constructors, Inc. v. Pena*, 115 S.Ct. 2097 (1995) the court again called for strict scrutiny in determining whether discrimination existed before implementing a federal affirmative action program. The majority of Supreme Court justices contended that the remediation of inequities through the use of race-based measures was constitutional in certain circumstances given "the unhappy persistence of both the practice and the lingering effects of racial discrimination against minority groups in this country."

White House Guidelines on Affirmative Action—President William J. Clinton expressed the need to reaffirm access by reforming affirmative action. He offered "mend it, don't end it" relative to mandating affirmative action because of the continuing existence of systematic discrimination in the United States. He asserted that affirmative action should remain, however, not include the use of quotas, create preferences for unqualified people, or create reverse discrimination, and that affirmative action programs should only persist until its equal opportunity purposes have been achieved.

1996   Once again attempting to resolve the case of *Hopwood v. State of Texas*, S.C. 95–1773 (1996) the U.S. Circuit Court of Appeals for the Fifth Circuit held that the Equal Protection Clause of the 14th Amendment does not permit an institution to establish preferential, race-based admissions policies. The Fifth Circuit also ruled that the University of Texas School of Law may no longer consider race in its admissions decisions.

1997   California Proposition 209, also known as the California Civil Rights Initiative, is enacted into law following a ballot measure to eliminate the use of affirmative action programs throughout state and local agencies including public colleges and universities.

1998   Washington becomes the second state to abolish state affirmative action measures when it passed Initiative 200, similar to California's Proposition 209.

2000   Governor Jeb Bush receives approval from the Florida legislature to ban race as a factor in college admissions and launches the One Florida Initiative ending affirmative action in the state. In *Gratz v. Bollinger*, 122 F. Supp. 2d 811. (E.D. Mich. 2000), the U.S. District Court for the Eastern District of Michigan, Southern Division, ruled that the University of Michigan's College of Literature, Science, and Arts use of race in its admissions decisions was a lawful and "narrowly tailored" way of achieving diversity.

2001   In *Grutter v. Bollinger*, 137 F. Supp. 2d 821. (E.D. Mich. 2001) the U.S. District Court for the Eastern District of Michigan, Southern Division, held that the University of Michigan Law School's use of race in its admissions decisions is unconstitutional. The university's policies violate both the Equal Protection Clause of the 14th Amendment and Title VI of the Civil Rights Act of 1964. This court also ruled that diversity is neither a "compelling interest" of the state nor a remedy for past discrimination.

2003   The U.S. Supreme Court upholds the use of race as one of many factors in university admissions. In a 5 to 4 decision the court supports the University of Michigan Law School's policy in the *Grutter* case as using race among a myriad of measures as diversity is a compelling state interest. In the *Gratz* case the Supreme Court ruled 6 to 3 that the University of Michigan's undergraduate admissions point system that awarded additional points to minorities must be modified as it did not meet strict scrutiny or was narrowly focused to provide individualized consideration of applicants.

2006   Michigan's Proposal 2 passes following voters' supporting a ballot initiative that comprehensively bans affirmative action in the state. This legislation parallels earlier initiatives in California, Washington state, and Florida. Labeled by some as misleading, Proposal 2, also referred to as the Michigan Civil Rights Initiative (MCRI), is really an anti-affirmative-action measure whereby voting yes to the MCRI equates to support for abolishing affirmative action. On December 22, 2006, the Michigan state constitution was amended disallowing the consideration of gender, race, ethnicity, color, or national origin for public employment, education, or contracting purposes. (Brunner, 2006a; Brunner & Haney, 2006).

Official Ballot Language Michigan Proposal 06-2

A proposal to amend the state constitution to ban affirmative action programs that give preferential treatment to groups or individuals based on their race, gender, color, ethnicity or national origin for public employment, education or contracting purposes.

The proposed amendment would:

Ban public institutions from using affirmative action programs that give preferential treatment to groups or individuals based on their race, gender, color, ethnicity or national origin for public employment, education or contracting purposes. Public institutions affected by the proposal include state government, local governments, public colleges and universities, community colleges and school districts.

Prohibit public institutions from discriminating against groups or individuals due to their gender, ethnicity, race, color or national origin. (A separate provision of the state constitution already prohibits discrimination on the basis of race, color or national origin.)

Should this proposal be adopted?

YES _____   NO _____

Source: Michigan Voter Guide 2006
Retrieved from http://www.lwvmi.org/documents/LWVGuide06p30.pdf

APPENDIX A.3

State of Michigan Constitutional Amendment[1]

ARTICLE I

Section 26.

1. The University of Michigan, Michigan State University, Wayne State University, and any other public college or university, community college, or school district shall not discriminate against, or grant preferential treatment to, any individual or group on the basis of race, sex, color, ethnicity, or national origin in the operation of public employment, public education or public contracting.
2. The state shall not discriminate against, or grant preferential treatment to, any individual or group on the basis of race, sex, color, ethnicity or national origin the operation of public employment, public education, or public contracting.
3. For the purposes of this section "state" includes, but is not necessarily limited to, the state itself, any city, county, any public college, university, or community college, school district, or other political subdivision or governmental instrumentality of or within the State of Michigan not included in sub-section 1.
4. This section does not prohibit action that must be taken to establish or maintain eligibility for any federal program if ineligibility would result in a loss of federal funds to the state.
5. Nothing in this section shall be interpreted as prohibiting bona fide qualifications based on sex that are reasonably necessary to the normal operation of public employment, public education, or public contracting.
6. The remedies available for violation of this section shall be the same, regardless of the injured party's race, sex, color, ethnicity, or national origin, as are otherwise available for violations of Michigan's anti-discrimination law.

[1] The passage of Proposal 2, amended Article I, of the state constitution with the new addition of Section 26. According to the Michigan Constitution, the amendment takes effect "at the end of 45 days after the date of the election at which it was approved." Subsequently, the amendment to ban affirmative action in the state of Michigan became effective December 23, 2006.

7. This section shall be self-executing. If any parts or parts of this section are found to be in conflict with the United States Constitution or federal law, the section shall be implemented to the maximum extent that the United States Constitution and federal law permit. Any provision held invalid shall be severable from the remaining portions of this section.

8. This section applies only to action taken after the effective date of this section.

9. This section does not invalidate any court order or consent decree that is in force as of the effective date of this section.

Instructional Supplement

Chapter Summary Outline, Discussion Questions, and Exercises for Further Thought[1]

Chapter 1

Navigating the Rocky Terrain of the Post–Civil Rights Era

Chapter 1 Premise: To fully assess the present climate for access policies, it is necessary to place the struggle for civil liberties in a historical context. By examining the antecedents to present-day challenges to affirmative action, one can more appropriately understand the varying interpretations of equal treatments and constitutional rights.

I. Over the years, U.S. society has become more culturally pluralistic because of immigration, birth rates, and so forth. However, two patterns were evident:

A. Prior to the civil rights initiatives of the 1950s and 1960s, there was very little racial/ethnic diversity in American organizations and on college campuses (Allen, 2004; Bowen & Bok, 1998; Fleming, 1984).

B. The expansion of opportunities in employment and higher education for minority populations, particularly African Americans, emerged during this era, increasing the participation for members of historically disadvantaged, disenfranchised, underrepresented groups.

II. Initially, civil rights policies and programs were established to redress discriminatory treatment African Americans suffered through the heinous system of slavery, Jim Crow, and continued de facto discrimination spanning more than three centuries.

A. The Dred Scott case is an example of legislation.

B. The Emancipation Proclamation was an attempt to prevent Civil War over slavery, not to grant Blacks rights.

---

[1] Compiled with assistance from T. Elon Dancy II, assistant professor of higher education, University of Oklahoma.

C. In 1865 the 13th Amendment to the U.S. Constitution abolished slavery, yet equal protection for African Americans (and other deprived groups such as Native Americans and women) was not guaranteed.

D. With the addition of the 15th Amendment to the U.S. Constitution the disparate treatment in voting was addressed in 1870, although injustices along racial lines persisted for many decades to follow.

E. The period following the Civil War and Reconstruction during 1861–1877 has been referred to as the point when the first affirmative action programs debuted.

   1. Representative John Coburn, Indiana Republican, coined the term.

   2. In this work, affirmative action is linked to safeguarding Black civil rights from the White affirmative action of state-sanctioned discrimination and refusal to stop White supremacist terrorism.

F. The National Labor Relations Act of 1935 referenced the need for affirmative action policy on behalf of union members and organizers who had been subjected to employment discrimination.

G. Colker (2005) refers to affirmative action policy as supportive of the antidifferentiation language of the Civil Rights Act as Congress provides protection against racial discrimination across the board.

H. In the early days of the enforcement of the Civil Rights Act, the courts did not have to consider whether it reflected an antisubordination or antidifferentiation perspective because the plaintiffs were racial minorities or women who had claims of discrimination under either legal theory.

   1. Courts soon concluded that the Civil Rights Act did not embody a pure antidifferentiation perspective.

   2. Result: Whites and men brought race and gender discrimination claims.

   3. Over time, however, the courts have more and more narrowly construed the ability of employers to institute affirmative action programs and hence have moved the Civil Rights Act to a purer antidifferentiation model.

I. In sum, while the government has promoted and encouraged affirmative action, employers and educational institutions have largely approached the implementation of affirmative action on a voluntary basis.

III.   Historical Accounts and Contemporary Clashes in U.S. Civil Rights
  A.   The 1950s began to lay the groundwork for what would become equal educational opportunity.
    1.   In *Brown v. Board of Education* (1954) the Supreme Court maintained that the precedent of "separate but equal" set in *Plessey v. Ferguson* (1896) was no longer constitutional.
    2.   The *Brown* decision began to dismantle K–12 public school segregation.
    3.   However, *Florida ex rel. Hawkins v. Board of Control* (1956) extended the unconstitutionality of "separate but equal" beyond elementary and secondary schools when enforcing higher education desegregation.
    4.   The late 1950s witnessed continued confrontations on integration with federal troops and the National Guard having to escort students, later referred to as the "Little Rock Nine," to Central High School in Little Rock, AR.
    5.   The Student Nonviolent Coordinating Committee (SNCC) began coordinating sit-ins. Congress of Racial Equality (CORE) organized freedom rides.
    6.   James Meredith enrolled at the University of Mississippi, which was surrounded by 5,000 federal troops called to respond to outbreaks of violence, rioting, and protest over integration of the flagship campus.
    7.   In the 1960s Congress amended the Constitution to extend suffrage to Blacks, passed four major civil rights bills, and funded numerous social welfare programs, including the War on Poverty.
       a.   These efforts to improve the situation of Blacks were successful: the economic status of Blacks improved, poverty declined, and on many indicators differences between races became much smaller.
       b.   But will this continue in coming decades?
    8.   During this period of civil unrest, racial and campus crises occurred at several colleges and universities, and efforts began to end racial divides through legal motions to ensure equality across racial/ethnic groups.

9. Concomitantly, the 1950s and 1960s gave birth to the idea of racial diversification and policy implementation as a national priority.
   a. President Lyndon B. Johnson signed the Civil Rights Act of 1964.
   b. Congress passed the Voting Rights Act of 1965.
   c. Executive Order No. 10925 was issued by Johnson and later evolved into Executive Order No. 11246, which evolved into a series of policies and programming commonly referring to affirmative action.
   d. More specifically, any organization conducting business with the federal government had to implement affirmative action by becoming more inclusive in its hiring practices.

B. Affirmative action was created to eradicate the legacy of discrimination and promote equal opportunity for African Americans in particular.
   1. By 1971 the formulation of affirmative action plans and programs were required at institutions of higher learning, particularly targeting predominately White institutions.
   2. Student affirmative action can be defined as special efforts directed toward African Americans, Hispanic Americans, Native Americans, and women to enlarge the applicant pool of potential students and to advocate for equal educational opportunities.
   3. In sum affirmative action evolved from Title VI of the Civil Rights Act of 1964 in an effort to provide more teeth to the 14th Amendment in solidifying equal protection for all citizens.
      a. K–16 educational institutions find themselves being charged to defend affirmative acts of inclusion targeted at the underrepresented and disadvantaged relative to hiring and admissions.
      b. The intent of affirmative action has been questioned and legally challenged since its inception irrespective of previous discrimination or its prior effects.
         i. legal tests illustrate the lack of consensus
         ii. critiqued as forms of preferential treatment or tokenism

IV. Demographic Realities and Participation Trends
A. The term *racial/ethnic minority* is a misnomer as there are more people of color than Whites worldwide.

B. From a Western perspective and U.S. context, the term racial/ethnic minority will become outmoded as people of color will collectively represent the majority of the U.S. population by the year 2050.

V.   K–12 Education
A. Enrollment in public elementary and secondary schools rose 22% between 1985 and 2004.
B. The percentage distribution by race/ethnicity for K–12 students represents an +0.6% increase for African Americans, +0.8% for Asian/Pacific Islander students, +5.8% for Hispanic students, only +0.1% increase for American Indian/Alaska Natives, and −7.4% decrease among White students.
C. High-stakes testing and the role of assessment have received greater attention.

VI. Postsecondary Education
A. College attendance is on the rise; enrollment at degree-granting institutions during 1982 and 1992 increase 17%—largely because of female attendees.
B. A 14% increase from 1976 to 2002 (15% compared to 29%) has been noted in the proportion of American college students who are members of racial/ethnic minority groups—largely Hispanic.
C. While the proportion of African American students fluctuated for most of the early portion of this time, the 9% enrolled in 1976 had only risen to 12% by 2002.
D. Participation of non-Asian students of color in higher education reflects stratification and differential completion rates.
E. Degree conferral is highest for Asian American students (62%), followed by Whites (58%), Hispanics (42%), with African American students falling last (36%).
F. By the year 2000, over half of undergraduates were women and little over two-fifths were 24 years or older, reflecting a growing nontraditional aged student demographic.
G. Community colleges have historically opened their doors to nontraditional students relative to age, gender, race/ethnicity, low-income, first-generation, people with disabilities, and so forth.
H. Two-year institutions have enrolled students of color, namely American Indian, African American, and Hispanic students in higher proportions than 4-year colleges and universities for over the last 20 plus years.

I. Four-year colleges and universities have enrolled lower proportions of African American and Hispanic students for the last 2 decades than 2-year institutions of higher learning.

J. Nearly half of all African American college students enrolled in postsecondary education 20 years ago attended community colleges, and the same holds true today with just under half of African Americans pursuing a college education doing so at a 2-year institution of higher learning.

K. Like African Americans, the number of Hispanics attending 2-year versus 4-year institutions has remained virtually unchanged over the last fifty years.

L. The participation and ensuing growth of women, African American, Hispanic, first-generation, and low-income students has largely been at 2-year institutions of higher learning.

M. Non-Asian students of color enter higher education at lower rates than their White and Asian American counterparts.

N. The literature has suggested continuance of "affirmative acts," in other words, special efforts to recruit, and once admitted, assist students of color in their postsecondary adjustment and transition given the shifting demographics of this country's populace.

VII. Retrenchment and the Politics of Access Policy Opinions
    A. Examples of various attempts to dismantle affirmative action are notable.
        1. The persistent climate of backlash surrounding affirmative action in higher education.
        2. Identity politics tend to surface in the differing political ideologies of students at various colleges and universities.
    B. Research is limited in examining student affirmative action attitudes as they relate to sociopolitical views by race, gender, and income.
        1. The literature has discussed in great detail the public opinion of Whites about affirmative action.
        2. A lack of consensus and little inquiry regarding people of color, their attitudes toward affirmative action, and political leanings—because of a belief that the thoughts are alike.
    C. Minority consciousness extends from conservatism to liberalism to radicalism.
        1. Liberals are considered to be individuals who question unequal participation of all citizens, advocate for governmental

intervention in assuring equity, and at the same time maintain a basic belief in economic, political, and social reform.

2. Conservatives generally echo preference of the status quo, while not challenging the distribution of societal resources or the stratification of their group's positioning in the present social order.

3. Radicals espouse the outermost rejection of the existing social order and link racism and sexism to the underlying principles of American politics.

D. The extant literature has noted that the driving force of American race relations is the degree to which Whites and people of color differ on social policy issues based on their values, absorption of pervasive stereotypes, and general beliefs about inequality.

VIII. Determinants of Stigma, Stereotypes, and Social Race Relations

A. Controversy surrounding affirmative action programs stems from the contention that diversity initiatives may be harmful to the intended beneficiaries.

B. In many circumstances the relationship of racial discrimination and stigma interact as a result of stereotyping.

C. Prevailing false beliefs that mark stigmatized groups have often worked against securing access and equal opportunities for individuals of that membership.

D. People with power are most commonly the markers who maintain the ability to exercise social control over stigmatized groups.

E. Stigma is thought to have a direct relationship with social inequities.

F. The institutionalization of stigma is systemic.

IX. The Scarlet Letter *A* and Affirming Diversity

A. Affirmative action is perceived by some as a disadvantage to women and minorities.

1. Critics suggest that stigmatization hampers the beneficiaries.

2. In a 1981 Stanford University study, 106 male and female undergraduates participated in a study on federal policies. The results revealed 41% of males and 31% of females expressed support for affirmative action.

3. Participants describe affirmative action in terms of fairness most in principle (Ayers, 1992).

4. The notion of affirmative action as tokenism is purported to imply the stigma of incompetence.

5. Research to date has not effectively illustrated the extent to which potential beneficiaries feel stigmatized as a result of affirmative action.

X.   The Impact of Stigmatization and Stereotyping on Affirmative Action

    A. The ability of stigmatized groups to alter society's image of them was developed in the last 30 years—via NAACP, the Urban League.

    B. Behind efforts to eliminate affirmative action lie stereotypes such as teacher's low expectations of students of color, the public's perception of the welfare queen, and so many other negative views that adversely affect and further marginalize students of color.

XI.   High-Stakes Testing, Stereotype Threat, and Affirmative Action

    A. Given the testing movement's checkered history beginnings, one should consider which came first—psychometric bias or social bias? Is it the long history of social bias, such as racial stereotyping, discrimination, and intolerance, that fuels psychometric bias to manifest itself? Or is it psychometric bias in the form of unreliability of the instrumentation, the variance in testing conditions, or structural inequities in the educational preparation of students by race/ethnicity, gender, and class that perpetuate oppressive circumstances for marginalized groups?

    B. While some African Americans have ascended into the middle class, overall there is still a Black-White achievement gap and a psychological realm unaccounted for, if assuming all things being equal, that the same factors for predicting White students' performance will align with Black student success.

    C. Scholars like Jacqueline Fleming (1984, 2000) and Claude Steele (2000, 2001) have published that the elimination of affirmative action would make the presumable objectivity of ACT and SAT college entrance exams more pronounced.

Chapter 1

Questions and Exercises for Further Thought

- What tensions persist between constitutional rights and civil liberties that continue to place African Americans and other people of color at the center of the struggle for educational access?

- Given the changing demographics, what are the implications for future access or affirmative action policies?
- With enrollment and graduation trends since the 1970s continuing to leave people of color at a disadvantage, how should campuses reshape their enrollment and retention policies?
- Research on attitudes toward affirmative action is limited. What research is needed to further understand the costs and benefits of affirmative action race-conscious policies?
- How can receipt of social benefits or access to social resources and education further marginalize students of color?

Exercise #1

The following exercises could be used in a graduate course (e.g., policy analysis, social justice, multicultural/pluralism courses) or may be used in a faculty/staff diversity workshop. Begin with the general question: *Is K–12 and/or postsecondary public education equal for all students in the United States? Why or why not?*

Split the group up into smaller groups and have them explain their K–16 educational experiences. In the small-group discussion the following questions could be proposed: Where did you go to school? What was the racial/ethnic makeup of your school? Were students of color overrepresented in any group of students (e.g., special education, discipline problems, athletics, etc.)? Were there any comprehensive discussions of race in the curriculum at your schools? The idea is to have the group begin to think about how K–16 organizations are a part of raced, classed, and gendered educational systems.

Exercise #2

With a medium- to large-size group, have each of the participants define the term *minority*. Ask them to discuss how the word is used in the larger context of the United States. Second, explain the demographics of the United States and provide general characteristics of the world's population. Explain that the population of the planet is predominantly people of color. Following this discussion, have them address why the term minority has become so prevalent in our language despite what we know about the rest of the world and the future projections of what the United States will look like racially and ethnically in the next few decades.

Chapter 2

The Language of Entitlement and Framing of Affirmative Action

Chapter 2 Premise: To problematize the notion of White entitlement and the compelling interest of the state. In so doing, the hope is to place affirmative action in an ideological perspective, with the hope of advocating for policies that recognize historical inequalities in higher education.

I.   Framing of Affirmative Action: Based on Race, Gender, or Need
   A.   Public opinion on social policies is often formed by how the issues are framed and presented to the public.
   B.   Race-based affirmative action is consistent with American ideas of fairness, as it has brought more people of color to the attention of employers and higher education admissions officers.
   C.   Affirmative action is often framed in Black and White.
   D.   Social policy implementation that is race targeted has become commonly referred to as *affirmative action programming*.

II.   Perceptions of Policy—Who Benefits?
   A.   People of different racial/ethnic backgrounds often perceive affirmative action differently.
   B.   Racial affect is displayed in subtle or overt expressions that reflect an individual's opinion regarding changes in social stratification and the status quo.
   C.   Research has noted that support for affirmative action among Hispanic students was dependent upon socioeconomic status (SES) and English as a second language. For Hispanic collegians, higher SES and/or English as the native language were indicative of resistance toward affirmative action in college admissions.
   D.   Smith (1993) conducted a study with 485 students at the University of Michigan regarding racial attitudes and views on affirmative action. The findings revealed that students enter college ambivalent about affirmative action, however, during the first year of study White males became less supportive of affirmative action while female support for these policies increased.
   E.   In examining whether gender inequality would prompt women to be more supportive of race-specific affirmative action, opposition to affirmative action among White women did not differ from White men.

F. Affirmative action is often viewed as a burden imposed on present-day society to address historical discrimination.

G. Need-based affirmative action is thought to be a potential compromise by some because policies would no longer target just racial minorities and women but extend to people from all racial backgrounds who demonstrated economic need.

    1. Feinberg (1996) argued that race- and gender-based affirmative action addresses three moral issues that need-based affirmative action policies do not adequately meet. Those three are (a) historical debt, (b) equality of opportunity, and (c) economics and the distribution of societal resources.

        a. This perspective only entertains the economic factors of affirmative action while not acknowledging previous injustices to people of color and women.

    2. Bowen et al. (2005) look at the issue of differential access by arguing for need-based affirmative action. The authors fail to acknowledge that poor Whites still have "the complexion for protection" and enjoy White privilege.

    3. It is negligent to suggest that there is comparative suffering or drawbacks between Whites and people of color when Whites make up three-fourths of the U.S. populace but roughly 8% live beneath the poverty level.

III. Views Regarding Race Relations, Diversity Policies, and Self-Interest

A. The rejection of affirmative action based on self-interest may be attributed to notions about unfairness regarding social policies and programs that seek to assist marginalized groups.

B. Kluegel and Smith (1983) describe self-interest as one's concern with the maintenance of the status quo.

C. Self-interest can be defined at the individual and group level.

D. Individual self-interest refers to private interests in rates of return or loss for a person and direct family members.

E. Group self-interest would involve making group-based appraisals when taking race-based policies into account based on one's categorical identification or affiliation.

F. Closely related to individual and group self-interest, economic self-interest refers to competitive and cooperative forms of self-interest.

G. The particular group a person ascribes to could bear some relationship to the person's racial identity and policy attitudes consider Bell's (1992) interest convergence.

IV. White Privilege and Racist Policy Formation
   A. Ideologically, affirmative action disrupts the privilege of Whiteness.
   B. Right-wing groups are quick to use Martin Luther King's quote concerning the judgment of people on the content of their character rather than the color of their skin. Simultaneously, they conveniently ignore King's (1964) opinion in *Why We Can't Wait*, arguing the importance of compensatory treatment for disadvantaged persons.

V. The Battle of Propaganda: CIR and the Discourse of Infringement

VI. Legal Antecedents Affecting Affirmative Action in Higher Education
   A. CIR language is explicit in supporting a conservative lean, maintaining the protection of individual and economic rights. It remains ironic that portions of CIR support come from institutions with White supremacy agendas.
   B. CIR in its rhetoric pushes for the removal of centers and programs for students of color under the guise that it promotes student segregation and divisions among groups on college campuses. What it fittingly overlooks is the idea that PWI campuses unfortunately are contested spaces that often serve as reflections of the society at large.
   C. The diversity segment of the CIR handbook contains a small section providing rationale on the legality of legacy admits (e.g., children of alumni admitted to an institution). Schools may also give preference to athletes and children from very affluent families.
   D. Language is of critical importance in the interpretation of access policies and programs.
   E. Black athletes serve the interests of predominately White universities through financial contributions—(Bell's (1992) interest convergence has conceptual utility here).

Chapter 2

Questions and Exercises for Further Thought

- How is White privilege or entitlement manifested on campuses of PWIs?
- What are the similarities and differences between need-based, race-based, and gender-based affirmative action policies? Discuss further

the parallels and disconnections between the tenets of the various forms of affirmative action programming.

- The affirmative action debate is extremely sensitive to language and terminology. Which terms are often used but elicit multiple meanings on different sides of the policy debate?
- Consider the policy community and all the various stakeholders/interest groups related to affirmative action. Which do you perceive to be the most active interest groups at the state and federal level (also including nongovernmental policy actors)?

EXERCISE #1

This exercise is useful as a supplemental conversation to racism as a system. This could be used in a group discussion format, possibly for a graduate course or professional development diversity workshop for faculty and/or staff.

Have the group define privilege. Ask group members if they view affirmative action policies as privilege or as special treatment. (Please note: This has the potential to be an extremely heated conversation—a skilled moderator will need to lead this discussion.)

Following this discussion explain the notion of legacy admits (i.e., the admission of students who are the relatives of alumni). Where this is often viewed as a protracted policy to solidify the alumni base for future contributions to the university, the policy reifies the structure of maintaining the admission of Whites. If a university is conducting this workshop, it will be important to find out whether the institutions' application for admission asks if the applicant has a relative who is a graduate. If it does, this question is weighted as part of the points given to the applicant during the admission process. This process also lessens the chance for first-generation students to be admitted (for more references, see Bowen & Bok, 1998).

EXERCISE #2

Debate—Break out into two small groups of 3–4 people for an affirmative action debate. One of the small groups will be pro–affirmative action and the other group is con. Have each group arguing its side/position on affirmative action to consider the status of the educational outcomes by race/ethnicity, gender, and class, as well as funding levels for diversity and patterns of government action or inaction in correspondence with formal laws. Additionally, have the group think about the politics of the policy process, and consider offering any alternatives group members think would be in the best interests of facilitating healthy participation and equity across marginalized groups.

Chapter 3

Accessing the Historical Repositories of Social and Cultural Capital in Higher Education

Chapter 3 Premise: To outline historical challenges to postsecondary educational equity and the construction of legal precedents that are key to understanding the practice of affirmative action in a contemporary context.

I. Legislative Antecedents Affecting Affirmative Action in Higher Education
    A. In the case of *DeFunis v. Odegaard* (1974) the trial court found the use of race in admissions at the University of Washington School of Law to be unconstitutional.
    B. Another early test of affirmative action was the *Regents of the University of California v. Bakke* (1978), which involved Alan Bakke who was twice denied admission to the University of California at Davis medical school and then sued the university on the grounds of reverse discrimination. The Supreme Court ruled that Bakke's civil rights had been violated in the use of strict set-asides.
    C. In *Mississippi University for Women v. Hogan* (1982) it was ruled that women's institutions were no longer justifiable.
    D. In *Podberesky v. Kirwan* (1994), the use of race-specific scholarships at the University of Maryland at College Park was questioned.
    E. Anti-affirmative-action legislation in California led to a more aggressive attack on affirmative action programs in higher education around the country. Concurrent with efforts to dismantle affirmative action in California was *Adarand Contractors, Inc. v. Pena* (1995). *Adarand* concerned the use of race in awarding construction contracts.
    F. *Hopwood v. State of Texas* (1996) concerned four White students who filed a suit against the University of Texas at Austin School of Law after being denied admission.
    G. The University of Massachusetts at one time provided an edge to African American, Hispanic, and American Indian applicants in admissions and financial aid decisions. The University of Massachusetts' decision to limit the use of race as a means of achieving

campus diversity was in response to the review and retreat of affirmative action efforts at peer institutions.

H. Similar to the University of Massachusetts, the University of California at Los Angeles (UCLA) has responded to the anti-affirmative-action climate with an educational venture referred to as the Early Start Program.

II. In April of 2000 the Governor of Florida, Jeb Bush, announced his One Florida Plan, also known as the Florida 20 Percent Plan. According to Bush, the One Florida Plan is an attempt to mend and not end affirmative action programs by eradicating racial preferences instead of establishing college admission that are completely color blind. NAACP's Kweisi Mfume called this "Jim Crow Jr."

III. Critical Race Theory (CRT) and Capital Inequities

IV. CRT is a useful conceptual lens to analyze the intersection of race, class, and gender.

A. Race matters at institutions of higher learning because it is an important factor in assessing campus climate.

B. The majority of students of color attend predominately White 2- and 4-year institutions where the campus climate is geared to the majority students.

C. Americans' beliefs about inequality illustrate a racial divide regarding policy implementation.

D. Because universities have larger enrollments than 4-year colleges on average, the findings suggest that increases in racial diversity are consistent with larger enrollment sizes.

E. The concept of capital describes an ability to generate wealth and promote means of production through social relationships.

F. Bourdieu (1986) states that cultural capital is everything one draws upon relative to knowledge, concepts, and ideas in participating in society. Hence, it embodies the views, techniques, and dispositions that are considered important to move ahead in society.

G. A second type of capital is financial capital, which refers to economic resources by means of income and wealth that an individual, family, or community possesses that may be used for educational advancement and further development. Health capital is the condition of your physical self; health matters can include the physical state as well as emotional/mental and spiritual integrity of a person.

H. Institutional capital refers to educational access, political acumen, and social networks.

I. Pedagogical capital is the extent to which one has the appropriate educational background and experiences in relation to transferring and receiving knowledge in school, home, and community settings.

J. Educational goals, career aspirations, personal disposition, awareness of power, and self-efficacy that individuals possess are referred to as personal capital.

K. Polity capital is the social concern and commitment shared by those who participate in a society relative to politics, economics, and so forth.

L. Social capital is prevalent with regard to cultural norms, social beliefs, and value orientations that operate within particular networks or relationships.

V. Given the unequal distribution of wealth and perceived scarcity of resources, it is obvious that every person does not have access to all the aforementioned capital types. In relationship to the affirmative action discourse, an individual who does not have access to a particular capital restricts subsequent rights of entry to social rewards and privileges.

Chapter 3

Questions and Exercises for Further Thought

- How have legal, political, and social challenges to affirmative action limited affirmative action policies? What does this trend imply for the future of affirmative action policy and equal access?
- Discuss the basic canon of CRT; additionally, consider the axiological, epistemological, and ontological tenets of this theory in contrast to the conceptual underpinnings of other theoretical perspectives used in shaping research on diverse populations (e.g., Black Feminist Thought, Human Capital Theory, etc.).
- What is the general concept of capital and how do the eight types of capital restrict or enhance educational access?
- Why are there differential levels of social capital across communities, and why have communities of color historically had limited access to various forms of capital?

EXERCISE #1

Various forms of capital are important assets to have in relationship to locus of control in goal achievement. While there is a private and public good of higher education, majority student populations more frequently have social capital that positions them to thrive while disenfranchised students have greater difficulty gaining access (e.g., to college, financial aid, other government services, gainful employment, etc.).

Construct a concept map of social and/or cultural forms of capital that diagrams relationships of these forms of capital in connection to (a) trust of people or organizations, (b) access to resources/basic necessities, and (c) social networks. Next, devise a draft of planned development interventions that takes culture into account in redressing the uneven access particular to people of color and women in education, the workplace, economic structures, as well as other systems.

EXERCISE #2

Conduct a racial/ethnic and gender history of your institution in correspondence to the following questions:

- When was the university founded?
- When did it admit the largest number of women?
- When did it admit the largest number of people of color? (Note: It will be important to disaggregate between U.S.-born and international students.)
- Since admission of the aforementioned groups, what are the retention/graduation rates for women and people of color since their admission?

Because data speaks to institutional history and the inclusion of students of color and women, discuss the implications of the historical and contemporary patterns of participation.

Chapter 4

From the Margins: Community College Student Opinions on
Affirmative Action

Chapter 4 Premise: Community colleges provide routes to baccalaureate degrees by filling existing gaps in educational access for those who may not have other options for postsecondary attendance.

I.   Two-year Student Demographics and Institutional Environment
    A. Rhoads (1999) asserts that institutions of higher learning illustrate the interconnectedness of culture, identity, and schooling.

B. Similar to people of color, however, women are overrepresented in 2-year institutions.

C. Women were also found to disproportionately attend institutions that were not their first-college choice.

D. The literature in reference to the enrollment status of women reports that a significant number enroll at community colleges as part-time students; many of whom are not traditional college age (i.e., ages 18–24) students.

E. Full-time baccalaureate degree aspirants attending 2-year institutions were twice as likely as part-timers to transfer to a 4-year college or university within 5 years.

F. Many African American and Hispanic students who are disproportionately concentrated at the 2-year level are located in urban areas, where they make up a significant percentage of the population.

G. Issues of access and school choice for students of color are often based on their local residence.

H. Institutions of higher learning within close proximity to where one lives and works as well as within one's financial reach are typically community colleges.

I. In addition, many urban community colleges boast large enrollments, and research has noted that the size and level of an institution can adversely affect student aspirations.

J. For students who look to 2-year institutions as the conduit to a bachelor's degree, critics have contended that the community college is not the optimal environment for those seeking a bachelor's degree.

K. The racial/ethnic background, gender, and enrollment status of community college students relate to the orientation of those attending, the campus climate, and institutional culture.

II. Catalyst or Deterrent to Baccalaureate Education?

A. The profile of community college students is unique as these collegians differ from those at 4-year institutions in terms of having dependents, full-time employment, or lag time prior to enrollment.

B. There is some degree of return on investment for those enrolling and completing postsecondary education. It is estimated that as many as 75% to 80% of community college students desire baccalaureate degrees and intend to transfer to a 4-year institution.

C. However, recent figures suggest that only one fourth of all students attending community colleges with baccalaureate degree aspirations actually earn one, though more than one-fifth of community college students transfer directly into 4-year baccalaureate programs.

D. College attendance has become increasingly important for individuals to self-actualize personally and professionally.

E. The demographic profile of community college students consists of many who bear characteristics of individuals that could potentially benefit from affirmative action initiatives.

F. Two-year institutions attempt to fill existing gaps in educational access for those who eventually plan to transfer in order to earn baccalaureate degrees.

III.   The Role of Affirmative Action in 2-Year Institutions

A. Absent in the literature is any discourse regarding how students attending community colleges (particularly those with baccalaureate or higher degree plans) respond to affirmative action in college admissions.

B. Researchers have noted that one way community colleges can reaffirm their position in higher education is by reforming and/or restoring the transfer function within their home institutions (transfer refers to numerous types of postsecondary transitions between levels of institutions).

C. There has been a steady decrease in the number of students transferring from 2-year to 4-year institutions over the last decade.

D. One way of addressing problematic transfer rates would be to develop admissions policies specifically targeting transfer students, as many share similar characteristics, such as being low income, disadvantaged, first-generation, and/or from an underrepresented group.

E. Issues of access for community college students should be considered by 2- and 4-year institutions of higher learning.

F. The community college is unique in that issues surrounding affirmative action have traditionally pertained to employment decisions.

G. Affirmative action tensions could manifest themselves through racial/ethnic issues within the community college curriculum via the various course offerings.

H. Concerns surrounding affirmative action at 2-year institutions have also extended to financial aid policies.

I. The assault on scholarships for students of color received great attention in *Podberesky v. Kirwan* (1994).

J. The case at Northern Virginia Community College is particularly problematic pending the court's determination of whether it is unlawful to administer race-specific scholarships if the scholarships are privately funded. (This case challenged race-specific scholarships.)

K. Given the threat of affirmative action retrenchment in college admissions, community colleges may face the possibility of serving a larger segment of first generation African American, Hispanic, and White students.

L. Community colleges refrain from discriminatory practices regarding student admissions by virtue of their open-door policies.

IV. Conclusions

A. The aim of this study was to investigate affirmative action views in association with the educational degree plans of students attending community colleges.

B. Results of this study suggest that variables such as race/ethnicity, gender, political views, and promotion of racial understanding have an impact on the odds of an individual's supporting the abolishment of affirmative action.

C. Students from higher-income families, having greater intentions of transferring, higher GPAs, lower college choice, and a greater belief that racial discrimination is not a problem had higher odds of supporting the abolishment of affirmative action in college admissions.

D. Students of color, women, liberals, and those placing importance on racial understanding had reduced odds of supporting the abolishment of affirmative action than other groups.

E. Race/ethnicity and gender factors into students' attitudes toward the use of affirmative action in college admissions.

F. White female students were less likely than White males to support abolishing affirmative action in college admissions.

G. Results revealed that African Americans and Hispanics approved of affirmative action at higher rates than did their White counterparts.

Chapter 4

Questions and Exercises for Further Thought

- What relevance does the affirmative action debate have for community colleges?
- The transfer function of the community college has consistently been critiqued. What strategies could community colleges implement to increase transfer rates and degree attainment for underrepresented groups (i.e., minorities, women, first generation, low income)?
- Why do students view and support affirmative action policies differentially? How do race, gender, and income factor into individuals' attitudes toward affirmative action?

EXERCISE #1

A culture audit takes stock of an organization's globalization, intercultural competence, and commitment to diversity. Based on available institutional data, conduct a culture audit of a community college, keeping in mind the degree of urbanicity (i.e., urban, suburban, or rural location) in strategically planning programs to better prepare 2-year collegians to transition to senior-level institutions. In fostering the upward mobility and status attainment of baccalaureate aspirants at community colleges, following your initial review, consider how the institutional culture at school may aid or hinder the multiplicity of goals held by different racial/ethnic, gender, social class, and/or ability microcultures. Based on your audit, outline a plan for action that would augment the policies, procedures, and practices to inform as well as improve articulation and transfer for diverse groups.

EXERCISE #2

The following exercise would be best suited for the administrative staff of a community college (e.g., enrollment services, admissions, transfer center, etc.). The data gathered could be used as background information for organizing a faculty/staff or student workshop on diversity. Use the following to serve as a jump start to discuss multiple group memberships and address curbing marginalization and increasing support mechanisms relative to the transfer function. (This may be best accompanied with a student survey designed to identify access to transition to 4-year institutions in relation to advising students into vocational/technical service sector employment.)

- Identify the racial/ethnic and gender demographics of the institution.
- Identify the racial/ethnic and gender demographics of faculty/administration positions in comparison to administrative and office staff

(maintenance may be able to be included in this equation if the institution hires its own maintenance staff).

- Identify the support mechanisms for transfer to 4-year institutions in comparison to support for transition into terminal service sector employment. Are the supports equal? What is the rationale for overrepresentation/underrepresentation in either of the groups?

Chapter 5

Access for Students with Disabilities: Infusing Affirmative Action in ADA Compliance

Chapter 5 Premise: The similar goals of affirmative action and the Americans with Disabilities Act (ADA; 1990) are similar in attempting to redress historical inequities of individuals who are members of stigmatized underrepresented groups in the United States. As such, this chapter pushes for reconceptualizing notions of diversity and reexamining antidiscrimination measures in protecting individuals with disabilities.

I.   Access to Employment
 A. Often most limiting and pervasive are the negative attitudes regarding people with disabilities that continue to permeate society.
 B. American employers have yet to keep pace with America's demographics and begin hiring members of marginalized groups.
 C. Traditionally, American educational institutions and businesses did not voluntarily strive for diversity among its participants. As a result, the vast majority of those who had access to educational opportunities and the workplace were White middle-class males.
 D. Legislative actions prohibiting discrimination on the basis of race/ethnicity, national origin, gender, and disability were then instituted.
 E. The U.S. federal government introduced policies to redress the lack of diversity and homogeneity of participants in the workplace as well as in higher education.
 F. Akin to underrepresented students of color and other disenfranchised collegians, the improvement of opportunities for students with disabilities calls for greater attention to postsecondary diversity initiatives in concert with the ADA.

II. Demographics of Students With Disabilities
 A. The greatest percentage of students with disabilities, irrespective of age group, was classified as having a learning disability (i.e.,

ranging anywhere from a little over 41% for ages 6–11, 62.3% for ages 12–17, and slightly over half of students 18–21 years old).

B. The population growth among students with disabilities parallels the overall increase in secondary education graduation rates.

C. A 13% gap exists in the conferral of high school diplomas between students with disabilities and their peers without disabilities.

D. Traditionally, students with disabilities are found in special education and developmental/remedial courses and frequently have been subject to lower expectations from instructional staff.

E. Students with disabilities at 2- and 4-year colleges and universities are primarily enrolled at medium- to large-sized publicly controlled postsecondary institutions.

F. A stratification of educational attainment occurs among students with disabilities enrolled in higher education.

G. Twelve percent of students without disabilities complete vocational certificates while roughly 20% of students with disabilities do the same.

H. Little over half of students with disabilities persist in their chosen postsecondary programs with 18% earning an associate degree and 33% of students with disabilities completing baccalaureate degrees.

I. Nearly two-thirds of students without disabilities persist in postsecondary education with 12% receiving vocational certificates, 7% awarded an associate degree, and just fewer than half obtaining bachelor's degrees.

J. Underuse of people with disabilities is manifested in the underemployment and unemployment of people with disabilities in the workforce.

III. The ADA in Meeting the Needs of People With Disabilities

A. As the civil rights of people with disabilities were limited prior to 1990, the establishment of the ADA is considered landmark legislation that makes sure the civil liberties and rights of people with disabilities are not so easily encumbered by pervading stereotypes and barriers to full integration into American life.

B. There are five titles under the ADA of 1990.

1. Title I focuses on employers and mandates that industry provide reasonable accommodations in all aspects of employment to protect the rights of people with disabilities.

2. Title II turns attention to public services by requiring aids and services to individuals with disabilities by all local, state, and federal agencies including the National Railroad Passenger Corporation and commuter authorities.

3. Title III addresses public accommodations and necessitates that all barriers to services in existing facilities be modified if not readily removed and that all new construction be fully accessible to people with disabilities.

4. Title IV places an emphasis on companies that provide telecommunication services and requires them to provide telephone services and devices for the deaf.

5. Title V provides provisions that prohibit retaliation, coercion, or threatening acts toward individuals with disabilities or those assisting by championing their rights.

C. Affirmative Acts in Challenging the Status Quo

1. Individuals opposing affirmative action generally view race/ethnicity, gender, or income as unimportant factors that are not germane to decision making relative to college admissions or hiring and promotion practices.

2. The overlap of these student attributes with disability has not been teased out.

3. As a result, the extent to which opportunity enhancement continues for students with or without disabilities across race/ethnicity, gender, or income via affirmative action policies and programs is highly questionable.

D. Mutually Distinct Yet Akin: Dilemma in Difference for the Underrepresented

1. Researchers suggest that people of color and individuals with disabilities are caught between two or more cultural extremes and must be bicultural in order to successfully participate in education, to be successful and effective at work, and to operate within their own respective communities.

2. Shapiro (2000) maintains that disability is relative and culture bound as legal definitions and cultural conceptualizations are made in reference to categories as opposed to individual cases.

3. Stigmatized in the same fashion as racial/ethnic oppressed groups, debunking stereotypes and fully integrating students with disabilities into postsecondary campus communities needs additional attention.

4. Shapiro (2000) asserts that the minority group model is appropriate for viewing disability issues in terms of the rights of individuals as opposed to the medical paradigm, which focuses on physical and social inferiorities.

5. There is a need for heightened awareness of cultural diversity in concert with the ADA. Considerations of culture should include race/ethnicity and gender, along with other nontraditional groups.

E. From K–12 Education to Postsecondary Access and Services

1. The ADA and Individuals with Disabilities Education Act (IDEA) Amendments of 1997

2. ADA and IDEA are two important federal laws that have an impact on an organization's ability to provide accommodations in educational and employment settings for people with disabilities.

3. In spite of funding problems, proposals have been approved that allow school districts to allocate 20% of their IDEA funding increases for purposes other than disabilities education efforts.

4. However, like other Federal policies, IDEA was another underfunded mandate and has not provided enough assistance to schools in covering the added expenses of educating students with disabilities.

5. While elementary and secondary schools have to conform to IDEA requirements, many of the services and accommodations that were received during the K–12 years are not necessarily available at the college level.

6. The campus climate is actually less supportive of practices that support the full participation of racial/ethnic minority students and collegians with disabilities.

7. The American Association for Community Colleges reports that disability services increased during 1992 to 1995. Just about 2% of students request disability services.

8. Although people with disabilities are not fully protected from employment discrimination, the ADA coupled with affirmative action measures could serve as a stronger response to signaling antidiscrimination.

9. Students with disabilities often feel academically and socially misaligned with their peers because of the continual obstacles

faced within postsecondary cultures limiting satisfactory engagement in the college setting.

10. Students with disabilities primarily attend community colleges where the dialogue regarding affirmative action in higher education is frequently relegated to employee hiring and promotion practices; by and large 2-year students are generally disregarded in policy debates regarding diversity initiatives such as affirmative action in college admissions.

F. Conclusions

1. With a scarcity of resources and limited state government allocations, it becomes increasingly difficult for learning institutions to maintain adequate disability support services, implement improvements, and sustain those improvements during periods of insufficient funding.

2. Although little literature has examined affirmative action (i.e., cultural diversity initiatives) in concert with ADA compliance, it is apparent that both policies and programs encourage nondiscriminatory practices against people with disabilities.

3. Making college environments inclusive of people with disabilities should entail more than providing "reasonable access" to higher education by expanding effectiveness of diversity initiatives to incorporate students with disabilities to enhance their collegiate years.

4. The politics of identity and political relations within and between groups are tempered by the frequent failure to accept cultural differences along lines of race/ethnicity, gender, disability, income, and so forth.

5. Double, triple, or possibly quadruple jeopardy face people of color with a disability given the interaction of race/ethnicity, gender, and disability contributing to further marginalization among those experiencing ableism, racism, classism and/or sexism.

Chapter 5

Questions and Exercises for Further Thought

- What are the parallels between affirmative action policies and the ADA?
- How does the notion of *bicultural* fit the experiences of individuals with disabilities versus people of color?

- What are the advantages and disadvantages of using a minority group model versus a medical model to address civil rights issues of those with disabilities?

EXERCISE

This exercise could be used for admissions, advising, or diversity offices at urban 2- or 4-year institutions of higher learning.

Conduct an inventory of students with disabilities at the institution, paying special attention to:

- How many students at the institution have self-identified as having a disability (physical, learning, emotional, etc.)?
- What services are provided for these students?
- How does the institution act in compliance with ADA as federal and university policy?
- What are the academic majors of students with disabilities?
- For community colleges, is the institution collecting data and/or tracking transfer students and what percentage of students with disabilities are transferring to 4-year institutions? How many are being referred to, and have been placed in, the vocational/technical service sector employment?

Chapter 6

Social Justice, Remediation, and Disputes To Diversity

Chapter 6 Premise: Given the increased competition for admission to elite public institutions and legal challenges to race-conscious admissions policies in higher education, the affirmative action debate intensifies and shifts from a discussion between racial preferences versus social justice to a discussion between racial preferences versus racial diversity.

I.   The Diversity Rationale: A Shifting Debate
  A. The debate regarding access and the use of race-conscious or race-sensitive policies to promote greater access for African Americans and other underrepresented groups persists in the higher education arena.
  B. Because various higher education constituencies, including parents and prospective students, believe the admissions process should be race neutral and based on merit, which translates into a system that considers students' talents and skills but not racial background in admissions decisions, the issues of racial discrimination and fairness become central to the debate.

II. The Antiracial Preferences Argument

A. While some constituents who oppose consideration of race argue that using race as a factor is unfair and discriminatory to White applicants, those who advocate for the need for racial consideration argue that accounting for race helps to minimize the unfair advantages White applicants are automatically given in the process.

B. Defenders of the social justice position also argue that elite public institutions have historically excluded and discriminated against minority student applicants by implementing policies and practices that favor White applicants.

C. Three key groups have been successful in advancing legal and political attacks against highly selective institutions that use racial preferences in admissions decisions. The three groups are (a) the Center for Individual Rights (CIR), (b) the American Civil Rights Institute (ACRI), and (c) the Center for Equal Opportunity (CEO).

D. Although these three organizations can be said to have very different missions and purposes, all three groups have taken steps to eradicate race-conscious policies across the country.

E. Awarding racial preferences to minority applicants is said to work against the sacred standards of academic excellence and the system of merit while creating polarized campus communities of students who are perceived as deserving and undeserving of admission to these top institutions.

III. Social Justice and Remediation

A. The social justice or remediation argument begins with different assumptions regarding who truly suffers from discrimination and who is being treated unfairly in the admissions process of these elite institutions.

B. Though the courts concede that societal discrimination exists and that economic and educational disparities persist along racial and ethnic lines, today's courts refuse to incorporate the historical record of discrimination and its legacy.

C. Selective schools are not vulnerable to lawsuits brought by African American plaintiffs because the courts do not seriously consider allegations of discrimination from Black plaintiffs and render them invalid.

D. Many advocates of the social justice position interpret the diversity rationale of *Bakke* as a retreat from remedial solutions,

solutions that are sorely needed to combat the ongoing legacy of educational, economic, and social discrimination.

E. With *Hopwood*, higher education was put on notice with respect to the diversity rationale.

F. In the 1996 *Hopwood* decision, racial diversity was considered no different or no more significant than eye color or other physical characteristics, leaving educators at a loss for evidence to justify why racial diversity was important.

G. While reasserting their expertise and role as educators, presidents and chancellors noted that diverse student populations or student bodies facilitate many interactions that are needed to enrich the educational experiences of students.

H. With the emergence of supportive allies among prominent corporations and the military, the diversity rationale was solidified and validated by segments of society that seem to matter most.

I. With the advent of *Gratz* and *Grutter*, "diversity as a compelling interest" now serves as the primary justification, dismissing social justice, equity, or remediation arguments.

J. The diversity rationale rather than social justice or remediation arguments garners more support and credibility.

IV. Diversity versus equity as an institutional value is perceived as less threatening and receives greater support because it benefits all students.

V. CIR and the Letter of the Law

A. The CIR completely denounced the use of racial preferences in admissions; however, other types of preferences were not ruled out (i.e., economically disadvantaged students).

B. While CIR spoke against racial preferences, campus diversity was a concept the organization did support in principle.

C. CIR's interpretation of the University of Michigan's admissions processes conveys that attempts to explicitly engineer racially diverse—rather than intellectually diverse—student populations at the undergraduate and law school levels were the same as instituting virtual quotas, which CIR sees as illegal and should not be the goal or outcome of diversity.

D. The National Association of Scholars also produced a report that contested the logic of Justice Powell's diversity rationale and concluded the diversity rationale must be rejected on the grounds "that a majority of the U.S. Supreme Court failed to reach agreement about the constitutional justification for racial preferences in University admissions" in *Bakke*.

E. The question remains: Can race, as one of the aforementioned factors designated by CIR, contribute to the diversity of an institution of higher education?

1. Under the old University of Michigan undergraduate admission system, 20 points (on an evaluation scale of 150) from a miscellaneous category would be given to a person who was a member of an underrepresented group, attended a high school serving predominantly people of color, or was a scholarship athlete.

2. Race, as a suspect category in the courts, is "strictly" scrutinized as a rationale to address past discrimination.

3. The Michigan cases were not about individual rights as much as they were about discrediting the use of race in college admissions. The Powell decision states race "cannot be systematically used to insulate the individual from comparison with all other candidates." In essence, CIR uses the Powell decision when convenient.

4. Numerical diversity in the form of quotas is a violation of the 14th Amendment as institutions that frame their affirmative action goals in specific numerical targets will be found not narrowly tailored.

5. The diversity argument is both strengthened and weakened by competitive individual versus group interests and self-interest versus cooperative politics.

6. And most important, the diversity rationale points to the social/utilitarian role that diversity can play in providing a broader, richer collegiate context for cross-racial socialization and learning.

7. Although never stated in CIR literature, the underpinnings of its legal interpretations are clear. The rights of Whites have been violated through the use of race in college admissions.

Chapter 6

Questions and Exercises for Further Thought

• The admissions process in college admissions requires examining the applications of many different types of students. From the perspective

of those who support race-conscious admissions policies, what are the key arguments to maintain race-sensitive policies? From the perspective of those who oppose race-conscious admissions policies, why should race not be considered?
- Compare and contrast three key organizations that have sought to dismantle affirmative action.
- How is the diversity rationale strengthened by the *Gratz* and *Grutter* rulings? How is it weakened?
- The diversity rationale is said to serve the interests of higher education. Define diversity and how diversity benefits educational environments.

Exercise #1

Revisit the admissions policy for your institution (this example is more applicable for 4-year colleges, particularly those with closed/selective admissions). Perform a critical analysis of the affirmative action policy in correspondence with the following questions:

- Does the university have a policy on diversity? If so, how does the admissions office understand and enforce the diversity policy in relationship to admissions?
- Has there been legal opposition to affirmative action policies at the university? If so, what has been the university's response? Since the threat or response to legal action, how has the university's population been affected with relation to diversity?
- On what criteria are applicants judged? Is race still explicitly included in the policy? If not, what policies have been put in place to ensure racial/ethnic diversity at the institution?
- If the institution has revoked affirmative action policy or has restructured its diversity policy, admissions and graduation data for students of color at the institution post–affirmation action will be critical to this analysis.

Exercise #2

University of California and University of Michigan Undergraduate Admissions
    As four states have officially passed anti-affirmative-action legislation and with many more subject to laws banning the use of race, ethnicity, gender, color, or national origin in consideration of university admittance,

please consider how as a public policy affirmative action should be assessed in relation to public higher education. As California was the first state to pass a ban on affirmative action by a ballot measure in 1996, and Michigan most recently did so in 2006, discuss how each state is similar and different relative to population characteristics, economy, labor market, school systems, and so on. Next, using the traditional techniques of policy analysis explore the issues, impacts, and implications that stem from abolishing affirmative action in each of these states.

Chapter 7

Affirming Acts for Increasing Access: Considerations for Policy, Practice, and Future Inquiry

Chapter 7 Premise: The implicit or explicit norm is to reduce, eliminate, or deny the manifestation of conflict in the academy, but higher education institutions avoid any meaningful action to do so.

I.   Percentage Plans Not Making the Mark
   A. The shift in White privilege and entitlement is modest at best given the stalemate and/or reduction experienced in participation of first-time, full-time racial/ethnic minority entrants at the undergraduate level, and more dramatically at the graduate/professional level.
   B. Second, substituting percentage plans for the top 4%, 10%, or 20% of students still narrowly defines meritocracy by reducing it to strict numerical standards without allowing other factors (such as race, gender, SES, etc.) in addition to class rank, GPA, and standardized text scores into consideration for admission.
   C. Third, percentage plans are not a panacea in guaranteeing equal access or outcomes, especially given the rationale that diversity is a compelling state interest.
   D. The initial goal of eradicating past overt discrimination of African Americans and other disadvantaged, underrepresented groups, in addition to eliminating the legacy and present-day effects of discrimination, is of little consequence and of minor importance under the percent plan alternative.
   E. The U.S. Commission on Civil Rights (2000) under the leadership of Chair Mary Frances Berry conducted an assessment of percentage plans and concluded that percentage plans are harmful to promoting and increasing enrollments among students of color.

1. Despite the U.S. Supreme Court ruling that race could be one of many factors considered in college admissions, there have been different institutional responses; some institutions with supportive campus cultures and climates have cheered while other institutions continue to hold firm to the notion that affirmative action should be abolished.

2. Texas A&M and the University of Washington prohibited race-conscious policies and programming.

3. It is apparent from the extant literature that color-blind policies in Washington and percentage plans in California, Florida, and Texas did not increase minority student participation in higher education.

II. Michiganders and the Next Act in Affirming Access

A. Even after the *Grutter* and *Gratz* decisions, Ward Connerly, who was instrumental in leading the charge to pass Proposition 209 in California, spearheaded a referendum campaign in the state of Michigan (and a few other states) to eliminate the consideration of race/ethnicity in admissions.

B. The poor economic landscape of Michigan was very much connected to perceptions of public policy and the MCRI agenda's receiving support.

C. A study from the W. E. Upjohn Institute for Employment Research (Bartik et al., 2006) found that regional economies with greater proportions of college graduates are more successful.

D. Michigan is above average in terms of high school graduates residing in the state but below average relative to its share of college completers (i.e., Michigan residents were 3.3% below the national average of people with college degrees—24.4% compared to 27.7%).

E. When applying the principle of ROI to educational attainment in the state of Michigan, increasing the number of college-educated residents would provide a social rate of return in attracting new industries that seek a highly capable, skilled workforce that is technologically competent and culturally diverse.

F. In turn, at the individual level, the societal benefit of increasing numbers of racial/ethnic minorities and women in postsecondary education and the workplace may not be readily seen or accepted in Michigan when working-class Whites have a heightened sense of perceived threat because of massive layoffs and/or a sense of entitlement with regard to their son's or daughter's college education.

III.   Theoretical Perspectives and Access Policy Research
   A. Political Culture Theory—Political culture is the way in which one's beliefs about what is proper policy and appropriate action merge into a collective response and way of viewing politics and the political process.
   B. Concerns Theory—Model seeks to more fully understand and describe the process of change in educational settings. More specifically, the model offers diagnostic tools to assess where people in the organization stand in relationship to adopting change or innovation.
   C. Liberal Egalitarian Theory—This perspective holds that the compensatory nature of education is a mandatory means of achieving social justice and eradicating past discrimination. This theory holds that until victims of previous racial/ethnic discriminatory acts and behavior have been compensated, affirmative action is necessary.
   D. Restorative Justice Theory—"is fundamentally concerned with restoring relationships, with establishing or re-establishing social equality in relationships" (Leung, 1999).

IV.   Acknowledging and Promoting the Panorama of Access
   A. Institutional strategies should focus on upholding diversity and defending affirmative action. They include:
       1. Dealing with Precollege Factors—Address college readiness, particularly with underserved groups, as there is a disproportionately high placement of African American and Hispanic students in special education and in remedial courses at the postsecondary level.
       2. Stepping Up Outreach Initiatives—More readily encourage people of color, women, and people with disabilities to apply for admission or employment at your institution.
       3. Intensifying Recruitment Efforts—Target students as early as the middle school grades in racially/ethnically diverse communities; partner with local K–12 districts and community colleges and capitalize on the transfer function to facilitate

greater participation from underrepresented students across disciplines.

4. Rethinking Scholarship Programs—Seek guidance and take note from the recent University of Michigan cases by exploring different forms of financial assistance that can assist diverse populations but can hold up to strict scrutiny and be narrowly tailored.

5. Mentoring Approaches—Infuse service-learning activities in the curriculum and volunteerism through student affairs to reach out to students from disenfranchised groups within disciplinary areas or along other interests. With a small commitment from your institution, prospective students will be more apt to feel an affinity for attending college and be affirmed in their decision to pursue higher education.

6. Looking Abroad—Affirmative action doesn't exist in a vacuum. Investigate what other countries are doing to adequately reflect the distribution of their population across groups. Although other countries may not have experienced the forms of discrimination or histories of oppression, insights could be gained from a comparative perspective that examines how higher education and industry outside Western contexts seek to affirm diversity.

Chapter 7

Questions and Exercises for Further Thought

- Define conflict.
- What are the components of activist leadership?
- Is the activist leadership approach better suited for public institutional leaders or private institutional leaders? Explain your response.
- What should higher education leaders understand about conflict? How can understanding conflict assist with creating more inclusive educational environments?

Exercise

Drawing on your experiences in education (e.g., as a student, faculty/staff, or administrator) write a case study (e.g., as short as one or two paragraphs, or multiple pages) that illustrates how inextricably linked leadership and diversity are in relationship to the discourse on affirmative action policy. More specifically, create a narrative that highlights how activist leaders can inform the policy process and foster social consciousness by actively working toward affirming diversity and remedying structural inequalities. In your case, outline the problems associated with diversifying policies, as well as creating and sustaining heterogeneity of participants across various sectors of public life. Additionally, your case may focus on the strategies/methods beyond those offered in the scope of this text that you feel are viable policy alternatives and actions for activist leaders to employ.

Chapter 8

Conflict, Diversity, and Activist Leadership

Chapter 8 Premise: Given the above, where do we go from here? What exists is a political, legal, and social quandary.

I.   Philosophical Approaches to Conflict and Conflict Management
   A. "In the 1950s, the organizational perspective on conflict was altered to the behavioral approach, which saw conflict as natural and encouraged people to accept conflict as an inevitable part of working together" (Holton, 1995b, p. 7).
   B. The modern view of conflict has somewhat departed from the original assumption that all conflict is detrimental to an organization and therefore is essentially a negative phenomenon.
   C. Negative perceptions and attitudes toward conflict are linked to notions of institutional governance models and leadership styles.

II. Governance Models, Leadership, and Perceptions of Conflict
   A. In particular, three governance models are relevant: collegial, bureaucratic, and political.
   B. According to the collegial model, conflict is not allowed and is considered abnormal; individuals attempt to eliminate conflict.
   C. The bureaucratic model, contrary to the collegial model, does not seek to eliminate conflict but to control it. Conflict is also perceived as abnormal, but if conflict emerges, allowances are made for it.
   D. In the political model, conflict is considered normal and is an essential element of organizational life.
   E. The political governance model is the only model that supports conflict as a normative behavior. The tendency to eschew this model will also promote the avoidance of conflict.

F. Higher education has been the battleground for opponents who wish to eliminate any form of opportunity targeting underrepresented minority students (i.e., debates over practices and policies).

III. Toward a Definition of Conflict

A. The term *conflict* has no single, clear meaning.

B. Different concepts posed in the conflict management literature provide useful frameworks that aid leaders in understanding the anatomy of a conflict scenario (Blake & Mouton, 1970; Donahue & Kolt, 1992).

C. The conflict literature clearly provides several concepts that educational leaders should understand in order to achieve affirmative access, racial diversity, and inclusion within their educational communities.

D. Positive conflict conditions and behaviors entail three essential elements: (a) the type of conflict, (b) the type of task being performed, and (c) behaviors in response to the conflict or conflict style behaviors.

1. Type of conflict
    a. Cognitive conflict is linked with cognitive disagreements related to performing a decision-making task.
    b. Affective conflict involves "personalized disagreement or individual disaffection" (Amason & Schweiger, 1997, p. 106).

2. Type of task being performed: Certain types of tasks complement cognitive conflict so that a positive relationship is likely to exist in order to generate a beneficial outcome or performance.

3. Conflict styles of avoidance and suppression negate the positive benefits that could emerge from conflict and lead to shared thinking, while problem solving and contending elicit more gains from conflict.

E. An environment of trust and openness must be established so that members of the unit, group, or organization feel free to engage in cognitive conflict without repercussions.

IV. Activist Leadership: An Introduction

A. An activist leadership approach is the paradigm that leaders must adopt to adequately confront the politics of affirmative access (equity and educational access). For example, activist leaders are willing to confront conflict and divisive issues that threaten diversity, specifically racial diversity, on their campuses and does not allow the press or activist opponents, such as CIR and CEO, to dictate practices and policies contrary to the institution's educational mission of equity and access.

B. Given the steady stream of lawsuits in the 1990s that challenged the constitutionality of affirmative action admissions, activist leadership is necessary.

C. Activist leadership moves beyond simply stating there is a commitment to equity, educational access, and racial diversity; activist leadership demonstrates through active engagement, within and outside the campus community, the importance and vital nature of moving the institution toward an inclusive community.

D. Steps Toward Activist Leadership:
   1. Taking a position is the first step.
   2. An activist leader should craft a clear message regarding the importance of the institutional values of diversity, equity, and educational access, followed by articulation of the message to the campus community and external stakeholders.
   3. An activist leader approaches the press regarding the importance of racial diversity.
   4. Activist leaders should encourage discussions about adversarial situations that concern minority students and other student populations.
   5. A team approach toward activist leadership should provide more benefits.
   6. An activist leadership approach requires revising or correcting failed strategies to advance the institution.
   7. Since taking on an activist leadership style is likely to engender conflicts rather than deter them, several higher education scholars and former executive officers have proposed that individuals in designated leadership roles learn to understand, analyze, manage, and use conflict.

V. Practical Policy Recommendations for Affirming Access
    A. Deal with precollege factors.
    B. Step up outreach initiatives.
    C. Intensify recruitment efforts.
    D. Offer more scholarships.
    E. Adopt mentoring approaches.
    F. Look abroad.

VI.   Activism and the Next Stage in the Battle for Civil Rights
    A. Although there are payoffs in terms of individual and societal rates of return for breaking down barriers for talented females to compete, similarly the progress of racial/ethnic minorities could reach a stalemate if institutions do not demonstrate a commitment to ensure access for those ready to vie for educational and professional opportunities.
    B. Michigan race relations are projected to worsen following the passage of Proposal 2.
    C. The state of Michigan officially banned affirmative action, amending the state constitution on December 22, 2006.

VII.   Extra steps will be necessary in sustaining diversity.

VIII.   New Chapters in Race/Gender Awareness
    A. Implications for the future of affirmative action post-*Grutter* are contingent on the Supreme Court's decisions on the *Meredith v. Jefferson County Board of Education* (2006) and *Parents Involved in Community Schools v. Seattle School District* (2006) cases.
    B. Race-conscious programs and policies are still vulnerable post-*Grutter*; one example is the current attack on Black male initiatives.
    C. Smiles (2002) reports that incarcerating minority men costs two to three times more than educating them.

IX.   Access, Immigration, and Contemporary Civil Rights Concerns
    A. Immigration policies have been desperately in need of reform, however, some of the restrictions of the new policies penalize students who have spent the majority of their growing years in the United States.
    B. Affirmative action and immigration should not be treated as distinct, unrelated policies but instead should be linked.

X.   Final Thoughts
    A. In this multiracial society, a new ethnic order has emerged in the United States. What must be considered a thing of the past is the Black-White dichotomy; with the growing number of Latinos and Asians, this binary frame of reference does not accurately depict today's global community.
    B. Converging in the post–civil rights movement are highly loaded, heated controversies across multiple access policy agendas. It is

our hope that readers of this text will be prompted to reexamine how affirmative action is framed, and for all intents and purposes alongside other civil rights policy clashes (e.g., EEEO, ADA, Immigration Reform) that necessitate better resolutions in an effort to protect minority civil rights in every respect.

C. With the shift in momentum favoring the anti-affirmative-action camp, business and educational leaders will need to maintain their resolve to affirm diversity through initiating/participating in grassroots efforts to increase awareness in the community about the benefits of diversity and how they align to improve the educational experience for majority and minority students.

D. In closing, the triad of conflict, diversity, and activist leadership is inevitable for higher education in the 21st century. Proclamations of affirmative access for all will be null and void without the aggressive leadership that is required to keep institutions on task and accountable to their constituencies of prospective students.

Chapter 8

Questions and Exercises for Further Thought

- What are the pros and cons of percentage plans?
- In higher education, what can be done to balance the competing interests of individual rights for Whites and a minority group's civil rights?
- How feasible are the recommended strategies? What additional strategies are needed?

Exercise

Diversity Policy and Activist Leadership Exploration

Following completion of the final chapter, please give further consideration to the conflicting political forces, various stakeholders, and divergent policy communities engaged in the debate over affirmative action. Now, from a pragmatic yet prescriptive angle, outline a course of action that puts forth mechanisms that can provide an effective response to affirming diversity. In forwarding a thoughtful, diagnostic framework for illustrating the utility of affirmative action as a public and private good, please distinguish between the strategies that would be most helpful in quelling the various challenges to authority in the form of activist leadership at the local, state, and federal level. Finally, as an activist leader, give thought to how you would advocate for marginalized minority communities by seeking to shape public policies affecting these communities in a post–civil rights environment.

Instructional Supplement

Recommended Readings[1]

Journal Articles

Antwi-Boasiako, K., & Asagba, J. O. (2005, December). A preliminary analysis of African American college students' perceptions of racial preferences and affirmative action in making admissions decisions at a predominantly White university. *College Student Journal, 39*(4), 734–748.

Baez, B. (2004, May/June). The study of diversity: The "knowledge of difference" and the limits of science. *Journal of Higher Education, 75*(3), 285–306.

Bowen, W. G., & Bok, D. (1998, Fall). Why race-conscious admissions make sense. *College Board Review, 186,* 8–11, 29.

Bridglall, B. L. (2006). A misguided debate about affirmative action? *Ohio State Law Journal, 67*(1), 15–35.

Brown, S. K., & Hirschman, C. (2006). The end of affirmative action in Washington state and its impact on the transition from high school to college. *Sociology of Education, 79*(2), 106–130.

Crosby, F. J. (2005). Understanding affirmative action. *Annual Review of Psychology, 57,* 585–611.

Davis, D. J. (2007). Race and diversity in higher education: An examination of race-based admission and its alternatives. *College & University, 82*(2), 25–30.

De la Torre, A. (2004, Fall). Race-neutral policies for professional school admissions: Are there strategies to enhance Latino enrollment? *Aztlán: A Journal of Chicano Studies, 29*(2), 155–169.

Donahoo, S. (2006). Derailing desegregation: Legal efforts to end racial segregation in higher education before and after Brown. *Equity & Excellence in Education, 39*(4), 291–301.

Flores, A., & Rodriguez, C. M. (2006). University faculty attitudes on affirmative action principles toward faculty and students. *Equity & Excellence in Education, 39*(4), 303–312.

Goldrick-Rab, S., & Shaw, K. M. (2005, Winter). Racial and ethnic differences in the impact of work-first policies on college access. *Educational Evaluation & Policy Analysis, 27*(4), 291–307.

Goldstein, J. K. (2006). Justice O'Connor's twenty-five year expectation: The legitimacy of durational limits in Grutter. *Ohio State Law Journal, 67*(1), 83–144.

---

[1] Compiled with assistance from Tamara N. Stevenson, doctoral fellow, Department of Leadership and Counseling, Eastern Michigan University.

Holzer, H., & Neumark, D. (2000). Assessing affirmative action. *Journal of Economic Literature, 38*(3), 483–568.

Holzer, H. J., & Neumark, D. (2000). What does affirmative action do? *Industrial & Labor Relations Review, 53*(2), 240–271.

Inkelas, K. K. (2003, September/October). Caught in the middle: Understanding Asian Pacific American perspectives on affirmative action through Blumer's group position theory. *Journal of College Student Development, 44*(5), 625–643.

Inkelas, K. K. (2003, November/December). Diversity's missing minority: Asian Pacific American undergraduates' attitudes toward affirmative action. *Journal of Higher Education, 74*(6), 601–639.

Lehmuller, P., & Gregory, D. E. (2005). Affirmative action: From before Bakke to after Grutter. *NASPA Journal, 42*(4), 430–459.

Morfin, O., Perez, V. H., & Parker, L. (2006). Hiding the politically obvious: A critical race theory preview of diversity as racial neutrality in higher education. *Educational Policy, 20*(1), 249–270.

Moses, M. S. (2006, September). Why the affirmative action debate persists: The role of moral disagreement. *Educational Policy, 20*(4), 567–586.

Nadel, M. (2006). Retargeting affirmative action: A program to serve those most harmed by past racism and avoid intractable problems triggered by per se racial preferences. *St. John's Law Review, 80*(1), 323–388.

Philip, E. (2002, April). Diversity in the halls of academia: Bye-bye Bakke? *Journal of Law and Education, 31*(2), 149–166.

Rose, H. (2005, Fall). The effects of affirmative action programs: Evidence from the University of California at San Diego. *Educational Evaluation & Policy Analysis, 27*(3), 263–289.

Selden, S. C. (2006). A solution in search of a problem: Discrimination, affirmative action, and the new public service. *Public Administration Review, 66*(6), 911–923.

Smith, D. G., Turner, C. S., & Osei-Kofi, N. (2004, March/April). Interrupting the usual: Successful strategies for hiring diverse faculty. *Journal of Higher Education, 75*(2), 133–160.

Smith, W. A. (2006). Racial ideology and affirmative action support in a diverse college student population. *Journal of Negro Education, 75*(4), 589–605.

Solórzano, D. G., & Yosso, T. J. (2002, May). A critical race counterstory of race, racism, and affirmative action. *Equity & Excellence in Education, 35*(2), 155–168.

Sullivan, P. (2006). Diversity, leadership, and the community college: A case study. *Community College Journal of Research and Practice, 30*, 383–400.

Thompson, F. T. (2003, November). The affirmative action and social policy views of a select group of White male private high school students. *Education and Urban Society, 36*(1), 16–43.

Vasquez, M. J., & Jones, J. M. (2007). Diversity is a compelling interest and affirmative action is an important strategy for achieving it. *American Psychologist, 62*(2), 146–147.

Books/Chapters/Monographs/Other Publications

Atkinson, R. C. (2006). Opportunity in a democratic society: Race and economic status in higher education. *Proceedings of the American Philosophical Society, 150*(2), 318–332.

Baez, B. (2002). *Affirmative action, hate speech, and tenure: Narratives about race, law, and the academy.* New York: Routledge.

Bailey, T. R., Leinbach, T., & Jenkins, D. (2005, January). *Community college low-income and minority student completion study: Descriptive statistics from the 1992 high school cohort.* New York: Columbia University, Teachers College, Community College Research Center.

Bailey, T., & Morest, V. S. (Eds.). (2006). *Defending the community college equity agenda.* Baltimore, MD: Johns Hopkins University Press.

Baldwin, A. (2007). *The community college experience plus.* Upper Saddle River, NJ: Pearson Prentice Hall.

Beckman, J. A. (Ed.). (2004). *Affirmative action: An encyclopedia.* Westport, CT: Greenwood Press.

Beckman, J. A. (2006). *Affirmative action now: A guide for students, families, and counselors.* Westport, CT: Greenwood Press.

Beckwith, F. J., & Jones, T. E. (Eds.). (1997). *Affirmative action: Social justice or reverse discrimination?* Amherst, NY: Prometheus Books.

Bensimon, E. M., & Polkinghorne, D. (2003). *Why equity matters: Implications for a democracy.* Los Angeles: Center for Urban Education, University of Southern California.

Bergmann, B. R. (1996). *In defense of affirmative action.* New York: Basic Books.

Bowser, B. P. (2006). *The Black middle class: Social mobility—and vulnerability.* Boulder, CO: Lynne Rienner.

Brown, M. K. & Associates (2003). *Whitewashing race: The myth of a color-blind society.* Berkeley: University of California Press.

Brown, O. G., Hinton, K. G., & Howard-Hamilton, M. (Eds.). (2007). *Unleashing suppressed voices on college campuses: Diversity issues in higher education.* New York: Peter Lang.

Cabrera, A. F., Burkum, K. R., & La Nasa, S. M. (2005). Pathways to a four-year degree: Determinants of transfer and degree completion. In A. Seidman (Ed.), *College student retention: A formula for success* (pp. 155–214). Westport, CT: ACE/Praeger Series on Higher Education.

Cokorinos, L. (2003). *Assault on diversity: An organized challenge to racial and gender justice.* Lanham, MD: Rowman & Littlefield.

Crosby, F. J. (2004). *Affirmative action is dead; long live affirmative action.* New Haven, CT: Yale University Press.

Davis, T. J. (2006). *Race relations in America: A reference guide with primary documents.* Westport, CT: Greenwood Press.

de la Torre, A. (2002). *Moving from the margins: A Chicana voice on public policy.* Tucson: University of Arizona Press.

Dipboye, R. L. & Colella, A. (2005). *Discrimination at work: The psychological and organizational bases.* New York: Routledge.

Dyson, M. E. (1997). *Race rules: Navigating the color line.* New York: Vintage Books.

Eisaguirre, L. (1999). *Affirmative action: A reference handbook.* Santa Barbara, CA: ABC-CLIO.

Fox, J. C. (1997). *Affirmative action plan workbook.* CCH Employment and Human Resources Management Professional Series. Chicago: CCH.

Garcia, M. (Ed.). (1997). *Affirmative action's testament of hope: Strategies for a new era in higher education.* Albany, NY: SUNY Press.

Gooden, J. M., & Blechman, R. S. (1999). *Higher education administration: A guide to legal, ethical and practical issues.* Westport, CT: Greenwood Press.

Gordon, E. W., & Bridglall, B. L. (Eds.). (2007). *Affirmative development: Cultivating academic ability.* Lanham, MD: Rowman & Littlefield.

Guinier, L., & Sturm, S. (2001). *Who's qualified?* Boston, MA: Beacon Press.

Hall, K. L., & Patrick, J. J. (2006). *Pursuit of justice: Supreme Court decisions that shaped America.* New York: Oxford University Press.

Higham, J. (Ed.). (1997). *Civil rights and social wrongs: Black-White relations since World War II.* University Park: Pennsylvania State University Press.

Hochschile, J., & Scovronick, N. (2003). *The American dream and the public schools.* New York: Oxford University Press.

Jacobs, B. A. (2006). *Race manners in the 21st century: Navigating the minefield between Black and White Americans in an age of fear.* New York: Arcade Publishing.

Jain, H. C., Sloane, P. J., & Horwitz, F. M. (2003). *Employment equity and affirmative action: An international comparison.* Armonk, NY: M.E. Sharpe.

Jordan, J. (1998). *Affirmative acts: Political essays.* New York: Anchor Books.

Karabel, J. (2005). *The chosen: The hidden history of admission and exclusion at Harvard, Yale, and Princeton.* New York: Houghton Mifflin.

Kellough, J. E. (2006). *Understanding affirmative action: Politics, discrimination, and the search for justice.* Washington, DC: Georgetown University Press.

Kozol, J. (2005). *The shame of the nation: The restoration of apartheid schooling in America.* New York: Crown.

Ladson-Billings, G., & Tate, W. F. (2006). *Education research in the public interest: Social justice, action and policy.* New York: Teachers College Press.

Laird, B. (2005). *The case for affirmative action in university admissions.* Berkeley, CA: Bay Tree Publishing.

Lawrence, C. R., & Matsuda, M. J. (1997). *We won't go back: Making the case for affirmative action.* Boston: Houghton Mifflin.

Levin, J. S. (2007). *Non-traditional students and community colleges: The conflict of justice and neoliberalism.* New York: Palgrave Macmillan.

Levine, S. (2007, May 30). Taking action to admit: UCLA tweaks its admissions process to stop the Black student enrollment decline. *U.S. News and World Report.*

Lindsay, B., & Justiz, M. J. (Eds.). (2001). *The quest for equity in higher education: Toward new paradigms in an evolving affirmative action era.* Albany, NY: SUNY Press.

Lipson, H. D. (2005). *Talking affirmative action: Race, opportunity, and everyday ideology.* Lanham, MD: Rowman & Littlefield.

Lowe, E. Y. (Ed.). (1999). *Promise and dilemma: Perspectives on racial diversity and higher education.* Princeton, NJ: Princeton University Press.

Lubiano, W. (Ed.). (1998). *House that race built: Black Americans, U.S. terrain.* New York: Vintage.

Mauro, T. (2005). *Illustrated great decisions of the Supreme Court* (2nd ed.). Oxford, UK: CQ Press.

Miller, J., & Garran, A. M. (2008). *Racism in the U.S.: Implications for the helping professions.* Belmont, CA: Thompson Brooks/Cole.

Moreno, P. D. (2006). *Black Americans and organized labor: A new history.* Baton Rouge: Louisiana State University Press.

Myers, S. L. (Ed.). (1997). *Civil rights and race relations in the post Reagan-Bush era.* Westport, CT: Greenwood Press.

Olson, J. S. (2003). *Equality deferred: Race, ethnicity, and immigration in America since 1945.* Belmont, CA: Wadsworth/Thomson Learning.

Ong, P. (Ed.). (1999). *Impacts of affirmative action: Policies and consequences in California.* Lanham, MD: AltaMira Press.

Orfield, G., Marin, P., & Horn, C. L. (Eds.). (2005). *Higher education and the color line: College access, racial equity, and social change.* Cambridge, MA: Harvard Education Press.

Page, S. E. (2007). *The difference: How the power of diversity creates better groups, firms, schools, and societies.* Princeton, NJ: Princeton University Press.

Perry, B. A. (2007). *The Michigan affirmative action cases* (Landmark Law Cases & American Society Series). LAWRENCE, KS: University Press of Kansas.

Rai, K. B., & Critzer, J. W. (2000). *Affirmative action and the university: Race, ethnicity, and gender in higher education employment.* Lincoln, NE: University of Nebraska Press.

Robinson, R. (2001). *The debt: What America owes to Blacks.* New York: Plume Books.

Shaw, K. M., & Heller, D. M. (2007). *State postsecondary education research: New methods to inform policy and practice.* VA: Stylus Publishing.

Sistare, C., May, L., & Francis, L. (Eds.). (2000). *Groups and group rights.* Lawrence: University Press of Kansas.

Sowell, T. (2004). *Affirmative action around the world: An empirical study.* New Haven, CT: Yale University Press.

Stohr, G. (2004). *A Black and White case: How affirmative action survived its greatest legal challenge.* Princeton, NJ: Bloomberg Press.

Williams, M. E. (Ed.). (2004). *Racism.* San Diego, CA: Greenhaven Press.

Wise, T. J. (2005). *Affirmative action: Racial preference in Black and White.* New York: Routledge.

Zweigenhaft, R. L., & Domhoff, G. W. (2003). *Blacks in the White elite: Will the progress continue?* Lanham, MD: Rowman & Littlefield.

Academic Publications/News Articles

Adam, M. (2006). The new diversity: Better or worse? *Hispanic Outlook in Higher Education, 16*(22), 34–37.

Ancheta, A. N. (2006). Civil rights, education research, and the courts. *Educational Researcher, 35*(1), 26–29.

Banerji, S. (2007, February 2). Black immigrant study puts spotlight back on affirmative action debate. *Diverse Issues in Higher Education, 24*(1), 24–25.

Berger, J. (2007, December 13). Adjusting a formula devised for diversity. *New York Times*, p. 7.

Black Issues in Higher Education. (2005, February 10). Connerly leaves California regents with warning: Don't reconsider affirmative action. *Black Issues in Higher Education, 21*(26), 14.

Black Issues in Higher Education. (2005, April 21). Grand Valley State University college republicans could face disciplinary action for "affirmative action" bake sale. *Black Issues in Higher Education, 22*(5), 15.

Cavanaugh, S. (2003, July 9). Affirmative action rulings seen yielding refinements in college-entrance plans. *Education Week, 22*(42), 29.

Chavez, L. (2007, April 29). Ending racial preferences [Editorial]. *Washington Times Daily*, p. 17.

Diverse Issues in Higher Education. (2006, January 12). Southern Illinois University faculty senate backs minority fellowships. *Diverse Issues in Higher Education, 22*(24), 8.

Drolet, L., & Brandenburg, J. (2003, August 1). Affirmative action creates division: Initiative to end racial preferences fights discrimination; affirming all people are created equal requires "divisive" debate. *Detroit News*, p. 11A.

Dunn, J., & Derthick, M. (2007). Affirmative action docketed. *Education Next, 7*(1), 11.

Galuszka, P. (2006). Turning up the heat on affirmative action policies. *Diverse Issues in Higher Education, 23*(22), 15.

Gardner, S. (2007, January). Today's courts re-conceive race and ethnicity in college aid and admissions. *Education Digest, 72*(5), 58–64.

Harris, M. (2007, May 29). Prison vs. education: Spending reveals California's priorities [Editorial]. *San Francisco Chronicle*, pp. B4, B5.

Jackson, C. (2006, December 11). Affirmative action, desegregation still vital [Editorial]. *Chicago Sun-Times*, p. 41.

June, A.W. (2007). Court tells Michigan universities to comply immediately with preference ban. *The Chronicle of Higher Education, 53*(19), A25.

Mangan, K. (2007, January 19). Education dept. will challenge law school accredi-tor's diversity standard. *The Chronicle of Higher Education, 53*(20), A23.

Mangan, K. S. (2003, June 6). Indiana U. Law School defends affirmative action. *The Chronicle of Higher Education, 49*(39), A12.

Martin, C. (2007, April 24). Race, sex emphasis in Colo. targeted vote eyed to quash affirmative action: A man who backed California's ban on minority preferences in hiring and admissions wants other states to follow suit. *Denver Post*, p. A01.

McGhee, L. (2007, May 5). Students speak out on lack of Latino professors. *Sacramento Bee*, p. B1.

Moore, N (2007). Michigan proposal 2 battle threatens scholarships. *Diverse Issues in Higher Education, 24*(2), 12–13.

Moses, M. S., & Chang, M. J. (2006). Toward a deeper understanding of the diversity rationale. *Educational Researcher, 35*(1), 6–11.

Moses, M. S., & Marin, P. (2006, January/February). Moving beyond Gratz and Grutter—the next generation of research: Informing the debate on race-conscious education policy. *Educational Researcher, 35*(1), 3–5.

Roach, R. (2006). The diversity mandate. *Diverse Issues in Higher Education, 23*(14), 26–28.

Schmidt, P. (2006). Michigan overwhelmingly adopts ban on affirmative-action preferences. *The Chronicle of Higher Education, 53*(13), A23–A24.

Schmidt, P. (2006, December 15). Supreme Court shows increased skepticism toward affirmative action. *The Chronicle of Higher Education, 53*(17), A20–A22.

Schmidt, P. (2007, February 23). Regents' diversity vote means trouble for U. of Wisconsin. *The Chronicle of Higher Education, 53*(25), A17–A18.

State programs violate affirmative action ban; 8 of 45 areas reviewed raise red flag, Michigan Department of Civil Rights says. (2007, March 8). *Grand Rapids Press*, p. B6.

Stuart, R. (2006, November 30). Michigan higher ed leaders look beyond Proposal 2. *Diverse Issues in Higher Education, 23*(21), 20.

Trotter, A. (2006, November 29). Michigan vote roils ground under K–12 race cases. *Education Week, 26*(13), 23, 25.

Turley, J. (2006, December 6). It's not Black and White; Affirmative action advocates should allow that someone can support minority advancement without endorsing flawed prescriptions. *USA Today*, p. 21A.

Walker, B. S. (2007). U.S. judge lets Michigan universities use affirmative action, for now. *Diverse Issues in Higher Education, 23*(24), 20.

Walsh, M. (2003, July 9). Justices give K–12 go-ahead to promote diversity. *Education Week, 22*(42), 1.

APPENDIX B.3

Instructional Supplement

Web-Based and Multimedia Resources[1]

Note: Every effort has been taken to verify the existence and access to the information presented in this compilation of Web-based and multimedia resources at the time of publication.

Reports

American Council on Education. (2000). Does diversity make a difference? Three research studies on diversity in college classrooms. Washington, DC: American Association of University Professors. Retrieved May 26, 2007, from http://www.acenet.edu/bookstore/pdf//diversity_report/2000_diversity_rep ort.pdf

American Council on Education. (n.d.). Making the case for affirmative action in higher education. Retrieved May 26, 2007, from http://www.acenet.edu/book store/descriptions/making_the_case/index.cfm

Affirmative action review: Report to the president. (1995). Retrieved May 26, 2007, from http://clinton2.nara.gov/WH/EOP/OP/html/aa/aa-index.html

The compelling need for diversity in higher education. Retrieved May 27, 2007, from http://www.vpcomm.umich.edu/admissions/legal/expert/index.html

Federal Glass Ceiling Commission. (1995). Good for business: Making full use of the nation's human capital. In A Fact-Finding Report of the Federal Glass Ceiling Commission. Washington, DC: U.S. Department of Labor. Retrieved May 26, 2007, from http://www.dol.gov/oasam/programs/history/reich/reports/ceiling.pdf

Office of Educational Research and Improvement, U.S. Department of Education. (1997, June 30). Diversity, affirmative action and higher education: Coordination, collaboration and dissemination of information. Retrieved May 26, 2007, from http://www.ed.gov/offices/OERI/PLLI/June30_web_version.html

President Bush discusses Michigan affirmative action case. Press release. (January 2003). Retrieved May 26, 2007, from http://www.whitehouse.gov/news/re leases/2003/01/20030115–7.html

Springer, A. (2005, January). Update on affirmative action in higher education: A current legal overview. American Association of University Professors. Retrieved May 26, 2007, from http://www.aaup.org/AAUP/protectrights/legal/topics/aff ac-update.html

---

[1] Compiled with assistance from Tamara N. Stevenson, doctoral fellow, Department of Leadership and Counseling, Eastern Michigan University.

U.S. Commission on Civil Rights. (2005, September). Funding federal civil rights enforcement: The president's 2006 request. Retrieved May 26, 2007, from http://www.usccr.gov/

The White House Initiative on Asian Americans and Pacific Islanders. (2001). Retrieved May 26, 2007, from http://www.aapi.gov/president.htm

Policy Analysis/Policy Groups

The Affirmative Action and Diversity Project: A Web Page for Research
http://aad.english.ucsb.edu/
Bibliographic reference on race, racism, gender, sexism, and affirmative action.

African American Policy Forum
http://www.aapf.org/focus/
A think tank that works to bridge the gap between scholarly research and public discourse related to inequality, discrimination, and injustice.

American Psychological Association Public Interest Directorate
http://www.apa.org/pi/oema/racism/homepage.html
Basic discussions of racism, stereotyping, and discrimination from a psychological point of view.

Center for Advancement of Racial and Ethnic Equity
http://www.acenet.edu/AM/Template.cfm?Section = CAREE
Monitors and reports on the progress of African Americans, Latinos, Asian Americans, and American Indians in postsecondary education, and engaged in efforts to improve their educational and employment opportunities in higher education.

Center for Higher Education Policy Analysis (University of Southern California)
http://www.usc.edu/dept/chepa/
Interdisciplinary research unit whose mission is to improve urban higher education, strengthen school-university relationships, and focus on international higher education, emphasizing Latin America and the Pacific Rim.

Center for Law and Social Policy
http://www.clasp.org/
Education, policy research, and advocacy organization seeking to improve the economic conditions of low-income families and secure access for the poor to the civil justice system.

Center for Research on Education, Diversity, and Excellence (University of California, Berkeley)
http://crede.berkeley.edu/index.html
A federally funded research and development program focused on improving the education of students whose ability to reach their potential is challenged by language or cultural barriers, race, geographic location, or poverty.

Center for Research on the Education of Students Placed at Risk (Johns Hopkins University and Howard University)
http://www.csos.jhu.edu/crespar/
Conducts research, development, evaluation, and dissemination of replicable strategies designed to transform schooling for students who are placed at risk because of inadequate institutional responses to such factors as poverty, ethnic minority status, and a non-English-speaking home background.

Community College Research Center (Teachers College, Columbia University)
http://ccrc.tc.columbia.edu/
Frames critical questions concerning the fundamental purposes, problems, and performance of community colleges and charts a course of strengthening scholarly research on the future of these important institutions.

Frederick D. Patterson Research Institute
http://www.patterson-uncf.org/
Research organization that focuses on improving the educational opportunities and outcomes of African Americans of all ages, from preschool through adulthood.

Higher Education Research Unit, Kellogg Forum on Higher Education for the Public Good
http://www.gseis.ucla.edu/heri/kellogg_public_good.html
In partnership with a number of organizations, institutions, researchers, and policy makers, the Kellogg forum is dedicated to increasing awareness, understanding, commitment, and action relative to the public service role of higher education in the United States.

Institute for Education and Social Policy (New York University)
http://steinhardt.nyu.edu/iesp/
Conducts scientific research about U.S. education and related social policy issues to help inform educational institutions and policy makers about the effectiveness of instructional programs, the impact of school reform initiatives, and the relationships between academic achievement, school finance, and socioeconomic and demographic factors such as poverty, ethnicity, and immigration status.

Institute for Educational Leadership, Inc.
http://www.iel.org
Seeks to improve education and the lives of children and their families by bringing together diverse constituencies and empowering leaders with knowledge and applicable ideas.

Office of Women in Higher Education
http://www.acenet.edu/AM/Template.cfm?Section = OWHE
Supporter of national leadership in the advancement of women into executive positions and campus presidencies.

Government Information and Resources

U.S. Department of Labor. Facts on Executive Order 11246—Affirmative Action.
http://www.dol.gov/esa/regs/compliance/ofccp/aa.htm

Regulations and Executive Orders

Civil Rights Act of 1964
http://www.historicaldocuments.com/CivilRightsAct1964.htm

The Civil Rights Act of 1991
http://www.eeoc.gov/policy/cra91.html

U.S. Department of Labor, Employment Standards Administration, Office of Federal Contract Compliance Programs. Compliance Assistance—Executive Order 11246.
http://www.dol.gov/esa/regs/compliance/ofccp/ca_11246.htm

Organizations/Other Resources

American Association for Affirmative Action
http://www.affirmativeaction.org/about.html
A national nonprofit association of professionals working in the areas of affirmative action, equal opportunity, and diversity.

Break the Glass Ceiling Foundation: Equal Opportunity for Women and Minorities
http://www.breaktheglassceiling.com/default.asp
A resource used by individuals to empower themselves for upward mobility.

By Any Means Necessary
http://www.bamn.com/
A mass, democratic, integrated, national organization dedicated to building a new mass civil rights movement to defend affirmative action, integration, and the other gains of the civil rights movement of the 1960s and to advance the struggle for equality in American society by any means necessary.

Chinese for Affirmative Action
http://www.caasf.org/
Designed to protect the civil and political rights of Chinese Americans in the interest of advancing multiracial democracy in the United States.

Civil Rights.org
http://www.civilrights.org/issues/affirmative/
A collaboration of the Leadership Conference on Civil Rights and the Leadership Conference on Civil Rights Education Fund, providing relevant and up-to-the minute civil rights news and information.

DiversityInc.
http://www.diversityinc.com/
Includes corporate news, reports, and advocacy on affirmative action.

DiversityWeb: An Interactive Resource Hub for Higher Education
http://www.diversityweb.org/
Designed to provide a comprehensive compendium of campus practices and resources for campus practitioners seeking to place diversity at the center of the academy's educational and societal mission.

Ethnic Majority
http://www.ethnicmajority.com/affirmative_action.htm
Dedicated to empowering African, Hispanic, and Asian Americans to advance in society and improve their quality of life, focusing on the major challenges that face people of color in a number of critical interest areas such as business, politics, civil rights, media/entertainment, the workplace, consumerism, housing, health care, and education.

National Association for the Advancement of Colored People (NAACP)
http://www.naacp.org/home/index.htm
Ensures the political, educational, social, and economic equality of rights of all people and works to eliminate racial hatred and racial discrimination.

National Center for Policy Analysis
http://www.ncpa.org/
A nonprofit, nonpartisan public policy research organization that works to develop and promote private alternatives to government regulation and control, solving problems by relying on the strength of the competitive, entrepreneurial private sector.

National Multicultural Institute
http://www.nmci.org/
Works with individuals, organizations, and communities in creating a society that is strengthened and empowered by its diversity.

National Organization for Women
http://www.now.org/issues/affirm/
Works to bring about equality and to eliminate discrimination and harassment in the workplace, schools, the justice system, and all other sectors of society.

Tolerance.org
http://www.tolerance.org
This Web site serves as a portal for educational materials to encourage valuing diversity, addressing bias, and challenging hatred and discrimination.

Understanding Prejudice
http://www.understandingprejudice.org/

Contains numerous resources and searchable databases and links relating to the causes and consequences of prejudice.
U.S. Commission on Civil Rights
http://www.usccr.gov/
An independent investigating commission, with no enforcement power, that investigates alleged civil rights violations around the country.

Multimedia (Print/Audio Transcripts)

PBS Online News Hour. (1997, August 18). Beyond Affirmative Action: Affirmative Reaction [Transcript]
http://www.pbs.org/newshour/bb/race_relations/july-dec97/affirm_8–18.html

PBS Online News Hour. (1997, December 3). Talking About Race: Beginning the Dialogue [Transcript]
http://www.pbs.org/newshour/bb/race_relations/july-dec97/town_12–3a.html

PBS Online News Hour. (1997, December 19). Talking About Race [Transcript]
http://www.pbs.org/newshour/bb/race_relations/july-dec97/race_12–19.html

PBS Online News Hour. (1998, April 1). Losing Diversity [Transcript]
http://www.pbs.org/newshour/bb/education/jan-june98/admissions_4–1.html

PBS Online News Hour. (1998, July 9). A Dialogue on Race with President Clinton [Transcript]
http://www.pbs.org/newshour/bb/race_relations/OneAmerica/transcript.html

Eboni M. Zamani-Gallaher holds a PhD in higher education administration with a specialization in community college leadership and educational evaluation from the University of Illinois at Urbana-Champaign. She is an associate professor and coordinator of the Community College Leadership Program in the Department of Leadership and Counseling at Eastern Michigan University (EMU). Prior to joining the College of Education at EMU, she held appointments as a faculty member at West Virginia University, was a fellow of ACT, Inc., and worked at Mathematica Policy Research Institute in Washington, DC. Her teaching, research, and consulting activities largely include psychosocial adjustment and transition of marginalized collegians, transfer, access policies, women in leadership, and institutional practices affecting work and family balance.

With a master's in experimental psychology, she often frames her research using a psychological and sociological conceptual lens to analyze educational problems and policy issues. She has presented numerous papers at national conferences and provides professional development consulting services through workshops and seminars with Gallaher Consulting Group. Her research has been published by various journals, including *The ASHE Reader on Community Colleges* and *New Directions for Student Affairs.*

Denise O'Neil Green received her PhD in public policy and postsecondary education from the University of Michigan, Ann Arbor. She is currently the associate vice president for institutional diversity at Central Michigan University. Before going to Central Michigan University, she was an assistant professor in the educational psychology department at the University of Nebraska-Lincoln and senior research associate in the Office of Qualitative and Mixed Methods Research.

As a diversity expert and qualitative methodologist, her research interests focus on developing and implementing qualitative research designs that aid researchers, policy makers, and administrators in understanding the complexities associated with diversity issues and diverse populations in the arenas of public policy, higher education, and K–12 education. To date, her publications have focused on affirmative action, institutional engagement, and campus diversity issues. Using a variety of qualitative approaches, her journal articles and book chapters emphasize strategies that are important to higher education's successful engagement in the policy arena, as educational leaders promote the importance of diversity and educational excellence. Her research has been published in *Educational Policy, Urban Education, National Association of Student Affairs Professionals Journal, Journal of College Student Development,* and *New Directions for Community Colleges.*

She was principal investigator of Documenting the Differences Diversity Makes, a project funded by the Ford Foundation at the University of Illinois at Urbana-Champaign. As PI she collaborated with a campuswide group of faculty, administrators, and students who were interested in ascertaining how diversity affects the campus at micro and macro levels. Green also served as a research associate for the Academic Pathways to Access and Student Success project funded by the Lumina Foundation that examined exemplar curricular pathways that enhance college access for minority students. Green has presented papers and workshops at national conferences, including the American Council on Education's Educating All of One Nation, the Association for Institutional Research, American Educational Research Association, and the Association for the Study of Higher Education. A native of Chicago, Illinois, she received her BA in behavioral sciences from the University of Chicago in 1985 and received her MA in public affairs, domestic policy, from the Woodrow Wilson School of Public and International Affairs at Princeton University in 1987.

M. Christopher Brown II is professor and dean of the College of Education at the University of Nevada, Las Vegas. He earned a national reputation for his research and scholarly writing on education policy and administration. He is especially well known for his studies of historically Black colleges, educational equity, and institutional culture. Brown previously served as vice president for programs and administration at the American Association of Colleges for Teacher Education, director of social justice and professional development for the American Educational Research Association, as well as executive director and chief research scientist of the Frederick D. Patterson Research Institute of the United Negro College Fund. He has also held faculty appointments at Pennsylvania State University, University of Illinois at Urbana-Champaign, and the University of Missouri-Kansas City. He has lectured and presented scholarship in various countries on six of seven continents—Africa, Asia, Australia, Europe, North America, and South America.

Brown is the author/editor of twelve books and monographs, as well as the author or coauthor of more than 100 journal articles, book chapters, and publications related to education and society. He has received research support from the Lumina Foundation, Spencer Foundation, AT&T Foundation, the Pew Charitable Trusts, the Sallie Mae Fund, as well as other foundations and corporations. He earned his BS in elementary education from South Carolina State University, his MSEd in educational policy and evaluation from the University of Kentucky, and his PhD in higher education from Pennsylvania State University with a cognate in public administration and political science.

David O. Stovall received his PhD from the University of Illinois at Urbana-Champaign in 2001. Presently he is an associate professor of policy studies in the College of Education at the University of Illinois at Chicago (UIC). His scholarship investigates four areas: (a) Critical Race Theory, (b) concepts of social justice in education, (c) the relationship between housing and education, and (d) the relationship between schools and community stakeholders. In the attempt to bring theory to action, he has spent the past three years working with community organizations and schools to develop curricula that address issues of social justice. His current work has led him to become a member of Chicago's Greater Lawndale/Little Village School of Social Justice High School design team, which opened in fall of 2005. Furthering his work with communities, students, and teachers, Stovall is involved with youth-centered community organizations in Chicago, New York, and the San Francisco Bay Area.

THE CASE FOR AFFIRMATIVE ACTION ON CAMPUS

THE CASE FOR AFFIRMATIVE ACTION ON CAMPUS

Concepts of Equity, Considerations for Practice

Eboni M. Zamani-Gallaher,
Denise O'Neil Green,
M. Christopher Brown II,
and *David O. Stovall*

Foreword by Lynn W. Huntley, Esq.
Afterword by Charles J. Ogletree, Esq., and Susan Eaton

STERLING, VIRGINIA

Published by Stylus Publishing, LLC
22883 Quicksilver Drive
Sterling, Virginia 20166–2102

Library of Congress Cataloging-in-Publication-Data
The case for affirmative action on campus : concepts of
equity, considerations for practice / Eboni M. Zamani-
Gallaher . . . [et al.] ; foreword by Lynn W. Huntley ;
afterword by Charles J. Ogletree and Susan Eaton.
    p.   cm.
  Includes bibliographical references and index.
  ISBN 978–1-57922–102–7 (cloth : alk. paper)—
  ISBN 978–1-57922–103–4 (pbk. : alk. paper)
    1. Affirmative action programs in education—United
States.   I. Zamani-Gallaher, Eboni M., 1971–
LC213.52.C37   2009
379.2′60973—dc22   2008025751

13-digit ISBN: 978 1 57922 102 7 (cloth)
13-digit ISBN: 978 1 57922 103 4 (paper)

Printed in the United States of America

All first editions printed on acid free paper
that meets the American National Standards Institute
Z39–48 Standard.

Bulk Purchases

Quantity discounts are available for use in workshops
and for staff development.
Call 1–800–232–0223

First Edition, 2009

10 9 8 7 6 5 4 3 2 1

Behold, I have set before thee an open door, and no man can shut it.

Revelation 3:8